THE
DEVIL'S
LANE

THE DEVIL'S LANE

Sex and Race
in the
Early South

◆

EDITED BY

Catherine Clinton and
Michele Gillespie

New York   London
Oxford University Press
1997

Oxford University Press

Oxford   New York
Athens   Auckland   Bangkok   Bogotá   Bombay
Buenos Aires   Calcutta   Cape Town   Dar es Salaam   Delhi
Florence   Hong Kong   Istanbul   Karachi
Kuala Lumpur   Madras   Madrid   Melbourne
Mexico City   Nairobi   Paris   Singapore
Taipei   Tokyo   Toronto

and associated companies in
Berlin   Ibadan

Published by Oxford University Press, Inc.
198 Madison Avenue, New York, New York 10016

Oxford is a registered trademark of Oxford University Press

Library of Congress Cataloging-in-Publication Data
The devil's lane : sex and race in the early South / edited by Catherine
Clinton and Michele Gillespie.
p.   cm. Includes bibliographical references.
ISBN 0-19-511242-3 (cloth) — ISBN 0-19-511243-1 (paper)
1. Southern States—History—Colonial period, ca. 1600–1775. 2. Southern
States—Race relations. 3. Sex role—Southern States—History—17th
century. 4. Sex role—Southern States—History—18th century. 5. Women
slaves—Southern States—Social conditions. 6. Afro-American women—
Southern States—Social conditions. 7. Women—Southern States—Social
conditions. I. Clinton, Catherine, 1952– . II. Gillespie, Michele.
F212.D48   1997   975'.02—dc21   96-39835

1 2 3 4 5 6 7 8 9
Printed in the United States of America
on acid-free paper

For our first born
Julian Drew Colbert
and
Michael Thomas Pittard

Contents

◄ Contributors

Carol Berkin is a Professor of History at Baruch College and The Graduate Center of the City University of New York. She is the author of *Jonathan Sewall: Odyssey of an American Loyalist* (1974), and the co-editor of and contributor to two volumes of original articles in women's history, *Women of America: A History*, with Mary Beth Norton (1979) and *Women, War, and Revolution*, with Clara M. Lovett (1980). Her most recent book, *First Generations: Women and Colonial America* (1996) provides a synthesis and overview of the experiences of Native American, African American, and European women in colonial American society.

Kathleen M. Brown is an Assistant Professor of History at the University of Pennsylvania where she teaches courses in colonial history. She is the author of *Good Wives, "Nasty Wenches," and Anxious Patriarchs: Gender, Race, and Power in Colonial Virginia* (1996). She received her Ph.D. from the University of Wisconsin-Madison and has taught at Princeton University, Rutgers University, and the College of William and Mary. She was a Postdoctoral Fellow at the Institute of Early American History and Culture.

Catherine Clinton is the Douglas Southall Freeman Distinguished Visiting Professor at the University of Richmond (1997–98). She is the author and editor of several books and anthologies, most recently *Tara Revisited: Women, War and the Plantation Legend* (1995), and the forthcoming *Civil War Stories*.

Paul Finkelman is Visiting Distinguished Professor at Hamline Law School. He is the author of *Slavery and the Founders: Race and Liberty in the Age of Jefferson* (1996), *Dredd Scott v. Sandford: A Brief History* (1996), *American Legal History*, with Kermit L. Hall and William Wiecek (2nd. ed., 1996), *Slavery in the Courtroom* (1985), *An Imperfect Union: Slavery, Federalism, and Comity* (1981), and the editor of *Slavery and the Law* (1996) and *His Soul Goes Marching On: Responses to John Brown and the Harper's Ferry Raid* (1995). He has held fellowships from the American Council of Learned Societies, the American Philosophical Society, the National Endowment for the Humanities, and Harvard Law School.

Kirsten Fischer received her Ph.D. from Duke University in 1994 and currently is an Assistant Professor of History at the University of South Florida. She is writing a book entitled *Dangerous Liaisons: The Politics of Illicit Sex in Colonial North Carolina*. Her essay, "'Disturbing the King's Peace': The Politics of Sexual Misconduct in Colonial North Carolina," will apppear in *Beyond Conventions*, a volume in the series on southern women's history sponsored by the Southern Association for Women Historians.

Michele Gillespie is an Associate Professor of History at Agnes Scott College. She received her Ph.D. from Princeton University and is the author of *Fruits of Their Labor: White Artisans in Slaveholding Georgia, 1790–1860* (forthcoming).

Virginia Meacham Gould is currently the research fellow for the Sisters of the Holy Family in New Orleans, where she works with the sisters on the Cause for Canonization of their foundress, the free woman of color, Henriette Delille. Her recent publications include "'If I Can't Have My Rights, I Can Have My Pleasures: And If They Won't Give Me Wages I Can Take Them': Gender and Slave Labor in Antebellum New Orleans" in *Discovering Women in Slavery*, edited by Patricia Morton (1995); "Free Creoles of Color of the Gulf Ports of Mobile and Pensacola: A Struggle for the Middle Ground," in *Creoles of Color of the Gulf South*, edited by James Dorman (1995); and "Urban Slavery—Urban Freedom: The Manumission of Jacqueline Lamelle," in *More Than Chattel: Black Women and Slavery in the Americas*, edited by David Barry Gaspar and Darlene Clark Hine (1996).

Joan R. Gundersen is Founding Faculty Professor of History and Women's Studies at California State University, San Marcos. She has published numerous articles on eighteenth-century Virginia, women's history, religion, and law. Her most recent work is *"To Be Useful Unto the World": Women in Revolutionary America, 1740–1790* (1996). She is currently working on a study of women in the Episcopal Church.

Gwendolyn Midlo Hall is the author of the prize-winning book, *Africans in Colonial Louisiana*; of *Social Control in Slave Plantation Societies: A Comparison of St. Domingue and Cuba*, and editor of *Love, War, and the 96th Engineers (colored)*. She was a Guggenheim Fellow for 1995–96; her forthcoming book is *Slavery and Race Relations in French, Spanish, and Early American Louisiana*. She is Professor of History Emerita, Rutgers University.

Kimberly S. Hanger received her Ph.D. in Latin American history from the University of Florida in 1991. Currently she is an Assistant Professor of History at the University of Tulsa and previously was historian and director of research for the Louisiana State Museum. She is the author of *Bounded Lives, Bounded Places: Free Black Society in Colonial New Orleans, 1769–1803* (1997), as well as numerous articles on Spanish New Orleans and the circum-Caribbean.

Jane Landers is Assistant Professor of History and a member of the Center for Latin American and Iberian Studies at Vanderbilt University. She is the editor of *Against the Odds: Free Blacks in Slave Societies of the Americas* (1996) and co-editor of *The African American Heritage of Florida* (1995), and has published essays on the African history of the Hispanic Southeast and of the circum-Caribbean in *The American Historical Review*, *The New West Indian Guide*, and *Slavery and Abolition*.

Cynthia Lynn Lyerly received her doctorate from Rice University and is currently an Assistant Professor at Boston College. Her book on Methodist women in the South is forthcoming.

Jon F. Sensbach is Assistant Professor of History at the University of Southern Mississippi. Previously he was a Postdoctoral Fellow at the Institute of Early American History and Culture in Williamsburg, Virginia. He is the author of *A Separate Canaan: The Making of an Afro-Moravian World in North Carolina, 1763–1840* (forthcoming).

Diane Miller Sommerville is a lecturer at Princeton University. She received her Ph.D. from Rutgers University in 1995. She is currently preparing a book on the intersection of race, class, and gender in the American South, 1800–1877.

Peter Wallenstein teaches history at Virginia Polytechnic Institute and State University. His publications include *From Slave South to New South: Public Policy in Nineteenth-Century Georgia* (1987); prize-winning essays in the *Georgia Historical Quarterly* (1985) and the *Journal of East Tennessee History* (1991); and two articles in the *Virginia Magazine of History and Biography*, entitled "'These New and Strange Beings': Women in the Legal Profession in Virginia, 1890–1990 (1993) and "Flawed Keepers of the Flame: The Interpreters of George Mason" (1994).

Betty Wood received her Ph.D. from the University of Pennsylvania. She is a Lecturer in the Faculty of History at the University of Cambridge and a fellow of Girton College. Her publications include *Slavery in Colonial Georgia, 1730–1775* (1984), *Women's Work, Men's Work: The Informal Slave Economies of Lowcountry Georgia, 1750–1830* (1995), and *The Origins of American Slavery: The English Colonies, 1607–1700* (1997). She is also the co-author, together with Sylvia Frey, of *Come Shouting to Zion: African-American Protestant Christianity in the American South and British Caribbean to 1830* (1997).

Peter H. Wood is a professor of early American history at Duke University and the author of the prize-winning study, *Black Majority: Negroes in Colonial South Carolina from 1670 Through the Stono Rebellion* (1974). With Karen Dalton, he co-authored *Winslow Homer's Images of Blacks: The Civil War and Reconstruction Years* (1988), and he has published a short survey of colonial black history for general readers entitled *Strange New Land, African Americans, 1617–1776* (1996). Dr. Wood holds degrees from Harvard and Oxford, and he has served on the editorial board of the *William and Mary Quarterly* and the *Journal of Southern History*.

◄ Introduction:
Reflections on Sex, Race, and Region

When Europeans settled within the early South, they quarreled over many things—but few imbroglios were so fierce as battles over land. Landowners might wrangle bitterly over boundaries with neighbors, and disputed areas became known as "the devil's lane." Violence or even bloodshed might befall those who ventured onto contested terrain.

We have borrowed this southern colloquialism to provide a provocative title with several intentions. Perhaps too many of us walk straight and narrow paths as scholars. We are taught to drive a hard stake when making a claim, to build strong fences and few bridges. Most academic training rewards territorial imperative. Southern history has remained a brawling, sprawling, convivial enterprise for many of us, and we want to welcome more into the fold as well as the feud. Compelling and extensive investigations in the area of race relations and gender studies have opened vast new horizons. At the same time, finding crossroads and blazing trails has been an arduous and drawn-out process.

We like to think that this volume is an example of the ways in which our interests as teachers and students, scholars and researchers, converts and skeptics converge. Our anthology brings together a variety of scholarly pieces: talks from conferences, case studies, overviews, previews of coming attractions. These original essays demonstrate the ways in which our fascination with sexuality, race, gender and region individually and collectively reshapes our thinking about the colonial experience and moves us toward dissolving artificial barriers.

As we expand our critical perspectives, we can transform boundaries and navigate uncharted territory. We recognize that some may well feel their carefully cultivated fields are "going to the devil." The demands on all of us grow exponentially, in a limitless, chaotic fashion. As we overload our circuits, we are increasingly bogged down by attempts to keep up with advances in scholarly specialties. Research findings seem more and more accessible—at the end of a modem. But with all these advances, our tasks become more challenging, not less difficult.

We recognize that information remains quite different from knowledge. To this end, we bring together fresh and intriguing highlights of trends in colonial southern history. Our collection is intended as an easy avenue into these new and complex areas of research and interest, showcasing the diverse viewpoints of contributors.

Academics rarely flock to taboo topics. Explorations of sexuality require delving into the most intimate and exploitable personal relationships, with sources difficult to locate and evidence tricky to interpret. Subtle and substantial recastings of the complex dynamics at play are required. This topic is well worth tackling and research is long overdue. Today individuals challenge the labels and "boxes" that society imposes, especially with regard to racial definitions. These kinds of definitions and disputes were a critical part of cultural evolution in the early South. We should not be surprised to find these contested issues of today so central to cultural debates nearly four centuries ago.

The broad influences of social contact are presentations of selves. Individual identity is not simply a result of our biological equipment and sexual orientation, our public and private racial designations, our region of origin and region of residence, but our responses to these factors within our projections of ourselves. With each added dimension (religion, color, class, to name a few), the mix gets refined and redefined. So these factors are not "simply" influences, but are the complex cluster of issues up for debate and reinterpretation. The formation of self and society reflects multiple layers. Think of sex, race, and region as circles that might overlap and blend to create patterns of identity and experience—but they shift kaliedescopically, according to dozens upon dozens of shadings and reshapings. One small fragment might recast the entire design. If we try to build our models to include all the elements, all the design possibilities, we discover that our categories are considerably more fluid than we initially conceived.

Think of sex as something about which many may be ambivalent. Although it can be a classification, it can also be an act. Gender roles, social conventions, and sexual orientation are embedded within nearly all aspects of public behavior, providing very distinct sets of expectations that shape and stylize human contact. An act is just an act, but society provides a label keyed to context: abomination, fulfillment of Biblical dictate, illicit desire, biological impulse, reproductive necessity. And one single act might be *all* the above, depending on the person or persons involved. Indeed, within early southern society, quite clearly a single sexual act between two persons might be interpreted, on occasion, as two very different acts in one: determined by the social constructions imposed on each individual.

The following essays confirm that sex and race must be situated at the heart of southern colonial history. The intersection between the two marks an essential point of departure. Our collection demonstrates that the dynamics created by colonization and nation-building cannot be fully appreciated without careful attention to both sex and race. Evidence may not always provide abundant clues, but always awaits a new generation of scholars eager to explore beyond the fences built by foremothers and forefathers.

In the early South, as in most societies, the legal system was one of the most visible arenas in which political and social dynamics played themselves out. How different sets of colonizers constructed legal systems to shape colonial attitudes and behavior is one of our central themes. Anglo-American laws against interracial sex were designed to reinforce slavery as an institution and to encode racism. The criminalization of interracial sex did not stem white desire or halt "immoral" or coerced interracial unions with enslaved women initiated by white masters. The law was designed to ensure the protection of slave property. Accordingly, white women who engaged in interracial liaisons —especially females of the lower class—were subject increasingly to punishment through these laws, while white men were not. Legal definitions of gender difference served to enhance white male authority and establish a strict social hierarchy based on Anglo-American values by the time of the American Revolution.

The Spanish Gulf maintained a social hierarchy of its own, based on perceived differences of class, race, gender, and status. The Spanish legal code bestowed rights and protections on both black and white women, giving them more legal parity than Anglo-American women because of their status before the bench. Moreover, unlike slave women in the Anglo-American South, enslaved women in the Spanish Gulf could use the legal system to challenge owners' illicit behavior, like cruelty and rape. Spanish law also protected female property rights, including their inheritances. Yet Spanish law was not without its restrictions: after 1776, the Spanish crown introduced legislation that made marriages between couples from different races and classes illegal, mirroring similar laws already in place in Anglo-America.

Law was not the only arena in which colonial societies defined social status. Religious institutions played a vital role in shaping people's relationships with each other. The Moravian Church exalted female spirituality and protected female sexuality across racial lines for a brief period in the late eighteenth century. At the same time Methodism, as patriarchal in organization as the Moravian Church, fostered a safe haven for southern women, white and black, who were free to express a gendered kind of religious enthusiasm. Southern evangelical churches in general encouraged churchgoers to respect each other across race and gender boundaries in the early Republic. In return, Afro-Baptists and Methodist men and women of color all across the South requested that their fellow white parishioners respect their rights as Christians.

Yet this respect had its limitations. While white women in these churches could engage in sexual expressions of religious ecstasy, slave women did not and could not. Slave women's overriding desire for freedom for themselves and their families, as well as white culture's willingness to cast slave women as immoral temptresses contributed to cultural censorship. Therefore, southern black women in biracial evangelical congregations tended to express religious ecstasy through liberatory visions, rather than the more overtly sexualized expressions of love for Jesus that white women exhibited. While the evangelical church encouraged its biracial congregations to consider the rights of all Christians, such spiritual considerations did not always transcend secular divides. The tensions that evolved from this disjuncture between belief and practice enabled evangelical enthusiasts to cultivate a distinctly southern and intensely personal relationship with God that complemented rather than challenged white society's interest in maintaining race and gender differences.

Social constructions of difference erected barriers reflected in the formal trappings of church and law through community and custom. One community's conviction that sexual identity was immutable compelled it to do battle over the sex of a resident whose behavior challenged notions of gender differ-ence. Sexual identity, the community decided, could take only one of two forms, male or female. Even when evidence defied their binary logic, they had no ability to adapt alternatives. Sexual identity, like racial identity, could be contested, but the normative values of dominant white society, steeped in European tradition, almost always prevailed.

Certainly the church and other governing bodies exerted enormous influ-ence over early southern communities. But as our research indicates, the bat-tles over land and questions of labor formed equally compelling influences on red, white, and black in early America. The arduous labor needed to produce crops within plantation society (tobacco, rice, indigo, and eventually short sta-ple cotton), the threat of armed clashes between natives and invaders, the ten-sions between the needs of settlers and the desires of plunderers provided competing agendas.

The sexual and racial divisions of labor were much more fluid and complex during the early colonial era. Several of the following essays highlight the fluidity in class, gender, and race relations. For example, a man's work and a woman's work was perhaps not so sharply divided until the development of a stable population (one that could reproduce itself) and a balanced sex ratio. A desperate shortage of bodies and the disproportionate number of men among Africans and Europeans throughout much of the era made the supplies and demands of the southern colonial economy peculiar, fostering unique cultural consequences.

With the maturation of colonial communities and the spreading stratifi-cation that accompanied this development, white attitudes toward perceived differences hardened. Racial, sexual, and gender roles grew increasingly rigid over time. Authorities used these perceived differences to marginalize large segments of any given community. Tracing these shifts, scholars can learn more about social hierarchy, political authority, economic opportunity, and the way in which individuals can fall victim to as well as exploit all three.

Most historians continue to define the colonial South as the point at which European white males landed at Roanoke in 1588. We do not wish to dispute this point, nor do we wish to begin with it, because we are concerned with "place" as well as time in this volume—the unifying geographical expanse redefined with each generation. Place is so important in our view of the American past. As southern historians we can *never* escape it, and as historians of the South, we may never want to.

We assembled pieces on the early South that focus on developments before the closing of the external slave trade in 1808. The chronological designation "early" provides a flexible time frame to cover over two centuries. We believe this neither limits nor narrows our volume, but allows a user-friendly frame-work.

Our essays tell us a great deal about different communities of women—black and white, slave and free. Many refine our appreciation of patriarchal patterns within newly settled plantation societies. What makes this set of essays especially exciting is the degree to which they deal with non-elite whites, the free black community and enslaved Africans in the upper and lower South, within Spanish, French, and British colonies, as well as within emerging southern states.

Scholars working on the nineteenth- and twentiethth-century South have stirred up considerable interest in race, color, ethnicity, status, class, sexuality, and gender, areas in which colonial historical forays are only beginning to yield riches. Yet the South being systematically deconstructed by researchers revising the nineteenth century—the single South paradigm—has been damaged, if not destroyed, through demographic and economic research demonstrating the multiple and colliding worlds within colonial southern settlements. So scholars of the early South are both behind and ahead of scholars chronicling later eras.

We decided to begin our volume with three very different essays, different from one another and decidedly different from the rest of the volume. Carol Berkin, Peter Wood, and Catherine Clinton allowed us to reproduce in written form talks they had delivered to scholarly forums. These scholars separately address the topics of race, gender, and sexuality.

We were grateful to have Wood and Berkin's perspectives as distinguished scholars who have been reflecting on colonial history for the past quarter century. They generously share theoretical insights, highlight transformations in academic inquiry and illuminate, through their own distinctive observations, the paths lying ahead. Including such material symbolizes our continuing quest for dialogue. We scholars endlessly speculate and invite discussion, in print and in person, unceremoniously or *en garde*—informed by who we are and what we seek.

Launching our volume with this informal section, with Broad Strokes, we hope to dramatize the open-ended quality of scholarly endeavor. We want to convince readers of our commitment to digging deeper in the past—not just scrambling up a twisted and often treacherous trail, to conquer dizzying academic heights.

Although we don't want readers dizzy, we do want them bedazzled by the methodological and interpretive bounty on display. These essays demonstrate the imaginative use of traditional sources such as census manuscripts, statutes, court records, legal documents, church records, pamphlets, sermons, wills, as well as letters and diaries. These investigations uncover a host of shifting relationships that revise current historical wisdom. These pieces collectively challenge the image of the colonial South as a fixed backdrop to events that led to the emancipation of enslaved African Americans in the nineteenth century. The earliest southern settlements often were triracial. Native Americans, European settlers, and enslaved Africans negotiated complex interactions between each other that at times belied but generally bolstered the power of European colonizers.

We decided to organize our remaining essays around regional categories, familiar designations that nevertheless allow us to explore beyond traditional boundaries. We do not use the label "the Chesapeake" in the way that it has been so successfully exploited by a previous generation of scholars working on the pre-Revolutionary South (i.e., the Chesapeake, and the non-Chesapeake). But we do include essays that cover Virginia and Maryland, in our first regional section, entitled the Upper South, a purely geographical—not cultural—designation.

These chapters feature new work in legal history—looking at questions of racial definition, gender definition, rape, miscegenation, crime, and punishment in the early South. Some pieces examine the circles that enclosed and the networks that bound women together in colonial settlements. Topics are as varied as state-mandated castration to one community's resistance to a cross-dresser. We know these essays might raise even more questions about tolerance and limitations, customs and exceptionalism, the individual and the community.

Part III, The Lower South, stretching from North Carolina to Georgia, proves equally bounteous and diverse. Essays trace the lives of African-American women through their presence in households and church pews. The psychosexual dynamics at play in biracial communities emerge by examining slander, piety, and other vital signs. We have strong evidence from private and public records about the significance of religion in the lives of women, black and white, in the early South. We appreciate the role played by females as culture brokers, especially those few Indian women who rise from the pages of southern history to tantalize us with their roles in colonial folklore This selection forms an important bridge to our fourth and final region.

We conclude with the Gulf South, delighted with the opportunity to give this historical stepchild some measure of the attention it deserves. We have charted the growing interest in this sprawling and complex region—from the far reaches of Spanish St. Augustine to the Mississippi Delta. We know these non-Anglo essays will prove engrossing and stimulating—from a case of infanticide in Florida, to the contested terrain of gender, race, and class in Louisiana during both French and Spanish rule.

This book addresses questions within the framework of southern colonial history, but our primary concern has not been to "fit" our pieces into the wider perspective of current scholarship on colonial America. Rather, we highlight the varied and distinctive experiences within the early South by the sheer force of our examples. This showcase of contemporary scholarship, this merging of exemplary research in the fields of race relations, gender studies, and southern colonial history has been very long in coming, yet we hope that the essays following will prove it was well worth the wait.

◄

The idea for this book was prompted by a lively discussion by scholars over margaritas and Mexican food during the June 1994 conference of the Southern Association for Women Historians. The excitement over research, the debate over ideas, the rising tide of enthusiasm drove one of us to distraction until she was able to find a co-editor to share her vision for an anthology capturing the intellectual heat generated by new work in southern colonial social history. This co-editor had a last name that would follow hers in the alphabet, a cheerful willingness to take on more work than she should have, and consistently exercised better professional judgment—like preventing her co-author from dedicating the volume to the *memory* of a legendary colonial historian who had taught at her undergraduate college—and was still living. This co-editor prevented many more mistakes from the dedication page onward, and together they were able to keep this book on the narrow but not so straight path to publication, on schedule and on target.

Although as graduate students the co-editors had prowled the same library stacks at Princeton, since they were from different generations, their paths did not cross until much later. But once they struck up a friendship, this partnership became an inevitable outgrowth of mutual regard.

We were blessed by the incredible crop of talented scholars willing to contribute essays to the volume. Many are very distinguished in their respective fields, and some are clearly destined for distinguished careers. Despite challenging requests for revisions, our contributors were tireless in their efforts to meet rigidly imposed deadlines and high standards. We salute them with gratitude.

Both Jacqueline Jones and Sylvia Frey took time from their busy schedules to read the entire manuscript at a critical juncture, and provided us with key suggestions. We appreciate their invaluable input.

Ellen Chodosh has been a terrific editor and we especially want to thank Carolyn Michelman, both of Oxford University Press. Their careful attention, generous enthusiasm, and patient guidance made working on this manuscript particularly rewarding.

Both of us would also like to thank Randy Sparks and the College of Charleston for supporting our work in southern history, women's history, and colonial history. We would each like to acknowledge the assistance we received individually. Catherine Clinton wishes to thank the W.E.B. DuBois Institute of Harvard University for its continuing support of her work and the Greenwich Public Library for its abundant resources. Michele Gillespie wishes to thank her colleagues in the history department as well as Agnes Scott College for its generous assistance and continuing support of her research.

While working together on this project over the past two years, one of us lost a mother, one of us got tenure, one of us recovered from Lyme disease, and both of us imposed on our husbands and children to finish this project in a timely fashion. Daniel, Drew, and Ned Colbert are Catherine Clinton's life-support system, for which she remains grateful—despite her inability to ever repay them for their countless sacrifices for her bloody books. Michele Gillespie is grateful to Kevin and Michael Pittard for their ever-present good cheer and patience throughout this project.

This project was an arduous undertaking, but also a collaboration that exceeded our expectations in terms of the intellectual and personal engagement it created. There was very little sense of give and take, no need for compromise—just a steady ebb and flow of leaning on one another, learning from one another. *The Devil's Lane* renewed our commitment to emerging scholarship and rekindled our interest in literary collaboration (if only with one another!). It represents shared burdens, shared affections, but, most of all, our hopes that future generations will find as much friendship and pleasure in exploring the past as we have in producing this book.

Riverside, Ct.   C.C.
Covington, Ga.   M.G.

Part I

BROAD STROKES

"THE FACTS SPEAK LOUDLY ENOUGH"

Exploring Early Southern Black History

One day in the mid-1980s, I received a phone call shortly after an article had appeared in the *New York Times* discussing the discovery of Fort Mose, the fortified eighteenth-century black village near Spanish St. Augustine. The piece mentioned that some of the fort's residents had escaped from the English colony of South Carolina around the time of the Stono slave uprising in 1739, and it cited my work on that revolt. "Hello," said a voice. "Are you the person who knows about the Stono Rebellion?" The caller introduced himself as a movie producer, and I jokingly told him that I had been awaiting his call for years. "This Stono thing sounds dramatic, Doc," the caller observed. "How can I find out about it? I'm leaving for the West Coast tomorrow."

"I guess the first thing you should know is that Stono was pretty violent," I replied; "People's heads were cut off and placed on poles." "Violence is no problem for Hollywood anymore," he responded briskly; "in fact they usually like it nowadays." "I've noticed," I answered, "but let me explain. You see, in this case several white storekeepers were murdered at the outset, and their severed heads were placed on the front steps of their store." There was a long pause at the other end of the phone line as the man considered that image. "I tell you what, Doc," he stated in a somewhat more distant voice, "why don't I just get back to you some other time, if anything happens to develop on this in the future." "Sure," I said, as the phone line went dead.

I offer this anecdote at the outset, because I intend to reflect briefly, and invite others to reflect, on the intractable, almost indigestible, nature of certain small hard facts as they continue to emerge in the growing field of early southern black history. The more we learn, the more we are faced by grim but undeniable details of this kind that simply do not fit well with our overall inherited picture of American—or southern—history. We can tell ourselves, as the producer apparently did, that our audience is not ready to deal with such details, or we can steadily adjust our understanding to incorporate fresh evidence, even when troubling new material undercuts cherished images and beliefs.

In exploring these thoughts, I make use of various personal recollections before turning, in the second half of this essay, to a brief but detailed case study. Occurring a generation after Stono, when the thirteen colonies stood on the brink of political independence, it involves another brief moment of intensified interracial violence in the colonial lowcountry that has interested me for a long time. This glimpse into several lost encounters at the outset of the American Revolution will provide a further chance to weigh new facts against traditional images in the eighteenth-century South. But first, let me begin with the simple reminder that our exposure to the complicated and troubling details of early black southern history, indeed to its very existence, is strikingly recent.

◆▷

Nearly thirty years ago, as a graduate student in history at Harvard, I traveled south to pursue research for a doctoral dissertation on slavery in colonial South Carolina. One afternoon at the state archives in Columbia, I set aside my file cards (this was long before the era of laptops) and picked up a local text for school students on the history of the Palmetto State. I was struck that it contained only two references to African Americans in the first hundred pages, for my note cards were already full of evidence concerning the lives of early black Carolinians. The moment strengthened my resolve to help put these people on the American map and to call my work, if I could ever finish it, *Black Majority*. After all, it had become clear to me by now that one of the thirteen original English colonies was more than half black by the time of the American Revolution.

Other southern history scholars of my generation were having similar challenging and exhilarating experiences in archives across the region and around the country. Not surprisingly, given the context of the Civil Rights Movement, we were finding that matters of race had always played a larger part in the story of southern history than many of the traditional mainstream chroniclers had acknowledged over the years. Moreover, this centrality could be documented, since far more records existed for the exploration of slavery and its aftermath than we had been led to expect. Even in Columbia, where Sherman's army had brought heavy destruction, diverse and underutilized resources abounded.[1] In my own case, though I had planned to move beyond the American Revolution, I found so much rewarding early material that

I ended my study with the bloody (and then virtually unknown) Stono Rebellion of 1739.[2]

In addition, we were also finding that usable records concerning enslavement stretched much further back in time than was generally assumed. Of course, certain important books, articles, and document collections existed regarding colonial slavery and white attitudes toward it. But, for the most part, "the peculiar institution" was regarded and discussed as an antebellum phenomenon. The attention of colonial historians was focused elsewhere, with the lion's share of scholarship continuing to concentrate in New England. When a few experts on the colonial South did turn to consider race-related issues, it was often as a result of political and social changes in the 1960s. For example, Wesley Frank Craven of Princeton, a pioneer among scholars of the early South, once noted that questions raised by visiting students from newly independent African countries first prompted him to examine the demography of enslaved black colonists in Virginia.

Much has changed in a short generation. An abundance of excellent scholarship has established beyond a doubt the centrality of race slavery to the first half of southern (and of American) history. Textbooks that once sidestepped the topic as a troubling contradiction to a vaunted "American consensus" now compete to underscore and analyze the issue. Suitable primary sources fostering further study are becoming better known and more accessible in the 1990s; thorough research aids and specialized bibliographies continue to proliferate. Moreover, the chronological longevity (as well as the geographical diversity) of American enslavement—especially in the South, where it shaped an entire culture—is slowly becoming more widely understood. And this transformation is due, more than anything else, to the slow accumulation of detailed and suggestive new evidence by scores of hard-working historians. In all sorts of valuable ways, the study of African-American life under enslavement has evolved into a mature field of scholarship.

The painful and impressive contours of early southern black history, from the Middle Passage through Emancipation and Reconstruction, are now more familiar and accessible in the academic community than they have ever been. But so far the broader public audience is gaining only glimpses of this landscape and is still being unduly sheltered from the harshest and most revealing aspects of the actual historical record. In part this is due to an unfortunate combination of seemingly opposite forces. On one hand, the same white conservatives who have challenged new American history standards on all fronts remain protective of the lingering myth of benevolent planters and incompetent Africans; they continue to oppose any perspective that might further undermine those cherished fallacies. On the other hand, a considerable number of African Americans, browbeaten by generations of white historical mythmaking, are equally unwilling to re-open the can of worms that is "slavery times," fearing that their ancestors, rather than the oppressors, might once again be demeaned by the process.

In short, there are those who, for varying reasons, would prefer to see the discussion of slavery dropped altogether from the historical agenda. (A few, it seems, would not be disappointed to return to the 1830s, when President

Andrew Jackson proposed a law preventing the circulation of material on slavery via the public post and Congress enacted a gag rule preventing debate on the subject.) But another, nearly opposite, set of forces may also prevent the American public from confronting the harshest elements of our own past. The very success of revisionist historians over the past generation has created pressures that seem to be dulling, rather than sharpening, our awareness of the slavery experience and its meaning.

As enslavement and the early black experience becomes a more widely acceptable topic in our schools and history texts, new pressures arise to moderate its presentation to suit differing ages and varied points of view. Ironically, as a more negative (and realistic) portrayal of "the peculiar institution" gains precedence over earlier (more benign and naive) interpretations, then more subject matter becomes available which many may wish to avoid, or to hide from others. For those who previously professed that whippings and rapes never occurred, that rebellions and revenge killings rarely took place, there was little to evade in a discussion of slavery. But once the documentation has been mustered, there is much provocative material available to be deflected, downplayed, or ignored.

If the maturing of early southern black history has brought new and unforeseen dilemmas, it has also brought significant gains. Perhaps the most positive feature of this steady evolution has been the rapid development of a diverse and talented new cadre of African-American historians of slavery. After a century of distinguished but isolated black pioneers—generally unheralded and all too frequently ignored—a generation of independent men and women has emerged since the 1960s to build collectively on the foundations laid by their predecessors. Their appearance in integrated classrooms and once-segregated research facilities promptly had a subtle but immeasurable impact; their steady rise as respected authors, tenured professors, and outspoken reviewers continues to enhance the study of U.S. history. Granted, their absolute numbers remain too small, their academic situation remains too precarious, and their varied voices are still not always heard in the mainstream culture, but their growing presence represents an important and hopeful shift on the scholarly landscape.

The integration of the historical workforce (including researchers, teachers, even movie directors) is proceeding steadily, if much too slowly. But this does not represent any magical solution in its own right. It is a partial means to an end, but the more difficult challenge lies elsewhere. It is one thing to express concern about who writes books and teaches classes and makes films regarding southern history—something we have heard frequently in recent years. But it is quite a different matter to worry, as all historians must, about how to present troubling material from the past to receptive but uncertain audiences in the present.

I recall how this issue was brought to my attention discretely, but forcefully, in 1971, when I submitted a draft chapter of my slavery dissertation to my Harvard advisor. Troubled by the widespread brutality that the South Carolina documents revealed, I had gone to considerable lengths to "spin" the narrative, inserting numerous adjectives and asides to indicate my feelings of righteous indignation. *"Sentimentality or 'understanding' will weaken rather than strengthen what you have to say,"* Bernard Bailyn scrawled in the margin beside one particularly irate paragraph. *"The facts speak loudly enough."* It was valuable advice, and I cut it out and saved it. More than twenty-five years later that faded scrap of paper is still taped to the desk lamp in my study.

Since that time I have done some work regarding enslaved blacks at the outset of the Revolutionary War. Although I have discussed this intermittent research in several articles over the years, new work by industrious scholars makes it possible to delve further into this topic. Most texts now give a brief summation of Lord Dunmore's proclamation in Virginia in November 1775, in which the colony's royal governor offered freedom to able-bodied African Americans who would leave their masters and join the British cause. But the implications of this controversial act still remain somewhat doubtful, inviting further local research in all the colonies south of Chesapeake Bay. In this context, consider the following incidents that took place along the southern coastline in winter 1775 and the early spring of 1776. Chronologically, they occurred in the tumultuous months between the battle of Bunker Hill in Boston and the signing of the Declaration of Independence in Philadelphia. But it remains hard to see them fitting neatly into most present-day representations of the patriot cause.[3]

News that black freedom had been sanctioned in Virginia had reached South Carolina by early December. On Sullivan's Island at the mouth of Charleston harbor, fugitives hopeful of escaping slavery were gathering near the so-called "pest house," the small structure beside the water supervised by a black man named Robinson and used to quarantine the sick off incoming ships from Africa and the Caribbean. Ironically, this was the spot where many of them, or their parents or grandparents, had first touched American soil as slaves. Now, in the wake of Dunmore's proclamation in Virginia, they hoped the small island might be their gateway to freedom. From the sandy beach, some refugees had already joined the British fleet and begun to participate in raiding parties to liberate their comrades, encouraged by the loyalist governor, Lord William Campbell. The patriot Council of Safety, chaired by the wealthy Charleston merchant and slave importer Henry Laurens, reported that "Campbell had gone [to] great lengths in harbouring & protecting Negroes on Sullivants Island from whence those Villains made nightly Sallies and committed roberies & depradations on the Sea Coast."[4]

On December 5, Captain Jacob Milligan of the sloop *Hetty* reached Charleston with a cargo of rum and sugar, but not before he had been seized and searched by Captain Tollemache of the *H.M.S. Scorpion*. The next day Milligan informed the Council of Safety "that there were considerable number of slaves upon Sullivan's Island, and that he learnt huts were building for them in the woods."[5] Almost immediately, Laurens and the Council of Safety commanded Colonel William Moultrie to dispatch a force of 200 men to Sullivan's Island "to seize and apprehend a number of negroes, who are said to have deserted to the enemy." The orders, issued on December 7, called for an attack "this ensuing night."[6] But the orders were not carried out for more than a week, probably because black workers on the other side of the harbor, who had been ordered to build a bulwark at James Island, were openly refusing to follow commands.[7]

These must have been anxious days for the growing contingent of people on Sullivan's Island. The British naval officers anchored so close at hand apparently lacked the space and the resolve to take more than a small portion of the refugees on board their ships, even though their long boats were visiting the Island regularly to refill their water casks. On December 10, Fenwick Bull, a prominent local citizen, reported to the Council of Safety that he had recently spoken with the commander of the man-of-war *Scorpion*, and Captain Tollemache "did not deny having some of our negroes on board, but said thay came as freemen, and demanding protection." Regarding these isolated and desperate persons the captain added, perhaps with only slight exaggeration, "that he could have had near five hundred, who had offered."[8]

> A few of these people were apparently granted shelter, for on December 14 the Council heard a first-hand report regarding some of the refugees "that a few days ago, when a report prevailed, that they were to be attacked upon Sullivan's Island, they were taken off the shore in boats sent from the ships. . . ." The eye-witness "declared that he saw a number of slaves belonging to the inhabitants of this town on board some of the ships of war, and on shore upon Sullivan's Island, several of which he knew," and the pressure for action from frustrated slave owners increased. Finally, on the morning of December 18, a party of 54 "Indian Rangers," directed by Lieutenant William Withers, carried out the orders to attack Sullivan's Island. According to the Council's initial hasty report, they made a descent on that Island burnt the House in which the Banditti were often lodged brought off four Negroes killed three or four & also took White prisoners four Men three Women & three Children destroyed many things which had been useful to those wretches in the Houses—many of the Men of Wars Water Casks, a great loss to them, exchanged a few Shot with Some of the Men of Wars Men & came off unhurt.[9]

A private letter written a month later may give a more candid and informed assessment of the operation. According to Josiah Smith, Jr., a force of fifty or sixty men staged a pre-dawn attack on the encampment and "early in the Morning sett fire to the Pest house, took some Negroes and Sailors Prisoners, *killed fifty of the former that would not be taken*, and unfortunately lost near twenty that were unseen by them till taken off the Beach by the Men [of] Warrs Boats" (italics added).[10] If fifty unarmed black refugees had in fact been massacred, preferring death over re-enslavement, the Council of Safety probably would not commit such a gruesome fact to paper in its report.[11] But its members, as we shall see, were not afraid to sanction such brutality where their own chattels were concerned. Indeed, this apparent outcome may even suggest a veiled meaning to the cryptic postscript in the original orders of December 7: "P.S. [Ordered by six members.] The pest house to be burned, and every kind of live stock to be driven off or destroyed."[12]

Embittered by the British "practice of harbouring & protecting our

Negroes on board" their ships, Charleston merchants "refused to Supply them" with provisions, and at the beginning of January several of the vessels set sail. South Carolina leader Laurens suspected they were heading to Savannah, where he feared they would seek supplies of "Bread & flour Beef & Pork" from a populace that remained lukewarm to the resistance movement building elsewhere. He rushed a letter to Archibald Bulloch (a Georgia planter taking a leading role in what Laurens ironically called "the hearty endeavours of a few to Save [the colonies] from Slavery"), warning the leader that the British may plan to "come into your River, for overawing the friends of Liberty & for giving energy to the projects for our Enemies." After all, various Georgians were hoping to violate Congress's non-exportation agreements by shipping their produce overseas under the protection of the British Navy.[13]

Moreover, the Council's concern grew that mounting disturbances would allow black workers to escape from their enslaved labor. A Spanish ship, the *San Miguel*, was delayed in Charleston harbor until February 3 because a passenger was discovered attempting to smuggle five fugitive slaves out of the colony as stowaways.[14] The prospects of black rebellion or escape seemed particularly strong in Georgia, with British ships off the coast and dissention and uncertainty dividing the whites on land. "It was a wise Step to Strip the Negroe Houses on both Sides [of] the Savanna of Arms & Ammunition," the Council wrote to the Georgia Council of Safety on January 19; "we highly applaud it & are now taking measures in concert with Colonel Bull for having an Armed force of 200 men in readiness. . . ."[15] A few days later, in response to messages from the beleaguered Georgia Provincial Congress, the Council ordered Stephen Bull to lead this contingent of South Carolina troops across the Savannah River to provide assistance.[16]

Henry Laurens, at the center of this maneuvering, felt particularly agitated. He had recently received news of the accidental death of his youngest son in England, and his mind was "further exercised by the prospect which the present S[t]ate of affairs opens to my view, in which I See my Country & my dearest connexions Standing on the brink of a precipice & tottering." He wrote to William Manning in London that South Carolina patriots felt besieged from all sides by colluding forces: "While Men of War & Troops are to attack us in front the Indians are to make inroads on our backs—Tories & Negro Slaves to rise in our Bowels." But he warned defiantly regarding this "present unnatural unjust & impolitic War on the part of Great Britain, that her Conquest will be her defeat."[17]

By this time Laurens was well aware of Lord Dunmore's proclamation, with its significant impact in the Chesapeake, and he was also conscious that the contents of his letter to Manning might well be reported to others in England. He stressed general patriot commitment by grandly claiming that Charleston residents were prepared "to put the torch" to their homes "with their own hands in preference to" allowing "the Houses in that fine Town" to ever serve as "Shelters for a Cruel Enemy." Similarly, the wealthy slave trader asserted (darkly and disingenuously): should England continue to threaten "to manumit & Set free those Africans whom She Captivated, made Slaves,

& Sold to us, the people are ready to anticipate the pious work." For emphasis, Laurens added a footnote: "I do not deliver these remarks as my own opinions[.] They are founded on declarations which I hear from the people every
day."[18]

Soon messages from Colonel Bull in Savannah would provide another test
for Laurens and his Council regarding how far they would go to keep their
"property" out of British hands. On March 12, Bull reported that "There are
in this town at present" from the "Creek & Euchee Indians about Seventy
men who are now Employ'd in the Service of the Province," plus many friends
of the patriot cause, "but there are a great many Torys" as well. He added that
about twenty-five blacks, including nine belonging to Mr. Arthur Middleton,
had gone aboard the British man-of-war *Cherokee* below Savannah.[19] The next
day's dispatch contained an update regarding Middleton's slaves: "am Sorry to
Acquaint you that I am well Informd between forty & fifty of his have Really
Deserted & above One hundred & fifty more the Property of others who are
now on Tybee Island" at the mouth of the Savannah River.[20]

The next day, when Bull dictated his next dispatch to Laurens, he added an
extraordinary paragraph regarding a matter of utmost secrecy. He urged
Laurens "*not* to have this last Paragraph read" to the entire Provincial
Congress, "but to be known only to the Council, for no one does, at least
ought to know, anything of the following matter but the Members of the
Council of Safety of this Province and myself, The matter is this," he wrote in
his own hand:

> it is far better for the Public and the owners of the deserted Negroes . . . who
> are on Tybee Island to be shot if they cannot be taken, [even] if the Public is
> obliged to pay for them; for if they are carried away, and converted into
> money, which is the Sinews of War, it will only enable an Enemy to fight us
> with our own money or property.[21]

Since members of the Georgia Council of Safety proved "timid" about
agreeing to such a brutal mission, Bull sought authorization from his own
home colony of South Carolina for dispatching a party of Indian allies to capture or kill the runaways. "I have just this moment had proper and certain
Assurance that a good Leader and party of the Creek Indians are willing and
desirous of going to take the runaway Negroes upon Tybee Island if I choose
it," he wrote. "But it must be kept a profound Secret, lest the Negroes should
move off, or they should ask for Arms, and so lay an Ambuscade for the
Indians." He told Laurens that "all who cannot be taken, had better be shot by
the Creek Indians, as it perhaps may deter other Negroes from deserting, and
will establish a hatred or Aversion between the Indians and Negroes."[22]

Bull's message reached South Carolina's revolutionary Council of Safety
late on the evening of March 16, and it was midnight when Laurens sat down
to compose a discrete reply. The Council had already dealt with a similar situation in the search-and-destroy mission to Sullivan's Island three months
earlier, so in answering Bull's request for permission to act, he chose his words,
repeatedly crossing out phrases. "Now for the grand we may say the awful

business contained in your Letter," he wrote; "it is an awful business notwith-standing it has the sanction of Law, to put even fugitive & Rebellious Slaves to death." Here Laurens penned in the margin, "the prospect is horrible." Then he continued,

> we think the Council of Safety in Georgia ought to give that encouragement which is necessary to induce proper Persons to seize & if nothing else will do to destroy all those Rebellious Negroes upon Tybee Island or wherever they may be found, If Indians are the most proper hands let them be employed on this service but we would advise that some discreet white Men were incorporated with or joined to lead them, the loss which may result, to proprietors ought to and must be borne by the Public.[23]

Laurens continued that "those Royal Miscreants," the British, bore full responsibility for "every inglorious unavoidable act of necessity which we may be driven to commit." Still anxious to justify the massacre that he was sanctioning, the future President of the Continental Congress went on to tell Bull, in the grandiose language of the moment, that if the interests of one person, or even one colony, were at stake,

> we might submit to suffer great injuries in both Cases in preference to giving Orders for such sanguinary measures as may follow in consequence of these—but when we consider that the loss of Georgia may be followed by the Loss of—Carolina & eventually work the defeat of the American Cause in which the happiness of ages unborn is included we dare not even hesitate whether we should order or perform any act which is required by the first Law of nature as well as by the Law of the Land.[24]

Apparently Colonel Bull left Savannah before this letter arrived, and he received word of it while on his way back to Charleston. "Could I have heard from you but twelve hours sooner," he wrote Laurens from Sheldon, South Carolina, on March 26, "I should not have left Savannah as soon as I have done, as there is one piece of service which I wanted to have put into execution, which I did not think myself properly authorised to do."[25]

In Bull's absence, however, the attack that he did not wish to name had already taken place the previous day. On March 25, a party of Georgia militiamen and roughly thirty Creek Indians invaded Tybee Island, burning what shelters they found and seizing several white Loyalists and black refugees. As with the Sullivan's Island attack, evidence of casualties remains sketchy; one British marine was killed and several others were apparently wounded. But thanks to the skillful editors of the *Laurens Papers*, we do know that "The British authorities condemned the patriots for committing atrocities during the attack. They claimed that the militiamen, dressed and painted like Indians, joined the Creeks in demonstrating 'signs of the most savage barbarity' that even 'exceeded the ferocity of the Indians.'"[26]

If the Hollywood producer mentioned at the outset backed away from the Stono Revolt, how would he feel about these grim incidents on the edge of the

American Revolution? After all, the Revolutionary Era remains the most closely guarded treasure in our national mythology. Adding too much realistic detail about the situation of African Americans at the moment when the colonies were declaring their independence might well, in the words of James Baldwin, "reveal more about America to Americans than Americans wish to know." Despite all that has changed in recent decades, lines that this distinguished black author composed in 1963 provide an appropriate close for a discussion of the disconcerting facts that underlie African-American history in the early South. Speaking of mainstream Americans, Baldwin observed, "They are, in effect, still trapped in a history which they do not understand; and until they understand it, they cannot be released from it."[27]

◀▷

Notes

This essay is an expansion of a talk given at the African-American Studies Center of the University of North Carolina at Chapel Hill in December 1995.

1. The silver lining to Sherman's dark cloud of destruction, I discovered, rests in the fact that he still serves as a scapegoat of truly monumental proportion. One day, when a genealogist requested the census of 1890 and it could not be found immediately, I heard a desk assistant explain with great earnestness and sympathy, "I am so sorry; General Sherman must have destroyed it."

2. Peter H. Wood, *Black Majority: Negroes in Colonial South Carolina from 1670 Through the Stono Rebellion* (New York: Knopf, 1974).

3. Some of the context for these events can be found in the following: Robert M. Weir, *Colonial South Carolina: A History* (Millwood, NY: KTO Press, 1983); Peter H. Wood, "'The Dream Deferred': Black Freedom Struggles on the Eve of White Independence," in Gary Y. Okihiro, ed., *In Resistance: Studies in African, Caribbean and Afro-American History* (Amherst: University of Massachusetts Press, 1986), 166–87; Sylvia R. Frey, *Water from the Rock: Black Resistance in a Revolutionary Age* (Princeton: Princeton University Press, 1991); Peter H. Wood, "'Liberty Is Sweet': African-American Freedom Struggles in the Years before White Independence," in Alfred F. Young, ed., *Beyond the American Revolution: Explorations in the History of American Radicalism* (DeKalb: Northern Illinois University Press, 1993).

4. Council of Safety to Richard Richardson, December 19, 1775, *Papers of Henry Laurens* 10:576.

5. "Journal of the Council of Safety," South Carolina Historical Society, *Collections*, III (December 6, 1775), 62–63.

6. "Journal of the Council of Safety," South Carolina Historical Society, *Collections*, III (December 7, 1775), 64–65. Also in David R. Chesnutt et al., eds., *The Papers of Henry Laurens, Volume 10, December 12, 1774–January 4, 1776* (Columbia: University of South Carolina Press, 1985), 546.

7. Major Barnard Elliott to the Council of Safety, December 7, 1775, *South Carolina Historical and Genealogical Magazine*, 3(October 1902), 194–197. (Also in *Papers of Henry Laurens* 10: 546–549.) A letter of Thomas Corbett to the Council of Safety, December 9, 1776, relates another incident that some might have read as sabotage. In treating several hundred pounds of valuable nitre "for the

making of Gunpowder," he reported that about 25 pounds "was blown up by the Carelessness of the Negroes who were curing it, & who were much hurt by the accident." *Papers of Henry Laurens* 10: 555.

8. "Journal of the Council of Safety," South Carolina Historical Society, *Collections*, III (December 10, 1775), 75.

9. Council of Safety to Richard Richardson, December 19, 1775, *Papers of Henry Laurens* 10:576. The editorial note (not the text) supplies the term "Indian Rangers" in quotation marks, leaving it somewhat ambiguous whether these are actual or would-be Indians. As for the date of the attack, the editors put it on December 19, and Sylvia Frey follows their lead in *Water from the Rock*, 64. But this letter of December 19th, complaining of the "Villians" on Sullivan's Island, states that "this alarming evil received Such a Check yesterday Morning [i.e., December 18] as will serve to humble our Negroes in general & perhaps to mortify his Lordship [Governor Campbell] not a little."

10. Josiah Smith, Jr., to James Poyas, January 19, 1776, in Josiah Smith, Jr., Letter Book, Southern Historical Collection, University of North Carolina, Chapel Hill. Frey omits this document from her discussion of the incident in *Water from the Rock*, 64–65.

11. The Council continued its silence about deaths in the incident, writing to the North Carolina Provincial Council on January 2, 1776, of "a descent made upon Sullivan's Island, where the house thereon was burnt, and some important prisoners taken." (The same letter observed that "as we are informed, thirty to forty negroes" had been taken up by Capt. Tollemache before his departure.) *Papers of Henry Laurens* 10:609.

12. *Papers of Henry Laurens* 10:546. Brackets in the original manuscript. In a previous sentence, the order itself had stated that "the detachment with their prisoners are to return to Charles-Town, with all possible dispatch." It may be that all on the twelve-member Council sanctioned reclaiming slave property, but only six were willing to endorse that black refugees be destroyed as a last resort.

13. Henry Laurens to Archibald Bulloch, January 2, 1776, *Papers of Henry Laurens* 10:606–607. For the Council of Safety's decision of December 16, 1775, "that all further supplies of provisions to the king's ships will be prohibited, unless the fugitive slaves . . . are forthwith delivered up," see *Papers of Henry Laurens* 11:49, note 1.

　　Regarding the departure of the British ships, Laurens wrote to Stephen Bull on January 20, 1776, "we have received certain information that every one of them carried off some of our Negroes, in the whole amounting to no inconsiderable number." *Papers of Henry Laurens* 11:50.

14. *Papers of Henry Laurens* 10:616, note 2.

15. South Carolina Council of Safety to Georgia Council of Safety, January 19, 1776, *Papers of Henry Laurens* 11:44.

16. South Carolina Council of Safety to Georgia Provincial Congress, January 24, 1776, *Papers of Henry Laurens* 11:60.

17. Henry Laurens to William Manning, February 27, 1776, *Papers of Henry Laurens* 11:122–28.

18. Henry Laurens to William Manning, February 27, 1776, *Papers of Henry Laurens* 11:123–24.

19. Letter from Stephen Bull, March 12, 1776, *Papers of Henry Laurens* 11:154. Arthur Middleton was a prominent member of South Carolina's Council of Safety who owned a plantation on the Savannah River.

20. Letter from Stephen Bull, March 13, 1776, *Papers of Henry Laurens* 11: 155. From the time the *Cherokee* departed from Charleston in early January, it had been known by whites, and undoubtedly by blacks in the region as well, "that the Cherokee is to go in at Tybee & to lye Some where in Savanna River." Henry Laurens to Stephen Bull, January 6, 1776, *Papers of Henry Laurens* 11:1.

21. *Papers of Henry Laurens* 11:163.

22. In closing, Bull added, "I have something farther to say on this Subject but defer it untill I come to Charles Town." *Papers of Henry Laurens* 11:163–64.

23. Letter to Stephen Bull, March 16, 1776, *Papers of Henry Laurens* 11:171–72. Both Bull and Laurens believed they were technically within the law in this matter, since violence and even death were sanctioned by statute in the pursuit of enslaved persons who were deemed fugitives or rebels. If such slaves were killed, their owners ("proprietors") were considered eligible for public compensation for the loss of their property.

24. Letter to Stephen Bull, March 16, 1776, *Papers of Henry Laurens* 11:172–73.

25. Letter from Stephen Bull to Henry Laurens, March 26, 1776, in Robert W. Gibbes, ed., *Documentary History of the American Revolution . . . Chiefly in South Carolina* (New York, 1853), 1:266–67.

26. *Papers of Henry Laurens* 11:173, note 7.

27. James Baldwin, *The Fire Next Time* (New York, Dial Press, 1963), 115, 22.

CLIO'S DAUGHTERS

Southern Colonial Women and Their Historians

My fourteen-year-old daughter, Hannah, owes her name to the many New England women I encountered in the 1970s as I leafed through the pages of Loyalist correspondence and pored over the diaries of Massachusetts women writing during the Revolution. This historical legacy has not prevented her, however, from preferring her mother's forays into the study of southern colonial women to any work on their northern counterparts. With a judgment born of intimate contact, she observes that "You think southern women are more interesting, Mom"; and with a flippancy that marks her as a true teenager, she adds, "and it's funny how your accent comes back while you study them."

There is a kernel of truth in both observations. A trace of the accent of my native Mobile, Alabama, does return when I focus on the lives of southern women—ah, but after thirty some years in New York City, it is little more than a hint of what used to be. And, it is not so much that I find southern women intrinsically more interesting than New England women, or the women of Pennsylvania and New York, but rather that the particular problems we confront in an effort to understand southern women are problems that tax our theoretical, methodological, and interpretive resources in the most interesting ways. It is in reconstructing the lives of southern colonial women that we are forced to confront the intersection of race and gender—it is possible (though of course not advisable) to avoid this relationship and still produce a respectable study of New England's seventeenth-century farm wives, or

Quaker women's culture. And it is here that the careful, precisioned application of quantitative methods has produced the finest demographic portraits of early American immigrants, female and male. Finally, the scholarship on southern colonial women forces a reinterpretation of any generalization we have developed—and canonized by usage—about gender ideals, and the impetus or motive forces behind their change or persistence.

What interests me as well, however—and this may reveal a certain cranky temperament—are the lacuna becoming evident in our research and our failure to escape certain traps and ruts that scholars of women in other regions fell into before us. This essay arises from the concern that, like my daughter's favorite childhood character, Milo of the *Phantom Tollbooth*, we have wandered into the doldrums and must, like Milo, "think" our way out.

Let me begin however—as I should—with the accomplishments in the years since Catherine Clinton, Jackie Hall, and I stood before an audience and read off our "wish lists" for scholarship on southern women.[1] I won't attempt a complete tour through the literature—even if you were willing to pitch your tents here in this room for several days, I could only accomplish an "if this is Tuesday, it must be Suzanne Lebsock's turn." Instead, I am going to exercise what Michel Foucault would call Power and my son the Little Leaguer would call a "fielder's choice"—I am going to focus on three areas of scholarship: demographic studies, legal studies, and the study of women's work roles, in the home and in the field. After singing the praises of work already done, I will take a little time to ask, as Lenin once did-what is to be done?

It was, of course, the demographers—Lorena Walsh, Lois Carr, Darrett and Anita Rutman, Allan Kulikoff, and Russell Menard—who slew the New England dragon and snatched the seventeenth century out of its Puritan jaws. Through their many articles and books, these scholars have provided us with a demographic portrait of the seventeenth- and early eighteenth-century Chesapeake colonizing population. They have traced the unfolding through time of their subjects' lives and the differences over time in the lives of successive generations. Their work has revealed the skewed sex ratio among the immigrant populations, both European and African, the abbreviated life expectancy for both sexes and races dramatized by the term "demographic disaster," the patterns of fecundity and population growth, and the process by which a Creole population emerged with its salient characteristics of a balanced sex ratio, greater longevity, and natural increase through earlier marriage and expanded childbearing years.[2]

The focus and the fruits of this scholarship do not lie exclusively within the domain of women's history. Yet, its value to us is unmistakable. First, there is the boost to our morale: we can glory in (or take momentary comfort in) the fact that women are an indisputable center of demographic questions and answers. No forced relationship here—no need to justify or explain, no need to insist on the legitimacy or the value of a new perspective—any study of human population and reproduction simply has to have "women" in its index.

In more scholarly terms, this demographic literature has provided us with knowledge about women's lives and experiences of equal weight if not of identical kind to that which New England diaries and sermons and letters earlier provided about women of the northern colonies. Insofar as the family was the core institution in white women's lives, the setting in which much of their time and their affective and physical energy was spent, then the effect of demographic patterns on the family tell us, perforce, much that is critical to our understanding of these women. From these scholars, we have learned how early death and speedy remarriage created the complex family structures captured in the phrase "now wives and Sons-in-law"—families constituted by stepparents and stepchildren, half brothers and sisters, at the heart of which a widow, or bride—a mother and wife—could most likely be found. And we can see how shortened life expectancy atrophied the normative patriarchy of the seventeenth century, led to a widow's receiving a greater share of and a greater control over her husband's estate, and to greater responsiblity for the welfare of her children and his heirs. In sum, we know much about the historically particular institutional environment in which colonial white southern women operated and about the social world in which they functioned. In the same vein, these scholars have outlined the demographic profile of African-American women in the early South—similar in many regards to that of white women insofar as sex ratio, childbearing, and mortality are concerned. Although the chronology of the establishment of African American family and community life is disputed within the literature, scholars like Gutman, Kulikoff, Cody, and Morgan have told us much about women's lives as wives, mothers, and daughters.[3] We know, among other things, that women were less likely to be separated from mothers and sisters than men on larger Chesapeake plantations, producing a multigenerational female community; that women in their prime were expected to be caretakers to the elderly and to the young; and that responsiblities and ties to family operated to diminish the number of female runaways.

As most of us recall, in the Bible Numbers is followed immediately by Deuteronomy. The study of laws and the legal status and identity they define is another way of locating women within the southern colonial past. One of the major contributors in this area is not a southern historian per se, for Marylynn Salmon's ambitious project has been to discover what women's legal rights and restrictions were, how they varied—both in theory and in practice—from colony to colony, particularly with regard to coverture and its impact on property rights and inheritance, and how they changed over time. In *Women and the Law of Property in Early America*, Salmon helped us understand the legal parameters within which women could make efficacious choices and the legal institutions that policed the perimeters of those choices.[4] Salmon revealed to us the great variation, both regional and among the individual colonies, in the laws that governed white women's lives, and she alerted us to the importance of distinguishing the options the law provided women—through, for instance, the courts of equity and prenuptial contracts—and the real circumstances—lack of resources, lack of knowledge, and the weight of custom and gender ideology—that made such options unlikely to be exercised. Salmon displayed a keen sense of the social impact of variations in the law, a sensitivity that has served us well

as we attempt to measure the economic autonomy possible for colonial southern women. For example, in her chapter on provisions for widows, she detailed
the consequences of the Chesapeake's persistence in the practice of granting
widows dower in personalty as well as realty. This tradition—which ensured a
widow absolute rights to between one-third and one-half of a husband's personal estate—died out in the English world by the end of the seventeenth century. It remained, however, in Maryland and Virginia. The significance for
women of both colonies was considerable—although its impact depended on
a second legal definition: that is, whether slaves were personal or real property.
Maryland law defined slaves as personal property, thus providing widows
with an absolute ownership of up to one half of their husband's labor force.
Virginia widows fared less well, for here slaves were considered real property
for the purposes of inheritance. Widows continued to receive their thirds in
personalty, but their society's most valuable property, its human labor force,
was theirs only for life. Southern historians have pursued the implications of
this Chesapeake idiosyncrasy further in recent years. Jean Lee, for example,
recalibrated the relative advantages of sons over daughters in Maryland
bequests to children, based on her shared understanding with Salmon that "in
plantation economies, bound laborers often were more valuable than the land
they tilled."[5]

Beginning with "The Planter's Wife," few scholars interested in women's
power within their society, in their economic authority and material comfort,
or in measuring the respect accorded them as adults, have failed to turn to the
transfer of property from husband to wife as a major yardstick.[6] What they have
concluded is that seventeenth-century southern white women could expect to
inherit more than dower, and be responsible for some considerable part of their
widowhood—as executrixes of their dead husband's estates—for the sustenance
and safekeeping of the family's wealth and property. Whether this continued
into the eighteenth century, and, if so, for how long and in what subregions of
the South, remains unresolved. What remains unresolved as well is the meaning of these inheritance patterns—to the individuals involved, to the larger
community, and to our understanding of gender relations in that era.

Whatever their number, and whatever their legal identities, white and
black women of the South spent much of their lifetime engaged in productive
(and reproductive) work. Women's historians have clearly recognized this—
even if their male colleagues sometimes overlook the fact entirely. Our most
thorough knowledge of those activities constituting "women's work"—including the processing skills of household and garden known as housewifery and
the service or maintenance chores such as cooking, cleaning, mending, and
washing—comes from New England scholars like Laurel Ulrich and from
broad studies such as Mary Beth Norton's *Liberty's Daughters*.[7] Scholars of
southern women, however, have appropriately refracted women's work
through the prism of region—showing that the cash-crop economies of the
South and the attendant slave labor system meant that this work was allocated
differently in this region and that women's relationship to their work—and to
each other—was different also. For example, Ulrich's "neighborliness" model

of the cooperative character of women's labor, with its exchanges of basic goods and services—and the skill specialization this cooperation permits—has little explanatory power for the larger plantation communities. Here the eighteenth-century mistress and her domestic slave women may sit together and spin or sew, but the relationship is not "neighborly"; skill specialization may exist, as some slave women are laundresses and others assist in the dairy, but this is not a voluntary division of labors. As historians have long pointed out, managerial skills were a critical part of the work repertoire of elite white women, and these skills, too, must be distinguished from those found in Ulrich's households. For in seventeenth- and early eighteenth-century New England, management is part of a mistress–apprentice relationship between housewives and their daughters or their neighbors' daughters, not between white mistress and black slave.

Probably the most significant scholarship by a southern historian on women's work has been by Lorena Walsh, who has noted the more sharply gendered division of labor based on social class among Chesapeake whites; the relationship between social class and the obligation to perform "housewifery" tasks (i.e., the concentration on housewifery by women in middling households, where there were fewer slaves to assign to such chores); and the emergence of a gendered division of labor among plantation slaves after 1750.[8] Her account of the factors leading to "female" and "male" work assignments for slaves bears particular mention. Walsh found that crop diversification and the introduction of the plow, coupled with the rise of craft activities on the plantations, operated to segregate man's work from women's work. The beneficiaries of these changes were the slave men who operated the plows and became the blacksmiths, brickmakers, coopers, and other artisans. Slave women continued to perform the most basic and monotonous field chores, chores that became synonymous with "women's work." Philip Morgan has found a similar trend toward gendered work in the rice colonies, where women were also required to perform the most grueling and monotonous of the tasks.[9]

This compressed and hasty review hardly does justice to the demographic, legal, or work literature on the prerevolutionary South. It excludes such interesting work as Jan Lewis's study of affect in the emerging genteel relationships of the eighteenth century, Jean Lee's challenge to the chronology of slave culture set forward by Kulikoff, and the limited literature on Native American women in the colonial era.[10] Yet, even talking much faster, I am afraid I can do no more.

Instead, I want to spend my last few minutes—and pages—on "what is to be done." After many years in the profession, I am keenly aware that it is often far easier to list what is missing than to suggest how to find it; easier to urge others into the archival fray than to walk it yourself. Nevertheless, it does seem to me that we make greater progress in our reconstruction and our understanding of the past if we share our assessments of what those missing pieces may be, cooperate on developing an agenda for the future, and open up for discussion how the problems and the opportunities raised might be approached. In historical scholarship, I am convinced that the cliché of "two heads are better than one" is more appropriate than the antithetical "too many cooks." So: here's what this head has to offer:

First, I believe we continue to be hampered in our work by mutations of the old "golden age paradigm." Southern colonial scholars these days rarely pass their time wondering if women declined or ascended into the industrial era; this notion of an edenic preindustrial life for women was always more gripping for scholars of New England. But, like the heart of an Anne Rice vampire, the heart of the golden age theory—that is, an evaluative comparison across time—threatens to beat forever. A comparative perspective inevitably limits the kinds of questions we ask and the types of evidence we seek—but when the comparison is judgmental rather than referential (and this is the legacy of the "golden age theory") it diminishes the interpretive power of our work. This seems to me to be the problem of both the new demographic work on southern women and the studies on women's legal status. With the publication of "The Planters Wife," a debate began over the comparative advantages enjoyed by seventeenth-century Chesapeake women over women of New England—and vice versa. Such a debate—which creates a comparison across space rather than time—offers little that is enlightening. In most cases, the unequal supply of information about key variables makes the comparison invalid. For example, the demographic data on southern women is more extensive and more sophisticated than that on other colonial women. In many cases, the factors examined are too narrowly defined to be satisfactory. And in all cases, the historian implicitly exercises a subjective value system in determining what is "better" and what is "worse" in a woman's life. Is it better, for example, for a single woman to have great discretion in marital selection because there are neither parents nor family members to consult or obey—as Carr and Green and others find in seventeenth-century Maryland and Virginia? Or does the advantage lie with the seventeenth-century New Englander, whose parents participate in this crucially important selection process? Are southern scholars correct in interpreting the fact that Chesapeake husbands leave their widows greater control over their estates as an indicator of higher esteem for women of this region than women in New England enjoyed or can we interpret the fact in the manner of Laurel Ulrich's *Good Wives* or more recently Lisa Wilson's study of Pennsylvania widows, *Life After Death*, who find that the assumption of such "male" duties is a burden rather than an opportunity to exercise independent judgment or enrich their lives?[11] What we come down to, despite a careful mustering of evidence, is an interpretation shaped by a subjective hierarchy of values.

"Better" or "worse"—no matter how elegantly or pedantically phrased—is a primitive tool of the historian's craft, reducing analysis to judgment. What is needed, instead, is a deeper, richer contexturalizing of what we know. And this, I would argue, leads us not simply to a careful look at modes of production, social class, and race (although these are essential). It also suggests a more materialist history. We need to look—as scholars like Gloria Main and Jim Deetz have done for colonial society in general—at the physical surroundings, the daily routines, the tools of work, and the medical resources that affect women's interactions and that particularize a life in real time and space.[12] If we seek, for example, to capture what motherhood meant to a Maryland woman, we might do well to know more about sexual practice and sexuality; what the physical process of childbirth was like; how infancy was handled; what childrearing methods were current in her social class or race; where children slept, ate, what they did in the course of a day, and so on. Some of this *is* known; but it remains unintegrated, underutilized. I think here of Karin Calvert's recent book *Children in the House* and the value it would have in the debate over parents' attitudes toward infants in colonial society.[13] We might be able to exercise more informed empathy if we can picture the material reality of swaddled infants and are familiar with the seventeenth-century belief that newborns were not fully human, and would not become so, without the consciencious and constant molding of both body and mind through a process of maturation. If, as Michel Foucault urged, we search for answers to the question "how do things happen?" we will place greater emphasis on the small matters of everyday life and the forces that shape material reality.

Second, we must resist a causal hierarchy that makes gender the necessary and sufficient variable in explaining women's lives. Elizabeth Fox Genovese's *Within the Plantation Household* offers a good example of the benefits gained when a scholar refuses to privilege gender above, or isolate it from, race or class. Fox-Genovese insists that gender is situational and thus her women are never just women, they are slave women, old women, young women, white plantation mistresses, or members of the yeoman class.[14] When Sarah Hughes attends to the overdetermination in women's lives in her article "Slaves for Hire: The Allocation of Black Labor in Elizabeth City County, Virginia," she shows us one of its exquisite ironies: by hiring out a slave woman, and thus separating her from her family and friends, a white widow was often able to hold her own family together.[15] We are correct to demand that the students of class and of race consider the gendered meanings of both; but we must take care to reciprocate, and carefully examine how class and race shape gender ideals and women's personal identities. Life, as country singer Rodney Crowell puts it, "is messy." The isolation of gender does not make it any less so.

Finally, let me make what is my own special pleading—that we write more biography where it is possible. Appreciating as I do that the bias in early American biography is toward the lives of the elite; appreciating as well that elite experiences cannot be transferred whole and complete to illuminate the lives of women of other classes and races—and sometimes cannot be transferred at all—let me nevertheless observe that historians must dig deep as well as cut broad swathes. A good biography is, in its own way, an exercise in materialist history, for through it we can learn how the abstract ideas that constitute ideologies take shape in the repeated experiences of a single life, in the repeated choices an individual makes, in her habitual responses to the events and people in her life. In short, a study of character is a window onto culture.

◄▷

Notes

This essay was prepared as a talk for the Southern Association for Women Historians' Third Southern Conference on Women's History, Rice University, Houston, Texas, June 3, 1994.

1. "Southern Women :Redefining Their Past," panel presentation at the Annual Meeting of the Southern Historical Association, Charleston, S. C., November 1983.
2. Lois G. Carr and Lorena S. Walsh, "The Planter's Wife: The Experience of White Women in Seventeenth-Century Maryland," *William and Mary Quarterly*, 3rd Series, 34, October 1977; Lois G. Carr and Lorena S. Walsh, "Economic Diversification and Labor Organization in the Chesapeake, 1650–1820," in Stephen Innes, ed., *Work and Labor in Early America* (Chapel Hill: University of North Carolina Press, 1988); Darret Rutman and Anita Rutman, *A Place in Time: Middlesex County, Virginia, 1650–1750.* (New York: W. W. Norton, 1984); Allan Kulikoff, *Tobacco and Slaves: The Development of Southern Cultures in the Chesapeake, 1680–1800* (Chapel Hill: University of North Carolina, 1986); Russell Menard, "The Maryland Slave Population, 1658 to 1730: A Demographic Profile of Blacks in Four Counties," *William and Mary Quarterly*, 3rd Series, 32, January 1975; Russell Menard, "From Servants to Slaves: The Transformation of the Chesapeake Labor System," *Southern Studies*, 16, Winter 1977.
3. Herbert Gutman, *The Black Family in Slavery and Freedom, 1750–1929* (New York: Vintage, 1976); Kulikoff, *Tobacco and Slaves*; Cheryll A. Cody, "Naming, Kinship, and Estate Dispersal: Notes on Slave Family Life on a South Carolina Plantation, 1786–1833," *William and Mary Quarterly*, 3rd series, 39, January 1982; Phillip Morgan, "Work and Culture: The Task System and the World of Lowcountry Blacks, 1700–1880," *William and Mary Quarterly*, 3rd series, 39, October 1982.
4. Marylynn Salmon, *Women and the Law of Property in Early America* (Chapel Hill: University of North Carolina, 1986).
5. Jean B. Lee, "The Problem of Slave Community in the Eighteenth-Century Chesapeake," *William and Mary Quarterly*, 3rd series, 42, July 1986.
6. Carr and Walsh, "The Planter's Wife."
7. Laurel Thatcher Ulrich, *A Midwife's Tale: The Life of Martha Ballard* (New York: Knopf, 1990).
8. Lorena Walsh, "The Experience and Status of Women in the Chesapeake," in Walter J. Fraser, Jr., Frank Saunders, and Jon Wakelyn, eds., *The Web of Southern Social Relations: Women, Family and Education* (Athens: University of Georgia, 1984).
9. Morgan, "Work and Culture."
10. Jan Lewis, *The Pursuit of Happiness: Family and Values in Jefferson's Virginia* (New York: Cambridge University Press, 1983); Lee, "The Problem of Slave Community."
11. Lisa Wilson, *Life After Death: Widows in Pennsylvania, 1750–1850* (Philadelphia, Temple University Press, 1992).
12. Gloria Main, *Tobacco Colony: Life in Early Maryland, 1650–1720* (Princeton: Princeton University Press, 1982); James Deetz. *Flowerdew Hundred: The Archaeology of a Virginia Plantation, 1619–1864* (Charlottesville: University Press of Virginia, 1993).

13. Karin Calvert, *Children in the House: The Material Culture of Early Childhood* (Boston: Northeastern University, 1992).

14. Elizabeth Fox-Genovese, *Within the Plantation Household: Black and White Women of the Old South* (Chapel Hill: University of North Carolina Press, 1988).

15. Sara Hughes, "Slaves for Hire: The Allocation of Black Labor in Elizabeth City County, Virginia, 1740–1790," *William and Mary Quarterly*, 3rd series, 35, April 1978.

WALLOWING IN A SWAMP OF SIN

Parson Weems, Sex, and Murder in Early South Carolina

South Carolina continues to lure us into its complex web: historians, tourists, preservationists, retirees, developers—promoting the exotic, the eccentric, the Edenic qualities of the region. As a scholar fascinated by matters symbolic as well as substantial, I periodically wade into South Carolina with enthusiasm and abandon. I might agree on South Carolina as a metaphorical Eden of colonial history. And if so, might suggest we explore not only Adam and Eve, but the equally compelling figure of the serpent, stand-in for Satan, Beelzebub, Lucifer, the Anti-Christ, King of the Underworld, the Devil himself.

I have been pondering early southern history for the past quarter century. I remember being asked during my first job interviews what kind of second study I might pursue, as a follow-up to my dissertation, "The Plantation Mistress." I came up with a grand proposal: investigating an early southern community, tracing its founding during the colonial period, developments during the Revolution, and transformations in the antebellum era: to provide thick and deep description of social change. Since I was anchored in a Yankee camp where New England communities were afforded lavish treatment, I longed for the Montaillou[1] treatment for some corner of Georgia, South Carolina, Florida—maybe even Louisiana—to receive this kind of nuanced, concentrated attention. A couple decades later, I'm still waiting.

I could carry on and on about the essays and volumes I'd *like* to see. Given the opportunity, I have promised myself a renewed acquaintance with the

South Carolina archives. Perusing rolls prepared by the county authorities offering depositions on crimes, tracking down some tantalizing evidence encountered in wills. Some day I would like to do justice to unresolved questions that continue to rattle around in my head: what possessed certain colonial communities to burn individuals at the stake and why were these individuals never white males? And why do these incidents seem confined to South Carolina and Virginia?

Fascinating work on gender and race and the intersection of the two topics in the colonial South has drawn me back into the seventeenth and eighteenth centuries for this volume. My interest was piqued several years ago by a book that began with the tale of an early nineteenth-century Carolina scandal that the author mistakenly claimed was popularized under the title "the Devil in Petticoats." When I began putting together a book with Devil in the title, memory drew me back to the supposedly sin-ridden South Carolina upcountry. By the time I discovered the layers of errors and exaggerations surrounding this particular scandal, it was too late—I was hooked, on the trail of the "virtual" South Carolina sensationalized in the works of the wildly popular Reverend Mason L. Weems, the inventor of George Washington's childhood cherry tree, affectionately known as Parson Weems.

You, like me, perhaps have only quaint or vague notions of who Weems was, what he represented to early Americans. I think we can't really grasp what a one-man wonder this industrious pamphleteer became—a true pioneer of tabloid sensationalism. Ministers railing at the decline in public morals were certainly nothing new, but the nature and extent of "putting the fear of God" into the hinterland became a revolutionary challenge after America won its independence. While the state disentangled itself from the church, religious affiliation declined and lapses in faith reputedly reached epidemic proportions. Before the early decades of the nineteenth century when the "Second Great Awakening" rippled through the countryside, divines, congregants and disbelievers were in turmoil. For the most elegant and erudite illumination of these issues, I can recommend Christine Heyrman's book, *Southern Cross: Reimagining Evangelicalism.* But for today, I am going to highlight the career of one young man who seized the day and forged his own brand of evangelical fervor: the very Reverend Mason Locke Weems.

Born in 1759 into a family of wealth and position in Arundel County, Maryland, Weems was the youngest of his father's nineteen children. Weems's father was born in England, a nephew of the Earl of Wymss. Young Mason was reared in Maryland by another uncle, a wealthy doctor who gave the Weems family a princely inheritance, including an estate at Marshes Seat. Mason Weems attended the Kent Free School before sailing for Scotland at the age of fourteen. He studied medicine and surgery abroad until 1776. Weems returned home, and, on the death of his father in 1779, inherited slaves that he chose to emancipate.

In 1782, Weems returned to England to study for the ministry and, with great difficulty, was ordained as an Episcopal priest in 1784 by the Archbishop of Canterbury.[2] He returned to Maryland to become rector of All Hallows parish in Anne Arundel County, a position he held for nearly five years.

Reputedly he would preach at the drop of a hat, or offer a prayer in a ball-room, but such demonstrations of piety were not always welcome. Indeed, many of his enthusiasms were ill suited to the Anglican community he served. Weems expanded his mission to open a school for girls, which was apparently well received. When he additionally offered sermons on alternate Friday evenings for the benefit of local African Americans, it is not difficult to imagine how the wealthy planter elite of his parish responded. While these activities marked him as energetic and restless, they also signaled that his days as a parish priest were numbered. Although we do not have any commentary from Weems himself or his contemporaries on this shift to evangelicalism, we know within a few years Weems drifted from an Episcopal post into a more radical and complex career.

By 1792 Weems was an itinerant minister and bookseller—and peddling what may have been his first literary effort, a tract entitled *Onania*. Weems believed countryfolk were keen for tales of sin and redemption and resolved to earn his living by meeting their needs in the pulpit and with his pen. He linked up with publisher Matthew Carey of Philadelphia and became Carey's agent in the South. He clearly tapped into the growing hunger in the young nation for religious revivalism.

After his marriage to Fanny Ewell, of Prince William County, Virginia, in 1795, Weems settled near her family home, Belle Air. His marriage at thirty-five, along with subsequent children, required a steady and growing income. He began to publish and distribute his own books, such as *The Lover's Almanac*. He hit on a winning formula with biographies of heroes of the Revolution, including Benjamin Franklin, William Penn, General Francis Marion, and a runaway bestseller on George Washington.

Weems's mythic *Life of Washington* remains the text for which he is best remembered, but during his own lifetime, he had an equally compelling reputation as a moralist, a populizer of the gospel who spread God's message in an appetizing, zestful manner. His sermons and didactic tracts stirred the passions of commonfolk. Through a series of provocative titles beginning in 1799 with *Hymen's Recruiting Sergeant*, Weems launched a tireless crusade: to vanquish debt through sales of his works. By 1807 his "immorality tales," re-rendering of notorious crimes laced with pastoral commentary, attracted a loyal readership and increased his bank balance. Weems had a flair for the melodramatic, with one finger on the pulse of the public and the other hand thrusting forth a fistful of colorful titles: *God's Revenge Against Murder* (1807), *God's Revenge Against Gambling* (1810), *The Drunkard's Looking Glass* (1812), *The Devil Done Over* (1812), *God's Revenge Against Adultery* (1815), *God's Revenge Against Duelling* (1821), and *The Bad Wife's Looking Glass* (1823). [Most of these tracts were roughly fifty pages and cost twenty-five cents. Some included a gaudy woodcut on the cover as well.]

Weems was indefatigable during his bookselling career. Perhaps he could ill afford to slow down with a burgeoning family of ten children, the first born in 1796 and the last in 1812. Only rarely did the peripatetic Weems settle in one place. In 1802 he preached for several months at the Pohick Church in

Fairfax County, Virginia—George Washington's family parish—which he promoted as Mt. Vernon Parish when he became the first president's biographer.

By 1809, even with acquisition of his wife's family estate, Weems remained on the road and considered relocating his family to Georgia, a more convenient home base for his travel schedule. During the period 1811–1814, he was away from his wife and children for a single stretch of twenty-three months. His sacrifice was great, but, in time, so was his fame.

Weems's formidable output fueled his popularity, and he became one of the best known clergy of his day. One critic observed "To an age that needed more of his kind, he preached virtue and decent living in language that gripped and seared and sickened."[3]

Weems cultivated a loyal flock during his southern sweeps. From his adopted homestate of Virginia, he branched out into the Carolinas and Georgia by 1804. In 1806 he spent the entire year in the deep South. This same year, Weems republished his *Life of Washington*, which, for the first time, included the infamous tale of young George and the cherry tree.[4] From this point, until his death in 1825, Weems was a popularly recognized author.

One scholar has suggested that Weems perhaps labeled his initial efforts "second editions" to offer the pretense of success to prospective buyers.[5] He may have been the first American author to boost sales through a book tour, although his career seems to have been in some ways a permanent book tour. It is not just his gift for promotion, but his product that commands our attention. An early twentieth-century critic argued:

He is the most delightful mixture of the Scriptures, Homer, Virgil and the back woods. Everything rages, and storms, slashes and tears. . . . It is in vain that the historians, the exhaustive investigators, the learned and the accurate rail at or ignore him. He is inimitable. He will live forever. He captured the American people. He was the first to catch their ear. He said exactly what they wanted to hear. He has been read a hundred times more than all the other historians and biographers of the Revolution put together.[6]

Indeed, for well over a century American schoolchildren have been entranced by Weems's George Washington. Only in recent years has lack of evidence and concern for accuracy tarnished Weems's halo.

Weems's eminence within his own lifetime was enhanced but not defined by his role as Washington's biographer. Paul Ford, Weems's biographer, suggests: "Weems is as typical a figure of the South as Cotton Mather is of New England . . . by painting crime with lurid colors he tried to lead the lawless and ignorant from their lives of excess. . . . His tracts were whips with which he lashed the brutal or self-indulgent classes of the South."[7]

As a recent convert to the Weems bandwagon, it is my observation that we can learn much from what I call his "wallowing in a swamp of sin," his canny choice of characters, his lurid portraits of moral mayhem. It was perhaps no accident that two of his most sensationalist tales were set in South Carolina, a state to which he frequently returned—the place where he retired when ill health overtook him, and the place where he died and was buried.[8] He wrote jokingly in 1821 as he was about to depart southward from Charleston on tour that "my friends here tell me to make my Will & order measure[s] of my Coffin before I set out—the country between being all made up of bogs & swamps & dens of death. But I feel a fearlessness about it, that is, to my mind tantamount to a good passport."[9]

His first foray into the tabloid style came with a juicy story of seduction and betrayal. Weems's publication *God's Revenge Against Murder* in 1807 was a rousing success, as the subtitle enticed through dozens of editions for over a decade: *or, The Drown'd Wife of Stephens's Creek, A Tragedy, lately performed with unbounded applause, (of the Devil and his Court) by Ned Findley, Esquire, one of the Company of Tragedians in the service of the Black Prince, who was so highly gratified with Ned's performance, that he instantly provided him Rooms in one of his Palaces, created him a Knight of the most ignoble order of the Halter, clapped bracelets on his wrists, and an ornament round his neck; and in a few days, promoted him to the ridge-pole of the gallows, at Edgefield Court-House, South Carolina*. The frontispiece included a poetic warning: "O Reader dear, I give you here/ A book to look upon,/ That you may pray, both night and day,/ Nor go, where NED has gone." (Again, this particular pamphlet had a special interest for me: Ned was a popular name in eighteenth-century nursery rhyme, frequently portrayed as a notoriously bad boy on British porcelain, and is the nickname for my own son, Edwin.)

Weems set the stage for this South Carolina scandal with vivid prose and anecdotes: "A gentleman who happened to be at Edgefield court, on its first session after the war [Revolution], assured me with his *own eyes* he beheld a defendant, on the suit's going against him, bounce out of the court-house like a shot out of a shovel, and stripping to the buff, went ripping and tearing about the yard like a mad man! damning both judge and jury for all the pick-pocket sons of b–tch–s he could think of! and daring them to come out, *only to come out*, and he'd shew 'em, *d—n 'em, what it was to give judgment against a gentleman like him!!* [10] (Weems was liberal with exclamation points and italics to heighten the impact of his language as well as using dashes to blunt the impact of profanity.) In his opening paragraph in this tract, Weems awarded a backhanded compliment: "Ned Findley, the hero of the following tragedy, was a native of Edgefield district, South Carolina. It may excite the surprise of some, that a district now so civilized should ever have given birth to such a monster. But that surprise will cease, when it comes to be remembered that Edgefield is a mere *nothing now* to what it was in days *of yore*."[11]

Edgefield was the fifth largest county in South Carolina. Snug against the Georgia border, the lower Piedmont portion of the South Carolina upcountry, Edgefield was a representative chunk of southern backcountry. During the colonial period the area directly north of Edgefield (now Abbeville County) became known as Long Canes, which one pre-Revolutionary claimed was "by far the most fruitful of all the back settlements."[12] By 1787, the top quarter of landowners in the district held three-quarters of the area's taxable property, with an average of seven slaves per household.[13] But Edgefield was mainly yeoman country, predominantly white farmers without slaves, well into the nineteenth century. And the white population of the upcountry jumped nearly 50 percent between 1790 and 1800.[14]

The backcountry settlements remained extremely cut off from the more populated coastal regions. At the turn of the century, life in the Piedmont was rough and tumble by comparison to lowcountry cousins: vagrants and bandits roamed the region. Rachel Klein's prize-winning study of South Carolina, *Unification of a Slave State*, offers us numerous and notorious examples of disorder: roads criss-crossed by marauding bands of highwaymen, gangs descending on magistrates' homes at midnight to drag them out for a dose of outlaw justice, fire-hunting (setting fire to a woods at night and driving out the animals for slaughter), and bandits willing to recruit runaway slaves, to break into isolated farmsteads to torture and rob.[15] Perhaps even more alarming, white women turned up as willing participants in some of these plundering hordes, which panicked authorities, determined to restore order and the good name of the region.

The cry went out for schools, which might have "good effect, the Youth in our Back Country w[ould] become valuable useful men, instead of being as they are at present, brought up deer hunters and horse thieves, for want of Education."[16] The desire for moral fortitude may have been sprouting, but it had a hard time taking root within a society where the gentry were so notoriously dissolute. A traveler commented that Carolina planters were climactically challenged: "The rays of their sun [seem] to urge them irresistibly to dissipation and pleasure."[17] Perhaps this was why Baptist ministers in the South did not demand abstinence from their flock, but merely censured church members who drank too much.[18] Even with these relaxed standards, historian Lacy Ford reports less than 8 percent of all white adults in the upcountry were church members in 1799.[19] Edgefield was a part of this lawless, irreligious corner of the state.

Weems's sketch of these "days of yore" is evocative: Edgefield citizens would "kick like so many . . . young Zebras hitched to a wagon" if even touched by the "trammels of the law."[20] After carrying on for pages about this degraded state, Weems blesses judges and ministers who reformed this den of iniquity. He regrets that his anti-hero, Ned Findley, was "destitute of the milk and honey of Canaan, how could he but long for the onions and garlic of Egypt—DRINKING, GAMBLING, AND LEWDNESS."[21]

In 1807, Weems transformed the tale of a woman murdered by her husband of eight weeks into an American fable: Cinderella meets the Prince of Darkness. When Polly Middleton and her sisters were left motherless, her father's remarriage and dereliction of paternal duty led to her fall from grace. His new wife exiled her stepdaughters to the kitchen: "There among the slaves, they lived and labored, coarse, ignorant and neglected for several years."[22] Ripe for ruin, Polly's vulnerability was exploited by a young man who took "advantage of her confidence in him, and in one fatal moment blasted her whole life's happiness."[23]

Pregnant and unmarried, Polly was turned out by her own family. She and her son lived hardscrabble in a cabin provided by her former lover. Then the boy tragically dies at the age of five. When Middleton died intestate, Polly unexpectedly came into a large inheritance, and naturally was the prey of for-tune hunters. She unfortunately accepted the proposal of Ned Findley—no stranger to seduction.

Weems paints Findley's early career as a drunken rake, highlighting Ned's aborted elopement with his employer's thirteen-year-old daughter. Within days of Findley's marriage to Polly, he ostensibly tired of her and planned "to rob her of her life! To hurl her out of *existence!!* that he might undisturbedly consume her treasures among strumpets and gamblers!!"[24]

One Sunday afternoon while they were alone in a canoe, having been mar-ried only eight weeks, Ned struck Polly with a paddle and knocked her over-board. Weems's depiction of the death scene is gory and sheer invention[25]: "he barbarously beat her hands from the canoe with his paddle, and then with the end of it against her breast, pushed her backwards, still *stretching out her arms to him*, and crying for *mercy*, as long as she could, till choked by the *bubbling, blood-stained* wave, her cries were silenced for ever!"[26]

Weems lays the blame squarely on her father who should not have followed blindly the *"Traditions of Elders,"* but should have broken with European con-ventions to find a more perfect, American ethic that might "melt down hatred with coals of love."[27] Forgiveness for the fallen woman was an extreme form of Christian benevolence, and a departure from orthodoxy for which Weems must be credited.

Findley's arrest and subsequent execution prompt Weems to warn, "Tender parents! think of the wretched Findley, and tremble for *your sons*! Like *there's* [sic], *his* face was once bright with the smiles of innocence."[28] Weems's last few pages are filled with visions of Polly's corpse: "Her long black hair, gather'd under her neck, was clotted with blood. —Her mouth which was open, still seem'd to plead for pity; and the horrors of *death* tho' past, were strongly painted on her ghostly countenance."[29] In his final paragraph, Weems chan-nels his redemptive message through Polly Findley herself: "These eyes, tho' darkened in death, shall see his glory. These, now bleeding ears, shall hear his voice—and this poor mangled body shall come forth, and with an immortal tongue, shall sing my *great Restorer's* praise for ever."[30]

This tract allowed Weems's reputation to soar. The celebrated historian David Ramsay wrote from his Charleston home on May 16, 1807: "I thank you for your much esteemed Pamphlet 'God's Revenge on Murder.' No man can read it without having his risible faculties often excited—No man can read it without having both his horror of *evil* and his respect for virtue increased. You have the art of blending instruction with amusement—while you keep your readers in high good humour by the frolicksomeness of your manner, you are inculcating upon them important moral and religious truths, conduc-ing to their present and future happiness." Excerpts from this endorsement, not surprisingly, appeared on the frontispiece of future editions.[31]

The success of *God's Revenge Against Murder* stimulated a traveling museum to incorporate not only "a Wax Figure, as Large as Life" of Mary Findley, "that was drowned by her husband only eight weeks after Marriage," but also a representation of "William, her beautiful Son, at the age of five years."[32] In a letter in March 1809 Weems reported that his tract on Mary Findley outsold *Robinson Crusoe* and *The Vicar of Wakefield*.[33] A year later he complained of his low stock: "[I have sold] near 800 Dolls [dollars] and no School books, no Religious books, nor even a Pilgrims progress & Washington & Findley all gone—People tearing me to pieces for the *first, and the last*."[34]

The same year Mary Findley made such a publishing sensation, another South Carolina woman, Rebecca Cotton, was publicly assassinated after being acquitted for her husband's murder in, yet again, Edgefield District. Weems's last pamphlet, published in 1823, only two years before his death, provided a colorful title: *The Bad Wife's Looking Glass or God's Revenge Against Cruelty to Husbands, exemplified in the awful history of the Beautiful but Depraved Mrs. Rebecca Cotton, who most inhumanly Murdered her Husband John Cotton, Esq. for which horrid act God permitted her, in the prime of her life and bloom of beauty to be cut off by her bother Stephen Kannady, May 5th 1807, with a number of Incidents and Anecdotes, most Extraordinary and Instructive*. Weems sent a part of this manuscript to Henry C. Carey in Philadelphia and "begg'd [him] to put it, *instantly* into the hands of some Artist good *at design* who wd give us at once the likeness of a very beautiful woman distorted or convulsed with Diabolical passion, in the act of murdering, with up-lifted axe, her husband in sleep." This commissioned frontispiece never materialized, but the sensational pamphlet was published in Charleston.

Weems sketched the pitfalls of John Cotton's beguilement with the beautiful young Rebecca Kannaday, his preoccupation with her physical rather than spiritual attributes. After many years of marriage and several children, Rebecca allegedly bludgeoned her sleeping husband to death with an axe. Put on trial for murder, she was acquitted. Still a striking young woman, she attracted the sympathy of a wealthy widower on the jury. Colonel Ellis proposed to her once he and his peers set her free. Rebecca became unhappy with Ellis, her new husband, and stirred up trouble. She got into a financial dispute with her brother Stephen, who had married one of Ellis's daughters, and feared the consequences of his sister's dissatisfaction, as he believed Becky was both capable of and guilty of murder. Deranged with fear that his sister was going to do him in, Stephen Kannaday made a preemptive strike and bashed in his sister's head with a rock—in broad daylight on the steps of the Edgefield courthouse—then ran away with his wife to the western frontier. The bare bones of the tale provided Weems with a field day.[35]

"The Beautiful but Depraved Mrs. Rebecca Cotton" continues as a mysterious figure, despite Weems's pamphlet. Despite my scouring probate and census records, marriage, death and cemetery notices, deed books, and newspapers of the region for the period, under any of her several names, Rebecca Cotton remains invisible. The men to whom she was related and those she married appear on occasion in the Edgefield County records. [One South Carolina retelling of the scandal alleges that Becky killed off two husbands before John Cotton. She supposedly dispatched her first spouse, Erasmus Smith, by stabbing him through the heart with a mattress needle, then poisoned her second husband, Joshua Terry, wed shortly after Smith's death.[36]

Weems offered riveting detail about so much of the Cotton saga that it's hard to believe he skipped over the "beautiful and depraved" one's knocking off her first two spouses, if there was any truth to this claim.]

In Weems's blow-by-blow description of the fable of Rebecca Cotton, the theme of physical allure and spiritual pollution abounds. Following Cotton's brutal slaying, Weems reminds readers: "Oh, learn the madness of those who prefer the Creature's to the *Creator's* love. How often do unthinking youth, caught by the beauties of the fair, forget HIM who lent all their charms; HIM who formed the snowy bosom—the ivory neck—the love breathing lips—the all conquering smile and eyes keen, darting their resistless glances to the ravished heart."[37] The way in which Weems dwells on Becky's physical attributes creates an erotic subtext for this southern soap opera.

In an unglamorous vein, Becky's twelve-year old brother helped her bury her husband's body in the potato vault. Neighbors are suspicious of his sudden disappearance and trap her young sibling into confession. By the time the body is dug up, Becky Cotton is long gone, leaving behind her children and dead husband. Captured and returned for trial, she escapes conviction.

Weems rages at her acquittal, claiming "her fair face saved her vile neck." Even more aggravating, Weems scorns "this self made widow [did] force her way through the sacred nettings of the law, even as a beetle drives through the slender webbings of a spider; not only extricating herself but enthralling her enemy." He bemoans that Ellis fell in love with her "at the tribunal, and while her hands were scarcely yet free from the scent of her husband's blood."[38]

But her deeds caught up with her, Weems intimates. And he offers an account, taken from an "eyewitness": Becky Cotton lingers for a day, placed on a bed in a nearby house while visitors watched her "brains constantly oozing from her fractured skull . . . and [she] would go into such strong convulsions that ten men were scarcely able to hold her, while at the same time she would pour forth such piercing shrieks and screams as were sufficient to call tears and blood from the hardest hearts."[39] Following this fantasmagorical deathbed scene, Weems "let[s] the curtain fall."

At the tract's close, Weems trots out allegories for good wives and counsel for married couples: eight pages of advice literature. This follows the thirty-plus pages of cinematic exposé of the bad wife's murderous career, replete with invented dialogue and vivid docudramatic renderings. Weems explains in his opening lines: "But how can the world learn wisdom unless those cruel *deeds* be *published* which provide God's judgments? And for what end so worthy, were writing and printing taught to mankind?"[40]

So his tracts overflowed with fiendish plots, debauched characters, grisly murders, forbidden tidbits. Weems riveted readers with layer upon layer of foul deed. Each tale showcases depraved sinners, graphic depiction of carnage, all under the banner of "exposing" evil.

Sexual acts remained off stage in these pamphlets, but lust and animal passion were front and center. Weems employed lengthy literary foreplay, leading up to climactic acts of perversity and violence. In his portrait of Becky Cotton, Weems paints a vampire-like hunger, as she like "any other wicked agent [who] raging with malice, *cannot rest on their beds unless they have shed innocent blood.*"[41] In Weems's version, Becky Cotton does not merely kill her husband with an axe, but, after a nap, strings him up from the rafters when she thinks he may still be alive.

Certainly the Bible features fiends and sinners. Weems makes inspired reference to Cotton as Samson and, by implication, Becky, his Delilah. Yet Weems knew the vinegar of Biblical truths might be sweetened by sugarcoating contemporary scandals with Christian commentary. Weems slaked the public's growing thirst for religious erotica, fulfilled his pastoral mission, and sold more books to boot.

Each and every text was loaded with didacticism, and Weems believed the ends justified the means. He fed the public a diet of crime and punishment to fortify their souls. If individuals were aroused by these stories of unbridled passions and profligate desecrations, how could he be blamed? If they gorged on his tawdry tales for the wrong motives, was Weems at fault?

Yes, Weems made the desires of his protagonists sparkle like shimmering mirages. Yes, he allowed his sinners to luxuriate in their plots and passions, to *wallow* in that swamp. But Weems also tore away the veil with prophetic rage. Offenses against God never went unpunished. Sinners could always repent and sin no more. But make no mistake about it, evil would be avenged. Justice might be postponed, guilt might be delayed, but eventually God evened the score. Weems preached the power of the Old Testament, alongside his Christian benevolence.

His message was embraced throughout the rural South, although William Gilmore Simms asserted that *God's Revenge Against Murder* "contained the offensive inscription—'Another Murder in Old Edgefield,'" and suggested, "It was a long time before the Edgefieldians forgave him this indignity."[42] Another South Carolina scholar charged that Weems characterized the county as "pandemonium," literally a home for devils.[43] Perhaps this perception of indictment led Weems to select a revival in Edgefield in 1809 as the topic for his epistolary tract, *The Devil Done Over*, published in 1812. Weems commended the fact that "seven hundred souls were added to the Baptist Church in nine months."[44] Finally, Edgefield soared like a phoenix during the Second Great Awakening, rising from the ashes of past infamy.[45]

Historian John Chapman described that with the preaching of Lorenzo Dow "no less than sixteen hundred persons in Edgefield joined the church" in 1809.[46] Chapman also credited the great earthquake of 1811 with deepening the religious convictions of residents in the formerly debauched region. Edgefield, once beset by scandal and corruption, transformed itself into a fortress against destructive elements, a region redeemed rather than condemned. And Parson Weems, the tireless advocate of Christian virtue, of rejecting things worldly in favor of spiritual renewal[47] might take comfort and pride in this sweeping southern revivalism. Armed with his fiddle, his preacher's passion, and his box full of tracts, Weems dove headfirst into the swamps of sin the post-Revolutionary backcountry provided, a lifeguard of souls with which to be reckoned.

Whether Edgefield was a ruined Eden or Weems took metaphorical liberties, whether Mary Findley's father or stepmother was more to blame for her demise, whether Becky Cotton did or did not nap while finishing off her husband: these are beside the point. When Weems embellished to increase his readership, we recognize his larger goals as a moralist, even while acknowledging his failings as an historian.

Weems set out to make sin and redemption the central contending forces within America. He urged Republican parents in the new nation to be more vigilant with their roles, to lead children away from lives of corruption and indulgence. He warned American youth to rein in their passions, to fulfill their Christian as well as secular promise. As the nineteenth century unfolded, swamps were drained, southern wilderness tamed, and Weems was laid to rest in South Carolina.

Having spent so much time with this cranky yet endearing parson, I wonder how Weems would translate in the modern era—not his work, but the man himself. Having read both volumes of his correspondence, I'm sure in the 1990s Weems would have his own Website and perhaps his own cable channel.[48] Weems would flourish now as then because the American appetite for scandal remains undiminished, our faith in our own righteousness seems unshakable, and South Carolina's Edenic aspirations still charm. In this spirit, I look forward to continued explorations of early southern history and future personal encounters with South Carolina's notorious and well-deserved reputation for hospitality.[49]

◄▷

Notes

This essay was prepared as a talk for the South Carolina Historical Association at its annual meeting in March 1997 in Columbia, S. C.

1. I am referring to Emmanuel Le Roy Ladurie's breathtaking bestseller *Montaillou*, which was translated into English and published in America by G. Braziller in 1978.
2. This ordination was only achieved after difficult negotiations, as Weems, among others, wanted to take vows, but was required to swear his allegiance to the Crown of England. He consulted Benjamin Franklin, among others, for advice. In August 1784, Parliament passed an Enabling Act that allowed "omission of the Oath in the ordination of persons intending to serve in foreign lands." See Lawrence Wroth, *Parson Weems: A Biographical and Critical Study* (Baltimore, Md.: The Eichelberger Book Company, 1911), 19–23.
3. Wroth, op. cit., 102.
4. It is difficult to determine this edition, which Weems claimed was the "5th," but we do know the book had been through more than one, if not indeed four editions before Weems added the infamous tale of young George's inability to tell a lie.
5. His bibliographer Paul Ford has suggested this is the reason why there are so few first editions of many of Weems's titles.
6. Emily Ellsworth Ford Skeel, ed., *Mason Locke Weems: His Works and Ways* (New York: privately published, 1928), Vol. III, 437.
7. Ibid.

8. Weems was later reinterred in Virginia at his family home, Belle Air.

9. Skeel, op.cit., Vol. III, 438.

10. Mason L. Weems, *God's Revenge Against Murder* (Baltimore, Bell & Cook, 1814), 8th ed., 4. [Hereafter cited as Weems, *GRAM*.]

11. Weems, *GRAM*, 3.

12 Rachel Klein, *Unification of a Slave State: The Rise of the Planter Class in the South Carolina Backcountry, 1760–1808* (Chapel Hill: University of North Carolina Press, 1990), 15.

13. Klein, 22–25.

14. Lacy K. Ford, Jr., *Origins of Southern Radicalism: The South Carolina Upcountry, 1800–1860* (New York: Oxford University Press, 1988), 31.

15. Klein, 51–64.

16. Ibid., 63.

17. Robert M. Weir, *Colonial South Carolina: A History* (Millwood, N. Y.: KTO Press, 1983), 260.

18. Klein, 294.

19. Ford, 21.

20. Weems, *GRAM*, 3.

21. Ibid., 9.

22. Ibid., 13.

23. Ibid., 19.

24. Ibid., 34–35.

25. Although Mr. Gilchrist came onto the scene shortly after Findley killed his wife and testified against Findley in court, this rendition of the death is pure speculation and vintage Weems.

26. Weems, *GRAM*, 39.

27. Ibid., 41–42.

28. Ibid., 50.

29. Ibid., 52.

30. Ibid., 54.

31. This was a well-worn ploy since Weems also solicited an endorsement in 1804 from Thomas Jefferson for his proposal to reprint excerpts from the writings of Algernon Sidney—and liberally made use of Jefferson's approval as well.

32. Skeel, ed., *Mason Locke Weems*, Vol. I, 198.

33. op. cit., Vol. II, 398–399.

34. op. cit., Vol. I, 197.

35. Weems may have postponed publicizing the case both because he had just sensationalized an Edgefield murder from a few years before, which was reportedly received with coolness in Edgefield itself. Weems had plenty of other scandals in other locales—gambling, adultery, dueling, and drunkenness—before returning to the infamous Becky Cotton nearly fourteen years after her death.

36. This tale of the first two husbands appears in *Devil in Petticoats or God's Revenge Against Husband Killing: a Tale of Eighteenth Century Edgefield*, Retold by Nancy C. Mims, in the Collection of the South Carolina Historical Society, Charleston, S.C. It is repeated in Nancy Rhyne's *Murder in the Carolinas* (Winston-Salem, N.C.: John F. Blair, 1988), 4–5, without any substantiation. I discount these accounts as folkloric exaggeration. Weems claimed an acquaintance with James Kannaday, the father of Rebecca Cotton, and would have known about earlier marriages.

37. Mason L. Weems, *The Bad Wife's Looking Glass or God's Revenge Against Cruelty to*

Husbands. (Charleston: 1823) 2nd ed., 19–20. [Hereafter cited as Weems, *The Bad Wife*.]

38. Weems, *The Bad Wife*, 27. Colonel Ellis is labeled as a "Major Gellis" in Weems's text, but otherwise his identifications seem accurate.

39. Ibid., 35–36.

40. Ibid., 3.

41. Ibid., 18.

42. Skeel, op. cit., Vol. I, 189.

43. John A. Chapman, *History of Edgefield County from the Earliest Settlements to 1897* (Newberry, S.C.: Elbert Aull, 1897), 73.

44. Skeel, op. cit., Vol. I, 232.

45. See Ford, 24–31.

46. Chapman, *History of Edgefield County*, 73.

47. Weems's letters are full of his fears and complaints about money. He frequently chastised Matthew Carey, reminding him of the difference in their stations: "You will do me Justice to remember that *I am not rich* . . . my daily bread depends on my daily revenue in your service. And when disasters come, they bring the most threatening aspect on *me*. You, thank God, are rich, & possessg wealth perhaps above one hundred thousand dolls. I am worth *nothing* but my Health & Spirits. And when I left Mrs. Weems, I left *her* in the last fortnight of gestation—in a town—with 12 in a family—a hard winter setting in and with only 40 dolls . . . I can hardly support my family, cannot give them the education they deserve." in Skeel, op. cit., Vol. II, 436. Naturally Weems was wheedling for advance money and perhaps exaggerating his claims; still, evidence confirms his claim that he struggled all his life with debt and turned his back on the comfortable life of a parish priest.

48. One can only imagine what Mason Weems would have done with the story of Susan Smith, the South Carolina mother convicted in 1995 of drowning her two sons.

49. I would like to thank Professor Randy Sparks and Carlin Timmons, both of the College of Charleston, for their assistance with this project. Michele Gillespie was a veritable midwife for this essay; her editorial skills, coaching talents, and unfailing good humor were essential for its completion.

◆　Part II

THE
UPPER
SOUTH

"CHANGED . . . INTO THE FASHION OF MAN"

The Politics of Sexual Difference in a Seventeenth-Century Anglo-American Settlement

In 1629, the gender identity of servant Thomas Hall stirred controversy among the residents of Warraskoyack, Virginia, a small English settlement located across the James River from what the English optimistically called "James Cittie." A recent migrant, Hall soon became the subject of rumors concerning his sexual identity and behavior. A servant man's report that Hall "had layen with a mayd of Mr. Richard Bennetts" may initially have sparked the inquiry that led to questions about Hall's sex. Although fornication was not an unusual offense in the colony—the skewed sex ratio of four men to every one woman and the absence of effective means for restraining servants' sexual activities produced a bastardy rate significantly higher than that in England—Hall's response to the charge and the subsequent behavior of his neighbors were quite out of the ordinary. When allegations of sexual misconduct and ambiguous gender identity reached the ears of several married women, Hall's case spiraled into a unique community-wide investigation that eventually crossed the river to the colony's General Court at Jamestown.[1]

Court testimony revealed that, while in England, Hall had worn women's clothing and performed traditionally female tasks such as needlework and lacemaking. Once in Virginia, Hall also occasionally donned female garb, a practice that confused neighbors, masters, and plantation captains about his social and sexual identity. When asked by Captain Nathaniel Bass, Warraskoyack's most prominent resident, "wether hee were man or a woeman," Hall replied that he was both. When another man inquired why he wore women's clothes, Hall answered, "*I goe in weomens apparell to gett a bitt for my Catt.*" As rumors continued to circulate, Hall's current master John Atkins remained unsure of his new servant's sex. But the certainty that Hall had perpetrated a great wrong against the residents of Warraskoyack led Atkins to approach Captain Bass, "desir [ing] that hee [Hall] might be punished for his abuse."

Unable to resolve the issue, Warraskoyack locals sent Hall's case to the General Court at Jamestown, where details of the community investigation and Hall's personal history were recorded by the clerk. Two witnesses testified to the community's multiple efforts to gather physical evidence. Hall, meanwhile, provided justices with a narrative history of his gender identity. Together, this testimony constitutes the main documentary trail left by the person known variously as Thomas or Thomasine Hall. Other colonial records reveal only a few additional details about this unusual servant and the unprecedented investigation of Hall's body, sexual history, and identity.

Despite the paucity of evidence, Hall's case presents a nonetheless richly detailed glimpse of an early modern community's responses to gender transgression, exposing to view a multiplicity of popular beliefs about sexual difference and the variety of uses to which they could be put by groups of people with different stakes in the social order. In contrast to most of the known European cases of gender transgression in the early modern period, the brief transcript of the Hall case contains a vivid description of the efforts of ordinary people (whom I define here as individuals who did not participate directly in formal legal, medical, or scientific theorizing about sexual difference) to determine a sexually ambiguous person's identity. Faced with an individual who did not conform to conventional gender categories, the residents of Warraskoyack gathered empirical evidence about Hall's physical body. The subsequent need to report their findings to a superior court compelled people who normally did not articulate their views on sexual difference to define the essence of maleness and femaleness. The Hall case not only provides documentary evidence of these beliefs, but offers an opportunity to reconstruct what we might call "beliefs-in-action." We can thus analyze each group's articulation of sexual difference by comparing it to their investigatory method, their claims (often implicit) to expertise, and their authority in the community.

Hall's case also offers a unique chance to compare popular concepts of sexual difference, about which little is known, with elite medical and scientific discourses, about which much has been written in recent years. Many early modern medical theorists and scientists worked within a predominantly Galenic framework that emphasized anatomical parallelism and the potential mutability of the sexes. Women were not a separate sex, according to this model of difference, but an imperfect version of men. Lacking the vital heat to develop external genitalia, women's deformed organs remained tucked inside. Early modern writers noted, however, that strenuous physical activity or mannish behavior could cause a woman's hidden testicles and penis to emerge suddenly, an occurrence contemporaries explained as evidence of Nature's unerring tendency toward a state of greater perfection.[2]

Scientific discourses that emphasized anatomical parallels and mutability ultimately left the lion's share of the work of producing gender distinctions to legal and religious institutions, local custom, and daily performance. Borrowing liberally from religious and medical texts that assumed women's inferiority, legal interpreters enshrined gender differences in the laws governing marriage, property, and accountability for crime. Christian theologians similarly reaffirmed gender differences in their divergent assessments of men's and women's capacity for reason and their condemnations of boundary violations as sinful and defiling. In daily life, meanwhile, family and neighbors naturalized gender boundaries by insisting on the continuity of identity established and affirmed through clothing, names, work, and the public approbation accorded to heterosexual relationships. Law, religion and custom thus stabilized gender, although they did so without access to a stable, biological concept of sexual difference.[3]

When challenges to early modern categories of manhood and womanhood arose in Christian Europe, as in the case of hermaphrodism or transvestism, the burden of explicating gender differences fell primarily to the law in consultation with academically trained doctors and scientific investigators. Legal constructions of gender difference were generally less ambiguous that those elaborated in the medical and scientific literature of the period because of the law's heavy reliance on gender categories to define and protect familial property. Concerned mainly with preserving clear gender boundaries rather than exploring anomalies, the courts also had the power to coerce individuals to alter their gender performances. Instead of insisting that the hermaphrodite had a "true" core sex that could be determined anatomically, early modern legal authorities urged the individual to adopt either a male or female identity. Echoing religious and philosophic treatises that categorized hermaphrodites as monsters, legal discourse reaffirmed gender boundaries by refusing to admit unstable or ambiguous sexual identities legally.[4]

Transvestism, which typically took the form of women dressing as men during the sixteenth and seventeenth centuries, represented a different sort of challenge. While the hermaphrodite embodied the slippery dualism of all sexual identities under the Galenic one-sex model, the transvestite undermined society's ability to use clothing to stabilize distinct sexual identities.[5]

Accounts of Hall's body and past, like most accounts of early modern gender transgression, were presented in a legal setting where they were subject to the needs of the court. Despite this legal context, the testimony in the Hall case still permits a comparison between community examinations of an ambiguous individual and the subsequent legal process. Energetic and heterogenous, the community investigations of Hall's identity reflected different philosophies and tactics from those used by Virginia's General Court. While justices inquired politely into Hall's past, seeking historical answers to the question of his identity, most of his neighbors responded to his fluctuating persona with aggressive curiosity about what lay hidden in his breeches. The settler population also had great difficulty reaching consensus; no single popular discourse of sexual difference informed their inquiries, nor did they agree about the meaning of their findings.

The location of Hall's case in a recently settled English colony may account in part for the extraordinary historical visibility and heterogeneity of the community's responses to Hall. In addition to its distance from the structures of metropolitan scientific and legal authority, Warraskoyack lacked both a parish church and a local court. As in most settlements in Virginia in the 1620s, such formal local institutions of authority simply did not exist. In their absence, the responsibility for producing and maintaining gender distinction fell almost entirely to laypeople. Popular ideas about sexual identity appear to have carried more weight in Virginia than in England, although they were perhaps more subject to challenge from other popular sources. The colonial site of Hall's case thus serves to illuminate not only the varieties of popular belief, but the fractures and fissures in the community's interest in preserving the gender order.

Perhaps the most compelling feature of Hall's case is Hall him/herself. Hall's life disrupted the attempts of justices and neighbors alike to treat gender as a set of natural categories. For Hall, the "performance" of gender identity appeared to be as malleable as a change of clothes and at least partially motivated by opportunities for employment. The burgeoning commerce, migration, and national rivalries of the early modern Atlantic world, moreover, had in many ways helped to produce Hall's complex personality. When asked to explain his/her gender identity, Hall recited a historical narrative in which the visible signs of gender were not the natural expressions of an internal identity, but communiques issued and manipulated for public consumption. Although Hall seemed utterly at ease with gender as a choice of self-presentation distinct from the issues of identity—a posture we will examine more closely—his metamorphoses provoked both his community and the colonial arm of the state to discover and affix a permanent identity.[6] Despite the brazenness of Hall's transgression and the importance of gender differentiation to the colonial economy, Hall received a comparatively mild punishment, raising additional questions about the significance of this case.

Let us turn now to the colony of Virginia and to Warraskoyack, the settlement where neighbors and plantation commanders found Hall's fluctuating identity so perplexing.

◄▷

By 1629, Virginia had enjoyed several years of peace and prosperity but was nevertheless considered an undesirable and dangerous place by many Englishmen and women. Two decades of warfare with local Indians culminated in an Indian attack upon the English population in 1622, a bloody event that tarnished the colony's early image as a paradise for settlers. Reports of rampant disease, maltreated servants, and backbreaking labor, moreover, filtered back to England, discouraged female migrants and exacerbated the skewed sex ratio and climate of lawlessness that prevailed among the colony's predominantly young, male, and unmarried settlers. The difficulty of attracting dedicated ministers and supporting churches in a region where the sparse European population was scattered over miles of riverine settlements rather than clustered in towns further contributed to the colony's reputation for godlessness and immorality. In addition, by 1629, the colonial economy was firmly committed to the production of tobacco, a New World commodity that had become fashionable in royal and aristocratic circles throughout Europe. Despite the efforts of local officials to encourage economic diversification, most of the colony's landowners devoted themselves to tobacco and procuring the labor necessary to its production. English laborers, especially men, were the preference of most planters, although by 1629 a newcomer to Virginia might have seen English women or African laborers, male and female, hoeing rows of tobacco.[7]

A fledgling plantation in a colony where everything was relatively new, Warraskoyack had been an English settlement for less than seven years when Thomas Hall arrived. Founded on the site of an Indian village, the settlement consisted of two plantations devoted to the production of tobacco. Bennett's Welcome, established in 1621 by London merchant and Virginia Company investor Edward Bennett, had suffered tremendous losses during an Indian attack in 1622 in which over fifty English men and women were slain. In 1628, command and ownership of Bennett's Welcome passed into the capable hands of the founder's nephew, Richard Bennett, who had arrived in the colony only recently but whose political star was already rising.[8]

Warraskoyack also included the plantation known as Basse's Choice. Founded a year after the Bennett Plantation, the Bass settlement narrowly escaped the ravages of the Indian attack. Captain Nathaniel Bass, plantation commander and proprietor, was a political player to be reckoned with. In 1624, he represented the plantation in the House of Burgesses; within one year after the Hall case, he became a member of the Governor's Council.[9]

Compared to the English cities and towns the Virginia colonists had left behind, Warraskoyack was a tiny community filled with newcomers. It is doubtful that the settlement ever exceeded 200 people during the 1620s. After the resettlement following the Indian attack of 1622, the population fell vulnerable to disease and its numbers again plummeted. By 1625, however, the settlement began to grow slowly through immigration, reconstituting itself with a steady stream of newcomers. Of the sixteen individuals named in the Hall testimony, seven can be positively identified as residents of the colony in 1625, four years before Hall came to the attention of the General Court. Of these, only three appear to have lived in Warraskoyack before 1627. When Hall moved to Warraskoyack that year, he was entering a community in which most members were as new to the area as himself.

Only two of those named in the court testimony could boast a lengthy tenure in Warraskoyack: Bass, the plantation commander, and Alice Long, who had married and born at least one child in Virginia since her arrival in the colony in 1620.[10] At thirty-nine and twenty-seven, respectively, both individuals were seasoned veterans of the south side plantations, embodying whatever traditions had endured the traumatic and disrupted history of English settlement. In 1629, while Bass enjoyed a position of political authority, Long claimed informal influence among the several dozen women in the settlement.

A few other individuals who became involved in the Hall case had been in the colony, if not in Warraskoyack itself, for several years before Hall's arrival. John Atkins, Hall's new master at the time of the inquest at Jamestown, arrived in the colony in 1623. Roger Rodes, who appears to have been living in Jamestown in 1625, was married to Dorothy Rodes, one of the matrons who assisted Alice Long in her investigation of Hall's body. John Tyos, described in the court testimony as a former master of Hall's, also had a history in the colony long enough to have included association with at least two men named Thomas Hall.[11] The other individual with a major role in Warraskoyack's attempts to determine Hall's identity was John Pott, the Governor of the Colony who presided over the colony's General Court. A medical doctor who had lived in the colony since 1620, Pott did not reside in Warraskoyack, but on one of several tracts of land he had acquired on the north side of the James River.[12]

The community investigations of Hall's body that took place in Warraskoyack in early 1629 occurred not at the behest of Governor Pott, however, but as a consequence of local concerns for social order. Lacking many of the traditional institutions of English village life, the small English community depended instead on highly personal forms of authority. Three converging lines of authority emerged as Warraskoyack residents mobilized personal networks to address Hall's transgression. The first—embodied by Bass and Bennett—derived its strength from the official mandates of the Governor, the General Court, and the Crown. The second, which included John Tyos and John Atkins, represented the community of masters and their interests in maintaining existing labor arrangements with servants. The third, a source of authority largely internal to the community, was constituted by women such as Alice Long and Dorothy Rodes.

Boasting nearly as much influence as its male counterparts, female authority in Warraskoyack accrued from the important role granted midwives and matrons by English law. In cases in which the condition of a woman's body could influence the verdict or sentence, English courts constituted an investigatory jury of women to conduct an examination. After searching the subject's body for evidence of recent sexual activity, pregnancy, or childbirth (or, in case of suspected witchcraft, suspicious marks), the matrons reported their findings to the court. With the exception of one fifteenth-century case in which a jury of women was summoned to arouse an allegedly impotent man to erection, these juries inspected only women's bodies. After 1500, Juries of Matrons who provided evidence in impotence cases did so as witnesses to the condition of the wife's genitalia. With minor deviations, the tradition of summoning the matrons' jury appears to have continued in Virginia. The testimony of a midwife might occasionally substitute for that of a Jury of Matrons at the colony's General Court or, after the establishment of the county courts during the 1630s, at a local hearing.[13]

The authority of the Warraskoyack matrons might also have derived from the heightened significance of their legal and historical functions in Virginia. In a small community that lacked rival institutions of historical memory, Long and Rodes could claim authority based on a historical and gender-specific construction of "experience." As witnesses to and participants in the births, weddings, illnesses, and deaths of Warraskoyack neighbors, women like Long and Rodes were repositories of information about community relationships, personal histories, and identities. These activities did not *naturally* constitute female authority. Rather, women's authority derived from constructions of tradition, and, more important, from their claims to interpret female bodies— a practice that required constituting the subjects of their inquiry (women) as well as their own authority to make sense of these bodies. Female authority to interpret female bodies depended in part, however, on the apparent natural- ness of sexual categories. Without the existence of two sexes, women's claims to special knowledge would have been unfounded and their unique roles in courtroom and community unnecessary. Women such as Long and Rodes thus had an important stake in protecting gender boundaries and enforcing the rules governing sexual behavior. Their authority resided in categories of sexual difference that Hall's changes of clothes threatened to undermine.[14]

This then was Warraskoyack in 1629, a community less than ten years old overseen by men and women with a maximum of six or seven years of colonial life under their belts, where intimate forms of authority diverged along gen- dered lines.

◀▷

The first to lay hands on Hall for the purposes of gathering information was a group of women whose interest had been piqued by a "report" that Hall was both a man and a woman. Groups of women usually searched only other women at the request of a local court; their authority to glean information from bodies rarely crossed gender lines and they did not usually initiate a search without the backing of local officials. With Hall's then-master, John Tyos, claiming his servant was female, however, the women decided that it was appropriate to intervene. After searching Hall's person for evidence of his sexual identity, Alice Long, Dorothy Rodes, and Barbara Hall concluded that "hee was a man." Despite this new evidence, Master Tyos continued to swear to Hall's female identity, provoking John Atkins, who was contemplating the purchase of Hall, to take the problem to plantation commander Captain Bass.[15]

Confronted with conflicting evidence—the rumors of Hall's hermaphro- dism and alleged fornication, Hall's master's claim that his servant was a woman, and the married women's findings that he was male—Bass asked Hall point blank "whether hee were man or woeman." Hall answered that he was both, explaining that although he had what appeared to be a very small penis ("a peece of flesh growing at the . . . belly as bigg as the topp of his little finger [an] inch long"), "hee had not the use of the man's parte." Hearing this con- fession, Bass ordered Hall to put on women's clothes. Male impotence was usually considered sufficient grounds for the annulment of marriages; for Bass, it was a sufficient condition for assigning female gender identity. An individual who lacked male sexual functions and sometimes dressed like a woman, Bass may have reasoned, could safely be classified as a woman.[16]

Bass's decision did not sit well with the group of married women who claimed to have seen evidence of Hall's manhood. But with Hall parading about Warraskoyack in the mandated female attire, they began to "doubt of what they had formerly affirmed." Trooping over to Hall's residence at the home of his new master John Atkins, the group searched the female-clad Hall while s/he slept, confirming their original judgement that he was a man. In an unusual breech of etiquette, moreover, they insisted that Master Atkins view the proof for himself. Atkins tiptoed to Hall's bed but lost his nerve when "shee" stirred in her sleep.

Tenacious in their quest to reveal the "truth" to Atkins and to two other women who had joined their ranks—and perhaps still harboring doubts themselves—the married women planned a third search of Hall's person. When Atkins finally saw the evidence of Hall's manhood he was unimpressed and asked Hall "if that were all hee had." Perhaps Atkins, like Hall himself, doubted the significance of the small "piece of flesh" protruding from Hall's belly and wondered whether there might be other anatomical clues. Describing his identity for the first time as the presence of female anatomy rather than as a lack or deformity of maleness, Hall told Atkins that he had "a peece of an hole." Atkins immediately insisted that Hall lie down and "shew" these female credentials. After searching together in vain for Hall's vagina, Atkins and the married women concluded that Hall could not be a hermaphrodite. Although Hall's penis may have been tiny and in poor working order, it became for Atkins and the matrons, in the absence of other "evidence" of femaleness, the dominant criteria for Hall's social identity. In sharp contrast to the language Hall used to describe his own freewheeling sense of chosen identities, Atkins ordered Hall to "bee put into" male apparel and urged Captain Bass to punish him for his "abuse."[17]

As soon as Captain Bass reversed his decision about Hall's gender identity and proclaimed him a man, Hall became fair game for the men of Warraskoyack. Hearing a "Rumor and Report" of Hall's tryst with Mr. Richard Bennett's servant Great Besse, Francis England and Roger Rodes took advantage of a chance meeting with Hall to conduct their own impromptu investigation. Rodes declared, "*Hall, thou has beene reported to be a woman and now thou are proved to bee a man, I will see what thou carriest.*" Assisted by England, Rodes threw Hall onto his back. England later told the General Court that, when he "felt the said Hall and pulled out his members," he found him to be "a perfect man."[18]

The declarations of evidence and the conclusions drawn from that evidence bring us as close as I believe we will ever be to ordinary seventeenth-century English people's articulated beliefs in the essence of sexual difference and their deployment of those beliefs to serve their own political and social interests. Three groups of people—the married women, Hall's former and present masters, and the plantation commanders—participated actively in these searches of Hall's person. In the absence of a county court and church, these groups represented the community's interests in determining Hall's sex. Significantly, each group also had a personal stake in defending the boundaries of maleness and femaleness. Married women who normally interpreted women's bodies for legal authorities intervened because Hall's crossing of gender lines challenged fundamental gender differences on which their authority was based. Hall's masters' interest in determining the sex of their servant suggested the significance of gender to the allocation of labor, an especially important issue in this new settlement so single-mindedly devoted to producing tobacco. Hall's gender identity may have affected Master John Atkins' decision to purchase a servant as well as his assignment of work, the sexual intimacies he did or did not attempt, and the company he allowed his servant to keep. Male servants would likely be pressed into militia duty at some point during their service. Male and female servants also received different freedom dues and were expected to assume different social and economic roles at the end of their terms. Charged with keeping order in the community, plantation commanders sought a permanent identity for Hall that would mollify the displeased masters and matrons of the community, restore Hall to his proper place in that community, and, above all, establish the commander's ability to resolve community conflicts successfully.

Roger Rodes and Francis England, whose interests in Hall's identity were slightly more attenuated but who nonetheless asserted their right to intervene, constituted a fourth group. Lacking any formal authority to search bodies except in the case of grand jury inquests into murder, Rodes and England could not claim the customary role or territorial interest of the matrons, the immediate interests of masters, or the political authority of the plantation commander. Marginal to the process of uncovering Hall's identity, Rodes' and England's belated search occurred only after the other groups had pronounced their interpretations of Hall's sex. Yet the two men still intruded themselves into the process, perhaps seeing the unprecedented nature of the case as an opportunity for expanding the scope of their own authority in the community, for satisfying their curiosity, or for punishing Hall informally for his masquerade.

The matrons of Warraskoyack, the community's plantation commander, and Hall's masters were initially at odds over the issue of his gender, issuing conflicting conclusions and repeating their processes of gathering evidence as they struggled to move toward a consensus. After the matrons' initial examination of Hall and their conclusion that he was a man, Captain Bass undermined them, reasoning from Hall's confession of impotence, rather than from the women's testimony, that Hall was a woman. The married women did not let this breech of their traditional legal role go unchallenged. To do so would have been to suffer a severe loss of credibility and influence. It seems that they may also have harbored doubts about the nature of the evidence they had uncovered, for they quickly instigated a second search. When this examination confirmed their initial pronouncement, they enlisted a man from the group of masters with an interest in Hall's case, thereby creating a coalition of women and men to confront Captain Bass. Despite their influence in Warraskoyack, women's word alone was not sufficient to lead Bass to change his mind. In league with Atkins, however, the married women's information persuaded Bass to contradict his own command and order Hall to don male clothes.

In addition to their difficulties with rival male authorities in their community, however, the married women faced the challenge of interpreting Hall's unusual body. As they did not describe their findings in detail—or those descriptions did not reach the records of the General Court—we can only speculate about their analysis of the evidence. The presence of a penis, however small and ineffective, seems to have weighed heavily in their initial conclusion that Hall was a man. But their articulated doubts and subsequent search for a vagina suggests the difficulty of fitting Hall's body into familiar categories.

Curiously, neither the matrons of Warraskoyack nor the male participants in the investigation chose to involve Great Besse, the servant rumored to have had a tryst with Hall, in their deliberations. In the absence of any additional information about Hall's alleged lover, we can only comment on the possible and probable reasons for her silence in the court record. Besse could possibly have been one of the tiny number of Africans who lived in the colony after 1619 and, as a consequence, may not have spoken much English; the chances are, however, that she would have been described in the testimony as a "negor" rather than as a "servant maid." It is less likely that Besse was an Indian, as few Indians were held as servants or slaves in the colony until the middle of the century. A less intriguing but more plausible scenario is that Besse was an Englishwoman whose link to Hall was so quickly proven to be unfounded that there was no need to pursue her testimony.

◄▷

Able to reach only a shaky consensus on the question of Hall's gender identity and unsure of how to punish his transgression, Warraskoyack locals sent Hall's case to the General Court at Jamestown. Under the leadership of the recently installed Governor John Pott, the General Court declined to initiate their own search of Hall's body. Pott may have been reluctant to embroil himself in a medical matter after having recently extricated himself from the seventeenth-century equivalent of a malpractice suit. Nor did the Court invite the married women to report their findings directly. They listened instead to Francis England's and John Atkins' accounts of Hall's gender mutability and then "examined" Hall juridically, eliciting a narrative of gender identity.[19]

Hall explained that he had been christened Thomasine in England and dressed accordingly in women's clothes. When "she" reached the age of twelve, an age at which many girls would have taken up residence with neighbors or relatives to learn housewifery, Thomasine was sent by her mother to London to live with an aunt. During her ten-year residence in the city, Thomasine might have witnessed the crossover of male and female aristocratic fashions that so disturbed James I. London's female street culture might also have had a profound impact on the young Thomasine, offering lessons in market savvy, sexuality, and marriage to all who listened to the ribald balladry of an itinerant performer or picked up a discarded broadside.[20]

If at this point in Hall's narrative justices harbored hopes that an established pattern of female identity, deeply rooted in Hall's childhood, would put an end to the confusion, they were to be sadly disappointed. Hall informed the justices that when her brother was pressed into military service, Thomasine "Cut of[f] his heire and Changed his apparell into the fashion of man" to become a soldier in the English force that intervened on behalf of French Hugenots at the Isle of Rhe. Twenty-four years old when he made this transformation, Hall was indeed lucky to survive his first year as a man, for the military adventure proved to be a debacle. Hall returned to England, where he "changed himself into woemans apparell," resuming both female identity and needlework. Residing in the port of Plymouth, which was by the mid-1620s a point of embarkation for many colonial voyages, Hall remained a woman until the opportunity arose to sail for Virginia. He "changed againe his apparell into the habit of a man and soe came over into this Country" sometime late in 1627.[21]

Both the evidence gathered by the community and Hall's own historical narrative of identity figured in the General Court's sentence of Hall. Compelling Hall to don men's breeches, the Court acknowledged the physical manifestations of sex that were of such importance to the diligent matrons of Warraskoyack. Governor Pott may have encouraged this anatomical interpretation of gender identity, having previously served the colony as a doctor. But the court found neither the physical evidence nor the sentence of an imposed (and permanent) male identity sufficient. Their order that the male-clad Hall should mark his head and lap with female accessories—"a Coyfe and Croscloth with an Apron before him"—attested to their power to punish by inscribing dissonant gender symbols on an offender, in this case, by demeaning a man with the visible signs of womanhood. Such a sentence mimicked Hall's crime of diminishing the integrity of his male identity with female garb. The sentence may also have been the justice's admission that self-confessed impotence, cross-dressing, and a history of female identity compromised an individual's claims to the political and legal privileges of manhood.

The Court's decision that Hall should wear male attire topped by the apron and headdress of a woman seems on one level to affirm Hall's claim to a dual nature by creating a separate category for him. Yet Hall himself never expressed his hermaphrodism in this fashion, choosing instead to perform his identity serially as either male or female. The Court's mandate of a permanent hybrid identity for Hall was thus both a punishment of Hall and an unprecedented juridical response to gender ambiguity. Denying Hall the right to choose a single identity—a marked departure from the usual European treatment of hermaphrodites—the judges asserted the importance of permanence for concepts of gender even as they failed to define its essence. They may have believed they had found a creative solution to the problem of defending the boundaries of both maleness and femaleness from Hall's transgressive behavior. That they chose to shame him rather than inflict brutal corporeal punishment also suggests that the Court recognized Hall's value to his masters and to the colony as a laborer.

The court never addressed the matter of Hall's culpability for fornication. Nor did it address the consequences of the court-ordered hermaphroditic identity for Hall's future sexual activity. Rather, it concerned itself with "publish[ing]" the fact that Hall was "a man and a woeman" in Warraskoyack so that "all the Inhabitants there may take notice thereof." In so doing the court may have sought to prevent unwitting men from committing sodomy with the ambiguous Hall. Perhaps, too, the justices were trying to warn unsuspecting women not to allow him too much intimacy. They did take the precaution of requiring Hall to find sureties for his good behavior until the local court of Warraskoyack discharged him. Good behavior in this case seems to have meant permanent compliance with the court-ordered signature of hermaphrodism, the mixture of male and female garb.

The General Court's interest in resolving the question of Hall's identity differed substantially from that of Hall's Warraskoyack neighbors, who had attempted to maintain gender boundaries by classifying Hall as one sex or the other. The Court's sentence, that Hall wear the clothing of both man and woman, did not solve the dilemmas that had initially compelled Warraskoyack residents to approach their plantation commander. Master Atkins, for instance, was probably no closer to determining Hall's work assignment or freedom dues than he had been at the beginning of the investigation. Sadly, we will never know just how Hall's community addressed the problems raised by the court's sentence.

Despite the differences between the General Court's focus on establishing identity from a narrative of performance and the Warraskoyack matrons' insistent search for readable physical evidence, the two groups may have shared a belief that the changeable physical bodies and legal identities of women mirrored changing female life histories. For the married women, beliefs that female bodies were constituted of pliable matter that bore the impressions of sexual activity made possible their own authority as interpreters of those bodies. Married women in most early European modern societies wielded influence in courtrooms in part because they had constructed a folk science of extracting sexual histories from female bodies by "reading" these marks. Virginity, recent sexual intercourse, rape, pregnancy, childbirth, sex with the devil—all carried corresponding physical signs in the science of midwifery and were probably equally significant, if not as systematically delineated, for matrons called upon by their communities to translate this evidence into legal testimony. When Hall's body proved resistant to being read, the married women may have been inclined to see the "piece of flesh" as a penis and to categorize "him" as a man. For the General Court, conversely, Hall's historical narrative of shifting sexual identities may have effectively obviated the possibility of declaring him a man. Having divulged a historicized and mutable sexual identity, in other words, Hall made it difficult for the court to assign him a legal identity defined by a presumed constancy of political and economic function and an invulnerability to changes in sexual status. Although courts across the early modern world recognized maturation to manhood as an inherently teleological feature of male identity, adult manhood brought a stabilizing conclusion, vulnerable only to age and death. Adult womanhood, in contrast, was viewed by the courts as an inherently episodic and unstable condition, subject to the changes of marriage, widowhood, and remarriage. Hall's changes of gender as an adult may thus have precluded him from the privileges of manhood, provoking the court to tag him with clothing that symbolized the mutable quality of female bodies and the tenuous nature of female legal existence.[22]

◀▷

Although it is easy to appreciate the unique features of the Hall case, it is no less important to identify the broad contours of early modern Atlantic history that are implicated in Hall's narrative of identity. Closer scrutiny of Hall's courtroom tale reveals that Hall's text, as well as the life represented in it, were emblematic of the destabilizing effects of military conflicts, imperial rivalries, and colonial projects on early modern Europeans.

Hall situated his account of shifting identities in the context of the major historical events of the early seventeenth century. In his narrative, English military mobilization was a stimulus for the initial transformation "into the fashion of a man." Military defeat and a return to England led to a reaffirmation of female social identity and domestic work. England's colonial aspirations in the New World created an opportunity for migration that Hall rather significantly decided to seize as a man.

Hall's mutability was also emblematic of the ambiguous and tentative identities of English peoples recently settled in the New World. Many conditions contributed to the instability of English identities in Virginia, but among the most significant challenges were the encounter with a Native American gender division of labor that differed significantly from that of the English, the demands of the colonial economy for a more flexible division of labor than that which existed in England, the difficulty of translating English symbols and institutions of political authority into a colonial idiom, and the existence of powerful women in a society committed to, but only partially able to replicate, English-style patriarchal institutions. Hall's self-fashioned gender identity presented a baffling challenge to these already shaky articulations of English identity and political authority. Reports of Hall's hermaphrodism led to public refutations of the conclusions of matrons, masters, and plantation commanders. Hall's ability to tangle the lines of authority, forcing residents of the Warraskoyack to improvise, was perhaps most evident in the unprecedented co-ed search for female genitalia. The attempts of community leaders and justices to define and "fix" Hall's identity reveals the complex ways in which the ideal of clear gender distinctions was an integral part of their vision of an orderly, stable society.

Hall's typicality among gender transgressors in the early modern Atlantic world points to the connections between sexual identities, as constructed and lived by individuals, and the major economic, political, and imperial events of the day. Hall and the other ambiguous and cross-dressing narrators of his day talked about gender contextually, representing their identities as interwoven with imperial rivalries for new territory, trade, and military supremacy. The similarities in their stories suggest that by the early seventeenth century, the Atlantic world may already have had its own sexual culture in which the narratives of gender identity and those of mercantilism and colonization had become mutually implicated in the practice of exploration, conquest, migration, and commodification.[23]

What distinguishes Hall from the other subjects of these tales is the identity revealed by investigation. In almost every other case of non-aristocratic gender transgression in the early modern period, the ambiguous or "passing" individual is revealed to be a hermaphrodite or a female transvestite. The end of Hall's story takes an unexpected turn, however, with the matrons' conclusion that Hall was really a man. Hall's atypicality as the rare non-aristocratic man discovered in woman's clothing—in the rough and tumble world of a British colony, no less—alerts us to another possible explanation for his otherwise difficult-to-fathom behavior. In a world in which dressing as a man brought women expanded economic and political opportunities, Hall found it difficult to suppress his female identity. Although he offered a pragmatic and environmental explanation for his cross-dressing that implied the occasional economic advantages of being a woman, very few of his contemporaries, male or female, would have agreed with him. Despite the attendant risks and disadvantages of being female in the seventeenth century, Hall found it personally useful, necessary, or comfortable to occasionally dress as a woman.[24]

Set against other transgression narratives of the period, Hall's stands apart both for the conclusions of his examiners that he was male and for the inability of seventeenth-century medical or economic theories to explain his transformation. Neither moving to a state of greater perfection nor adopting a more expansive social role, Hall left his contemporaries—and indeed, leaves us—baffled. We might hypothesize that early colonial Virginia, a settlement in which English women were scarce, may have afforded enough opportunities for upward mobility to tempt an individual like Hall to try to take advantage of them. He had, after all, renounced his male identity when such opportunities presented themselves in England. Yet such a theory raises as many questions as it answers. If early seventeenth-century Virginia was so favorable a place for women, why didn't more women flock to the colony or more men attempt to pass as female? A more plausible explanation may lie with Hall himself. Perhaps "his" female identity was so deeply imbedded as a consequence of a childhood and adolescence of female training and identification that he could *not* shed it. His cross-dressing episodes in Virginia appear then *not* as an opportunistic effort to achieve upward mobility, but as quite the opposite: as episodes of selective, intermittent declension, compelled by an identity deeply rooted in a history of female performance.

◄

We can only speculate about what, if anything, the different conclusions about Hall's sex may have had in common. I have suggested that community investigations and legal examinations may have shared a belief in the historicity and changeability of femaleness and the functional constancy of maleness, even though this conceptualization of difference ultimately led them to different conclusions. It is important to note that this concept of female historicity provided no firmer grounding for gender differences than early modern scientific theories, as male maturation to manhood was a crucial process in contemporary definitions of maleness. The problem with using a construct of historicity to define sexual difference only underlines the importance of performativity for understanding Hall, his narrative, and his complex sexual identity. As the perplexity of Hall's neighbors and the sentence meted out by the General Court suggest, ordinary people's concepts of sexual difference could not be easily reconciled with the behavior of an individual who periodically "changed himself . . . into the fashion of man."

◆▷

Notes

1. For bastardy rates in the Chesapeake, see Lois Green Carr and Lorena S. Walsh, "The Planter's Wife: The Experience of White Women in Seventeenth-Century Maryland," *William and Mary Quarterly*, 3rd Series, 24, October 1977, 542–71; Herbert Moller, "Sex Composition and Correlated Culture Patterns of Colonial America," *William and Mary Quarterly*, 3rd Series, 11, April 1945, 113–53. For comparison to New England, see Mary Beth Norton, "The Evolution of White Woman's Experience," *AHR*, 89, June 1984, 593–619; Roger Thompson, *Sex in Middlesex: Popular Mores in a Massachusetts County, 1649–1699* (Amherst, Mass.: University of Masschusetts Press, 1986), 13, 70. The text of the Hall case can be found in H. R. McIlwaine, ed., *Minutes of the Council and General Court of Colonial Virginia* (Richmond, 2nd ed., 1974), 194–95. Unless indicated otherwise, all references to the testimony in the Hall case is from this source. The case is discussed in Alden Vaughan, "The Sad Case of Thomas(ine) Hall," *Virginia Magazine of History and Biography*, 86, 1978: 146–48; Jonathan Ned Katz, *Gay/Lesbian Almanac: A New Documentary* (New York: HarperCollins, 1983), 71–72; Ivor Noel Hume, *Martin's Hundred* (New York: Knopf, 1982), 133–34; Kathleen Brown, "'Changed . . . into the fashion of man': The Politics of Sexual Difference in a Seventeenth-Century Anglo-American Settlement," *Journal of the History of Sexuality*, 6, 1995, 171–93; Mary Beth Norton, *Founding Mothers and Fathers: Gendered Power and the Forming of American Society* (New York: Alfred A. Knopf, 1996), 183–97.

2. Michel Foucault, *Herculine Barbin: Being the Recently Discovered Memoirs of a Nineteenth-Century French Hermaphrodite* (New York: Pantheon, 1980), vii–xvii; Stephen Greenblatt, "Fiction and Friction" in Greenblatt, ed., *Shakespearean Negotiations: The Circulation of Social Energy in Renaissance England* (Berkeley, Cal.: University of California Press, 1988), 66–93; Ludmilla Jordanova, *Sexual Visions: Images of Gender in Science and Medicine between the Eighteenth and Twentieth Centuries* (Madison, Wisc.: University of Wisconsin Press, 1989); Thomas Laqueur, *Making Sex: Body and Gender from the Greeks to Freud* (Cambridge, Mass.: Harvard University Press, 1990); see also Ludmilla J. Jordanova, ed., *Languages of Nature: Critical Essays on Science and Literature* (New Brunswick, N.J.: Rutgers University Press, 1986); Ian McLean, *The Renaissance Notion of Woman: A Study of the Fortunes of Scholasticism and Medical Science in European Intellectual Life* (Cambridge: Cambridge University Press, 1980), 28–46; Ann Rosalind Jones and Peter Stallybrass, "Fetishizing Gender: Constructing the Hermaphrodite in Renaissance Europe," in Julia Epstein and Kristina Straub, eds., *Body Guards: The Cultural Politics of Gender Ambiguity* (New York: Routledge, 1991), 80–111, especially 88.

3. MacLean, *Renaissance Notion of Woman*, 6–27; Pierre Darmon, *Trial By Impotence: Virility and Marriage in pre-Revolutionary France*, trans. Paul Keegan (London: Chatto & Windus, 1985), 40–58; Laqueur, *Making Sex*, 122–42; Jones and

Stallybrass, "Fetishizing Gender," 88–89; Mary Elizabeth Perry, *Gender and Disorder in Early Modern Seville* (Princeton, N.J.: Princeton University Press, 1990), 123–35; Roger Thompson, "Attitudes Towards Homosexuality in the Seventeenth-Century New England Colonies," *Journal of American Studies*, 23, April 1989, 27–40; Richard Godbeer, "'The Cry of Sodom': Discourse, Intercourse, and Desire in Colonial New England," *William and Mary Quarterly* 3rd Series, 52, April 1995, 259–86.

4. MacLean, *Renaissance Notion of Woman*; Greenblatt, "Fiction and Friction," 66–93; Jones and Stallybrass, "Fetishizing Gender," 80–111; Darmon, *Trial By Impotence*, 40–58; Laqueur, *Making Sex*, 122–42; Katharine Park and Lorraine J. Daston, "Unnatural Conceptions: The Study of Monsters in Sixteenth- and Seventeenth-Century France and England," *Past and Present*, August 1981, 20–54.

5. Early modern theologians denounced transvestism as a violation of prohibitions spelled out in Deuteronomy 22:5, "the woman shall not wear that which pertaineth unto a man, neither shall a man put on a woman's garment, for all that do so are abominable unto the Lord thy God." Legal institutions similarly attempted to police gender boundaries by harshly punishing cross-dressing. The penalities remained less severe in England, however, with its tradition of transvestite theater than they did on the European continent, where the crime was a capital offense. Unlike the hermaphrodite, who was usually allowed to choose a permanent identity, the transvestite's wrongdoing could be rectified only by the restorative power of punishment. See Vern L. Bullough and Bonnie Bullough, *Cross Dressing, Sex, and Gender* (Philadelphia: University of Pennsylvania Press, 1993), 94–101; Rudolf M. Dekker and Lotte C. van de Pol, *The Tradition of Female Transvestism in Early Modern Europe* (New York: Macmillan, 1989); Jean E. Howard, "Cross dressing, the Theatre, and Gender Struggle in Early Modern England," *Shakespeare Quarterly* 39, 1988, 181–210. See also Mary Douglas, *Implicit Meanings: Essays in Anthropology* (Boston: Routledge & Keegan Paul, 1975), xxx, 49–70; idem., *Purity and Danger: An Analysis of the Concepts of Pollution and Taboo* (New York: Praeger, 1966), 5; Marjorie Garber, *Vested Interests: Cross-Dressing and Cultural Anxiety* (New York: Routledge, 1992), 17.

6. See Judith Butler, "Gender Trouble," in Linda J. Nicholson, ed., *Feminism/Postmodernism* (New York: Routledge, 1990), 336–39, for her discussion of gender as performance. See also Stephen Greenblatt, *Renaissance Self-Fashioning: From More to Shakespeare* (Chicago: University of Chicago Press, 1980), 1–9.

7. Edmund S. Morgan, *American Slavery, American Freedom: The Ordeal of Colonial Virginia* (New York: W.W. Norton, 1975), 3–179; Charles E. Hatch, Jr., *The First Seventeen Years: Virginia, 1607–1624* (Charlottesville, Va.: University Press of Virginia, 1957); Jordan Goodman, *Tobacco in History: The Cultures of Dependence* (New York: Routledge, 1993), 59–89; Kevin Kelly, "'In Dispers'd Country Plantations': Settlement Patterns in Seventeenth-Century Surry County, Virginia," in Thad W. Tate and David L. Ammerman, eds., *The Chesapeake in the Seventeenth Century: Essays on Anglo-American Society and Politics* (Chapel Hill, N.C.: University of North Carolina Press, 1979), 183–205; James Horn, "Servant Migration to the Chesapeake in the Seventeenth Century," in ibid., 51–95; Carville V. Earle, "Environment, Disease, and Mortality in Early Virginia," in ibid., 96–125.

8. McIlwaine, ed., *Minutes of the Council*, 120, 169; Nell Marion Nugent, ed., *Cavaliers and Pioneers: Abstracts of the Virginia Land Patents and Grants*, 3 vols. (Rich-

mond, Va.: Dietz Printing Company, 1934), I: 23, 45; Annie Lash Jester and Martha Woodruff Hiden, eds., *Adventures of Purse and Person: Virginia 1607–1625* (2nd ed., n.p., 1964), 91; Hatch, *First Seventeen Years*, 86–89.

9. Jester and Hiden, eds., *Adventurers*, 46; McIlwaine, ed., *Minutes*, 192; Nugent, ed., *Cavaliers*, 10; Hatch, *First Seventeen Years*, 89.

10. David R. Ransome, "'Wives for Virginia, 1621," William and Mary Quarterly, 3rd Series, 48, January 1991, 4–5, 10.

11. Jester and Hiden, eds., *Adventurers*, 40; McIlwaine, ed., *Minutes of the Council*, 6, 96, 158–164, 202.

12. McIlwaine, ed., *Minutes of the Council*, 7, 58–59.

13. Julia Cherry Spruill, *Women's Life and Work in the Southern Colonies* (Chapel Hill, N.C.: University of North Carolina Press, 1938, rpt. 1972), 327–330; James C. Oldham, "On Pleading the Belly: A History of the Jury of Matrons," *Criminal Justice History: An International Annual*, vol. VI (Westport, Ct.: Greenwood Press, 1985), 1–64; Martin Ingram, *Church Courts, Sex and Marriage in England, 1570–1640* (New York: Cambridge University Press, 1987), 172–73; Darmon, *Trial by Impotence*, 141–73; Audrey Eccles, *Obstetrics and Gynecology in Tudor and Stuart England* (Kent, Ohio: Kent State University Press, 1982); R. H. Helmholz, *Marriage Litigation in Medieval England* (New York: Cambridge University Press, 1974), 87–91.

14. Joan Scott, "Experience," in Judith Butler and Joan W. Scott, eds., *Feminists Theorize the Political* (New York: Routledge, 1992), 22–40. Scott's important critique of the explanatory power of experience for historians and the unexamined assumptions of what it embodies should not lead us to avoid the term, but rather to seek to analyze it as a specific cultural production that bolstered claims to authority.

15. Jester et al. eds., *Adventurers*, 47; John Camden Hotten, ed., *The Original Lists of Persons of Quality . . . and Others Who Went From Great Britain to the American Plantations, 1600–1700* (London, 1874; reprint Baltimore: Baltimore Geneological Publishing, 1986), 184.

16. McIlwaine, ed., *Minutes of the Council*, 195. The ellipses in the quotation represent testimony missing in the published version of the original. Hall's use of the word "belly," his claim of impotence, and the response of Captain Bass have informed my interpretation of this partial evidence as Hall's manifestation of a small penis-like appendage. See also Darmon, *Trial by Impotence*; Ingram, *Church Courts*, 172–73, 187; Oldham, "Pleading the Belly," 4–5; Helmholz, *Marriage Litigation*, 87–91. For New England see Roger Thompson, *Sex in Middlesex*, 116, 154. For a different interpretation, see Norton, *Founding Mothers and Fathers*, 183–97

17. Laqueur, *Making Sex*, 126–28; Jones and Stallybrass, "Fetishizing Gender," 86–88.

18. Nugent, ed., *Cavaliers*, 140, 147, 183, 261.

19. McIlwaine, ed., *Minutes of the Council*, 7, 58–59.

20. See "Hic Mulier" (London, 1620) and "Haec Vir" (London, 1620), excerpted and reprinted in Katherine Usher Henderson and Barbara F. MacManus, eds., *Half Humankind: Contexts and Texts of the Controversy about Women in England, 1540–1640* (Urbana: University of Illinois Press, 1985); Joy Wiltenberg, *Disorderly Women and Female Power in the Street Literature of Early Modern England and Germany* (Charlottesville, Va.: University Press of Virginia, 1992); Margaret Spufford, *Small Books and Pleasant Histories: Popular Fiction and its Readership in*

Seventeenth-century England (Athens: University of Georgia Press, 1982), 61–65, 158–159, 184–185.

21. Background on the conflict at the Isle of Rhe can be found in David Ogg, *Europe in the Seventeenth Century*, (London: A. and C. Black, 1954) 65–66, 191–192; M.S. Anderson, *War and Society in Europe of the Old Regime, 1618–1789* (New York: St. Martin's Press, 1988), 38, 41, 50.

22. Eccles, *Obstetrics and Gynecology*; Darmon, *Trial by Impotence*, 147–153. For an example of gynecological and obstetrical terms used by midwives, see Laurent Joubert, *Popular Errors* [1579], trans. Gregory David de Rocher (Tuscaloosa, Al.: University of Alabam Press, 1989).

23. Bullough and Bullough, *Cross Dressing*, 94–101; Greenblatt, "Fiction and Friction;" Dekker and van de Pol, *Tradition of Female Transvestism*. Perry, *Gender and Disorder*, 127–35. Spufford, *Small Books*, 8–12, 53–54. For examples of scholarship documenting early modern Atlantic sexual cultures, see Perry, *Gender and Disorder in Early Modern Seville*; Richard C. Trexler, *Sex and Conquest: Gendered Violence, Political Order, and the European Conquest of the Americas* (Ithaca: Cornell University Press, 1995); Kathleen M. Brown, *Good Wives, Nasty Wenches, and Anxious Patriarchs: Gender, Race, and Power in Colonial Virginia* (Chapel Hill, N.C.: University of North Carolina, 1996).

24. Garber, *Vested Interests*, 68–70, refers to this type of explanation for transvestism as a "progress narrative."

INDIAN FOREMOTHERS

Race, Sex, Slavery, and Freedom in Early Virginia

Two women, both of them black according to twentieth-century racial categories, had a conversation in 1937. Susie Byrd, a writer with the New Deal's Works Progress Administration, was looking for former slaves to share their recollections, and had asked a Virginia woman named Octavia Featherstone for her story. Featherstone talked about her triracial background—part white, part black, and part Indian—and about how, though legally nonwhite and born during slave times, she had, in fact, never been a slave. She closed the interview with an explanation: "I forgit to tell you how and why we was free. You see Gramma bein' a Indian, she came of de Indian Tribe which cause our freedom. You know Indians was never slaves, so dey chillun was always free, dat is cordin' to law."[1]

According to Featherstone, her Indian ancestry—and not her white forebears—made it possible for her to be born free and live free in the 1850s. Her tale raises questions worth pursuing. How did the law of slavery and freedom lead, despite her African ancestry, to her free birth? What exactly was the legal significance, if any, of her Indian ancestry? Her account, dating from the twentieth century, points back toward other stories from the years between the 1760s and the 1810s.

Race, sex, slavery, and freedom commingled with Virginia's society, economics, politics, and law in various and changing ways. In 1607, just before three ships arrived from England to establish the colony of Virginia, the many residents were all Native Americans. Over the next two centuries, newcomers and their progeny from both Europe and Africa soared in numbers, while Indians seemed to vanish.[2] If the patterns had been more simple than they were, it might be possible to speak as though everyone was either white or black, and as though all blacks were slaves, whether in 1760, 1810, or 1860. But such was not the case, and boundaries were not so clear. Indians refused to vanish,[3] and many Virginians were multiracial. Some mixed-race Virginians, though born unfree, were designated to remain so only for specific periods, though lengthy ones—eighteen, twenty-one, thirty, or thirty-one years. And many nonwhites, though born into lifelong slavery, gained their freedom, especially in the quarter-century beginning in 1782.

This essay focuses on the years between 1760 and 1810, especially the 1790s. It explores each of these complicating features of Virginia's social landscape. It emphasizes one group, those claiming Indian foremothers, a group that highlights the complexity of race, sex, slavery, and freedom in Virginia during those years. Finally, it focuses on Virginia east of the Blue Ridge, a region whose population, in the years between 1760 and 1860, was roughly half white and half nonwhite, half free and half slave. Yet, in many counties and for the region as a whole, it was often true that, while only a minority was white, at the same time only a minority was slave. Tilting the balance was a middle group of people who were free but not white. This essay takes another look at their origins—who they were and how, though many of them had been born into slavery, they came to be free.

◀▷

Multiracial Virginians originated as early as the 1610s, when John Rolfe and Pocahontas married and had a son, Thomas. No law then specifically governed interracial marriages or multiracial children. When such laws emerged, lawmakers mostly had black Virginians in mind, though some laws specified Indians as well, and some that did not nonetheless affected Indians too. In 1662 the Virginia legislature, feeling compelled to define the status of the children of black women and white men, declared that such children would follow the status of their mothers. Thus slave women would have slave children, regardless of who the father was, while free women, whether white or not, would have free children, again no matter who the father was.[4]

The 1662 law might have put an end to such questions, so that the crucial question remained who was the mother, but again such was not the case. Race and sex would combine in other patterns, too, to determine the racial and social identity of the children of Virginia. A 1691 statute addressed the question of mixed-race children of white women. First, the act in effect banned interracial marriage by providing that any white person who married a nonwhite—whether black, Indian, or multiracial—must permanently leave the colony within three months. But perhaps, then, legislators mused, an occasional white woman, even though unmarried, would have a child whose father was "negro or mulatto" (here lawmakers did not include Indians). If so, she would be fined, and, if unable to pay the fine, would be sold as a servant for five years. Regardless of whether she retained her freedom, she lost her child, who would be bound out as a servant until the age of 30. An act passed in 1705 changed the child's indenture to 31 years.[5]

By the eighteenth century, two major rules had come into play to determine the destinies of mixed-race children. If the mother was black and the father white, the law wanted only to know the status of the mother, for the child's status, slave or free, would follow the mother's. But if the mother was white, then the law inquired the identity of the father. If the father was black, then the mother was penalized—fined or sold into five years of servitude—and the child entered a very long period of unfreedom as a servant.

In 1723, the law went further by applying the penalties to the next generation—the mixed-race, nonslave grandchildren of white women with mixed-race daughters. Speaking of young women, whether mulatto or Indian, who were serving terms of thirty or thirty-one years as the mixed-race children of white mothers, the new law said that, if they happened to have children during their servitude, "every such child shall serve the master or mistress of such mullatto or indian, until it shall attain the same age the mother of such child was by law obliged to serve unto."[6] Now the terms of 30 or 31 years were inherited, from mother to child. In effect, a third category had been established with reference to the 1662 law, and just as slave women bore slave children, and free women bore free children, these long-term servants bore long-term servants.

The rules changed again in the 1760s. Declaring the terms of thirty or thirty-one years for mixed-race children of black men and either free white mothers or women servants—that is, either the first or subsequent generations—to be "an unreasonable severity to such children," in 1765 the legislature reduced the terms to eighteen years for females and twenty-one years for males. These were the same numbers the legislature applied when unmarried white women, whether servants or free, had white children who would otherwise become public charges.[7]

One family's story illustrates the complexity. An unnamed "Christian white woman" had a daughter, Betty Bugg, whose father was black. Under the 1705 Virginia law, Betty Bugg became a servant to the age of thirty-one. During her servitude, she had a son, who, while in his twenties, brought suit for his freedom. Against that effort, his master's lawyer argued successfully in 1769 that the 1705 statute required that mixed-race children like Betty Bugg (whose mothers were not slaves) be bound out for thirty-one years but, silent on the status of their children, presumably left them free. The 1723 act required children of that next generation, too, to live as servants to age thirty-one, and, since Bugg's son was born after 1723, he was subject to that law. The 1765 law, which set shorter terms of servitude, could not help him, because he was born before its passage. Born after 1723 but before 1765, he was born too late to gain his freedom at birth and too soon to obtain it at age twenty-one. Yet his bondage was not defined in terms of life, for he, like his mother, would become free at age thirty-one.[8]

Sarah Madden and her family demonstrate a variant version of the Virginia laws of race and sex at work. Her mother, Mary Madden, who probably came to Virginia from Ireland in the 1750s as an indentured servant, gave birth to a mulatto daughter, Sarah, on August 4, 1758. Sarah Madden, bound out until the age of thirty-one, finally gained her freedom in 1789 (the year the U.S. Constitution went into effect). In the meantime she had children of her own, beginning with Rachel in 1776 (the year of the Declaration of Independence), who presumably gained her own freedom at the age of eighteen in 1794. Another child, David, born in 1780, likely gained his freedom at the age of twenty-one in 1801, soon after his sister Betty, born in 1782, reached the age of eighteen and shortly before Polly, born in 1785, did so.[9]

Sarah Madden's seventh child, Fanny, came along on July 6, 1789, just weeks before Madden turned thirty-one. Had Fanny been born a month later, she would have gained her freedom at birth, instead of only in 1807. Nelly and Nancy, by contrast were born in 1793 and 1796, so they were born free, as was Willis, born in 1799. As for Sarah Madden's daughters, they appear to have waited until at least the age of eighteen before having any of their own children. Thus Sarah Madden's grandchildren (more precisely, her daughters' children)—like her own children born in the 1790s, but unlike herself and unlike the children she bore between the Declaration of Independence and the U.S. Constitution—were born free.[10]

The decade between the Declaration of Independence and the Constitutional Convention of 1787 brought important changes to the law of race and slavery in Virginia. In 1778, during the American Revolution, the legislature of the new state of Virginia passed a law declaring that "hereafter no slave shall be imported into the Commonwealth by sea or land"—that is, whether from outside the United States or even from another state. "Every slave imported contrary to . . . this act shall become free." The children of slave women would continue to be born into lifelong slavery, but the only other way for new slaves to come to inhabit Virginia would be if their owners moved with them from another state into Virginia.[11] Sarah Madden's children showed, however, that long-term, mixed-race servants could still be born to women of the same description under the series of laws that began in 1691 and continued through 1705, 1723, and 1765.

Four years later, in 1782, the state legislature went beyond curtailing the growth of slavery through commerce and provided authority, for the first time, for slaveowners to free their slaves. Owners could, without restriction, emancipate slave women between the ages of eighteen and forty-five and slave men between the ages of twenty-one and forty-five, provided the new freedpeople were "of sound mind and body." Otherwise, the new right carried significant restrictions. Slaves younger than eighteen or twenty-one and older than forty-five, as well as slaves between those ages who were not "of sound mind and body," could be freed only if the former owners "supported" them, that is, saw that they did not become charges of the county. George Washington, for one, freed all his many slaves. The law held without material change until 1806, when the legislature mandated that, in the future, slaves who gained their freedom must leave the state within a year or forfeit their freedom. County officials could still permit newly freed people to stay, but it had become more doubtful, and by that time the willingness of slaveowning Virginians to manumit some of their human property had receded.[12]

Beginning in 1782, therefore, slavery in Virginia was, in effect, redefined. Enslavement was still defined as lifelong, and it was still inherited from a slave mother, but owners could now free their slaves. As had been the case ever since the 1662 law clarified matters, nonwhite women, if free, would bear free children. In all those years there had never been many free nonwhite women, so there had never been many nonwhite children born free. Beginning in 1782, through manumission, the number of people in Virginia who, though nonwhite, were free began rapidly to grow. Whether slavery proved to be lifelong had become contingent—it now depended on how the new legal environment in Virginia affected that individual. After growing rapidly in the twenty-five years beginning in 1782, Virginia's free nonwhite population, though it continued to rise each decade from the 1810s through the 1850s, did so at a much more modest pace.

As early as 1790, the number of free nonwhite Virginians reached 12,766, or 4 percent of all nonwhites in Virginia. By that time, several Eastern Virginia counties had populations in which the middle group—people neither white nor slave—tipped the balance, so that more residents were free than slave, even though more were black than white: Henrico, Northampton, Northumberland, Southampton, and Surry.[13]

During the last half century of Virginia slavery, approximately one in ten nonwhite Virginians were free. The number of free nonwhites grew by more than 50 percent in the 1790s to 20,124, and then to 30,570 by 1810. The number of counties increased in which that middle group made it possible for a majority of residents to be free even though only a minority of residents were white.[14]

◄

There were three ways, not just two, in which the number of nonwhite Virginians grew in the late eighteenth century. Certainly some people were born to free nonwhite mothers, and certainly far more Virginians gained their freedom from owners who, whatever their motivation, determined to manumit one or more of their slaves. Yet a third group consisted of people who went to court to force the question—contested the matter with people who had every intention of remaining in the slaveowning business—and in that manner won their freedom.

The courts were solicitous of such efforts. They demonstrated a willingness to consider the freedom claims of Virginians and, with some frequency, to come down on the side of freedom. Perhaps the relative prevalence of a long-term, but finite, status of unfreedom—an intermediate station between slave and free—helps explain why the courts felt obligated to scrutinize freedom suits as possibly meritorious. The possibility that white people might get caught up in slavery offers another explanation. Still another reason for their willingness to often side with the plaintiffs who sued for their freedom, relates to ideas of human liberty that came out of the Revolution.

In one case, Nanny Pagee, who was held as a slave, along with her children, sued for her freedom on the grounds that she had been brought illegally into

Virginia from North Carolina as a slave after 1778 and thus should be free and, moreover, that she was a white woman. The court, finding her (from inspection) white, and with no evidence introduced to show her to be the daughter of a slave woman, declared her free—after having been held as a slave for over thirty years—and thus her children (though mixed-race offspring of a slave father) free as well.[15] But now we return to the matter of Virginians who claimed Indian ancestry.

◄

A court document from the year 1790 offers another take on the questions that Octavia Featherstone's account of her free birth raises. In 1790, a white man from Stafford County named James Howarth granted his slave Amy her freedom, on condition that she first work for him another three years with no pay except "necessary Clothes and Victuals." In the spirit of the 1782 law, he went on to pledge that, after the three years had passed, "should the said Amy be incapable of maintaining herself through Age, Sickness, or Misfortune, I will allow her a Sufficiency to subsist to prevent her" from becoming so poor that the county would have to support her as a pauper. Then, offering a clue to his motive in this gift of freedom, he noted: "Amy says she is originally entitled to her freedom, being descended of Indian parents as her colour somewhat shews." Howarth recognized that Amy might seek, and perhaps with success, to "prove her right and title to her freedom."[16] Both of them saw the possibility under Virginia law at that time. She no doubt accepted the deal so she would not need to sue and take the chance she might lose, while perhaps he made the offer because he would immediately lose her if she sued and won.

Late-eighteenth century Virginia newspapers contained advertisements for people who were claimed as slaves, identified as claiming Indian ancestry, and understood to have claimed their right to be free on the basis of that ancestry. In October 1772, for example, Paul Michaux advertised from Cumberland County for "a Mulatto Man named Jim, who is a Slave, but pretends to have a Right to his Freedom." Michaux explained that Jim's "Father was an Indian, of the name of Cheshire," and Jim would likely "call himself James Cheshire, or Chink." About twenty-seven years old, he had "long black hair resembling an *Indian's*," and "When he went away I expected he was gone to the General Court to seek his Freedom." In April 1773, a twenty-two-year-old man named David left his Dinwiddie County owner, William Cuszens, who then advertised that this "Mulatto Slave," who "says he is of the *Indian* breed," had gone "down to the General Court, as I imagined, to sue for his freedom, but has never returned."[17]

Other documents from eastern Virginia help fill in more of the picture of race, sex, slavery, and freedom in the years around 1800. These are court cases in which slaves acted to gain their freedom on grounds of Indian ancestry, as Howarth anticipated that Amy might, and took their owners to court. More often than not, they won their freedom, to judge from the cases that went all the way to the Virginia Supreme Court of Appeals. At trial, slaves won those cases, but then their owners, putting up more resistance than James Howarth seemed inclined to, appealed the decisions to Virginia's highest court. And those cases left a trail of records—though a more scant trail than historians two centuries later might wish—showing the racial complexity of society in general, and slavery in particular, in eighteenth-century Virginia.

All these cases originated in eastern Virginia (i.e., that is east of the Blue Ridge) where slavery was so dominant an institution, affected so many people's lives, that in many counties slaves constituted a majority of all residents, and most white families owned one or more slaves. Each time a slave or group of slaves gained their freedom, they tilted the ratio among Virginians a little less toward slavery and a little more toward freedom. The growing number of Virginia residents in a special category, neither white nor slave, resulted in part from a window of freedom that Virginia judges opened in the way they interpreted the past as they decided what to do about suits for freedom in the present. The following cases show how.

Robin v. *Hardaway*, a court case that arose in 1772 as relations between the colonies and England made their way toward the American Revolution, offers a glimpse of how the ideas of the American Revolution could affect thinking about slavery and freedom for nonwhite Virginians. It also makes very clear that slaves with Indian ancestry might draw on that background—their ancestry and those ideas—to make a bid for freedom. Finally, it shows that such bids made their way into the Virginia courts, where judges and juries had to decide what to make of such arguments. Robin and his co-plaintiffs sued for their freedom, in part claiming they were descendants of Indians. According to the surviving records, Attorney Mason argued for their freedom:

> The Indians of every denomination were free, and independent of us; they were not subject to our empire; not represented in our legislature; they derived no protection from our laws; nor could be subjected to their bonds. If natural right, independence, defect of representation, and disavowal or protection, are not sufficient to keep them from the coercion of our laws, on what other principles can we justify our opposition to some late acts of power exercised by the British legislature? Yet they only pretend to impose on us a paltry tax in money; we on our free neighbors, the yoke of perpetual slavery.[18]

Among cases similar to Robin's, another reached the Virginia Supreme Court of Appeals in 1792, its record scant, its significance large. A number of slaves owned by William Jenkins, among them one named Tom, "an Indian," sued for their freedom. They claimed descent from two Indian women, Mary and Bess, one the grandmother of the other, who, decades before, had been brought into Virginia and kept—wrongfully—as slaves. Given the general rule under Virginia law, that each child inherited the status, free or slave, of his or her mother, Bess's children all grew up as slaves. In similar fashion, her daughters' children were all slaves, and so on. But if Bess had been free, her children, too, would have all been born free, and thus her daughters' children.[19]

In Northumberland District Court, Jenkins's lawyer took the position that, under a 1753 statute, Virginia clearly permitted such enslavement, but the court corrected him. He was informed—to use the words reported in 1792—that "he misstated the law." The judge agreed that "there was a time at some period in the last century" when a law permitted the enslavement of Indians under certain conditions and, under that law, "many Indians were made slaves, and their descendants continue slaves to this day." But, he went on, "this law was some time after repealed; from which period, no American Indian could be sold as a slave, and . . . all such as had been brought into this country since that time, and who had sued for their freedom, had uniformly recovered it." The jury found for the plaintiffs, that they should be free. Their putative owner appealed the decision, but Virginia's highest court upheld the District Court.[20]

Pursuant to this single case, Jenkins lost his slaves, and Tom and the unnamed others gained their freedom. But that case outlines a story that relates to far more individuals than Jenkins, Tom, and those unnamed others. As the lower-court judge stated, first, under a seventeenth-century law "many Indians were made slaves" but, second, "all such [Indians] as had been brought into [Virginia as slaves] since [its repeal], and who had sued for their freedom, had uniformly recovered it."

Moreover, cases like Tom's continued to come before Virginia's highest court as late as 1831. In 1793, for example, Dick and Pat obtained their freedom from Williamson Coleman. The court ruled that a 1705 statute constituted "a compleat repeal of all former laws on the subject, and that since that period, no American Indian, can be reduced into a state of slavery."[21]

In the twenty years between 1792 and 1811, the Virginia Supreme Court of Appeals heard eighteen cases in which one or more Virginians challenged their enslavement. Six of those cases, or one-third of them, involved plaintiffs who called themselves Indians and who relied on their Indian ancestry as the basis for their claim to freedom.[22] In every instance, the trial court or the appeals court or both sided with the plaintiffs and declared their right to freedom.

Those cases point up the complexity as well as the operations of the law of slavery and freedom in post-Revolutionary America. How, to begin with, did these kinds of cases ever get into the courts? Moreover, they identify an intriguing type of resistance to North American slavery. Resistance, after all, could take many forms,[23] and surely taking one's master to court—seeking a legal victory in a demand for freedom—was one such form. In addition, they indicate a continuing strand in American social and cultural history that relates to the presence of a group in eighteenth-century Virginia called at that time "native American Indians."[24]

Virginia law permitted people held in servitude to challenge their bondage and sue for their freedom, as had Nanny Pagee as well as Tom, Dick, and Pat. A 1795 statute spelled out the procedure. On presentation of a petition for recovery of freedom, the court assigned the person counsel, whose duty it was to investigate and "make an exact statement to the court of the circumstances of the case, with his opinion thereupon." If persuaded that the case should go forward, the court summoned the owner ("or possessor") to answer the complaint. Pending a trial, the owner had to give security, "to the full value" of the "complainant," to permit the plaintiff to appear in court. The court phrased the right in emphatic, though restrictive, terms: "Persons in the *status* of slavery have no civil rights, save that of suing for freedom."[25]

The same law that offered a remedy as well as procedural protection to the slave, however, offered protection to the owner. Historian Robert McColley has said of late-eighteenth century Virginia's "true emancipators"—especially Quakers—that such people "diligently investigat[ed] the legal titles by which Negroes were held, and su[ed] for freedom whenever such titles were doubtful."[26] To counteract such activities, the 1795 law provided that, for each plaintiff who lost his or her case, anyone who had helped bring the suit was liable to pay the owner $100. And a subsequent amendment stipulated that no "member of any society instituted for the purpose of emancipating negroes from the possession of their masters" could serve as a juror in such a case.[27]

In formulating a response to suits for freedom by people who claimed Indian descent, Virginia judges created a history to guide their deliberations. As late as 1682, they knew, the Virginia legislature had provided for the enslavement of Indians.[28] Yet a 1705 act had authorized "a free and open trade for all persons, at all times, and at all places, with all Indians whatsoever." In a 1787 case, in which Hannah and other Indians sued for their freedom, the General Court decided that "no Indians brought into Virginia" since 1705, "nor their descendants," could be held as slaves there.[29] In a brief account of these developments, St. George Tucker wrote a few years later that he had encountered an act apparently passed in 1691 with the same language as the 1705 law, and thus "it would seem that no Indians brought into Virginia for more than a century [since 1691], nor any of their descendants, can be retained in slavery in this commonwealth."[30]

A frequent figure taking the cases of Indian plaintiffs in manumission suits, at least on appeal, was George Keith Taylor. Reputed to be one of the great orators of his generation, Taylor was a Federalist politician who served his native Prince George County in the state House of Delegates in the 1790s. He was also a son-in-law of Chief Justice John Marshall.[31] In the years that followed, this gifted orator took several leading cases to the Virginia Supreme Court of Appeals. One was the case of Jacky Wright and her family.

In 1805, Jacky Wright and her children—Maria, John, and Epsabar—brought suit to recover their freedom from Holder Hudgins. They won, and Hudgins appealed to the Virginia Supreme Court of Appeals. St. George Tucker was now a member of that court, where he propounded his thesis that the acts culminating in 1682 had been repealed in 1691, rather than 1705, that is, after only nine years rather than twenty-three. His colleague Spencer Roane found Tucker's position plausible, but concluded that accepting the earlier date was unnecessary in this case to find for the Wrights. A unanimous court, agreeing that Jacky Wright and her children were entitled to their freedom, affirmed the lower-court ruling.[32]

The case of *Hudgins* v. *Wrights* gave judges occasion to speak to several major questions about presumption and evidence in suits for freedom. That case came to the Virginia Supreme Court of Appeals from the High Court of Chancery, where George Wythe presided and where, on two separate grounds, he had ruled in favor of the Wrights. He pointed to section one of the Virginia Bill of Rights—what he called the state's "political catechism"—that began with the declaration "That all men are by nature equally free and independent." Thus, as his words were later reported, "freedom is the birthright of every human being," and, "whenever one person claims to hold another in slavery, the onus probandi [burden of proof] lies on the claimant." Quite aside from that line of argument, witnesses had testified that the family descended, in the female line, from "an old Indian called Butterwood Nan," and her daughter Hannah "had long black hair, was of the right copper colour, and was generally called an Indian by the neighbours, who said she might recover her freedom, if she would sue for it." Chancellor Wythe inspected members of the family there in the courtroom and concluded that they—three generations of females—appeared more or less Indian, not at all African, and, in the case of Jacky Wright's youngest child, "perfectly white." Thus—without even having to rely on his radical statement of broader grounds for emancipation—he decided that they were entitled to their freedom.[33]

On appeal to the state supreme court, George Keith Taylor, counsel for the Wrights, argued: "From the beginning of the world till the year 1679, all Indians were, in fact as well as right, free persons." And if, he declared, "the appellees [the Wrights] are descended from Indians, it is incumbent on the appellant [Hudgins] to prove that they are slaves; the appellees are not bound to prove the contrary."[34] In effect, the court agreed, though it "entirely disapprov[ed]" Chancellor Wythe's reasoning as it might apply to black Virginians. Judge Tucker made clear his premise that the Virginia Bill of Rights applied to "free citizens" and by no means "overturn[ed] the rights of property." And yet he—and the rest of the court—had no difficulty affirming the substance of Wythe's decree. The Wrights must benefit from a presumption of freedom; the burden of proof fell on Hudgins. The Wrights should go free.[35]

Judges Tucker and Roane each wrote an essay on "natural history" and elaborated on how "mere inspection" might establish a prima-facie case—a presumption of slavery or freedom, to be rebutted by opposing evidence if such could be supplied. Judge Tucker concluded that "all American Indians are prima facie free; . . . where the fact of their nativity and descent, in a maternal line, is satisfactorily established, the burthen of proof thereafter lies upon the party claiming to hold them as slaves. To effect which, according to my opinion, he must prove the progenitrix of the party claiming to be free, to have been brought into Virginia, and made a slave between the passage of the act of 1679 and its repeal in 1691." Judge Roane's version went as follows: "In the case of a person visibly appearing to be a negro, the presumption is, in this country, that he is a slave, and it is incumbent on him to make out his right to freedom; but in the case of a person visibly appearing to be a white man, or an Indian, the presumption is that he is free, and it is necessary for his adversary to shew that he is a slave." And yet, Roane pointed out, Hudgins "brings no testimony to shew that any ancestor in the female line was a negro slave or even an Indian rightfully held in slavery."[36]

In a cluster of cases, twenty-two slaves, among them Pallas, sued for their freedom in 1807. They produced evidence that they were "descendants in the maternal line of a native American Indian named Bess" who had been "brought into Virginia in or about the year 1703." The plaintiffs' lawyer urged that the jury be instructed that "no native American Indian brought into Virginia since the year 1691, could, under any circumstances, be lawfully made a slave." Instead, the lower court placed the date at 1705. Thus, Pallas and her colleagues lost the case, but they appealed to the state supreme court. There, counsel for the putative owners urged the judges to uphold the lower court and, moreover, overturn the decision in *Coleman* v. *Dick and Pat* that the 1705 statute had, in fact, repealed such laws as permitted reducing Indians to slavery. But Judge Tucker and his colleagues, as Spencer Roane put it, "could not agree that solemn decisions of the Court should be stirred." As Tucker observed, "the only question" was whether the act of 1691, as he had urged in *Hudgins* v. *Wrights*, was "to be regarded as the law of the land." The court ruled that the crucial date was, in fact, 1691 and not 1705. Pallas and the others were thus entitled to a new trial.[37]

The same appeals court that ruled in favor of Pallas and the Wrights had difficulty achieving a libertarian outcome in another case. A slave named Isabell sought to obtain her freedom from Elizabeth Pegram, and she had won at trial in Petersburg District Court. She claimed to be an Indian, and she showed that her mother, Nanny, had won a freedom suit, on the basis of her Indian ancestry, back in 1799. Pegram's attorney argued, though, that Isabell might have been born before Nanny gained her freedom and thus the previous case, even if it could be admitted as evidence, could hardly be conclusive in supporting Isabell's claim. Isabell's lawyer, George Keith Taylor, countered that, as an Indian, she had a right to her freedom regardless of when she was born. A unanimous court of appeals rejected that claim and ruled the record of the lower court "too imperfect" to reach a determination. A second trial at Petersburg ended as the first one had, with a judgment for Isabell but an appeal by Pegram. The court of appeals reversed this decision, too, and sent the case back for yet a third trial. Still to be determined, as Pegram's counsel had insisted, were two questions: On what basis had Nanny obtained her freedom? And had she given birth to Isabell before or after her being emancipated? Isabell's struggle no doubt continued, though her case did not rise again to the state's highest court.[38] According to the law, if Nanny had been freed on the basis of her Indian ancestry, her children, whether born before or after she gained her freedom, should have become instantly free too.

◀▷

Isabell's tenacity supplies a metaphor for Virginia slaves' quest for freedom in the years between the 1760s and the 1810s. George Keith Taylor's efforts on her behalf were representative of one white Virginian's struggle in the early nineteenth century to adapt the law to the cause of freedom. His arguments regarding Indian ancestry sometimes sufficed, sometimes not, to win freedom for his clients. Either way, they gave evidence time and again that Indian ancestry was, as Octavia Featherstone knew, connected with a greater likelihood of freedom among nonwhite Virginians.

The Indian plaintiffs in Virginia's manumission cases were among America's "new people"—biracial, even triracial, descendants of people who originated in Europe, Africa, and America.[39] Most slaves, even of Indian descent, had no means of manipulating the legal mechanism that Virginia law provided for a time to some descendants of Indian women. The child of a son of an Indian woman could not hope to win a case on that basis, as only an unbroken maternal line would satisfy the requirement. Thus most slaves in Virginia, even among those with some Indian ancestry, could not hope to make their way through that escape hatch from slavery to freedom. Some could, and did, make their cases in the courts and find their paths to freedom. Some no doubt retained that freedom, once they gained it. Moreover, free mothers gave birth to free children, so the multiplier effect of emancipating a slave woman continued to operate into the 1860s.[40] And, more often than not, antebellum free nonwhites carried advantages in their cultural and economic baggage—in literacy and propertyholding, for example—into the post-Civil War world.[41]

If we place the plaintiffs themselves at the center of the story, then the "true emancipators" were slaves themselves. Favorable outcomes in several of these cases—and the resulting rise in the number of free nonwhite Virginians—came as a consequence of actions that slaves themselves took. Emancipation, in this view, rather than resulting from initiatives taken by slaveholders large or small, had its roots in resistance by slaves against those masters. In these cases, emancipation resulted from actions taken not by owners but by their slaves *against* those owners.[42]

Most nonwhite Virginians who lived free, though born slaves, gained their liberty only in the convulsive events of the 1860s, but having Indian foremothers provided a means for some slaves to obtain their freedom much earlier. As late as the twentieth century, some Virginians displayed an awareness of that dual fact—that they had Indian ancestry as well as African, and that it had made all the difference in determining the slavery or the freedom of their ancestors. What has tended generally to fade from view, nonetheless, is the complex past of the eighteenth century, when three races continued to mix, whatever the binary premises of later understanding, and when there were intermediate stations between slavery, lifelong and inherited, and freedom from slavery.[43]

Octavia Featherstone has led us back to identities other than only black or white, African or European, among Virginians. And she has reminded us not only that some nonwhite Virginians were free during slave times, but that they had to use the law to maintain or even create their opportunities. They may have crafted those opportunities out of unpromising materials, but they crafted them nonetheless.

Between them, Sarah Madden and Jacky Wright embody the triracial nature of Virginia society as late as the American Revolution and the Early National era. Between them, they demonstrate the enormous power that race and sex, in various combinations, could have in shaping people's lives, in determining whether, when, and on what conditions they might live their lives in freedom. Sarah Madden exemplified the long-term unfreedom that some Virginians experienced, a status midway between starting out life free and being born slave. The daughter of a European American and an African American, she had to wait until the age of thirty-one to gain her own freedom in 1789 and another eighteen years before the last of her unfree children became free in 1807. Jacky Wright showed that, though born into lifelong slavery, one might still obtain freedom. Wright, who had Indian ancestry, whatever European and African ancestry she or her three children had, was a grown woman before she succeeded in wresting freedom for herself and her children in 1805 from Holder Hudgins.

In the years to come, the daughters of Sarah Madden and Jacky Wright would no doubt have children of their own, and those children, born to free mothers, would be born free. The Maddens would finally shake free of the burdens of the 1691 law and its successors. The Wrights would finally see the law of 1662 operate to produce free Virginians rather than slaves.

◀▷

Notes

1. Charles L. Perdue, Jr., et al., eds., *Weevils in the Wheat: Interviews with Virginia Ex-Slaves* (Charlottesville: University Press of Virginia, 1976), 91.

2. By 1860, on the eve of the Civil War and the end of slavery, the state of Virginia counted only 112 "civilized" Indians in a total population of 1,596,318. Whites numbered 1,047,299, and Virginians of African ancestry 548,907—490,865 of them slaves and 58,042 free. U.S. Census Bureau, *Population of the United States in 1860* (Washington D.C.: Government Printing Office, 1864), 598–604.

3. "People Who Refused to Vanish," in Helen C. Rountree, *Pocahontas's People: The Powhatan Indians of Virginia through Four Centuries* (Norman: University of Oklahoma Press, 1990), Chap. 8.

4. Virginia's laws can be found in William Waller Hening, ed., *The Statutes at Large, Being a Collection of All the Laws of Virginia, from the First Session of the Legislature in the Year 1619* (13 vols.; 1809–1823; reprint Charlottesville: University Press of Virginia, 1969), but in this essay they are cited, when possible, from June Purcell Guild, *Black Laws of Virginia* (1936; reprint New York: Negro Universities Press, 1969); the 1662 act is at 23–24.

5. Guild, *Black Laws of Virginia*, 24–26; the quotation is from Hening, *Statutes at Large*, 3: 87. For a fuller discussion see Peter Wallenstein, "Race, Marriage, and the Law of Freedom: Alabama and Virginia, 1860s–1960s," *Chicago-Kent Law Review* 70, no. 2, 1994, 371–438.

6. Hening, *Statutes at Large*, 4:133.

7. Guild, *Black Laws of Virginia*, 27–28.

8. *Gwinn* v. *Bugg*, Jefferson 87 (1770). Another such case immediately follows: *Howell* v. *Netherland*, Jefferson 90 (1770).

9. T. O. Madden, Jr., with Ann L. Miller, *We Were Always Free: The Maddens of Culpeper County, Virginia, a 200-Year Family History* (New York: Norton, 1992), 2–26, 37.

10. Ibid., 35–39.

11. Purcell, *Black Laws of Virginia*, 60.

12. Ibid., 61, 72; James Thomas Flexner, *Washington: The Indispensable Man* (Boston: Little, Brown, 1974), 385–94.

13. U.S. Census Office, First Census, 1790, *Return of the Whole Number of Persons* (Philadelphia: Childs and Swaine, 1791), 48–50.

14. By 1830, to take a midpoint sighting, a host of counties displayed population data of that sort, particularly in the Tidewater, a region where, as a whole, 48.6 percent of all residents were slaves and 7.6 percent were free nonwhites. Nine counties in the Tidewater area had such patterns: Henrico, Isle of Wight, Nansemond, Northampton, Richmond, Southampton, Surry, Westmoreland, and York. So did the cities of Richmond and Petersburg. In the Piedmont, where slave percentages tended to be higher and free black numbers smaller, the counties of Amherst, Campbell, and Fauquier showed a similar pattern. The figures are most accessible in Alison Goodyear Freehling, *Drift Toward Dissolution: The Virginia Slavery Debate of 1831–1832* (Baton Rouge: Louisiana State University Press, 1982), 265–69.

15. *Hook v. Nanny Pagee and her Children*, 2 Munford 379 (1811).

16. Register of Free Negroes, Stafford County, p. 5, 20 July 1790, City Library, Fredericksburg, Virginia.

17. *Virginia Gazette*, 26 Nov. 1772, 15 July 1773.

18. *Robin v. Hardaway*, Jefferson 109 (1772), 114.

19. *Jenkins v. Tom and Others*, 1 Washington 123 (1792); Virginia Supreme Court of Appeals, Order Book 2 (1790–94), 187 (microfilm, Library of Virginia, Richmond, Virginia).

20. *Jenkins v. Tom and Others*, 124. Attorneys for both sides in *Robin v. Hardaway* had spoken of the large numbers of Indian slaves in Virginia in years past. Hardaway's lawyer, Colonel Bland, declared that, even before the laws of the 1670s permitting Indian slavery, "great numbers of Indian captives were held in slavery, every man thinking himself entitled, under the law of nature, to his captives in war." Mason, for his part, had it that his interpretation of the law had been the "universal opinion in this country . . . and under that persuasion hundreds of the descendants of Indians have obtained their freedom, on actions brought in this court." *Robin v. Hardaway*, 119, 116.

21. *Coleman v. Dick and Pat*, 239; Order Book 2: 255. The court divided 2–2 on the particulars of the case and thus affirmed the outcome in the lower court, where a jury had found for the plaintiffs.

22. Helen Tunnicliff Catterall, ed., *Judicial Cases Concerning American Slavery and the Negro* (5 vols.; Washington, D.C.: Carnegie Institution of Washington, 1926–37), contains a history and analysis of the Virginia laws and the cases that arose from them (1:61–71) as well as abstracts of the Virginia cases (1:76–265); the cases regarding manumission of Indians are at 1:91–166 passim. The cases from 1792 through 1811 are at 1:99–122. For a full analysis of judges, slaves, and the legal system in a regional context see A. E. Keir Nash, "Reason of Slavery: Understanding the Judicial Role in the Peculiar Institution," *Vanderbilt Law Review*, 32, January 1979, 7–218.

23. For other treatments of this period, though not of this type of resistance, see Gerald W. Mullin, *Flight and Rebellion: Slave Resistance in Eighteenth-Century Virginia* (New York: Oxford University Press, 1972), and Sylvia R. Frey, *Water from the Rock: Black Resistance in a Revolutionary Age* (Princeton: Princeton University Press, 1991). See also George M. Fredrickson and Christopher Lasch, "Resis-

tance to Slavery," *Civil War History*, 13, December 1967, 315–29, one of various treatments that focus on the later period; Philip J. Schwarz, *Twice Condemned: Slaves and the Criminal Laws of Virginia, 1705–1865* (Baton Rouge: Louisiana State University Press, 1988), a study of criminal law that posits slave crime as a political statement against slavery; and Brenda E. Stevenson, *Life in Black and White: Family and Community in the Slave South* (New York: Oxford University Press, 1996).

24. The phrase is from *Pallas v. Hill* (and other cases), 2 Hening and Munford 149 (1808).

25. Shortly before enactment of the 1795 measure, the president of the Supreme Court of Appeals, Edmund Pendleton, observed: "Although suits for freedom may be instituted without the leave of the court, yet it is usual to petition for such leave. The court, generally require the opinion of the counsel upon the plaintiff's right; and if it appear, that the plaintiff has probable cause for suing, the court will make special orders for the purpose of protecting the plaintiff from the master's resentment, or ill treatment, on that account, and for allowing him reasonable time to prepare for this trial." *Coleman v. Dick and Pat*, 239.

   Such a right to sue for freedom prevailed throughout the South (Nash, "Reason of Slavery," 101–102). See also J. Thomas Wren, "A 'Two-Fold Character': The Slave as Person and Property in Virginia Court Cases, 1800–1860," *Southern Studies*, 24, Winter 1985, 419–20; Adele Hast, "The Legal Status of the Negro in Virginia, 1705–1765," *Journal of Negro History* 54 (July 1969): 234–35; Tommy Lee Bogger, "The Slave and Free Black Community in Norfolk, 1775–1865" (Ph.D. diss., University of Virginia, 1976), 90–93.

26. Such "true emancipators" also freed their own slaves, if any, and provided the impetus to enactment of the 1782 measure that facilitated such private manumissions as theirs and George Washington's (McColley, *Slavery and Jeffersonian Virginia*, 159–60). An earlier statement, with additional detail, is John H. Russell, *The Free Negro in Virginia, 1619–1865* (1913; reprint New York: Dover, 1969), 46–65.

27. Virginia Code (1819), I: 482; McColley, *Slavery and Jeffersonian Virginia*, 159–61. One might hypothesize that this measure, by imposing punitive fines in failed manumission suits by Indian plaintiffs, heightened the stakes for any people who helped bring such cases—and thus that, if they lost at trial, they would have had a financial interest in appealing such a decision. But, of all the reported cases recounted in this essay that the measure might have applied to, except for the case of *Pallas v. Hill* (which was lost at trial but reversed on appeal), every one that reached the state supreme court had been *won* by plaintiffs at the lower level.

28. Edmund S. Morgan, *American Slavery, American Freedom: The Ordeal of Colonial Virginia* (New York: Norton, 1975), 328–30.

29. See Catterall, ed., *Judicial Cases*, 1:61–71; on *Hannah* see also Charles T. Cullen, *St. George Tucker and Law in Virginia, 1772–1804* (New York: Garland, 1987), 67. An earlier account, less reliable, is Almon Wheeler Lauber, *Indian Slavery in Colonial Times within the Present Limits of the United States* (1913; reprint New York: AMS Press, 1969), 312–15.

30. St. George Tucker, *A Dissertation on Slavery: with a Proposal for the Gradual Abolition of It, in the State of Virginia* (1796; reprint Westport, Ct.: Negro Universities Press, 1970), 34–37. On Tucker, see Winthrop D. Jordan, *White over Black: American Attitudes toward the Negro, 1550–1812* (Chapel Hill: University of

North Carolina Press, 1968), 551–60. See also W. Stitt Robinson, Jr., "The Legal Status of the Indian in Colonial Virginia," *Virginia Magazine of History and Biography*, 61, July 1953, 247–59.

The way in which a judge might happen upon a statute, or be oblivious to it, helps explain why, after W. W. Hening approached the legislature in 1807 seeking support for a full reprinting of all the laws passed in Virginia's history, he gained approval and funding in 1808 (see Hening, *Statutes at Large*, 1: xi, xxiii). The first volume appeared in 1809, and as Virginia's legislative history became complete, judges needed only worry about how to interpret and apply the statutes, not wonder what the statutes were.

31. *William and Mary Quarterly*, 2nd Series, 10, October 1930, 349–50; Richard R. Beeman, *The Old Dominion and the New Nation, 1788–1801* (Lexington: University Press of Kentucky, 1972), 223; Cynthia Miller Leonard, comp., *The General Assembly of Virginia, July 30, 1619–January 11, 1978: A Bicentennial Register of Members* (Richmond: Virginia State Library, 1978).

32. *Hudgins v. Wrights*, 1 Hening and Munford 134 (1806); Virginia Supreme Court of Appeals, Order Book 5 (1804–07), 345, 348; Catterall, *Judicial Cases*, 1: 65, 99–100, 112–13.

33. *Hudgins v. Wrights*, 134; Robert M. Cover, *Justice Accused: Antislavery and the Judicial Process* (New Haven: Yale University Press, 1975), 50–55.

34. *Hudgins v. Wrights*, 135.

35. Ibid., 144, 141.

36. Ibid., 139, 141, 142.

37. *Pallas v. Hill*, 149, 152, 157; Virginia Supreme Court of Appeals, Order Book 6 (1808–11), 26; Catterall, *Judicial Cases*, 1: 66, 116–17.

38. Judge William Fleming explained in the court's second decision in the case: "Although it is admitted, that laws should be liberally construed in favour of the rights of freedom, yet the rights of property ought to be respected and preserved." *Pegram v. Isabell*, 1 Hening and Munford 387 (1807); *Pegram v. Isabell*, 2 Hening and Munford 193 (1808), 208; Virginia Supreme Court of Appeals, Order Book 5 (1804–07), 415, and Order Book 6 (1808–11), 30. Other cases regarding freedom suits by Indian slaves, after 1811, were *Butt v. Rachel*, 4 Munford 209 (1814); *Gregory v. Baugh*, 4 Randolph 611 (1827); and *Gregory v. Baugh*, 2 Leigh 665 (1831).

39. The phrase, though not the specific application, is Joel Williamson's: *New People: Miscegenation and Mulattoes in the United States* (New York: Free Press, 1980).

40. Cover, *Justice Accused*, 67–75; Ira Berlin, *Slaves Without Masters: The Free Negro in the Antebellum South* (New York: Pantheon, 1974), 15–50.

41. Luther Porter Jackson, *Free Negro Labor and Property Holding in Virginia, 1830–1860* (1942; reprint New York: Atheneum, 1969); Berlin, *Slaves Without Masters*, 381–95.

42. Suzanne Lebsock notes that, increasingly in the first half of the nineteenth century, it was free blacks who secured the freedom of slaves: *The Free Women of Petersburg: Status and Culture in a Southern Town, 1784–1860* (New York: Norton, 1984), 94–96.

43. For a provocative interpretation of the missing Indians and their continuing presence, see Gary B. Nash, "The Hidden History of Mestizo America," *Journal of American History*, 82, December 1995, 941–62. For discussions of "Part-Africans and Part-Americans as *Mulatos*" and "The Classification of Native Americans as Mulattoes in Anglo-North America," see Jack D. Forbes, *Africans*

and Native Americans: The Language of Race and the Evolution of Red-Black Peoples (2nd. ed.; Urbana: University of Illinois Press, 1993), Chaps. 6–7. Regarding what he called "the problem of racial identity," see James Hugo Johnston, *Race Relations in Virginia and Miscegenation in the South, 1776–1860* (Amherst: University of Massachusetts Press, 1970), 191–215. The antebellum cases were related as frequently to the racial identity, and thus the rights, of a free person—white or mulatto—as to whether he or she should be free.

RAPE, RACE, AND CASTRATION IN SLAVE LAW IN THE COLONIAL AND EARLY SOUTH

In the late summer of 1810, a Prince William County, Virginia, jury—all–white, all–male, as would be expected—was summoned to hear the Commonwealth's case against an eighteen–year–old slave who, it was charged, had attempted to rape a young white woman, Elizabeth Vickers. The rape of a white female by a slave was indeed a capital crime in Virginia as well as the rest of the slaveholding South at this time.[1] Attempted rape by a slave, however, was not yet punishable by death in Virginia. Instead, slaves convicted of the attempted rape of a white female were castrated.[2] Ben, the property of Major Thomas Ewell, thus faced castration for his alleged attempt on Elizabeth Vickers if found guilty.

A guilty verdict, and the concomitant punishment of dismemberment, however, was not a foregone conclusion, even in the racist, slaveholding South. While Vickers's race accorded her sufficient status to have had her complaint officially received by local officials, and thus taken seriously, her whiteness did not shield her from an investigation into her personal life, specifically her past sexual history. Elizabeth Vickers testified that Ben, who had frequently passed by the home she and her mother shared, had on occasion addressed her in "very familiar language," inquiring about "the number of sweethearts" Vickers had. On the day of the alleged attack, Vickers told the court, Ben had passed by her house and again spoke to her "in the same familiar terms." She ignored the affront and later—she did not such how much time had elapsed—after having gone some distance from her home, Ben attacked her. When she offered resistance, Ben drew a knife with which he "cut and disfigured" her clothing.[3]

It seems probable that Vickers's testimony about Ben's improper conduct—his use of "familiar language" with Vickers—was offered up as proof that the slave had harbored sexual designs toward her for some time and then acted on them at the first opportunity. James E. Heath, defense counsel employed by Ben's owner, however, turned Vickers's own testimony against her by insinuating that her failure to report the "insulting language" to the brazen slave's master actually had invited Ben's attempt. Heath also demanded to know why, if she really had struggled to resist Ben's attack as she claimed, were there not "the slightest marks of violence" on her body? Clearly, through this line of questioning the defense intended to weave a version of the attack that suggested the incident was not an unwanted assault, but rather a consensual act.[4]

The legal stratagem adopted by Ben's counsel has been frequently employed in sexual assault trials throughout American history continuing to the present day, regardless of the race of the accused and the accuser. In this particular case, the defense attack of the accuser was seemingly bolstered by neighbors' testimony maintaining that Vickers had earned a reputation for cavorting with both black and white men. Hewel A. Perry testified, for instance, that Vickers and her mother, Ann Vickers, "kept a house upon the main Road where Waggoners, black as well as white frequently rested." Seen in the best light, the Vickers women may have earned their living servicing weary travelers who passed by their house located on a busy "publick Road." A more cynical, less favorable interpretation of the circumstances would have Elizabeth and Ann Vickers prostituting themselves. This latter version was buttressed by Perry's testimony. He informed the court that Elizabeth Vickers had given birth to a "Bastard Child" and was supposed by others to be "addicted to those practices which would naturally produce Children."[5]

Despite the presentation of what the defense perceived as mitigating factors, namely, the accuser's reputation for sexual deviance, Ben was convicted of attempted rape and ordered to be castrated. A sympathetic court, however, at the behest of Ben's master, attached a recommendation for mercy to the verdict.[6] Although apparently convinced that Ben indeed had attacked Elizabeth Vickers, the court nonetheless was persuaded that inappropriate, indecent behavior by the accuser had been partially responsible for Ben's affront. In the eyes of the white male jury members and court officials, Vickers's status had been degraded because of her own intimate relations with black and white men outside of marriage. Her charge of attempted rape, therefore, was not taken as seriously as that by a white woman who had not ventured outside the boundaries of acceptable sexual behavior.

This specific case of attempted rape by a slave of a white female serves to make several points this essay will elaborate. First, this court case exposes the fallibility and inadequacy of relying solely on statutory law to draw conclusions about the extent to which the white male population was animated by deep–seated fears of black male sexuality. A very influential and highly revered body of work premised on statutory evidence has argued for the presence of widespread sexual anxiety among whites, citing as evidence laws that treated convicted slave rapists and would–be rapists of white females harshly, as evidenced by slave codes; specifically, punishments of death and castration usually reserved for African Americans. While in this case the accused slave was convicted and sentenced to a harsh punishment, such claims fail to account for the behavior of southern whites during and after Ben's trial who vigorously sought a reprieve for him. Most notably, Ben's owner had plenty of incentive to keep his slave—and property—healthy and alive.

Other factors, for example, the formidable prejudices about poorer women who did not conform to societal conventions of appropriate sexual behavior, help explain why some whites lent their support to Ben, a black male accused of sexually assaulting a white female. Elizabeth Vickers had behaved badly in the eyes of her community, and that was, for some, grounds for the rough treatment she received at the hands of a slave. Statutes, of course, made no accommodation for mitigating circumstances. Yet juries and judges in the early slave South frequently made such distinctions and fashioned their decisions accordingly. A closer look at such cases, therefore, enables us to gauge more accurately the racial, sexual, and class dynamics of a community in a way that slave criminal statutes alone cannot.

In addition, closer scrutinization of those statutes that prescribed castration for slave sex offenders and a look at the criminal proceedings of slaves charged with rape or attempted rape yields findings that are incompatible with those that regard castration as a manifestation of white sexual anxiety. Rather, I argue that a multiplicity of factors and conditions account for the prescribed punishment of castration. Furthermore, I contend that even when castration was the stipulated punishment for convicted slave offenders, white community members and/or courtroom participants sometimes sought to circumvent the letter of the law and worked to spare convicted slave sex offenders from dismemberment or death.

Colonial and early American rape laws that held out either castration or death for convicted blacks frequently are posited as proof that whites harbored widespread anxiety about black male sexuality. Winthrop Jordan, for instance, wrote that the "white man's fears of Negro sexual aggression were . . . apparent in the use of castration as a punishment in the colonies."[7] One historian even asserted that castration of slaves who made sexual advances on white women was virtually axiomatic. "It almost goes without saying that the penalty for a slave who dared lust after white women's flesh was castration, first by the law of the slave code, later by community justice alone."[8] More recently, Peter Bardaglio has argued that "anxieties of southern white males about black sexual aggression found their most morbid expression" in the castration of black males for the rape or attempted rape of white females.[9]

While it is true that slaveholders and local officials at times utilized castration as a means to control errant slaves, the punishment was never exclusively used in cases of alleged sexual affronts. Indeed, at least three southern colonies legally sanctioned castration of African-American men for an array of offenses.[10] Anxiety about black rape, however, was not the chief motivating factor for prescribed castration. Initially at least, castration was not even reserved for black rapists. In South Carolina, slaves who ran away for the fourth time could be castrated.[11] Virginia lawmakers sanctioned dismemberment for troublesome "outlying" slaves.[12] In fact, a North Carolina statute excepted black rapists from castration, which was reserved for first–time offenders of serious crimes *other than rape* and murder.[13] Historians Marvin L. Michael Kay and Lorin Lee Cary have documented nineteen cases of North Carolina slaves sentenced to castration from 1755 to 1767. In only five cases were the crimes of the offending slaves stated and none of these were sex crimes. Offenses included breaking and entering, stealing, poisoning, and arson.[14] Legally sanctioned castration of slaves, then, was hardly a punishment reserved for the rape or attempted rape of white females.

Furthermore, some of the earliest legislation imposing castration on sex offenders encompassed nonblacks. A New Jersey measure passed in the first decade of the eighteenth century, for example, directed that any slave, whether "Negro, Indian or Mallatto," be castrated for attempted rape. The wording of the statute suggests that slaves, whether of Indian or African descent, were the object of this directive. Importantly, free blacks do not appear to have been encompassed by this law.[15] Pennsylvania's statute permitted castration of white men, although there is no evidence that the punishment was ever carried out on whites.[16] That some colonies legally sanctioned castration for Indians and even whites calls into question the claim that the castration penalty for sex crimes in the colonies was motivated primarily by white stereotypes about black lasciviousness.

The myopic reliance on southern rape statutes to gauge white sexual anxiety about blacks has proved an inadequate and problematic approach. Because southern rape statutes have historically been race–specific, or perhaps more accurately bondage–status specific, some historians have been too quick to make the causal connection between law and societal behavior. Several qualifications are in order. First, judging by colonial rape statutes it would appear that southern legislative bodies took sexual assault very seriously, regardless of the race of the alleged perpetrator. Several southern colonies, and later states, held out the death penalty for both black and white rapists. In Virginia, for example, prior to 1796 the law was equally harsh to free and unfree, European and African descended rapists; death could be prescribed for both.[17] Likewise, colonial South Carolina sentenced black and white rapists to death.[18] Among southern colonies that did in fact treat black and white sex offenders differently were Georgia, Maryland, and North Carolina.[19] The norm, however, for all British America seemed to hold out capital punishment for all rapists regardless of color.

Second, experts in legal history have cautioned against making sweeping generalizations about society on the basis of statutes alone. William M. Wiecek, for one, asserts that "statutes are not evidence of actual societal conditions. When a statute prohibits a certain type of behavior . . . it is no more reasonable to infer from the enactment of the statute that such behavior was common than to infer that it was rare."[20] Moreover, as evidenced by the attempted rape trial of Ben, implementation and prosecution of the law were entirely different matters.[21]

The castration of slaves as a form of punishment emerged and continued not so much out of fears about black male sexual ardor but rather out of the slaves' condition as property. In the colonial South, numerous crimes when committed by slaves or African Americans were considered capital.[22] Since the colonial treasuries were required to compensate slaveowners for executed slave criminals, some colonies looked to dismemberment as a means not only of punishing slave offenders and detering would–be slave criminals, but doing so at minimal cost.[23] The punishment of castration was serious, yet spared the colonial governments the costly burden of compensating slave masters for the loss of slave lives. One North Carolinian in 1737 complained about the high cost of reimbursing masters for executed slaves:

> [T]he Planters suffer little or nothing by it, for the Province is obliged to pay the full value they judge them worth to the Owner; this is the common Custom or Law in this Province, to prevent the Planters being ruined by the loss of their Slaves, whom they have purchased at so dear a rate[;].[24]

The policy of reimbursing masters for condemned slaves came under closer scrutiny during the French and Indian War when the cost of the war strained colonial coffers even further. In an attempt to reduce the huge sums paid in compensation for executed slaves, the North Carolina legislature in 1758 passed a law that substituted castration for execution in all but cases of murder and rape.[25] During the years in which the law was in place, 1759 to 1764, officials castrated sixteen slaves.[26] Once the war was over and dire economic conditions eased, the North Carolina assembly rescinded the castration clause and executions of convicted slave criminals resumed.[27]

By the end of the eighteenth century, official use of castration to punish recalcitrant slaves diminished substantially.[28] In 1769, the Virginia legislature severely circumscribed the use of castration as punishment, reasoning that "dismemberment is often disproportionate to the offense." Thereafter, castration of slaves was forbidden, except in cases of attempts to ravish a white woman.[29] Philip Schwarz, in his survey of crime among Virginia slaves, could locate only four instances of officially sanctioned castration after passage of this law.[30] Among these, a Northampton County, Virginia, slave was castrated in 1782 after the court was convinced he had attempted to rape a white woman.[31] Six months later another Virginia slave, Bob of Southampton County, was castrated for the rape of his owner's mother.[32]

Although difficult to gauge, it seems likelier that castration would have been utilized more extensively by masters as a private means of retribution and punishment or as a way to curtail "high spirits."[33] In a dispute over damages arising from the sale of three slaves in 1818 that found its way before the South Carolina supreme court, we learn of a belligerent slave who had been castrated, presumably by private individuals, not officials. The slave appears to have been castrated not for any sexual improprieties, but because of a "malicious and vindictive" temper which had manifested itself as thievery and running away.[34]

Not all white southerners approved of castrating slaves. Charles Janson reported that in his travels through North Carolina, probably in the late 1790s, he came across a planter/doctor who had been pressed into service by a slaveowner plagued by a slave who had made repeated "attempts on the chastity of his female neighbors." The doctor reluctantly performed the castration on the slave but refused to accept payment, it seems, a reflection of the doctor's uneasiness.[35]

Other white southerners shared the doctor's apprehensions and misgivings about the propriety of castration as an acceptable form of slave control, and it was perceived by some eighteenth–century southerners as cruel and inhumane. As evidence, in 1784, officials in Mecklenburg County, Virginia, outraged that a local slaveowner had directed one of his slaves to castrate another, slapped him with a warrant. Henry Delong appeared before the county court charged with "cutting and destroying the testicles of his Negro man Will." While Delong confessed to having ordered his slave Ned to castrate Will, the court found the crime was not a felony and thus discharged Delong. Although in the end Delong escaped punishment for his action, the fact that he was ordered to appear before the court demonstrates that certain officials felt the slaveowner had exceeded his authority.[36]

As late as 1850, authorities in Tennessee prosecuted a slave master who castrated one of his slaves, again, not for any sexual infractions, but due to a "turbulent, insolent" disposition. Gabriel Worley, described as a yeoman, "somewhat advanced in life," and who was "remarkable for his kindness and humanity toward his slaves," had grown weary of Josiah's repeated escapes and harassment of other slaves. Worley banished all the female family members from the premises, and with the assistance of his son and a "certain razor" "did strike, cut off, and disable the organs of generation" of Josiah. Worley then summoned a physician to dress the wound, with the court noting that Josiah recovered quickly. Local officials nonetheless charged Worley with mayhem, an act outlawed by Tennessee statute and sentenced him to two years in jail. Tennessee supreme court judges, sufficiently repulsed by the owner's actions, upheld his conviction and jail term.[37]

The personal use of castration at the hands of slave masters, as in these several instances, most likely represented attempts to curb more general turbulent behavior in male slaves in much the same way that a farmer might neuter a bull or horse. That masters would borrow from the pages of basic husbandry manuals advising castration of unruly male livestock and apply these same principles to their slaves, frequently regarded as chattel, should surprise no one. Simply put, castration of slaves as a means to modify behavior and curtail unruliness was an entirely logical extension of some of the most basic elements of agrarian culture.

Yet the fact remains that many slaves did receive castration or death sentences for the crimes of rape and attempted rape. In 1738, Jemmy, a slave owned by James Holman of Goochland County, Virginia, was tried and convicted for raping Elizabeth Weaver. The court sentenced him to hang.[38] Two years earlier, one of Richard Bradford's slaves, Andrew, was also sentenced to die for raping Elizabeth Williams, the wife of Joseph Williams of Caroline County, Virginia.[39] When the alleged victim of a rape was a member of the slaveowner's family, retribution came even swifter. In 1775, Lancaster County slave Natt was sentenced to die for raping Sarah James, the daughter–in–law of his owner, Walter James.[40] Sometimes death alone was deemed an insufficient deterrent to other would–be slave rapists. In the second year of the eighteenth century, one Virginia slave hanged for the rape of a married white woman. His head was subsequently placed on a pole as a warning to deter "Negroes and other Slaves from Committing the Like Crymes and Offences."[41] In 1777, the body of Titus, a North Carolina slave, was burned after he was hanged for the crime of rape.[42]

Despite the harsh tenor of Virginia's colonial rape statutes and the documented executions of convicted black rapists, some convicted slave rapists actually got off relatively lightly. In 1724, Caesar, a slave owned by Gawen Corbin of Spotsylvania County, appeared before the court charged with the attempted rape and buggery of a four–year–old white girl. Although Caesar was convicted, he received merely corporal punishment: twenty–one lashes, one–half hour standing at the pillory, and both ears severely cropped.[43] This was a rather common form of punishment in the early eighteenth century, but hardly one we would have expected to have been levied on a black slave convicted of attempted rape and buggery of a four–year–old white girl.

A similar account involving a free African American was recorded in 1737 in the *Virginia Gazette*. The Isle of Wight court convicted him of the attempted rape of a seven–year–old white girl. The man was condemned, not to die, but to receive twenty–nine lashes, an hour in the pillory, and then to be sold in order to pay court costs and fees. The paper reported that he was "pillory'd and much pelted by the Populace; and afterwards smartly whipp'd."[44]

Daniel, a slave belonging to John Brummall of Chesterfield County, Virginia, likewise cheated the executioner. Having stood trial in the fall of 1753 for raping Mary Danfork [?] he was sentenced to death by the jury. Daniel eluded the hangman's noose, however, by escaping from jail. Officials soon recaptured him and wasted no time reinstating the original guilty verdict; however, this time the court attached an addendum recommending the governor reprieve Daniel. It seems that since Daniel's flight, the court had obtained information that caused it "to suspect the veracity of the witness upon whom his testimony he was convicted." The governor acceded to the court's wishes.[45] A Maryland slaveowner also proved successful in receiving a pardon for his slave who had been convicted for breaking and entering, stealing, and attempting to ravish a white woman. The pardon was granted contingent upon the slave's departure from Maryland within ten days.[46]

And in the same Virginia county where in 1775 a slave hanged for raping his master's daughter–in–law, roughly one week later the court heard testimony in a similar case involving Tom, a slave owned by Nancy Dameron of Northumberland County. Tom purportedly attempted to rape a white woman, Chloe Carter. But rather than execute Tom the court decided that he should:

> suffer the Punishment of having each of his Ears nailed to the Pillory, & then cut out, to be branded on the Cheek with a hot Iron & to receive thirty nine Lashes well laid upon his bare Back at the publick Whipping Post.[47]

Occasionally, slaves who were brought up on charges of rape found themselves judged guilty of lesser crimes. In 1742 Virginia slave Jack was put on trial for raping a white woman. Instead, he was convicted of assault and given 39 lashes.[48]

These cases of African Americans convicted of rape or attempted rape of white females but who were not executed demonstrate that justice meted out to convicted black rapists was not universally harsh.[49] Even though the statutes dealt with black rapists in an unequivocally severe manner, the end result was not routinely a death sentence.[50] Ample opportunity existed for community members and government officials, motivated by various concerns, to spare the life and limb of a black man convicted of sexually assaulting a white female. If a white woman accusing a slave of rape or attempted rape had a reputation for illicit sexual relations, either outside the bonds of marriage, or across the color line, such as Elizabeth Vickers had, members of the white male community at times utilized the discretion accorded to them by the law and worked to forestall the implementation of the most severe punishments of death or dismemberment. In short, southern white elite males who displayed considerable contempt for women of their own race, but not of their own class, sometimes aided convicted black rapists and worked toward the amelioration of harsh punishments.

Events unfolded in just this manner following the conviction in 1808 of a Virginia slave for the attempted rape of a white woman, Patsey Hooker. The slave, Peter, was sentenced to be castrated. Although no depositions or court minutes from the trial have survived, we do learn something of the case from white citizens of Hanover County who petitioned the governor of Virginia to pardon Peter. Governor William H. Cabell's office received two petitions on Peter's behalf, one signed by fifty-seven county residents, the other by numerous freeholders including four magistrates who presided over the trial and the attorney representing the Commonwealth in the case. Both letters present that the accuser was a "common strumpet" and a "common prostitute," a fact alleged to have been conceded by the prosecuting attorney. In court, Hooker admitted to having given birth to "several bastard children," but she adamantly denied ever having "been intimate with any negro." While her illicit sexual activities, established by the birth of children outside marriage, were irrefutable, Hooker vociferously repudiated the change that she had had sexual relations with men of color. The accuser's murky sexual history helped shape the decision of the all-white jury, which rendered a guilty verdict and handed down a sentence of castration, the only recourse available to the court given the conviction. Yet Hooker's actions elicited some degree of empathy and support for the accused whose fate of castration the petitioners believed unwarranted and too severe.[51]

◆

In sum, the treatment of black males in southern rape statutes reflects not white anxiety about black rape but rather the codified belief that blacks, specifically slaves, had to abide by a different, stricter set of legal standards to ensure greater control of the region's bonded labor force. Specifically, the punishment of castration enabled colonial and state governments to spare their treasuries the exorbitant costs of compensating slaveowners for condemned slaves convicted of serious crimes, among which were rape and attempted rape. Castration served the dual purpose of saving money while maintaining control over the slave population; it allowed colonial authorities to punish felonious slave behavior and deter future slave crime while minimizing the financial losses to individual slave owners and the colonial or state governments.[52]

Arguing that pardons and light sentences given to convicted African-American sex offenders were common in the early South does not insinuate that such men were treated "fairly" by southern courts.[53] In fact, black males accused of sexually assaulting white females did experience a high conviction rate. Philip Schwarz, in his comprehensive study of Virginia slave crime, has found that between 1706 and 1785, fifty-nine slaves were accused of rape and attempted rape. Of those fifty, or 84.7 percent, were convicted. Still, a high conviction rate of black rapists does not necessarily prove that white colonials and early Americans were obsessed with fears of black rapists. Slaves charged with hog–stealing, for example, experienced a higher conviction rate than those charged with rape and attempted rape.[54] Slaves brought before the courts in the South in general were dealt with more harshly than the white population. Slave rapists were no exception.

Instead, the evidence and arguments presented in this essay are meant to question frequently repeated, but largely untested, assumptions about race and sexuality in the experience of the American South. Historical analysis of race and rape in the early South that focuses on rape statutes alone runs the risk of reducing the region's peoples to one–dimensional actors, Disneyesque automatons programmed to respond purely on the basis of racial categories. Such was not the case. Members of white communities recognized slave rape laws as harsh and thus scrutinized circumstances of an alleged assault to determine whether or not death or dismemberment of the accused was warranted. The race of the accuser and accused was certainly material, but numerous other considerations weighed in, foremost among them the social standing of the accuser: Was there any evidence of sexual transgression? Had she given birth out of wedlock? Did she have a reputation for promiscuity or prostitution with members of either race? Well–off white southerners believed poorer women, especially those without husbands, to be innately depraved.[55] Thus, the life of a slave was balanced against not merely the race of the accuser, but by her behavior and demeanor as well. If an accuser fell short on any account, as in trials initiated by Elizabeth Vickers and Patsey Hooker, white juries and neighbors might well have circumvented the decreed harsh punishment prescribed by law by any number of means including acquittal, finding the accused guilty of a lesser offense, or petitioning the governor for reprieve or pardon. Such actions taken by whites expose at once divisions along class and gender lines as they reflect contempt for poor white women who in their eyes made unfortunate, improper sexual choices.

◀▷

Prior to emancipation, African American men posed no political threat to white patriarchal rule of the South. With the demise of slavery, however, and the enfranchisement of black men, whites began to conflate politics and sexuality and to associate newly won black political rights with black manhood.[56] During Reconstruction, a time of considerable uncertainty and anxiety for whites when social and political roles remained in flux, incidents of sexual mutilation of black men rose. By contrast, the early South, characterized by relative social, racial, and political stability, which hinged in large measure on racial slavery, afforded white southerners the luxury of siding with slaves who were charged with rape or attempted rape of white females. The postbellum South, not the colonial or even early American South, unleashed the social and political vertigo that eventually gave rise to the white obsession with black rape of white women.

◀▷

Notes

The author would like to acknowledge Jan Lewis and Philip J. Schwarz for their gracious assistance in the preparation of this essay, as well as that provided by the co–editors, Catherine Clinton and Michele Gillespie.

1. On rape statutes for nonwhites in the colonial and early South, consult Diane Miller Sommerville, "The Rape Myth in the Old South Reconsidered," *Journal of Southern History*, 61, August 1995, 492–93; Diane Miller Sommerville, "The Rape Myth Reconsidered: The Intersection of Race, Class and Gender in the American South, 1800–1877," Ph.D. dissertation, Rutgers University, 1995, 82–84, 89–98, 102–04; Peter W. Bardaglio, "Rape and the Law in the Old South: `Calculated to Excite Indignation in Every Heart,'" *Journal of Southern History*, 60, November 1994, 753–55; and, Peter W. Bardaglio, *Reconstructing the Household: Families, Sex, and the Law in the Nineteenth–Century South* (Chapel Hill: University of North Carolina Press, 1995), 64–66. For documents relating to the trial of Ben, see August 1–10, 1810 folder, box 168 (August–September 1810), Virginia Executive Papers (hereafter VEP), Library of Virginia (hereafter LVA), Richmond, Virginia.

2. William W. Hening, ed., *The Statutes at Large, Being a Collection of All the Laws of Virginia* (13 vols.; Richmond: Samuel Pleasants, 1809–23), VIII, 358–61 (Act of 1769). The law, designed to curtail dismemberment of "outlying" slaves, a punishment deemed "disproportioned to the offence," limited castration to those slaves who attempted rape. See also Philip J. Schwarz, *Twice Condemned: Slaves and the Criminal Laws of Virginia, 1705–1865* (Baton Rouge: Louisiana State University Press, 1988), 21–22. Throughout this essay I rely solely on the word castration when referring to the surgical removal of testes from males. Other synonyms, most notably the word emasculation, may insinuate a link between the surgical procedure and the social, political, and personal issues of empowerment and masculinity that I do not wish to convey.

3. August 1–10, 1810 folder, box 168 (August–September 1810), VEP, LVA.

4. Ibid.

5. Ibid.

6. Ibid.

7. Winthrop D. Jordan, *White over Black: American Attitudes Toward the Negro, 1550–1812* (1968; rpt. New York: W. W. Norton, 1977), 154.

8. Bertram Wyatt–Brown, *Southern Honor: Ethics and Behavior in the Old South* (New York: Oxford University Press, 1982), 50.

9. Bardaglio, "Rape and the Law in the Old South," 752. This influential "psycho-sexual" explanation of castration in the slave law has even permeated fields outside history. A sociological study of racism and sexuality in the administration of white justice also cited the historical use of castration as evidence of white anxiety about a black sexual threat: "It is noteworthy that even as early as the 1700s, the white man's anxiety and fear of the Black man's sexual aggression were expressed in the codes. This situation is evidenced by the peculiarly sexual aspect of the rise of castration as a lawful punishment in some of the early colonies." In Coramae Richey Mann and Lance H. Selva, "The Sexualization of Racism: The Black as Rapist and White Justice," *Western Journal of Black Studies* 3 (1979), 171.

10. Hening, ed., *Statutes at Large of Va.*, III, 461 (Act of 1705); Walter Clark, ed., *The State Records of North Carolina* (16 vols; Winston and Goldsboro: State of North Carolina, 1895–1906), XXIII, 489 (Act of 1758); Thomas A. Cooper and David J. McCord, eds., *Statutes at Large of South Carolina*, (10 vols.; Columbia, S.C.: A. S. Johnson, 1836–1841), VII, 359–60 (Act of 1712).

11. Cooper and McCord, *Statutes at Large of S.C.*, VII, 360.

12. Hening, *Statutes at Large of Va.*, III, 461 (Act of 1705).

13. Alan D. Watson, "North Carolina Slave Courts, 1715–1785," *North Carolina Historical Review*, 60, January 1963, 34.

14. Marvin L. Michael Kay and Lorin Lee Cary, *Slavery in North Carolina, 1748–1775* (Chapel Hill: University of North Carolina Press, 1995), 80–85.

15. Bernard Bush, comp., *Laws of the Royal Colony of New Jersey, 1703–1745*, vol. 2 of *New Jersey Archives*, 3rd ser. (Trenton: New Jersey State Library, 1977), 30.

16. J. T. Mitchell and Henry Flanders, eds., *Statutes at Large of Pennsylvania from 1682 to 1801*, II, 77–79 (Act of 1700), as cited by Jordan, *White Over Black*, 155n39, and Kay and Cary, *Slavery in North Carolina*, 84n46. The Pennsylvania statute called for the castration of married men convicted of sodomy, bestiality, or rape for the second time. The law was repealed shortly thereafter. See *Statutes of Pa.*, II, 178, 183–84 (Act of 1706). On the punishment of castration in colonial Pennsylvania consult Karen A. Getman, "Sexual Control in the Slaveholding South: The Implementation and Maintenance of a Racial Caste System," *Harvard Women's Law Journal*, 7, Spring 1984, 134–54, and A. Leon Higginbotham, Jr., *In the Matter of Color: Race and the American Legal Process. The Colonial Period* (New York: Oxford University Press, 1978), 282.

17. A. Leon Higginbotham, Jr., and Barbara K. Kopytoff, "Racial Purity and Interracial Sex in the Law of Colonial and Antebellum Virginia," *Georgetown Law Journal*, 77, 1989, 2008.

18. Cooper and McCord, *Statutes of S.C.* II, 422 (Act of 1712).

19. Horatio Marbury and W. H. Crawford, comps., *Digest of the Laws of Georgia* (Savannah: Seymour, Woolhapter, Stebbins, 1802), 430 (Act of 1770); Clark, *State Records of N.C.*, XXIII, 23, 489 (Act of 1758). Colonial Maryland regarded rape by whites as a capital offense, relying on the authority and precedence of English law. Its legislature, however, provided the death penalty for slaves convicted of rape but did not enact similar legislation for white rapists. See C. Ash-

ley Ellefson, *The County Courts and the Provincial Court in Maryland, 1733–1763* (New York and London: Garland Publishing, Inc., 1990), 290.

20. William M. Wiecek, "The Statutory Law of Slavery and Race in the Thirteen Mainland Colonies of British America," *William and Mary Quarterly* 34, no. 2 (1977), 279. Likewise, Winthrop Jordan, while relying heavily on laws as evidence, acknowledged the danger in "assuming that laws reflect actual practice." Jordan, *White over Black*, 587. Timothy H. Breen and Stephen Innes also counsel against scholarly use of statutes in making generalizations about "white" society. "To what degree did a planter elite set the cultural standards for less affluent whites?" in *"Myne Owne Ground": Race and Freedom on Virginia's Eastern Shore, 1640–1676* (New York: Oxford University Press, 1980), 119n14 and 23–26.

21. See, for example, the cases and statistics cited in Arthur P. Scott, *Criminal Law in Colonial Virginia* (Chicago: University of Chicago Press, 1930), 207–208.

22. Because South Carolina was sluggish in revising its harsh legal code and because it had no penitentiary until after the Civil War, numerous crimes were capital, even for whites. In 1813 there were 165 capital crimes. See Michael S. Hindus, *Prison and Plantation: Crime, Justice, and Authority in Massachusetts and South Carolina, 1767–1878* (Chapel Hill: University of North Carolina Press, 1980), 196. A perusal of antebellum Virginia criminal codes reveals sixty offenses for which blacks could receive the death sentence but free whites did not. In George M. Stroud, *A Sketch of Laws Relating to Slavery in the Several States of the United States of America* (1856; rpr. New York: Negro Universities, 1968), 77–80.

23. On the practice of colonial and state governments compensating slaveowners for executed slaves, see Wiecek, "The Statutory Law of Slavery and Race," 275; Daniel J. Flanigan, "The Criminal Law of Slavery and Freedom, 1800–1868," Ph.D. dissertation, Rice University, 1973, 66; Schwarz, *Twice Condemned*, 20, 52–53; Michael S. Hindus, "Black Justice Under White Law: Criminal Prosecutions of Blacks in Antebellum South Carolina," *Journal of American History* 63, 3, 1976, 595; Jeffrey Crow, *The Black Experience in Revolutionary North Carolina* (Raleigh: Division of Archives and History, 1983), 25–26; John Spencer Bassett, *Slavery in the State of North Carolina* (Baltimore: Johns Hopkins University Press, 1899), 14; R. H. Taylor, "Humanizing the Slave Code of North Carolina," *North Carolina Historical Review* 2, 1925, 329; John Edwards, "Slave Justice in Four Middle Georgia Counties," *Georgia Historical Quarterly*, 57, 1973, 266; Ulrich B. Phillips, *American Negro Slavery* (New York: D. Appleton & Co., 1918), 491–92; Donna Spindel, *Crime and Society in North Carolina, 1663–1776* (Baton Rouge: Louisiana State University, 1989), 133–34; Clark, *State Records of N.C.*, XXIII, 489; and, Philip J. Schwarz, "The Transportation of Slaves from Virginia, 1810–1865," *Slavery and Abolition: A Journal of Comparative Studies* 7, 1986, 224–26. While slaveowners were usually compensated for condemned slaves, rates generally did not always reflect fair market value, masters thus had financial motives to save the lives of their slaves despite the policy of compensation. See Sommerville, "The Rape Myth in the Old South Reconsidered," 504–566.

24. John Brickell, *The Natural History of North Carolina* (Dublin, 1737; reprint ed., Murfreesboro, N.C.: Johnson Publishing Co., 1968), 273.

25. Clark, *State Records of N.C.*, XXIII, 488–89. On North Carolina's use of castration of slave criminals during the French and Indian War, see also Crow, *The Black Experience in Revolutionary North Carolina*, 25–26; Taylor, "Humanizing the Slave Code of North Carolina," 324; Spindel, *Crime and Society in North Carolina, 1663–1776*, 134; Jordan, *White over Black*, 157; Watson, "North Carolina

Slave Courts," 32; Kay and Cary, *Slavery in North Carolina*, 89–90; and, Kirsten Fischer, "Dangerous Acts: The Politics of Illicit Sex in Colonial North Carolina, 1660–1760," Ph.D. dissertation, Duke University, 1994, 262–64.

26. Marvin L. Michael Kay and Lorin Lee Cary, "'The Planters Suffer Little or Nothing': North Carolina Compensations for Executed Slaves, 1748–1777," *Science and Society*, 40, n. 3, 1976, 298; Kay and Cary, *Slavery in North Carolina*, 84.

27. After the end of the war, executions of slaves quadrupled and only two castrations can be documented for the period 1765 to 1772. In Kay and Cary, *Slavery in North Carolina*, 90.

28. Eugene D. Genovese, *Roll, Jordan, Roll: The World the Slaves Made* (New York: Random House, Vintage Books, 1975), 67. There was renewed interest in castration of slaves, especially among the "western" slaveholding states later in the nineteenth century. In Missouri during the antebellum period, men of color faced castration for rape and attempted rape of white females. See Mo., *Rev. Stat.* (1844–45), ch. 47, art. 2, sec. 31, 349. Two Missouri slaves convicted of sex crimes appealed their castration sentences to that state's supreme court. See *Nathan v. State*, 8 Mo. 631 (July 1844) and *State v. Anderson*, 19 Mo. 241 (October 1853). An 1855 Kansas law went so far as to require castrated blacks or mulattos to reimburse officials for the cost of the procedure. In Jennifer Wriggins, "Rape, Racism, and the Law," *Harvard Women's Law Journal*, 6, April 1983, 105n8.

29. Hening, *Statutes*, VIII, 358. A 1792 revision of the Virginia slave code left the castration punishment for attempted rape intact. Samuel Shepherd, ed., *The Statutes at Large for Virginia* (3 vols; rpt. New York: AMS Inc., 1970), I, ch. 41, sec. 18, p. 125 (Act of 1792). An 1805 law provided that "if any slave shall hereafter attempt to ravish a white woman, and shall be thereof lawfully convicted, he shall be considered guilty of a felony, and shall be punished as heretofore." Shepherd, *Statutes at Large*, III, ch. 5. sec. 11, p. 119 (Act of 1805). Not until 1823, however, did the death sentence replace castration for the crime of attempted rape of a white female by a slave. In Virginia, *Acts* (1823), ch. 34, sec. 3, p. 37 (Act of February 14, 1823); and, Joseph Tate, comp., *Digest of the Laws of Virginia* (Richmond: Smith & Palmer, 1841), 127–28 (Act of 1823). See also Schwarz, *Twice Condemned*, 206; and, Bardaglio, "Rape and the Law in the Old South," 753n13. Winthrop Jordan incorrectly stated that castration of slaves convicted of attempted rape ended with the 1805 legislation. See Jordan, *White over Black*, 473.

The era of the American Revolution and the subsequent founding of the new nation precipitated the amelioration of some of the more severe features of colonial law, for both blacks and whites. Legal reform as well as the overhaul of judicial systems became the focus of many Americans during this era, including Virginians. And, importantly, the numbers of crimes considered capital when committed by slaves diminished as did the rigorous enforcement of harsh slave codes in the nineteenth–century South. Due to these developments, castration declined as a form of officially sanctioned punishment for slaves in southern states along the Atlantic seaboard, although it did not entirely disappear. See Schwarz, *Twice Condemned*, 22–23; and Genovese, *Roll, Jordan, Roll*, 67. For a discussion on the impact of the American Revolution on criminal law in Virginia, see Kathryn Preyer, "Crime, the Criminal Law and Reform in Post–Revolutionary Virginia," *Law and History Review*, I, 1983, 53–85. For a more general assessment of the impact of the American Revolution on the new nation's black population see Higginbotham, *In the Matter of Color*, 371–89; Jordan, *White over Black*, 269–311; and Ira Berlin, "The Revolution in Black Life," in Alfred F. Young, ed., *The American Revolution: Explorations in the History of American Radicalism*, (DeKalb: Northern Illinois University Press, 1976), 349–82.

30. Schwarz, *Twice Condemned*, 152.

31. Trial of Peter, January 5, 1782, Northampton County Court Minute Book (hereafter CCMB) (1777–83), 334–35 (microfilm reel #50) (hereafter reel), LVA.

32. Trial of Bob, June 13, 1783, Southampton County Court Order Book (hereafter CCOB) (1778–84), 336, (reel #27) LVA.

33. Genovese, *Roll, Jordan, Roll*, 67.

34. *Mathews v. Sims*, 2 Mill 103 (May 1818).

35. Charles William Janson, *The Stranger in America, 1793–1806* (1807; rprt. New York: The Press of the Pioneers, 1935), 386–87.

36. Trial of Henry Delong, April 9, 1784, Mecklenburg CCOB, (1779–84), 530 (reel #35), LVA. Philip Schwarz also located the case of a York County, Virginia, slavemaster who was examined for having castrated a slave. Cited in Trials, November 18, 1773, York CCOB (1774–84), 411 (reel #33), LVA in Schwarz, *Twice Condemned*, 162–63.

37. *Werley v. State*, 30 Tenn. (11 Humphreys) 171 (1850), 172–75 [Werley and Worley are used interchangeably throughout the published decision]; Tennessee, *Acts . . .*, Chap. 23, sec. 55 (Act of 1829) reads "no person shall unlawfully and maliciously, by cutting or otherwise, cut off or disable the organs of generation of another, or any part thereof." Tennessee was not alone in outlawing castration and bodily mutilation. See also William A. Hotchkiss, *A Codification of the Statute Law of Georgia* (Augusta: Charles E. Grenville, 1848), tit. I, ch. 28, art. 3, sec. 6, 708–709; Bartholomew Moore, Asa Briggs, et al., comps., *Revised Code of North Carolina* (Boston: Little, Brown & Co., 1855), Chap. 34, sec. 4, 203; William S. Oldham and George W. White, comps., *Digest of the General Statute Laws of the State of Texas* (Austin: John Marshall & Co., 1859), ch. 4, art. 505–506, 521. Bertram Wyatt–Brown reports yet another case of local officials admonishing a slaveowner for castrating a slave. A poor North Carolina farmer who owned one slave was jailed and fined $20 in 1831 for castrating that seventeen–year–old slave. Wyatt–Brown, *Southern Honor*, 376.

38. Trial of Jemmy, July 13, 1738, Goochland CCOB (1735–41), 327 (reel #21), LVA.

39. Trial of Andrew, May 28, 1736, Caroline CCOB (1732–40), 349 (reel #13), LVA.

40. Trial of Natt, September 6, 1775, Lancaster CCOB (1778–83), 7–8 (reel #30), LVA. This case is also related in Schwarz, *Twice Condemned*, 158–59. For other colonial cases of Virginia slaves sentenced to die for rape or attempted rape of white women or girls, see the trial of Harry, Lancaster CCOB (1713–21), 334–36 and February 25, 1723 (1721–29), 136–37, 141–42 (reel #27); and trial of Jack, June 12, 1772, Mecklenberg CCOB (1771–73), 257 (reel #34), LVA.

41. Trial of Daniel, property of Henry Hatcher, in 1701, quoted in Schwarz, *Twice Condemned*, 72. Similar fates fell on two condemned slave rapists from North Carolina: George, of Duplin County in 1770, and Ben, in 1775, both recounted in Spindel, *Crime and Society in North Carolina*, 109, 134–35. See also the case of a runaway Virginia slave who, along with an another runaway, was found guilty of breaking into and entering the home of a married white woman, where he purportedly beat the woman and, in the mind of the court, probably intended to

kill or ravish her. Trial of Olan, June 12, 1744, and Trial of Tom, August 6, 1744, Westmoreland CCOB (1737–43), 34a, 37a, LVA, and in Schwarz, *Twice Condemned*, 133.

42. Trial of Titus, August 25, 1777, Onslow County, Miscellaneous Records, North Carolina Department of Archives and History, Raleigh (hereafter NCDAH), as cited in Watson, "North Carolina Slave Courts," 33n38. It should be pointed out that convicted rapists were not the only slave criminals to suffer such horrific postmortem treatment. A North Carolina slave found guilty of murder in 1785 was decapitated and his impaled head placed on a pole for public display. Also in Watson, "North Carolina Slave Courts," 33.

43. Trial of Caesar, November 18, 1724 Spotsylvania CCOB (1724– 30), 37 (reel #43), LVA.

44. *Virginia Gazette*, August 26, 1737, as quoted by Marion Dargan, "Crime and the Virginia Gazette, 1736–1775," *University of New Mexico Bulletin*, Sociological Series 2, May 1934, 43–44.

45. Trial of Daniel, September 23, 1753, and November 28, 1753, Chesterfield CCOB (1767–71), 1–2, 14–15 (reel #39); and *The Journal of the House of Burgess* (1752–55), 115 and (1756–58), 270, as quoted in Schwarz, *Twice Condemned*, 163n55.

46. Re Negro Abraham, *Md. Arch.*, XXXII, 368–79 (June 1770).

47. Trial of Tom, September 14, 1775, Lancaster CCOB (1778–83) (reel #30), LVA. The reluctance of courts to execute condemned slaves is noted in the diary of Virginia planter Landon Carter. Carter complained that a grand jury that met on May 6, 1772, failed to hold over an errant slave (his alleged crime is not stated) although "every presumption [of guilt] was as strong as could be." Carter further groused about a "New law," the impact of which was that "a Negro now cannot be hanged, for there must be four Judges to condemn him; And such a court I am persuaded will never be got." Carter's allusion was to a law passed in 1772 that required a majority of justices vote for the sentence of death in capital cases of slaves. (Hening, *The Statutes at Large*, VIII, 522) Carter speculated the motivation for such a reform was rooted in fiscal concerns. "I understand the Public frugality occasioned this law that they might not have too many slaves to be paid for." In Jack P. Greene, ed., *The Diary of Col. Landon Carter of Sabine Hall, 1752–1778* (2 vols.; Charlottesville: University of Virginia Press, 1965), II, 676.

48. Scott, *Criminal Law in Colonial Virginia*, 161n208.

49. Other cases of black men charged with rape or attempted rape in the colonial South include "Robin," who was being sought by Virginia officials in 1677 for the ravishment of a white woman. Robin was captured, convicted, and sentenced to death; however, his master intervened on his behalf. Robin's life was spared. In H.R. McIlwaine, ed., *Minutes of the Council and General Court of Colonial Virginia*, 2d ed. (Richmond: Virginia State Library, 1979), 520. Jack Kecatan, a black servant in Charles City County, Virginia, had a reputation in the neighborhood for seducing or raping English servants, including one or more of his own master's female servants. Kecatan appears never to have been brought to trial for his alleged infractions (Schwarz, *Twice Condemned*, 71). Harry, a North Carolina slave, was convicted of raping a sixteen–year–old white girl and sentenced to hang (Spindel, *Crime and Society in North Carolina*, 76, 109) and Wills, a Dobbs County, North Carolina, slave and conjurer, knowledgeable in herbs and concoctions, was charged with using his potions to seduce and impregnate a white woman in 1769. This may have been an attempt by the accuser to cover up

a consensual relationship with the slave (Crow, *The Black Experience in Revolutionary North Carolina*, 38–39).

50. Eugene Genovese's brilliant analysis of the hegemonic function of the law is valuable in understanding this contradiction. Genovese argued that slaveholders, in fashioning strict slave codes, never intended rigorous enforcement. Instead, severe legislation was meant to serve as a device to be used at their discretion during times of crisis and emergency, such as a slave insurrection. Genovese, *Roll, Jordan, Roll*, 40–41.

51. Petition of fifty-seven citizens of Hanover County, n.d., and petition of twenty-seven citizens of Hanover County, box 157 (October–December 1808), VEP, LVA.

52. Higginbotham, *In the Matter of Color*, 168.

53. On this historiographical debate, consult Sommerville, "The Rape Myth in the Old South Reconsidered," 483n7.

54. Schwarz, *Twice Condemned*, 39.

55. See Victoria E. Bynum, *Unruly Women: The Politics of Social and Sexual Control in the Old South* (Chapel Hill: University of North Carolina Press, 1992), 7, 10, 109, and especially Chap. 4, "Punishing Deviant Women: The State as Patriarch"; Martha Hodes, "Sex Across the Color Line: White Women and Black Men in the Nineteenth–Century American South," Ph.D. dissertation, Princeton University, 1991, 2, 41, 60–61; and Catherine Clinton, *The Plantation Mistress: Woman's World in the Old South* (New York: Pantheon Books, 1982), 204. It is worth noting that poor white males also were regarded as naturally promiscuous. On the rape trials of poor Irishmen in antebellum Virginia, refer to Sommerville, "The Rape Myth Reconsidered," 255–58.

56. Martha Hodes, "The Sexualization of Reconstruction Politics: White Women and Black Men in the South after the Civil War," *Journal of the History of Sexuality*, 3, 3, 1993, 404.

KITH AND KIN

Women's Networks in Colonial Virginia

When Dorothy Henry of St. Anne's Parish in Essex County, Virginia, died in 1709, she appointed "My very good friends Mr. John Boughan and his wife Susanna and Thomas Lee" as her executors. Sixty years later, Mary Jones signed a series of letters addressed to Frances Bland Randolph "Your Unalterable Friend and Affectionate Cousin." The gulf between these two uses of the word "friend" is more than the simple passage of time. Dorothy Henry's trusted friends were two men and a woman, a reflection of the integrated world of men and women in which she had lived. She understood friendship as built on kinship and day-to-day contact. Friends were people Henry could trust with her economic affairs. In contrast, Mary Jones and Fanny Randolph built their friendship on kinship and emotional support, what another Virginia woman referred to in 1772 as being a "Sister of my Heart."[1] The redefinition of women's friendships in eighteenth-century Virginia is part of a larger reorientation of men's and women's lives that led women to retreat to a private world where women's special friendships flourished.[2] The transformation from a gender-integrated world to a gender-segregated one gradually emerged as a product of kinship ties, women's literacy, and exclusion from the new, sophisticated commercial economy. That transformation had different implications for black and white women. Black women created their own networks without the support system available to whites. Ironically, however, black women served as a means for maintaining ties between white women.

Fanny Randolph's friendship with Mary Jones is readily recognizable to historians of women as similar to those described by Nancy Cott, Carroll Smith-Rosenberg, Anne Firor Scott, and other historians of post-Revolutionary America.[3] These friendships developed most strongly between women of the same age and race and provided support even after marriage. Women used intimate, personal letters to maintain this closeness when separated. Dorothy Henry's patterns of friendship are less well understood, for there has been little exploration of the patterns of women's social connections before the era of the American Revolution. The main source of evidence for later friendships—letters and journals of women—are notably scarce for the colonial period. There are no such collections of letters for Virginia women before the middle of the eighteenth century. Historians, while admitting that colonial white women lived in a web of neighborliness, have argued that they led isolated lives, tied closely to the house and devoid of networks of support.[4] Such historical judgments, however, have measured the colonial period against definitions of friendship and support created in the nineteenth century. When historians look specifically at the patterns of social contact of early eighteenth century women, a different world view emerges.

This essay explores the crucial period (1700–1775) during which women's social contacts moved from an integrated circle of family, neighbors, servants, slaves, and mistresses to a dual system. Many women developed more extended networks shaped by class lines, while continuing to participate in a set of local contacts that transcended class and race. Because the traditional sources for friendship studies—letters and diaries—are a product of the transformation under study, such materials are available only for the latter part of the period. Thus, this study has sought glimpses of women's lives between the lines of deeds and wills and the diaries of daily activities kept by men, and the result is a partial reconstruction of patterns of women's lives as they began to invest female friendships with new meaning. This transformation is generational, and involves both social and economic factors. Most surprisingly, the evidence suggests that the factors historians often consider isolating—illiteracy, childbirth, and housework—could generate social contacts, and continued to do so for women who were not part of the elite.

Dorothy Henry lived in a world that did not separate spaces or roles into public and private spheres. Colonial homes often had only one to four undifferentiated rooms. The typical Virginia plantation in 1709 consisted of one to two rooms on the main floor and lofts above. Work, play, sleeping, eating, and entertaining all took place in the same physical space. Men and women pursuing their separate tasks did so in a shared space. The physical arrangements of colonial homes thus mitigated against gender or functional segregation. A French visitor who attended a Virginia wedding in the 1680s, for example, found himself bedded for the night in a room reserved for women and children who were guests. The mixed sleeping arrangements, however, scandalized no one. Much of Chesapeake life went on in a gender-integrated space.[5]

These social networks crossed racial lines in a number of ways. As several of the essays in this volume document, interracial sex was a part of colonial life, involving elites and non-elite whites with Indians and Africans. The very ability of some enslaved people to sue for their freedom based on their descent from a free woman is a measure of the integrated nature of a neighborhood. Those bringing such suits could often find whites in the area who could testify about their family background because neighborhood social networks in the years before 1776 gave whites opportunity to know personal information about mixed race individuals.[6]

The 600-acre Henry plantation was home to at least fourteen people (excluding overseers), including eight women, one white (Dorothy) and seven black. Among the slaves were Nan and her daughter Beck. Dorothy's and Nan's world was integrated by both gender and race. Slaves lived in two communities whose permeable boundaries allowed passage from one to the other every day. Even if Nan and her husband Tom lived in their own cabin, she crossed into Dorothy Henry's world on a daily basis. The enslaved women not only hoed tobacco and corn with each other and the men, but they would have worked with Dorothy Henry to milk the more than eight cows and prepare cheese or butter. At night or in the winter, the women worked together on making the sheets and bed furnishings Dorothy Henry carefully passed on to her grandchildren.[7] The particular restraints of slave life meant that black women were marginal members of these integrated networks. Dorothy Henry, after all, set the parameters for the work they did together, and she reaped more of its benefits. The women may have worked together stuffing a featherbed, yet when they were done, Dorothy slept on the bed, not Nan. Separate networks centered on black women kin and neighbors would develop as the slave population became larger and increasingly native born. Interestingly, the development of these networks for black women occurred simultaneously with the development of a new privatized set of friendships for white women, but for different reasons.[8]

Women's first lines of social contact were drawn in the neighborhood. Local visiting could prevent isolation and be rewarding; seventeenth-century Virginians relied mostly on local contacts. As a Huguenot visitor to Virginia in the 1680s noted, "When a man has fifty acres of ground, two man-servants, a maid and some cattle, neither he nor his wife do anything but visit among their neighbors." The visitor noted with surprise that "women ride their horses at such a gallop when traveling that I marvelled they could keep so well seated." Whether at a gallop or a walk, Dorothy Henry rode a horse to visit neighbors and willed the animal to her grandaughter Susan. In the eighteenth century, elite families shifted their focus to a colony-wide network of others with similar social standing. This wider geographic network continued to be gender integrated, however, for several decades. For more ordinary people (both black and white), the neighborhood remained the center of social networks, although there is evidence to suggest that during the eighteenth century their kin networks also spread beyond parish or county lines.[9]

Neighborhood visits crossed class lines. In the wedding attended by the Huguenot visitor, many, but not all, of the guests were "of social standing." Kin could be of a different social station. Chesterfield County Justice of the Peace Abraham Salle owned fifty-seven slaves in 1783, for example, while his cousin Joseph Salle was a yeoman farmer who worked his land with one slave. Neighborhood visiting included attendance at church by people of all ranks and trips to nearby farms to exchange goods and services. Local women with skills in sewing, weaving, or other special household crafts might spend several days at a neighboring plantation plying those skills. Work brought women of different classes (and races) together.[10]

Neighborhood visiting among the galloping horsewomen of Virginia was in part ritualistic. Certain occasions, such as childbirth, death, and the arrival of a distant visitor to a neighbor's house required visits by local women. These were supplemented by more formal occasions such as parties, weddings, funerals, and baptisms. Although many of these events had religious functions, Virginians celebrated them in the home where women played important roles in planning and directing them.[11] All these events, except for childbirth, were gender integrated and provided opportunities for women to meet both with other women and with men. Slaves attended the events as servants to whites. Weddings and funerals were public events to which families invited strangers. In 1754, for example, Mrs. Salkeldat invited the sister of an officer in the British army to her husband's funeral even though the women had never met before. Mrs. Salkeldat treated her husband's funeral as a ritualistic social occasion appropriate for first social contact among strangers. African Americans had their own funeral rituals, but from the number of comments by whites on slave funerals, it is clear that these, too, were integrated occasions.[12]

Childbirth was the only ritual purely a woman's event. It, too, cut across racial lines. White women sometimes served as midwives for blacks, and black women attended the deliveries of whites. Both Frances Bland Randolph and her sister were expecting children in 1771 when her mother wrote to Frances

> Your sister Banister has been very ill but I thank god she is now well again but very bigg and heavy. She says you may have Cate as soon as she is delivered, pray Let me know when you'l want her if you are detirmin'd not to come down, which wou'd give us great satisfaction. if it will be as convenient to you both if not & it pleases God to permit me I'll come up as soon as your sister can be left with safty.

In this case, Cate, a family slave and possibly a midwife, shared in the births of her mistress's family at the expressed request of the white women. The letter also makes clear that the impending births would result in female travel no matter what Frances Bland Randolph decided. Many women chose to travel during their pregnancies. For example, Anne Rose was five months pregnant when in June 1749 she went with her clergyman husband, Robert, to visit distant members of his frontier parish. Four months later, Anne Rose rode all day in a lurching carriage to reach her parent's home in Stafford County in order to have her mother near as Anne gave birth. The Rose diary provides evidence that other women made similar trips. The Roses had moved to the frontier when Anne had her last child in 1749. With her mother dead and family distant, Anne relied on friends in her new location for help. Elizabeth Gaines and

Martha Harvey not only hosted Robert on his travels, but they visited Anne at least four times during her pregnancy and came to help the day after the baby was born.[13]

Although having children to care for might discourage female slaves from running away, pregnancy did not. For example, Moll, "very big with Child," and her husband Roger escaped from John Shelton's plantation in Hanover County at the end of September 1739. One-quarter of the sampled advertisements in the *Virginia Gazette* for escaped female slaves noted their pregnancy. Moll and Roger may have run away in order to claim freedom for their child or prevent it from being sold. Perhaps they, too, sought the comfort of kin. (Moll was Virginia born.)[14]

The earlier patterns of local visits and ritualistic occasions continued throughout the century, even as some women began to develop more intense friendships. The diary of Madame Browne, sister of a British officer in Virginia during the 1750s, records that visits began before she had even moved in to rented lodgings. Three weeks later she set out with her brother and James Wood to meet his daughter. They arrived at 6:00 A.M. "but to great Disappointment she was out; but her Mother receiv'd us with a friendly wellcome." Schoolmaster John Harrower's journal from 1776 records a number of these more spontaneous occasions when he and housekeeper Lucy Gaines paid unannounced calls on local small planter families. These calls were part of rituals of visiting used by yeoman and elite families to establish and maintain local networks. Spontaneous visits were a major factor in maintaining networks among slave women, since many of their opportunities to visit neighboring plantations (and thus friends and kin there) came while on errands for their white masters or mistresses. Thus they had less control over the timing of visits than free women, and made visiting less of an elaborate ritual.[15]

Colonial women built their closest friendships within the intersecting sets of neighborhood and kinship. For many women, the two might be nearly identical. Dorothy Henry's and Mary Jones' uses of the term "friend" are equally revealing on this point. Henry used the term in her will to refer to her granddaughter, grandson, and the granddaughter's husband. Mary Jones coupled "Friend" with "Cousin." Virginians used "friend" to refer collectively to an assortment of relations and neighbors. When Magdalene Chastain died in 1732, her will specified choices for the residence of her three teenaged children. All could live with their older brother Jacob Trabue, or daughter Magdalene could live with her godmother Elizabeth Dutoy, daughter Judith with her Aunt Mary Flournoy, and son John James with his godmother Susanna Farcy. All lived in the immediate neighborhood. In addition, so did seven of Magdalene's stepbrothers and sisters, her stepfather's brother, another brother and his wife's family, and numerous other kin. The neighborhood was her family.[16] Family density increased over time. More than half of those who married found their partner within five miles of home. By 1773, 70 percent of Prince George County, Maryland, families shared a surname with another family in the county. Such measures cannot disclose how many more families shared ties through female lines. Ironically, frontier migration simultaneously removed women from their neighborhoods. The reorientation of elite families to a colony-wide social network had the same effect. Women of all classes left their home area after marriage. Kin networks stretched far beyond the neighborhood, and families traveled to maintain family ties. Such visits were not limited to members of the elite. Dorothy Pankey, a Cumberland County widow who supported herself by weaving, died in 1772 while on a visit to her sons in Lunenburg County, for example.[17]

Slave women also found themselves living in dense networks of kin that coincided with their neighborhood by the middle of the eighteenth century. Throughout the eighteenth century, natural increase complemented importation as Virginia moved steadily toward a population half black by 1775. As the population climbed, so did the opportunities to build viable communities. As the number of Virginia-born slaves rose, so did the number of slaves with family networks in Virginia. Unlike most enslaved women at the beginning of the century, Nan did not have to leave the plantation to be with her husband, but after Dorothy Henry died, the small community of African Americans on her plantation was scattered among five grandchildren on four nearby plantations. Visits on Sundays and while taking care of errands helped the separated keep in touch. Ironically, the very process that threatened slave families helped to establish larger networks and communication lines, but left their ability to maintain these ties dependent on the very masters and mistresses who had caused the separation. Many of the enslaved women who ran away went to join kin. Three of the five women whose escapes from slavery prompted their owners to place advertisements in the *Virginia Gazette* were presumed to be living openly in the state as free women, or traveling with forged passes. The implications of the advertisements are clear: African American women had networks that could hide and sustain them off plantation; there were enough black women traveling that the escapees were not conspicuous, and they had literate (presumably white) connections willing to forge a pass.[18]

When long-distance geographic separation occurred, however, slaves had fewer opportunities to maintain connection with family and friends. Their ability to visit depended on the travel plans of their owners or special leave. The experience of one Albemarle County mulatto woman may help illustrate both the possibilities for networks and the constraints placed on black women. When John Thompson died in 1765, the woman claimed to be a free person, The evidence suggests that she was born near Petersburg and taken to frontier Albemarle County to work on a new quarter of land claimed by Thompson. Although the woman had friends in Petersburg who might help her case, she needed a pass from a justice of the peace to travel safely to seek them out.[19] What is especially significant about the ties this incident uncovers is that the whites also recognized that these kin and neighbor networks existed and thus were willing to give permission for the travel.

The experience of William Byrd's wife Maria Taylor Byrd and his daughters, Mina, Molly, and Anne shows how neighborly visiting, when reinforced by class, could begin to form closer friendships. Maria Taylor Byrd seldom traveled, except in the immediate neighborhood. Tradition relates that her family would meet the Robert Carter family under a tree where their properties adjoined. There the women would picnic and quilt together. While the only evidence for this tradition is an heirloom coverlet, William Byrd's diary records that the most frequent place that his wife or daughters visited was Shirley, the Carter plantation. In turn, Elizabeth Carter was the fourth most frequent visitor at Westover. If Maria Byrd seldom traveled, others came to her. At least forty-three women made a minimum of ninety-nine visits to Westover in a two-year period, including a cousin of Maria's who had been abandoned by her husband. The most frequent visitor was Frances Pinkard, who lived directly across the James River from the Byrds.[20] Maria Taylor Byrd thus had a small inner circle of frequent visitors and close friends and a larger network of occasional and ritualistic callers.

Weather and seasonality of work could hinder visiting. Most traveling by women, either to court, or on visits, was done between February and August. (See Charts A and B.) In general women stayed home in December and January during the worst rainy and cold weather. But they traveled during the spring when rain could turn roads to quagmires and soak clothes packed carefully in a travel trunk. While bad roads and mud could render travel more difficult, women persisted. In 1775, Elizabeth Feilde expected a female friend to visit even though roads were too bad for Feilde's husband (a minister) to get to church. What did deter women was heavy seasons of household work (such as harvest) and poor health. July, August, October, and January were traditional months of illness.[21]

Visiting was an essential part of the oral culture that shaped Dorothy Henry's life and that of her slave Nan. In the first third of the eighteenth century, only a third of white women and about two-thirds of white men could write. Hence, people had to deal face-to-face.[22] Letters obviously played a lesser role in maintaining networks between those who could not write. Dorothy's news and business depended on oral communication with friends and neighbors. Visiting was more than a social amenity—it was essential if she (or Nan) were to sell surplus butter, market the tobacco raised by Nan and the other slaves, or know someone who could draft her will.[23] Thus the low literacy rates for both men and women helped to encourage travel. Couples who needed help with legal documents, for example, traveled together to county courts where they could find someone to draw up their legal documents. Thirty percent of women's participation in legal documents came on such occasions. In the Essex sample at the beginning of the century, every document drawn up at court involved an illiterate woman.[24]

Wills and deeds recover fragments of the gender-integrated networks of women such as Dorothy Henry. The deathbeds of both men and women attracted friends of both sexes, if the witnesses to deathbed wills are any indication. Analysis of the deed and will books of Essex and Henrico Counties covering the year of Dorothy Henry's death shows that while white women participated as signatories 159 times in the two books, there was no pattern of women witnessing for women. Women served as witnesses on thirty-four occasions, but 80 percent of the time they witnessed men's documents and only 20 percent of the time did they witness documents for other women. Women, however, were direct parties in more than 20 percent of the transactions. The records for 1728–1731 reveal no change in this pattern.[25]

Women participated in these legal arrangements because they were part of the world in which the documents were made. Men and women gathered to support a dying neighbor—this was a standard social call of the day. Thus, the most common kind of witnessing women did in this early period was of wills. On the other hand, Virginians negotiated land sales over a mug of small beer in their homes, then if one of them felt confident of the legal forms, that person drew up the deed and called on those present in the house to witness it. The document was not part of a larger ritual requiring the presence of women. If women happened to be present, as Judith Bingley was when John Ford and the Lansdons sat down with her husband to draw up deeds, they might then be witnesses, but the pattern of signatures does suggest a preference for male witnesses. Women signed only when there were less than three (the number needed for witnesses) men present. Enslaved women, of course, had no legal standing in such transactions (unless they were the property being transferred), even though one might have poured the small beer Joseph Bingley and William Lansdon sat drinking. Enslaved women could not testify in civil matters at court, although indentured women could.[26]

Along with knowledge of business transactions and court procedure, attendance at county court days provided women with social opportunities. Consider the families who gathered for business at Goochland County Court in May 1729. William and Esther Lansdon, Anthony and Elizabeth Benin, and Joseph Bingley came to court to prove a series of interrelated land transactions negotiated and signed at home. All had modest farms in the King William Parish area. The Lansdons and Bingley took those deeds with them to court on May 20. There they met with Esther's sister and brother-in-law, Elizabeth and Anthony Benin, to arrange a swap of lands the sisters had inherited. At court they found other neighbors, widow Susanne Kerner and James and Sarah Holman, who also were there selling land. The women had time to visit, catch up on local news, and discuss the health of Elizabeth Benin, who was in the last trimester of pregnancy. This tangle of land transactions brought neighboring women together both before and during court days. Of this group only the Holmans might be considered members of the elite.[27]

By mid-century this integrated world was receding, especially for more elite, literate women. Analysis of the wills of fifty-two women who lived near King William Parish shows women had a gender-integrated view of family and community before 1750. After 1750, women increasingly favored other women in bequests and sought witnesses among female relatives and neighbors. Women born before 1690 showed some preference for other women in their wills only one-quarter of the time. This rose to 40 percent for the women born between 1700 and 1730. About two-thirds of women in the next three decades favored other women. For the generation born after 1730, female preference became the norm.[28]

The new emphasis on female friendships came as women withdrew from public activity after 1750. The county court was an integral part of the commercial system of Virginia. Here land transactions became final, estates were settled, and debts collected. Court days traditionally provided a time and place for people to meet and conduct business. The Virginia economy and court procedure became more complex in the eighteenth century as a commercial credit economy involving hiring of money, and local book-debt moved beyond a simple barter and exchange system.[29] From a distance of two centuries it is impossible to determine the extent to which the withdrawal was by choice or coerced. The courts and taverns increasingly served as arenas for the acting out of a competitive male culture that might seem a hostile environment to women who held different values.[30] But such evidence does not explain why male and female social rituals or values diverged. In addition, separation between men and women was incomplete. Older patterns of community work and visiting continued, alongside the new.

Legal records documenting the clearance of women's dower claims to land show a decline in women's physical presence in court. Clearing dower rights was the single most common reason for white women of all classes to appear in court—that is what had brought Elizabeth Benin and Esther Lansdon to Goochland Court in 1729, for example. The most common (and statutory) method was to have husband and wife jointly sign a deed, then the wife attend court where the judges privately interviewed her to ensure that her consent was voluntary and informed. A majority of couples chose this method at all times before 1778. However, the practice was in decline, and used mostly by the small farmer, illiterate group that still relied on oral networking.

Logically, one would expect distances in sprawling frontier counties to deter women from coming to court, but rates dropped after 1750 when all the sampled counties were more compact and the courthouse more convenient. In Essex and Henrico Counties during the first decade of the century, 70 percent of dower releases were done in person at the court. In mid-century, in Goochland County (carved from Henrico), over 90 percent of the releases were done in person. However, by 1775–1777, the rate of personal releases returned to 70 percent, despite further shrinkage in the size of the county and more settled conditions. In Lancaster, the decline was even more precipitous. There only 35 percent of the women appeared in court to relinquish dower rights.[31]

Early in the century, some of the minority of women avoided coming to court by using powers of attorney or affadvits declaring their willingness to relinquish dower. By mid-century, legal changes prevented use of powers-of-attorney in land transactions. As women stayed away, the courts began appointing several justices to visit a woman and examine her at her home. Sixty-five percent of dower releases were home interviews in Lancaster County during 1775–1777. In Goochland 11 percent of women relinquished their claims to family property in this way. Another 19 percent simply signed the deed at home. The court and home spaces became gendered in ways unknown to white women twenty years before.[32]

A variety of historical studies have documented that women less often received appointment as sole administrator or executor of their husbands' wills after 1750, thus reducing another common appearance in court. They also received less economic independence in the bequests left to them by their husbands, and this changed economic status meant that fewer women had reason to appear in court because they had less property to protect or sell. Furthermore, the changes in bequests and naming of executors suggest that fewer husbands after 1750 saw their wives as competent actors in management of the family assets. This was especially true for wealthier families who practiced more sophisticated forms of commercial transactions. Women participated infrequently in these new forms of commerce.[33]

Court appearances carried a very different meaning for enslaved black women. Unable to legally inherit or transfer property (although they may have had small quantities of personal goods), black women appeared in court as a form of property (as children imported from Africa needing their ages determined, as runaways being held until claimed by an owner, or as property offered for sale during court days) or as a criminal defendent. Except for those black women who sold things at the markets held in conjunction with court days, enslaved women did not voluntarily attend county courts. Ironically, white women's withdrawal from the courts thus minimized the differences between women with property and women who were property.

Just as illiteracy had encouraged women to attend court where they participated in an integrated world of social and business relationships and had an opportunity to visit with friends, growing rates of literacy provided women with a way of avoiding court and still maintaining female friendships. Women's literacy rates in Goochland County had reached 50 percent in 1750. Twenty-five years later, three-quarters of the women who appear in court records in Goochland and Lancaster Counties could sign their names. Thus they could turn to letter writing to sustain friendships between visits. (See Chart C).

The process of becoming literate could also help to form friendships. Many Virginia women received part of their educations in someone else's home. John Harrower, an indentured schoolteacher, took addtional boarding students for his own profit. He accepted both boys and girls who then boarded with the Dangerfields. Maria Carter had been sent to her grandmother's for schooling. Maria lived in a small world of women (black and white), with only the intrusion of tutor Thomas Price.

> I am awaked out of a sound Sleep with some croaking voice either Patty's, Milly's or some other of our Domestics with Miss Polly Miss Polly get up, tis time to rise, Mr Price is down Stairs, & tho' I hear them I lie quite snugg until my Grandmama raises her Voice, then up I get, huddle on my Cloaths & down to Book, the to Breakfast, then to School again, & maybe I have an Hour to my self before [Dinner] then the same Story over again till twi-Light, & then a small [free] time before I go to rest.

Anne Blair took charge of her sister's child Betsy so that the girl might take lessons in Williamsburg. The advantage of the Blair household was access to social occasions, which were another part of the education of a girl from an elite family.[34] A girl's education was in part an initiation into a network of women, even if seldom in a formal school.

Eighteenth-century letter writing was an art. Form books suggested proper ways to handle all social situations while setting standards for language, behavior, and humor. The description of Maria Carter's day was actually her response to the challenge to write a "comical" letter. It was part of her education. Virginia women, however, used a more personal style in letters to peers than any of the models in form books. Anne Blair's letters to her sisters are filled with lively images, funny scenes (such as two girls firing bursts of flatulence at each other in a "duel" over a British navy officer's attention), and direct addresses to the reader. Letters to non-kin friends remained closer to the forms, but expressed more affection than the forms called for. Elizabeth Feilde, for example, addressed Maria Armistead as "Dear Madam." But in the body of the letter she interjected the less formal "Oh! My Dear Friend."[35]

Women relied on these networks to pass along news and help in their household duties. The surviving letters from Virginia's elite women are filled with mentions of small favors, such as finding material for a cap or women to hire, acquiring sheet music, and swapping garden roots and seeds. In other words, they were used to extend the old neighborhood patterns based on women's work. Some needs of elite women, however, could not be met by neighbors from a different class. Mary Blair Braxton would find few of her near neighbors with spinets or music, but her sister Anne in Williamsburg would know what to look for in the local shops.[36]

The letters themselves suggest that non-elite women were part of these networks. Frances Bland thought her daughter Frances Randolph would be interested in the death of Betty Carlos's maid. Elizabeth Feilde discussed the skill of a woman who was dyeing thread for Maria Armistead as though both knew the woman. Women sometimes witnessed the deeds of women from families of much greater status in the county. They were available because they were present either visiting or working.[37] Enslaved women might carry letters or gifts between distant friends. As they furthered the long-distance (literate) friendships of their mistresses, the (illiterate) enslaved women could maintain their own face-to-face visiting networks. Either way, the evidence suggests that women's networks crossed race and class lines, but special friendship required the safety and security that came with equals, especially relatives.

The role of religion in the changing patterns of friendship is unclear. The generation of women who came of age in 1750 to 1770 was both the most affected by the Great Awakening and by women's withdrawl to a more private sphere. Neither the withdrawal nor the new emphasis on women's friendship correlate to an attachment to the Awakening. While religion may not have had a causal role in forming this new women's culture, the networks of women did affect the spread of the Awakening, and church was a place that women gathered. Before the Revolution, Virginia churches did not develop women's organizations or parish community life, but an informal social life did develop as families visited after church and invited neighbors home for meals.[38]

For African-American women, religion offered a precious opportunity for visiting. It also continued their participation in community networks that crossed lines of race and class. Proportionately more black women joined churches than men. After 1760, a number of Methodist and Baptist congregations in the southside and piedmont areas of Virginia had a majority of members who were black. Methodist mid-week classes and Baptist prayer meetings offered additional chances for women to meet together. Methodist classes were often single sex. Integration, however, does not imply full equality. Even in the most open congregations, various practices reminded black women both of their inclusion and their marginality by adapting church discipline to fit circumstances of slave lives, by segregating seating, or by limiting their participation in church decisions. Thus women were welcomed into a new kind of "sisterhood" but one with limits.[39]

By mid-century there were other signs in Virginia of a growing private world for the elite. The very wealthy built new houses with more rooms. Parlors and bedrooms became the public and private places for receiving friends. Receiving friends, however, was a different process than neighbors dropping in with some extra butter to sell. Women cemented friendship over cups of tea served on special tables and with special dishes designed for this occasion. Even more modest households began to acquire these small luxuries associated with the rituals of friendship. Widowed Elizabeth Porter of Cumberland County could serve tea or coffee to neighboring women in her china cups in 1767, but since she could not write, she still depended on the traditional face-to-face contacts of friends. Her friends were drawn from kin and the neighbors with whom she had grown up and worshipped. Her world was still an integrated one, but women had clearly become more important than they had been to Dorothy Henry. The neighbors who gathered to help her write and witness her will in 1772 were neighbors Sukey and Haskins Lendrum and Sukey's father. Sukey and Elizabeth probably attended a Methodist women's class together. Women with time to pursue friendships bought that time with the labor of other women, especially slaves who had assumed tasks in the household, gardens, dairies, and fields that might otherwise have fallen to those now receiving friends. In Elizabeth's case that work was done by three women and a boy. Not yet influenced by the growing literature on women's private role, she nonetheless had withdrawn from the courts. Elizabeth had been absent from county court records for fifteen years since she had appeared to present her husband's estate inventory.[40]

The integrated world of Dorothy Henry, in which all aspects of life had public connotations, had by the American Revolution begun to separate into a private and public world. For women such as Elizabeth Porter, or the slaves who supported her, that separation was partial. Accompanying it was a growing connection to other women. For the literate elite, this could be friendship selected within a narrow class scattered through Virginia. For more middle-class women like Elizabeth Porter or for her slave Jude, connections remained tied to the neighborhood, but with increasing emphasis on gendered space and friendships. Men staked out new, exclusive claims to the public sphere; thus women began to cultivate a private garden of emotions and friends. The process was still tentative. Women's networks were still based upon neighborhood and kinship. The neighborhood ties still expressed a public kind of social contact where social unequals might meet, gossip, and negotiate about work. As families spread over larger geographic areas, women had to travel longer distances to maintain the ties to kin. Eventually growing literacy gave women a tool to maintain contact when visits were impossible. The inner circles of kin provided a safe place where a woman could drop formalities and release emotions. Thus, as women began to form more intense friendships, they developed first within the security of kinship and then radiated outward into the community. Largely illiterate, poor white women and black women found their friends and support among kin and neighbors, but increasingly only from those of similar status. Virginia women's networks became increasingly stratified by race, gender, and class as elites fashioned a romanticized world of female friendship.

Number of Visits

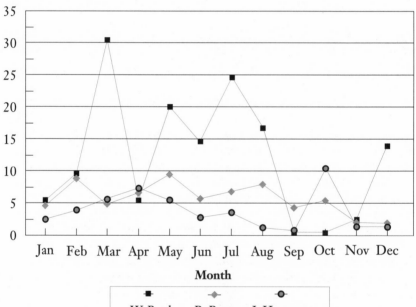

Chart A: **Visits Between Women**

Compiled from the diaries of William Byrd II, Robert Rose, and John Harrower.

Number of Visits

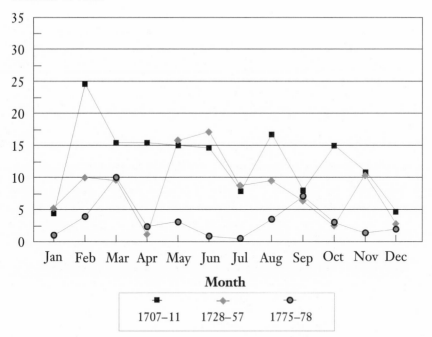

Month

■	◆	◉
1707–11	1728–57	1775–78

Chart B: **Court Appearances**

Compiled from the court records of Henrico, Essex, Goochland, and Lancaster Counties.

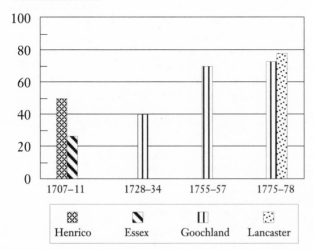

Percent Literate

▨	◣	‖	⬚
Henrico	Essex	Goochland	Lancaster

Chart C: **Women's Literacy**

Notes

1. Dorothy Henry will, December 19, 1709, recorded January 1, 1709–10, Essex County Deeds and Wills 1709–10, Virginia State Library (hereafter VSL); Mary Jones to Frances Bland Randolph, April 10, 1769, and May 10, 1769, and Kitty Eustace Blair to Anne Blair Bannister, July 18, 1772, Tucker-Coleman Papers, College of William and Mary (hereafter TCP).

2. This essay uses five methods to help determine the patterns of women's social contacts: sampling of county deed and will records at regular intervals, charting of all visiting recorded in three diaries, analysis of women's wills in a particular community, a sample of advertisements for runaways from the *Virginia Gazette*, and the reading of surviving letters between women. The sample of advertisements consists of all advertisements for women servants or slaves that appeared in the *Virginia Gazette* from 1737 to 1739, and from April 1768 to March 1769. The county record samples are drawn at generational intervals (1706–1711, 1728–1731, 1748–1755, 1775–1777) from the piedmont area originally in Henrico County and later in Goochland. The earliest and latest samples were matched with comparable records from the tidewater counties of Essex and Lancaster. There are no women's diaries for colonial Virginia (excluding those of a few travelers). Thus I chose to look at three men's diaries, to see what they revealed about women's visiting. The diaries were those of William Byrd II from 1739–1741, Robert Rose from 1748–1750, and of John Harrower from 1773–1776. The will analysis contains all wills written by women with a connection to King William Parish during the eighteenth century.

3. Nancy Cott, *The Bonds of Womanhood: Woman's Sphere in New England, 1780–1835* (New Haven: Yale University Press, 1977); Carroll Smith Rosenberg, "The Female World of Love and Ritual," *Signs*: 1:No. 1, 1975; Anne Firor Scott, "What, Then, Is the American: This New Woman?" *Journal of American History*, 65 December, 1978, 679–703.

4. Laurel Ulrich, *Good Wives: The Lives of Women in Northern New England, 1670–1750* (N.Y.: Knopf, 1982); Lorena S. Walsh, "The Experiences and Status of Women in the Chesapeake," in Walter J. Fraser, Jr., R. Frank Saunders, Jr., and Jon L. Wakelyn, eds., *The Web of Southern Social Relations: Women, Family and Education* (Athens, Ga: University of Georgia Press, 1984), 14; Allan Kulikoff, *Tobacco and Slaves: The Development of Southern Culture in the Chesapeake, 1680–1800* (Chapel Hill: University of North Carolina Press, 1986), 229–31. Daniel Blake Smith argued that Virginia women had close, emotional friendships, but his book is set after 1750, with most evidence coming from after 1770. Daniel Blake Smith, *Inside the Great House: Planter Family Life in Eighteenth-Century Chesapeake Society* (Ithaca, N.Y.: Cornell University Press, 1980), 74–76, 175–230.

5. Gilbert Chenard, ed., *A Huguenot Exile in Virginia or Voyages of a Frenchman Exiled for his Religion with a Description of Virginia and Maryland* (New York: The Press of the Pioneers, 1934 [reprint of 1687 ed.]), 137. For homes, see Darrett B. Rutman and Anita H. Rutman, *A Place in Time: Middlesex County, Virginia, 1650–1750* (New York: W.W. Norton & Co., 1984). For gender integration, see, for example, Michael Zuckerman, "William Byrd's Family," *Perspectives in American History*, 12, 1979, 288. Smith, *Inside the Great House*, 175–230.

6. Peter Wallenstein's chapter documents suits for freedom. Paul Finkleman and Diane Sommerville's chapters provide evidence of interracial sex, especially between slaves and lower-class white women.

7. Dorothy Henry will, December 19, 1709, recorded January 1, 1709/10, Essex County Deeds and Wills 1709/1710, VSL.

8. Allan Kulikoff, "The Beginnings of the Afro-American Family in Maryland," in Aubrey C. Land, Lois Green Carr, and Edward C. Papenfuse, eds., *Law, Society, and Politics in Early Maryland* (Baltimore: Johns Hopkins University Press, 1977); Allan Kulikoff, "The Origins of Afro-American Society in Tidewater Maryland and Virginia, 1700–1790," *William and Mary Quarterly*, 3rd series, 35 April 1978; Joan R. Gundersen, "The Double Bonds of Race and Sex: Black and White Women in a Colonial Virginia Parish," *Journal of Southern History*, 52, August 1986.

9. Chenard, *A Huguenot Exile*, 111, 123, 137; Walsh, "Women in the Chesapeake," 11; Darrett and Anita Rutman, *A Place in Time*, 234–47.

10. Kulikoff, *Tobacco and Slaves*, p. 287. Joseph and Abraham Salle were grandsons of Abraham and Olive Salle, Huguenot immigrants. For their slave holdings, see Powhatan and Chesterfield Counties, Department of Commerce and Labor, Bureau of the Census, *Heads of Families at the First Census of the United States Taken in the Year 1790. Records of the State Enumerators, 1782 to 1785*. Virginia, 1908. For an example of a work visit see "Diary of a Little Colonial Girl," *Virginia Magazine of History and Biography*, 11, 1903–04, 212–14.

11. Joan R. Gundersen, "The Non-Institutional Church: The Religious Roles of Women in Eighteenth-Century Virginia," *The Historical Magazine* of the Protestant Episcopal Church, December 1982; Smith, *Inside the Great House*, 194–97.

12. Sarah Browne Diary entry, May 29, 1755, Fairfax Harrison, ed."With Braddock's Army: Madame Browne's Diary in Virginia and Maryland," *Virginia Magazine of History and Biography*, 32, October 1924, 305–20; For African-American funeral customs, see Sylvia Frey, *Water From the Rock: Black Resistance in a Revolutionary Age*, (Princeton: Princeton University Press, 1991), 31–37 and Mechal Sobel, *The World They Made Together: Black and White Values in Eighteenth-Century Virginia*, (Princeton: Princeton University Press, 1987).

13. Gundersen, "The Double Bonds of Race and Sex," 367. Frances Bland to Frances Bland Randolph, n.d. [1771], TCP; Ralph Fall, ed., *The Diary of the Reverend Robert Rose* (Verona, Va.: McClurc Press, 1977). See the entries for August 3, 1747, August 17, 1747, April 2, 1749, April 17, 1749, May 10, 1749, and October 8, 1749. Because Rose was absent so often, it is possible that Anne actually had many other visitors who went unrecorded.

14. Another of the pregnant runaways, Tabb, was presumed by her owner to be passing as free. *Virginia Gazette*, November 16, 1739, 4 and November 17, 1768, 3.

15. *Ibid.*, diary entry May 21, 1755; Edward Miles Riley, ed. *The Journal of John Harrower: An Indentured Servant in the Colony of Virginia, 1773–1776*, (Williamsburg, Va., 1963), passim. See particularly the entries for March 26, 1775, October 29, 1775, November 4, 1775, April 7, 1776, and April 14, 1776. Smith has argued that Virginia planters stripped dependent kin from their networks as they began to value privacy. The Rutmans, however, suggest that a person has a finite number of close friends. When the nuclear family was truncated, Virginians then turned to neighbors and extended kin, and when life expectancy increased and families grew larger, Virginians had less need to go outside the immediate family. This insight seems eminently more reasonable. However, when neighbors are kin, there is no need for either/or choices of friends. Smith, *Inside the Great House*, 175–77, 226. Darrett B. and Anita H. Rutman, *A Place in Time, Explicatus*, (New York: W.W Norton, 1984), 107–16.

16. Magdalene Chastain will, June 2, 1729, recorded May 7, 1731, Henrico County, Deeds and Wills; Peter Chastain will, October 3, 1728, recorded November 20, 1728, Goochland County, Deeds and Wills; Stephen Chastain will, January 10, 1732, recorded August 21, 1739, Goochland County, Deeds and Wills, VSL.

17. Kulikoff, *Tobacco and Slaves*, 241–50. Despite Kulikoff's argument that patriarchy dominated all aspects of family life, his evidence shows families naming children more for maternal kin. Dorothy Pankey will, November 12, 1772, Lunenburg County Wills, Will Book 2, VSL.

18. Gerald W. Mullin, *Flight and Rebellion: Slave Resistance in Eighteenth-Century Virginia* (Oxford: Oxford University Press, 1972), 105–12. *Virginia Gazette*, August 4, 1768, 3, September 22, 1768, 4, November 17, 1768, 3, December 22, 1768, 2–3.

19. The advertisement does not give the woman's age, but describes her as a "tall mulatto wench, slim made, has long hair and is about 30 years old." Given that children born to white mothers and black fathers were often indentured until age thirty, her claim fits the evidence. She was expected to be near Petersburg, if still in the colony. Between 1740 and 1765 a number of families moved west along the James River valley to Albemarle County. *Virginia Gazette*, August 4, 1768, 3.

20. Maude H. Woodfin, *Another Secret Diary of William Byrd of Westover, 1739–1741, with Letters and Literary Exercises 1696–1726*, trans. by Marion Tinling, (Richmond, Va.: Virginia State Library, 1942), passim. Byrd records only formal visits or those in which he was involved. William Waller Hening, ed., *The Statutes at Large; Being a Collection of All the Laws of Virginia* . . . (Richmond, Va.: Virginia State Library, 1809–1823), V, 294–95, 216–18. Greenhill eventually succeeded in getting a private act passed through the legislature to declare her a feme sole.

21. As the experiences of Anne Rose and others indicates, pregnancy was not considered ill health. Elizabeth Feilde to Maria Armistead, June 5, 1775, ACP, Earl Gregg Swem Library, College of William and Mary; Anne Blair to Mrs. Eustace, July 17, 1772, TCP, College of William and Mary. Kulikoff, *Tobacco and Slaves*, 209–12. The diary and court evidence cited above suggests that elite families increased long-distance visiting and that neighborhood visiting remained constant rather than local visiting increasing after 1740 as Kulikoff thought. The court evidence of travel to court does not support Smith's supposition that small planters would travel more in the off season. Smith, *Inside the Great House*, 200–201.

22. Rutman and Rutman, *A Place in Time*, 94–127.

23. Literacy rates were calculated using women's signatures on deeds, wills, and inventories. See also Kenneth Lockridge, *Literacy in Colonial New England: An Enquiry into the Social Context of Literacy in the Early Modern West*, (New York: W.W. Norton, 1974), 88–92.

24. Essex and Henrico County records for the first sample period included 230 legal records (other than estate inventories) signed by women. Sixty-four of these were signed within one day of being proved in court. Essex County court officer, Salvatore Muscoe, witnessed over a quarter of such documents. Essex County, Deeds and Wills, 1707–1711, and Henrico County, Deeds and Wills, 1706–1709, VSL.

25. Henrico County, Deeds and Wills, 1706–1709; Essex County, Deeds and Wills, 1707–1711; Goochland County, Deeds and Wills, Book 1, 1728–1734; Goochland County, Deeds and Wills, Book 6, 1748–55; Goochland County,

Deeds and Wills, Book 11, 1775–1777; Lancaster County, Deed Book 19, 1770–1782; Lancaster County, Will Book 20, 1770–1783, VSL.

26. None of the participants was among the elite. Although William and Ester Lansdon swapped several parcels of land, much of it was unimproved. William's estate when he died in 1743 was valued at £40.14.4, Goochland County, October 18, 1734, Deeds and Wills. Joseph Bingley was murdered in 1761. His estate was not valued, but its itemized listing is similar in quantity of items and slaves to that of neighbor Anthony Lavillan whose estate was appraised at £258.12.9. Cumberland County, July 23, 1750, Cumberland Wills. John Ford worked a small farm in Goochland County.

27. There is, of course, no way to determine what was said that day. Goochland County, May 20, 1729, Deeds and Wills, Book 1, VSL. Isaac Benin, son of Anthony and Elizabeth, was baptized at King William Parish August 9, 1729. King William Parish Register, 1721–1745 in R. A. Brock, *Documents Chiefly Unpublished, Relating to the Huguenot Emigration to Virginia and to the Settlement at Manakin-Town,* ... (Richmond, Va: Virginia State Library, 1886).

28. I scored wills on two criteria: women witnesses, and special bequests. A woman made a special bequest to a female relative or friend if she had male heirs and made no similar bequests to males. The wills, excepting two filed in Prince Edward County, one in Amelia, and one in Lunenburg, are from the area around present Powhatan County (then Henrico, Goochland, Cumberland, and Chesterfield Counties). They were filed between 1703 and 1800.

29. Smith, *Inside the Great House*, 81. For the economic transformation in the colonies, see John J. McCusker and Russell R. Menard, *The Economy of British America, 1607–1789* (Chapel Hill: University of North Carolina Press, 1985) 60, 124, 127–33, 139, 277–94; Timothy H. Breen, *Tobacco Culture: The Mentality of the Great Tidewater Planters on the Eve of Revolution* (Princeton: Princeton University Press, 1985) 124–59; Edward Perkins, *The Economy of Colonial America* (New York: Columbia University Press, 1980) 101–20.

30. The classic statement of this male culture is found in Rhys Isaac, *The Transformation of Virginia, 1740–1790* (Chapel Hill: University of North Carolina Press, 1982).

31. For changes in the size of Henrico, Goochland, and Essex Counties, see Martha W. Hiden, *How Justice Grew: Virginia Counties, An Abstract of Their Formation* (Charlottesville: University of Virginia Press, 1957).

32. One-half of Henrico County women's powers-of-attorney in 1706–1709 were by four Quaker women who thus avoided the hassles of the court over Quaker insistence on affirmation rather than swearing of oaths.

33. Joan R. Gundersen and Gwen Victor Gampel, "Married Women's Legal Status in Eighteenth-Century New York and Virginia," *William and Mary Quarterly*, 3rd series, 39 January 1982, 114–34; Smith, *Inside the Great House*, 231–48. For evidence of women's withdrawal from court and economic activities in other colonies see Dayton, "Women before the Bar," 83–88.

33. Maria Carter to Maria Carter, March 25, 1756, ACP; Jean Blair to Mrs [Mary Blair] Braxton, October 14, 1769, Blair, Bannister, Braxton, Horner, Whiting Papers, Earl Gregg Swem Library, College of William and Mary (hereafter BBB).

34. For example, see *The Ladies Complete Letter-Writer: Teaching the Art of Inditing Letters on Every Subject That Can Call for the Attention, as Daughters, Wives, Mothers, Relations, Friends, or Acquaintances,* (London, Printed for the editor, and sold

by T. Lownds, 1763). Anne Blair to Mary Braxton, August 21, 1769, BBB; Elizabeth Feilde to Maria Armistead, January 3, 1776, ACP.

35. See Elizabeth Bannister to Frances Randolph, June 19, 1772, Jean Blair to Mary Braxton, October 14, 1769, Anne Blair to Mary Braxton, n.d. [1768], Anne Blair to Mary Braxton, August 21, 1769, Anne Blair to Mary Braxton, September 4, 1769, BBB.

36. Frances Bland to Frances Randolph, n.d. [1771], and Mary Jones to Frances Randolph, February 28, 1769, TCP; Elizabeth Feilde to Maria Armistead, January 3, 1776, ACP, College of William and Mary; "Diary of a Little Colonial Girl," *Virginia Magazine of History and Biography*, 11, 1903–04, 212–14.

37. Before 1776, there is little evidence of any collective action by women in Virginia churches or any denomination, but heavy involvement in family religious choice and family worship. Thus Virginia women did not have the female religious spaces noted in later essays in this collection. Joan R. Gundersen, "The Non-Institutional Church: The Religious Roles of Women in Eighteenth-Century Virginia," *Historical Magazine* of the Protestant Episcopal Church, 51, December 1982, 347–58.

38. Sylvia Frey, *Water from the Rock: Black Resistance in a Revolutionary Age*, (Princeton: Princeton University Press, 1991), 19–35, 37; Sobel, *The World They Made Together*, 180–203.

39. Rutman and Rutman, *A Place in Time*, 234–39; Thomas Porter will, April 27, 1767, Thomas Porter inventory, July 27, 1767; Elizabeth Porter inventory, August 18, 1772; Deed, William Short to John Landrum, May 1752, Chesterfield County Records, and John Landrum to Thomas Smith, July 6, 1764, Cumberland County Records Deeds and Wills, VSL; Haskins Lendrum took the state loyalty oath in 1777 as a Methodist preacher. Thomas Porter owned nineteen slaves, but their household goods would have given them a middle-class lifestyle.

"FOR THEIR SATISFACTION OR REDRESS"

African Americans and Church Discipline in the Early South

Baptist and Methodist ministers who served in the early South seldom experienced the public disgrace and humiliation of being dismissed from their posts, but this was to be the fate of Reverend John Chalmers. In 1812, following a thorough investigation of the charges brought against him, a specially convened meeting of the Quarterly Conference of the Baltimore Circuit had no compunction in relieving Chalmers, a white preacher, of his ministerial responsibilities for the biracial Methodist congregation in Annapolis.[1] The trial and punishment of John Chalmers by his white peers constituted a most unusual occurrence. What was even more remarkable about this episode, however, was that the case against Chalmers had been initiated by Charity and Forty, two enslaved women members of his congregation, who alleged that their minister had made unacceptable sexual advances toward them.

The case of John Chalmers is instructive for several reasons, but principally because it sheds significant light on what remains a largely unexplored dimension of the disciplinary structures and proceedings of the early South's biracial evangelical Protestant churches. During the last two decades of the eighteenth century, the black membership of these churches grew at a dramatic rate and, in most congregations, enslaved people heavily outnumbered free people and women heavily outnumbered men.[2] Recent scholarship has tended to emphasize what are usually depicted as the largely successful efforts of white Baptists and Methodists to impose their value systems, their morality, and particularly their ideal of a gendered sexual morality, on their enslaved coreligionists.[3] Behavioral conformity was sought, and church records suggest that it was often achieved through the use of sanctions that ranged from private admonition and public censure to the ultimate punishment of excommunication. Inadvertently, perhaps, the impression can all too easily be conveyed that the disciplinary mechanisms of the biracial evangelical Protestant churches had a single function, that their principal, if not their sole, purpose was to reorder the moral priorities and behavior of enslaved church members who meekly submitted to the demands being made of them by their white coreligionists.

Even the most cursory examination of the records of biracial Methodist and Baptist congregations located throughout the eighteenth- and early nineteenth century South reveals these disciplinary mechanisms in a rather different light. They could be, and were, employed by Afro-Baptists and Methodists on their own behalf, often with a considerable degree of success.[4] After all, it was an appeal to the disciplinary mechanisms of their church by two enslaved women that was to cost Reverend John Chalmers his career and his reputation. The Chalmers' case also exemplifies another crucial point: Although religion is often depicted as a tool for the ongoing oppression of women, under certain circumstances it could be employed by women as a liberating and an empowering force.

While it is true that in the vast majority of biracial Methodist and Baptist churches the names of enslaved church members appear in the disciplinary records far more often as defendants than as plaintiffs, and that in some churches they seem to have initiated no charges at all against their white coreligionists prior to the early nineteenth century,[5] this should not be allowed to obscure the significance of the number, character, and outcome of the charges they did bring. Indeed, given the composition of the disciplinary bodies that, by the late eighteenth century, were dispensing justice in most evangelical Protestant churches, the remarkable thing is not that Afro-Baptists and Methodists initiated so few charges but that they initiated as many as they did.

Disciplinary structures and procedures that had as one of their main purposes the regulation and control of enslaved church members provided their intended subjects with a crucially important means by which and through which they could articulate and assert their own understanding of the rights, rather than the privileges, they believed that their common religion, their continuing church membership, entitled them to. As Mechal Sobel has observed, and as Charity and Forty's successful complaint against Chalmers so amply confirms, the right claimed by Afro-Baptists and Methodists to use the disciplinary structures of their churches on their own behalf, for their own reasons and purposes, "was not simply an abstract right."[6]

First and foremost among the rights claimed by Afro-Baptists and Methodists were the often closely related demands for the right to an equality of respect from their coreligionists and the right to protection against any form of abuse, be it verbal, physical, or emotional, perpetrated against them by any other of their fellow church members. Significantly, Afro-Baptists and Methodists sought to secure these twin rights of respect and protection not only from their white coreligionists but also from one another. This dual concern brought into often sharp focus imperatives and demands that could be differentiated as much on the basis of gender as they were on the basis of race and status. Moreover, the contest to secure the rights they sought, the charges brought by Afro-Baptists and Methodists, could produce what, on the face of it, might seem to be some improbable, and possibly only temporary and expedient, alliances that cut across differences of race, status, and gender.

By the 1790s, the inescapable reality facing any church member, white or black, elite or underclass, female or male, who contemplated pressing a charge against one of their coreligionists of a different gender, race, or status was that ultimately they might find themselves being forced to confront a white male authority whom at best they might expect to be sceptical, and at worst entirely unbelieving, of their claims.[7] In at least some churches, however, this had not always been so.

In 1802, for example, the Dover Baptist Association of Virginia expressed its concern and distaste at the fact that some of its constituent churches "admitted to their church meetings, even for discipline and government, all the members of the church, male and female, bond and free, young and old. Others admitted all male members, whether slave or free."[8] For some years before 1802, however, the formally recognized authority in disciplinary matters enjoyed in some biracial congregations by women and enslaved church members had been coming under ever-increasing, and generally successful, attack from white male Baptists and Methodists. In 1783, for example, the Charleston Baptist Association had declared quite categorically that "female members may, when called upon, act as Witnesses in a Church; and when aggrieved are to make known their Case . . . but they are excluded from all Share of Rule or Government in the Church." [9] A decade later, when it drew up its Rules of Decorum, Virginia's Black Creek Baptist Church decreed that "No Woman shall speak in church, except it be by a Friend, otherwise asked questions, & called upon to give evidence."[10] Also in Virginia, the Emmaus (New Kent) Baptist Church declared that the free white male members of the congregation would convene on the first Saturday of every month to arbitrate on disciplinary matters. Cases would be decided by a majority of those present and voting.[11]

Some churches and associations acknowledged that white women could have a role, albeit a strictly limited role, to play in disciplinary proceedings. In 1801, for instance, the Dover Baptist Association conceded that white women church members might be "very useful in certain stages of discussion" and that if individual churches so determined they "may admonish, reprove or rebuke, either singly or united to others, others meaning a right to cite refractory members to appear before the church & may act as witnesses for or against them." The constituent churches of this association were also advised that, if they thought the nature or gravity of the charge brought against one of their members warranted it, they might first bring the matter to the attention of a committee composed of persons whose sex was "similar to that of the offender." The churches were further advised that it would be appropriate were they to appoint "the most considerable & experienced" of their members to such committees.[12] The language employed by the association strongly suggests that social status, as well as the duration of church membership, would be a decisive factor in the composition of any committees appointed by white male church members. A woman's prestige, her reputation, would determine whether or not she was invited by the white men in her congregation to sit in initial judgment on one of her church sisters. But, as the Black Creek Church insisted in 1803, although they would be allowed to speak in church "for their own satisfaction or Redress in any matter," and to testify against white male church members, under no circumstances would any woman, however "considerable & experienced" she might be, be permitted "to use authority over man."[13] And what was true of white women was equally true of enslaved Baptists and Methodists.

In 1802, for instance, the Dover Baptist Association declared quite unequivocally that it was wholly unacceptable for enslaved church members to sit in judgment on the morality and behavior of any of their white coreligionists. The association sought to rationalise the exclusion of bondpeople from participation in the formal disciplinary proceedings of its member churches on the grounds that "The degraded state of the minds of slaves render[s] them totally incompetent to the task of judging correctly respecting the business of the church, and in many churches there [is] a majority of slaves; in consequence of which great confusion often arose." Clearly this proposal had not gone entirely unopposed because it was only after "some debate" that the delegates agreed "by a large majority" to recommend to the association's constituent congregations that "although all members were entitled to privileges, yet none but free male members should exercise any authority in the church."[14] Enslaved church members had been effectively stripped of the right that obviously some of them had previously enjoyed of formal participation in the disciplinary proceedings of their congregations.

In some Baptist and Methodist churches, however, and in many ways parallelling the limited involvement in disciplinary matters granted to white women, African-American men, but never African-American women,[15] were appointed to serve as deacons and as class leaders. In addition to the ritual and educational duties that these offices entailed, those appointed were usually entrusted with another important responsibility by their white coreligionists: "to have the oversight of our black members & to admonish [them]."[16] In effect, class leaders and deacons constituted a powerful intermediary layer of authority, of black male authority, between Afro-Baptists and Methodists and the white male government of their churches.

If the African-American deacons and class leaders of the early South kept written accounts of their disciplinary dealings with the enslaved members of their churches, and there is no firm evidence that they did, then the same have not survived the passage of the years. However, it would seem entirely reasonable to suggest that from the perspective of Afro-Baptists and Methodists, and particularly perhaps from the perspective of enslaved women, the power vested in the hands of class leaders and deacons was by no means inconsequential. But, like the power exercised by white male church members, the formal authority exercised by an albeit minuscule number of black deacons and class leaders was double-edged.

On the one hand, black deacons and class leaders were expected by the white men who had appointed them to keep a close and constant watch on, to pry into, the morality and behavior of those placed under their charge. If they thought it appropriate, they could counsel, caution, or censure those who were brought to their attention without recourse to the higher white male authority of the church. Those who might have felt dissatisfied with the treatment they had received at the hands of their class leaders and deacons, and who wished to take the matter further, had only one official recourse open to them: to take their case to the white male dominated disciplinary bodies of their church. With good reason, many might have believed that such an appeal would be likely to fall on deaf ears; that their word would not be accepted against that of a class leader or a deacon.

However, there was another, and from the standpoint of those black church members who might find themselves in need of it, more positive and benign use to which the authority of class leaders and deacons might be put. By definition, the power vested in them to admonish their erring brethren, and if necessary to report them to the disciplinary bodies controlled by white male church members, meant that they constituted a potentially powerful source of justice and protection for those enslaved church members who had been unable to secure these either by their own efforts or through the intervention of a family member or a friend. Indeed, for those who had fallen out with, or felt in need of protection from, a family member, their class leader or deacon might seem to be either the best or the only person to whom they could turn for help. Although impossible to document, it may be safely assumed that if the evidence produced by the plaintiff was not incontrovertible, if there were no witnesses, and if a defense was offered by the accused, then the outcome of the case was likely to depend on what weight the deacons and class leaders concerned attached to the credibility, the prestige, and the reputation of the accuser and the accused.

If there were occasions, albeit an unknown number of occasions, when the credibility, prestige, and reputation of enslaved church members assumed a crucial importance in the disposition of cases dealt with by black deacons and class leaders, then these same qualities, or the perceived lack of them, could be of even greater significance in the determination of those cases that brought them into direct contact with the white male authority of their church. Afro-Baptists and Methodists who, for whatever reason or motive, contemplated bringing a case to the attention of that authority had first to consider two weighty questions, particularly if their case involved an accusation against one of their white coreligionists: Would they be believed and what might be the repercussions, the possible cost to themselves, of making such an approach?

By the turn of the eighteenth century, even the most pious, respectable, and honest enslaved church members must have entertained some doubt as to whether their word would be taken against that of any of their white coreligionists. Those doubts were well founded because the validity of slave testimony was called into open question, and debated at length, by the white membership of some congregations. Lyville's Creek Baptist Church, in Augusta County, Virginia, was more explicit on the matter than most. In 1807, in a quite categorical and entirely unapologetic assertion of the inequality that would now mark its disciplinary proceedings, the church declared that it would no longer "hold the testimony of a black member valid as a white member."[17]

Significantly, however, neither Lyville's Creek nor any other biracial Baptist or Methodist church traveled the entire route to an exact duplication of secular justice for their enslaved members. That is, Afro-Baptists and Methodists were never denied the right—or as their white coreligionists had come to regard it by the turn of the eighteenth century, the privilege—of presenting their grievances to the disciplinary bodies of their churches. Moreover, although its authenticity and worth might be called into serious question, enslaved church members retained the critically important, and potentially potent, right of testifying against their white coreligionists, something universally denied them in the world outside their churches. The continued willingness of Afro-Baptists and Methodists to exercise that right was a profoundly significant aspect of their struggle to resist total domination, whether spiritual or temporal, by their white coreligionists.

The cases that were initiated by Afro-Baptists and Methodists, and heard by the white men who composed the disciplinary boards of their churches, can be subdivided into two main categories: those that they brought against one another and those that they brought against white members of their congregations. But they can also be subdivided in another way: according to the gender as well as to the status of plaintiff and defendant. There were several possible scenarios. For example, charges might be brought against a white woman church member by an enslaved man or an enslaved woman; an enslaved woman might bring charges against another bondwoman or bondman as well as against one of her white coreligionists.

Arguably the dynamics, as well as the outcome, of particular cases were strongly influenced, if not largely determined, by issues of gender just as much as they were by issues of race and status. In the process, all church members, women and men, as well as free and slave, could be made to confront, to assess, and sometimes to amend the prejudices and stereotypes they held of one another; they could be forced to rethink and reorder their own morality and behavior.

No doubt many enslaved church members thought long and hard before initiating a formal charge against one of their coreligionists, particularly if that individual was of a different gender or status. At the very least, and this might well have deterred some from proceeding, they would have to confront the gender, as well as the social and racial, prejudices of the white men who would sit in judgment on them. Indeed, with such serious doubt being cast on their reputations, on their honesty and credibility as witnesses, by the late eighteenth century, Afro-Baptists and Methodists had some reason to doubt whether they could ever secure the justice and protection they sought from their white male coreligionists. Yet in ways that must have confirmed their hopes, if not their expectations, the church records reveal that many of the cases brought by enslaved church members against their white coreligionists were determined in favor of the black plaintiff. That this was so reflected a combination of various, and often essentially local, considerations that included the reputation and prior record of both the defendant and the accused; the pragmatic private agendas, as well as the consciences and self-images, of the white men who sat on the disciplinary boards; and the kind of public image they sought to project of themselves and their church.

There were two fundamental forms of protection, one physical, the other emotional and psychological and undifferentiated by gender, that male and female Afro-Baptists and Methodists alike sought from their churches. The records suggest that they were to find the former somewhat easier to obtain than the latter. Where slave and owner belonged to the same congregation, the disciplinary mechanisms of the church were there to be employed by those bondpeople who were desperate enough, and determined enough, to seek relief from various forms of physical abuse being perpetrated on them by their master or mistress. Of course, there was always the possibility that, regardless of its outcome, the mere fact of initiating such a case could result in even more punishment being heaped on the head of the plaintiff. But bondpeople persisted in bringing charges against those of their coreligionist owners who were physically maltreating them and, as a consequence, kept alive the question of the nature of the disciplinary relationship between Christian master and Christian slave. Was that relationship to be characterized by the virtually unencumbered power granted to slaveowners by secular law or should different rules and standards apply to coreligionists?

Some congregations formally debated the theoretical issues posed by the physical disciplining of their enslaved members; others were forced to confront that same issue as a direct result of charges that were initiated either by or on behalf of their enslaved members. In 1772, for example, the white church members of the Meherrin (South Side) Baptist Church in Lunenburg County, Virginia, debated whether it was "lawful to punish our servants by burning them & in any case whatsoever." The reason they did so was because one of their slaveowning number, Charles Cook, had been charged, by whom it is not recorded but possibly by the bondperson concerned, with "burning one of his Negroes." Apparently without a dissenting vote, and probably because the evidence against him was incontrovertible, the disciplinary body of the church agreed that Cook's behavior was totally unacceptable and that his church membership should be suspended.[18]

The case brought against Cook was rare but not unique.[19] Moreover, charges of physical brutality were made against female as well as against male slave owners. In 1797, for instance, South Carolina's biracial Turkey Creek Baptist Church expelled one of its white women members "for impiously abusing her servant."[20] The unspecified violence meted out by this woman to one of her bondpeople conformed neither to her white male coreligionists' expectations of someone of her sex nor to the restraint they deemed appropriate from one of her social standing in the religious community.

Whoever initiated them, cases that charged Baptist and Methodist slaveowners with the physical mistreatment of their bondpeople neither promised nor implied that in future they and other owners would desist from employing physical force when it came to disciplining and punishing their bondpeople. There seems seldom, if ever, to have been any doubts raised by white

Baptists and Methodists as to the legitimacy of the physical punishment of their enslaved coreligionists and, in this sense, the rights claimed by the slave-owning members of biracial churches remained largely intact. But the cases brought by, or on behalf, of Afro-Baptists and Methodists had a significance that went way beyond their number. They forced all white church members, and not simply slaveowning ones, to confront the nature of the disciplinary relationship between owner and slave and to persuade them that personal constraint was both a necessary and a desirable condition of continued good standing in the church. Sometimes in formal statements, and sometimes less formally through the disposition of particular cases, congregations laid down clear guidelines that sought to govern the use of physical force by their slave-owning members.[21]

As far as enslaved church members were concerned, they could not expect, and perhaps many of them did not hold out much hope, that their church membership would necessarily provide them with complete immunity against the possibility of being physically chastised by their coreligionist owners. What they could reasonably hope for, however, was that their churches might be persuaded to offer them a significant degree of protection against excessively brutal treatment. The best that those Afro-Baptists and Methodists whose owners did not share their church affiliation could hope for was that their white coreligionists might be willing to intervene on their behalf, to provide a buffer of sorts between themselves and their owners.

Precisely the same was true when it came to the second form of protection, a second right, sought by Afro-Baptists and Methodists from their churches: the right to personal relationships in keeping with those sanctioned by their churches; the right to a secure, unbroken, family life. Their white coreligionists employed the disciplinary mechanisms of their churches, mechanisms of their own devising, in order to impose on black church members their own ideal of a gendered Christian sexual morality: a morality that demanded virginity followed by a monogamous lifetime marriage. The only acceptable alternative was lifelong chastity. In every biracial Baptist and Methodist congregation, everywhere in the early South, it was the failure, in one way or another, of enslaved church members to live up to these ideals that accounted for the vast majority of the disciplinary charges initiated against them by their white coreligionists.[22] However, the fact that alleged or proven sexual improprieties comfortably topped the list of accusations brought against Afro-Baptists and Methodists should not be allowed to obscure two highly significant, and closely connected, points: first, these charges involved a comparatively small number of black church members and, second, the vast majority of Afro-Baptists and Methodists wanted nothing more than the comfort and the security of assured partnerships and family lives. Their agenda, what they sought from their churches, from their white coreligionists, was perfectly simple: the right to a marriage partner of their own, rather than their owners', choosing; the right to parenthood and to family life that would be unimpaired by the enforced separation of husband and wife, parents and children. These were rights that in theory, and all too often also in practice, went totally unrecognized in the secular world; they were rights that would receive only limited protection by virtue of church membership.

The dilemma for white Baptists and Methodists was that the sexual morality, and particularly the Christian marriage, they demanded of enslaved church members ran directly counter to the property rights claimed by owners and had absolutely no validity in civil law. Many churches explicitly acknowledged those rights by declaring that any of their enslaved members who sought to marry must have the prior permission of their owners.[23] Some congregations intervened in other ways in the choice of marriage partners. For example, around the turn of the eighteenth century, the Sharp Street Methodist Church in Baltimore excommunicated some of its number who had insisted on marrying "unawakened" partners.[24] A few years earlier, in 1794, the disciplinary board of Smith's Creek Baptist Church, in Shenandoah County, Virginia, considered a case brought by Margaret Harrison, one of its white women members, against an enslaved man named Joe. According to Harrison's account, Joe had spread "a scandalous report, as a truth." The church records do not reveal the substance of this alleged "report," but the initial inclination of the board was to believe Harrison. Joe was duly censured but, a few weeks later, and possibly because of an appeal made directly by him or on his behalf by another church member, a second hearing was convened at which he was called on to give his side of the story.

As far as Joe was concerned, the results of this second hearing were mixed. On the one hand, his reputation was vindicated because "upon hearing his relation, the church was of opinion, that there was as much cause for [Harrison] being suspended as him." A formal vote was taken as to whether he should be restored to full church membership and she suspended, with a majority voting for "suspending her w. him." But this was not to be the end of the matter because, a month later, Harrison and Joe negotiated a settlement with the church board that entailed both of them being restored to full church membership. For Harrison, the price to be paid was the embarrassment of forgiving Joe for bringing charges against him but she demanded something of him in return. She agreed "that he might keep his Place in the Church, as well as herself . . . but this she undertook on Condition that said Joe should not have the Previledge sic of her wench Dine, as his Wife." In what must have been an immensely harrowing decision for him, when forced to choose between his church and his prospective wife, Joe agreed to the condition laid down by Harrison, and sanctioned by the church board, and was restored to full church membership.[25]

Joe's case is indicative of the fact that enslaved church members could not necessarily expect from their churches a cast-iron guarantee of their right to marry a partner of their own choosing. However, there was another side to the coin: they could appeal to their churches for, and sometimes receive, support and protection in those cases that did not infringe on the rights claimed by their owners. In 1805, for example, Joe and Milly, enslaved members of Burruss' Baptist Church, in Caroline County, Virginia, accused three of their black male coreligionists of "interfering improperly in a proposed marriage."

The records reveal neither who was involved in this "proposed marriage," whether it was Joe and Milly, their children or other of their family members, nor the nature of the "interfering" being brought to the church's attention. But perhaps because no vested slaveowning white interests were involved, the disciplinary authorities found in Joe and Milly's favor and the three defendants were found guilty as charged and their church membership suspended.[26]

Assuming that their choice of marriage partner meet with their owners' and their church's approval, the form of the ensuing marriage ceremony varied somewhat from congregation to congregation, but it always involved the couple concerned "entering into obligations to each other."[27] The problem for white church members, and all too frequently the source of immense personal agony for their enslaved coreligionists, was the force of these "vows" in societies where slaveowners were legally free to dispose of their human property at will. In some cases, where they were held in bondage by their coreligionists, if it ever became necessary, enslaved husbands and wives—and presumably parents and children also—were able to use the disciplinary mechanisms of their churches to secure an important degree of protection against their enforced separation. In 1772, for instance, "two Black Brethren," members of the Meherrin Baptist Church, successfully charged a white woman church member, Rebekah Johnson, with "the sin [of] . . . offering something like parting of a Black brother & sister (Man & Wife)."[28]

Albeit with variable results, formal or informal pressure might be brought to bear on slaveowning members of biracial congregations to recognize the integrity of slave marriage and family life. But, as with cases of physical brutality, those Afro-Baptists and Methodists who did not share church membership with their owners lacked any formalized institutional means of securing the protection they so desperately sought. Those, the many who were forcibly separated from their loved ones by their owners and who, after varying lengths of time, might seek to forge new sexual relationships sanctioned by their churches, met with varying responses from their white coreligionists.

The disciplinary boards of some churches were adamant that, however painful for those concerned, and however pious and respectable they might be, the enforced separation of enslaved couples provided no justification whatsoever for breaking their "vows of mutual constancy." Other congregations took a more realistic, and more compassionate, approach and decreed that marriage vows remained in force "until death or removal." Almost without exception, though, Baptist and Methodist churches were entirely unsympathetic, and seldom allowed the remarriage of the innocent party, in those cases where a marriage had irredeemably broken down.[29]

Appeals made to their churches by enslaved church members for protection against physical abuse and for the rights they associated with marriage and family life met with mixed results, but they were appeals that were made by bondmen and women alike; they were not gender-specific claims and assertions. Unsurprisingly, perhaps, there was one appeal that was, by its very nature, gender specific: the right claimed by Afro-Baptist and Methodist church women for protection against any and all forms of sexual harassment and abuse that might be perpetrated against them by their male coreligionists, white or black; their assertion of a right totally denied them in civil law, the right to their own bodies.

Any disciplinary charge initiated by an enslaved church member invited a public examination of their own, as well as the defendant's, character and standing in the community; this was a particularly crucial consideration in the bringing and determination of cases of a sexual nature. Enslaved women church members who wished to press a charge of sexual misconduct against one of their male coreligionists, especially if he was white, must have known, and some might have been deterred from proceeding by the fact, that they would be confronted by the gender, as well as by the racial, prejudices of those white men who would try the case. Those gender prejudices raised the distinct likelihood that they, just as much as the men they charged, would be the ones placed on trial; that in all probability their integrity and motives would be called into question; that they would be forced to defend themselves against either the implicit or the explicit suggestion that they must have encouraged the defendant in some way, that ultimately it was they who were responsible for his behavior toward them. Women not only had to prove male culpability—no easy task in cases that were usually of such a private nature—but also to demonstrate beyond any shadow of a doubt their own innocence.

We can never know exactly how many enslaved church women were deterred from bringing formal charges of sexual abuse against their male coreligionists or how many of their complaints might have been resolved by informal pressure being brought to bear on the accused, perhaps by the woman's family and friends, perhaps by other church members. But, perhaps because of the absence or the failure of such informal pressure, there were women who were confident enough, or angry or desperate enough, to take their cases to the disciplinary boards of their churches. In keeping with these women's hopes, but contrary to what some of them might have feared, they were not always denied the justice and the protection they demanded from these boards.

Sometimes the justice or the protection sought by enslaved women church members involved the initiation of formal charges against enslaved men in their congregation who were sexually harassing them in ways that they found unwelcome, inappropriate, and, quite possibly, also frightening. We do not know, for example, what steps Dinah, a member of the Albermarle Baptist Church, might have taken to try to deter York before bringing formal charges against him for "attempting her chastity (or something of that kind)." Neither do we know what defense, if any, York offered or if either party to the case summoned witnesses to testify on their behalf. All the church records reveal is that the disciplinary board fully accepted Dinah's account, completely exonerated her of any blame, and excommunicated York.[30]

That the bringing of formal charges might be indicative of the failure of informal methods of dissuasion is suggested by the case of Jim and Milley, two enslaved members of Burruss' Baptist Church, who belonged to the same owner, a Mrs. Minor. Any appeals that Milley might have made to Mrs. Minor, and any action that Mrs. Minor might have taken on Milley's behalf, proved fruitless because Milley formally accused Jim of making "improper solicitations and advances." As in the case brought by Dinah, the disciplinary board of Milley's church accepted her account. Jim, however, received a lesser, but nonetheless still a humiliating punishment than York. His church membership was suspended but, within a few months, he proved sufficiently contrite to be readmitted to the congregation.[31]

At the same time that they constituted demands for protection, cases such as those brought by Dinah and Milley represented powerful assertions of the standards of sexual morality set for themselves by enslaved church women. Moreover, they were insistent that these standards should be acknowledged as right by all their male coreligionists, regardless of their race or status.

As the case of John Chalmers so clearly demonstrates, neither religious nor secular status automatically protected a white male church member from formal charges of sexual misconduct being made against him by an enslaved church woman. Neither did religious or secular status automatically predetermine the outcome of the case in the man's favor. One might have expected, and no doubt such a thought would also have crossed the minds of Charity and Forty, that accusations of sexual impropriety brought by an enslaved woman against their minister, arguably the most respected and respectable figure in any church, would have shocked most members of the congregation and been dismissed out of hand by the church's disciplinary board. Many members of Chalmers' congregation might have been horrified by Forty and Charity's allegations, and some might have sought to silence or discredit the two women. Others, including perhaps women whom Chalmers might also have pestered but who were too afraid or too embarrassed to make publicly known the fact, may well have applauded Charity and Forty's action and done whatever they could to support them. However, it was crucially significant that the revelations of these two enslaved women were taken seriously by one person who was both willing and able to press their charges against Chalmers.

Unfortunately, the records do not reveal how Reverend Guest, a white preacher, first heard of the allegations being made against Chalmers by Charity and Forty. The two women might have approached him for advice and help; alternatively, he might have heard rumors and sought them out to hear their side of the story. But, whatever the circumstances of their meeting, Guest was convinced by what Charity and Forty told him. He may or may not have remonstrated privately with Chalmers, but if so he was clearly skeptical of his colleague's explanation and possible assurances about his future conduct because he determined to take the matter further. Guest summoned a meeting of local preachers who were prepared to consider the charges against Chalmers. Those present concluded that, although without "criminal intention," Chalmers' behavior with Charity "was highly imprudent & derogatory to the character of a Christian and minister." As for Forty, Chalmers' "conduct, *with a woman professing religion*, was calculated to excite her to sin, and was very reprehensible in him, both as a preacher and a man professing religion." [32]

There is no transcript of the proceedings of the meeting that heard the case against Chalmers or any record of whether the verdict to convict him, and to strip him of his ministry, was a unanimous or a majority decision. One may safely surmise, though, that it was not a decision taken lightly. But that it was taken at all owed much to a factor that arguably was crucially significant in many of the cases brought by enslaved church members, men as well as women, against their white coreligionists: the support of an influential backer. It took an enormous amount of courage on Forty and Charity's part to make public their grievances against their minister and clearly they were viewed as reputable witnesses by the white preachers who found in their favor; without Reverend Guest's backing, however, those grievances might not have been resolved in the way they were.

Enslaved church members brought a variety of cases against one another and against their white coreligionists, and those cases had a significance out of all proportion to their number. Albeit in profoundly different ways, cases that were resolved in favor of enslaved plaintiffs sent out a clear message to every church member, black and white, slave and free, man and woman, as to the morality and behavior that was demanded of them if they wished to continue as members of the church. If they deemed it necessary or appropriate, Afro-Baptists and Methodists who were in dispute with one another turned to their churches, in effect to the white male authority of their churches, for the justice or the protection they felt entitled to. But as far as enslaved church members were concerned, the disciplinary mechanisms of their churches served another, and arguably an even more significant, function.

Afro-Baptists and Methodists employed the disciplinary mechanisms of their churches not to directly challenge the relationship between Christianity and bondage, not to assert their right to secular freedom, but to publicly articulate their understanding of their rights as Christians. They demanded the protection of their persons and their most highly cherished personal relationships; they demanded from their white coreligionists an equality of respect and esteem in their capacity as fellow Christians. They insisted on these not as privileges but as rights. The struggle to secure these rights both reflected and stemmed from the determination of Afro-Baptists and Methodists to play an acknowledged part in shaping the character, the morality, and the behavior of the religious communities they voluntarily co-inhabited with whites. This not always entirely fruitless struggle would continue to characterize the South's biracial evangelical Protestant churches for the remainder of the antebellum period.

◀

Notes

1. Baltimore Circuit, Methodist Episcopal Church, Quarterly Conference Reports, 1794–1815 [Steward's Book], 154–55. These Reports are to be found in the United Methodist Historical Society of the Baltimore Annual Conference Library and Museum, Lovely Lane, Baltimore [hereafter Lovely Lane]. This case was unearthed by Professor Sylvia R. Frey. I am most grateful to Professor Frey for allowing me to cite this material, together with other data that she amassed for our collaborative work, *Come Shouting to Zion. African American Protestant Christianity in the American South and British Caribbean to 1830* (Chapel Hill, The University of North Carolina Press, forthcoming).

2. For the appeal of the Baptist and Methodist churches to enslaved African Americans, see Sylvia R. Frey, *Water from the Rock. Black Resistance in a Revolutionary Age* (Princeton, N.J.: Princeton University Press, 1991), 284–325. For the preponderance of women, see Frey and Wood, *Come Shouting to Zion*, Chap. 5.

3. See, for example, Rachel N.Klein, *Unification of a Slave State. The Rise of the Planter Class in the South Carolina Backcountry, 1760–1808* (Chapel Hill and London: University of North Carolina Press, 1990), esp. 293–301 and Stephanie McCurry, *Masters of Small Worlds. Yeoman Households, Gender Relations, and the Political Culture of the Antebellum South Carolina Low Country* (New York and Oxford: Oxford University Press, 1995), esp. 138–48.

4. For cases brought by Afro-Baptists in eighteenth-century Virginia, see Mechal Sobel, *The World They Made Together. Black and White Values in Eighteenth-Century Virginia* (Princeton: Princeton University Press, 1987), 190–97. See also Daniel, W. Harrison, "Virginia Baptists and the Negro in the Early Republic," *Virginia Magazine of History and Biography*, 80, 1972: 60–69, and William W. Sweet, "The Churches as Moral Courts of the Frontier," *Church History*, 2, 1933: 3–21.

5. Klein, *Unification Of A Slave State*, 297.

6. Sobel, *The World They Made Together*, 191.

7. Frey, *Water from the Rock*, 270–71.

8. Proceedings of the Dover Baptist Association Meeting (1802) cited in Robert A. Semple, *A History of the Rise and Progress of the Baptists in Virginia* (Richmond, Va.: John O'Lynch,1810; rev. and ext. by Rev. G. W. Beale, Richmond, Va. Pitt & Dickinson, 1894), 130.

9. Proceedings of the Charleston Baptist Association (1783) cited in Klein, *Unification of a Slave State*, 279.

10. Rules of Decorum, February 22, 1792, Black Creek Baptist Church, Southampton County, Va., Minute Book, 1774–1804, Virginia Baptist Historical Society, Richmond, Va. [hereafter VBHS].

11. Rules, 1792, Emmaus (New Kent) Baptist Church, Minutes, 1792–1841, VBHS.

12. Proceedings of the Dover Baptist Association (1801), cited in Semple, *History of the Rise and Progress of the Virginia Baptists*, 129–30.

13. April 30, 1803, Black Creek Baptist Church, Southampton County, Va., Minutes.

14. Proceedings of the Dover Baptist Association (1802), cited in Semple, *History of the Rise and Progress of the Virginia Baptists*, 130.

15. No evidence has been unearthed of an African-American woman who served in either of these capacities in the biracial churches of the eighteenth- and early nineteenth-century South. For a more extensive discussion of this point, see Frey and Wood, *Come Shouting to Zion*, Chap. 6.

16. June, 1809, Antioch Baptist Church, Minutes, VBHS.

17. March 8, 1807, Lyles (Albermarle) Baptist Church Minutes, 1800–1835, VBHS.

18. June, September, November 1772; May 1773; July 1774; June 1775; January 1777, Meherrin Baptist Church Minutes, cited in Sobel, *The World They Made Together*, 194.

19. For other examples from eighteenth-century Virginia see ibid., 196–97. See also Frey, *Water from the Rock*, 274.

20. November, 1797, Turkey Creek Baptist Church, Minutes, cited in Leah Townsend, *South Carolina Baptists, 1670–1805* (Florence, S.C.: Florence Printing, 1935), 257.

21. Sobel, *The World They Made Together*, 194; Townsend, *South Carolina Baptists*, 257.

22. For a detailed analysis of the disciplinary charges brought by white Baptists and Methodists against their enslaved coreligionists in the biracial churches of the late eighteenth- and early nineteenth-century South, see Frey and Wood, *Come Shouting to Zion*, Chap. seven. See also Sobel, *The World They Made Together*, 190–93; Klein, *Unification Of A Slave State*, 293–301; and McCurry, *Masters of Small Worlds*, 138–48.

23. In 1802, for example, the Goshen Baptist Church, in Lincoln County, Georgia, drafted as its Seventh Rule the stipulation that any black church member who wished to marry must "first make it known to their master, mistress or overseer." Lincoln County, Georgia. Goshen Baptist Church Records. Minutes 1802–1869 and Miscellaneous Records to 1911. Indexed. (Typescript, Hargrett Rare Book and Manuscript Library, University of Georgia), vii–viii.

24. Sharp Street Methodist Episcopal Church (Baltimore City Station), White and Colored Classes, 1799–1812, Lovely Lane.

25. 1794, Smith's Creek Baptist Church, Shenandoah County, Va., Minute Book, 1779–1805 (photocopy), VBHS.

26. 1805, Burruss' Baptist Church, Caroline County, Va., Minutes, 1779–1819, VBHS.

27. Queries by Euhaw Church to the Charleston Association of Baptist Churches, *Minutes of the Charleston Association, October 17, 1788* (N.p., N.d.), 2. See also Daniel, "Virginia Baptists and the Negro," 65; Frey, *Water from the Rock*, 272–74 and Frey and Wood, *Come Shouting to Zion*, Chap. 7.

28. February 22, 1772, May 30, 1773, June 7, 1773, Meherrin (South Side) Baptist Church, Lunenburg County, Va., Minute Book, 1771–1844, VBHS.

29. For examples of the different stances adopted toward enforced separation and remarriage, see Minutes of the Dover Baptist Association, 1801, 1804; Berryville Baptist Church, Minutes, 1803–1814, 1807; Wiccomico Baptist Church, Northumberland County, Va., Records, 1807–1847, VBHS; and *Minutes of the Georgia Baptist Association* (Savannah, 1809), 2. See also Frey and Wood, *Come Shouting to Zion*, Chap. 7.

30. May 18, 1777, Albermarle Baptist Church, Albermarle County, Va., Minutes, 1773–1779. VBHS.

31. 1805, Burruss' Baptist Church, Caroline County, Va., Minutes, 1779–1819, VBHS.

32. Baltimore Circuit, Methodist Episcopal Church, Quarterly Conference Reports, 1794–1815 [Steward's Book], 154–55 [emphasis in original].

CRIMES OF LOVE, MISDEMEANORS OF PASSION

The Regulation of Race and Sex in the Colonial South

From the beginning of European settlement sexual activity in the South was multiracial. In the first years of the Virginia colony almost all the settlers were male. This was generally true in other southern colonies as well. Thus, while this essay focuses mostly on Virginia, the patterns I discuss apply to other places as well.[1] Just as Virginia led the way in creating slavery in what became the United States, so too did the first colony lead the way in stigmatizing and criminalizing love, and sometimes sex, between the races. Thus, in trying to understand the contours and twists of the "devil's lane," it is both appropriate and necessary to begin in Virginia.

◂▹

Throughout the seventeenth century there were far more European men than European women in Virginia. The first three boats to arrive at Jamestown had only men on them. Women began to trickle in after 1608, but they were few in number. In the 1630s, for every six men sailing to Virginia only one woman embarked. By the 1650s, the ratio of emigrants was down to three to one.[2]

Given the paucity of white women, it is not surprising that early on some Englishmen had relations with Native American women. Most famous was John Rolfe who married Chief Powhatan's daughter, Pocahontas. This high-level union between an Indian "princess" and an English leader had obvious political implications. But Rolfe's affection for his bride seems to have been genuine. His eager courtship suggests that English attitudes toward race were hardly firm or preconceived in the early seventeenth century. Indeed, even in the twentieth century, Virginians displayed an unexpected tolerance for Indian heritage among people who were otherwise "white."[3] This tolerance of some Indian "blood" was necessary because more than a few "white" Virginians in fact had some Native American ancestry. Nevertheless, for a variety of reasons, including Indian disinclination to choose English spouses, there were in the end relatively few Indian-English marriages in early Virginia.[4]

The arrival of Africans broadened the base for this multiracial society; whites and blacks developed liaisons that flowered into love and marriage. This happened among all classes of whites, but increasingly interracial marriage blossomed between servants. Starting in the 1620s, a growing number of blacks, as slaves and servants, worked side-by-side with white indentured servants. English indentured servants accepted black co-workers with little regard for their race, and "the unfamiliar appearance of the newcomers may well have struck them as only skin deep." As Edmund Morgan has noted, "The two despised groups initially saw each other as sharing the same predicament. It was common, for example, for servants and slaves to run away together, steal hogs together, get drunk together. It was not uncommon for them to make love together."[5]

These interracial affairs of the heart affected only a few people. The small number of interracial relationships may have been mostly a result of the relative shortage of women in early Virginia. White men always outnumbered white women in colonial Virginia. In 1625, when all but a handful of the settlers were white, an incomplete census found that there were nearly six men for every woman in the colony. By the end of the century the white population of the colony was still 60 percent male, and among adults it may have been as high as 70 percent male. Gary Nash notes that in comparison to the colonies in Latin America and the Caribbean, sex ratios among whites in Virginia were almost reasonable. But, for the third or more of Virginia's white males who were unlikely to find a European wife, the fact that they were not as poorly situated as their Caribbean counterparts offered little consolation. Black men were even worse off. In the seventeenth century they outnumbered their female counterparts four to one, and for at least the first two decades of the eighteenth century, two new African males arrived for every new female.[6] Given these demographic constraints, lack of opportunity, if nothing else, limited interracial romance in the early colonial period.

But opportunities did present themselves, and men and women of both races, to paraphrase George Washington Plunkett, "seen their opportunities and they took 'em." In 1656, Elizabeth Key, a woman of mixed ancestry, married her white attorney, who had successfully sued for her freedom. At about the same time Francis Payne, a free black male, married a white woman, while sometime before 1671 Francis Skiper, a white man, married a black woman. Scattered records suggest other marriages between whites, of both sexes, and blacks of both sexes. Sex was of course not limited to marriage. In 1649, a white man and a black woman did public penance in Norfolk for "fornication." Between 1690 and 1698, at least seven white women were punished in just Westmoreland and Norfolk Counties for bearing mulatto children. Similarly, between 1702 and 1712 white women gave birth to nine illegitimate mulattoes in Lancaster County.[7]

In early Virginia, there were enough instances of interracial sexual liaisons to trouble the authorities, once they decided that such relationships threatened the social order. This fear did not emerge, however, until notions of race were directly tied to status and political power. As the number of exploited workers grew in Virginia, the leaders of the colony became increasingly fearful of a servile rebellion. After 1660, when the black population began to grow more rapidly, the fears of the elite increased. As Edmund Morgan has persuasively argued, racism became a tool for driving a wedge between the black and white segments of the lower classes. After Bacon's Rebellion, in 1676, the "wave of the future" in Virginia was to "subdue class conflict by racism" that "would sweep Virginians into their paradoxical union of slavery and freedom in the eighteenth century."[8] A major component of this creation of racism was the concerted effort of the Virginia House of Burgess to prevent or control interracial sexual relations.

The fear and ultimately the criminalization of interracial sex also stemmed from the creation of slavery. Slavery was unknown in English law.[9] Virginians initially legitimized bondage because the slaves were "heathens," who had been purchased as slaves in their own country. A traditional defense of slavery was that "captive heathens" were "really unfit for freedom." As early as the thirteenth century, Europeans began to conclude that "true slavery was appropriate only for pagans and infidels." Initially Virginia applied this rule to Africans. Those who were Christian and "civilized" might be treated as other Englishmen. Thus, in 1624, a Virginia court allowed a black named John Phillip to testify in a proceeding involving whites because he was "A negro, Christened in *England* 12 years since."[10] However, by the 1660s this justification for slavery made no sense. Some masters, prodded by conscience or the Anglican clergy, baptized their slaves. Similarly, some Africans saw conversion as a way out of their bondage and willingly accepted Christianity. In 1667, the Virginia House of Burgesses solved this potential problem with a law "declaring that baptisme of slaves doth not exempt them from bondage."[11]

As religion and foreignness receded as justifications for slavery, color or race took over. If slavery was tied to color, then racial separation had to be maintained. Otherwise, it would soon become impossible to tell the slaves from their masters. Often laws reflect social norms. This may have been the case when colonial Virginia began to proscribe interracial sex. However, the evidence suggests that the process was reversed. Virginia's lawmakers quite deliberately set out to alter social norms involving sex, in order to encourage racial separation to both justify enslavement and encourage landless whites to believe that they could rise in the social hierarchy at the expense of blacks. Once legal mechanisms made it clear that interracial sex came with penalties, it was only a small step to the development of social norms that precluded, or at least frowned on, such relations.

◀

The earliest regulation of race and gender had little to do with sex or love; it was, oddly enough, a tax law. In 1643, the House of Burgesses provided that black women servants would be taxed at the same rate as male servants. White female servants remained untaxed.[12] This law was probably a recognition that most African women were being used as field servants and should be taxed accordingly. This law did not directly affect the black women, since their masters paid the tax. But, because the master had to pay taxes on African women as though they produced as much as European or African men, the master had a strong economic incentive to send African women into the tobacco fields, even if that was not his initial intention when he purchased them.

In hindsight, this law can be seen as the beginning of a distinction between black and white women. Unlike white women, black women—so the law seemed to say—were fit only for the fields. While initially designed to reflect the kind of work African female servants and slaves did, this statute had the pernicious affect of lowering the status of blacks within Virginia society. These extra taxes created a "cost of color"—a sort of civil penalty for being black. This made life more difficult for free blacks who also had to pay this tax. If they could not afford this cost, then they presumably would have been sold into temporary servitude until the amount was paid.

This law also placed a tax on interracial marriage between white men and black women. At the time this law was passed, such marriages were legal. Thus, the 1643 law led to the bizarre outcome that Francis Skiper, a white Virginian, had to pay a tax for his black wife Ann.[13] He would not have had to pay a similar tax for a white wife. Presumably other white men who married black women also faced this marriage tax.

In the next two decades the Virginia lawmakers seem to have ignored the small, but growing, number of black women in the colony. However in this period Virginia, for the first time, openly acknowledged the existence and legality of racially based slavery. Once recognized, the institution had to be regulated. The status of black and mulatto children and the increase in interracial sex that came with a growing black population, called for special legislation.

In 1662, Virginia took its most important step in stamping the mark of the law on people of African ancestry. The title of the act—"Negro womens children to serve according to the condition of the mother"—only partially explains the nature of the law. The full statute provided:

> WHEREAS some doubts have arrisen whether children got by any English-man upon a negro women should be slave or ffree, *Be it therefore enacted and declared by this present grand assembly*, that all children borne in this country shalbe held bond or free only according to the condition of the mother, *And* that if any christian shall committ ffornication with a negro man or women, hee or shee soe offending shall pay double the ffines imposed by the former act.[14]

This statute applied to black human beings the civil law concept of *partus sequitur ventrem*—which William Blackstone accurately explained meant that: "Of all tame and domestic animals, the brood belongs to the owner of the dam or mother." The law was a clear break from the English common law rule that a child follows the status of the father (*partus sequitur partem*).[15]

Despite the origin of this rule, it would be wrong to assume that the Virginia Burgesses had purposefully dehumanized blacks by saying that the children of black women should be treated, in term of their status at law, in the same way animals were treated. Rather, this law should be seen for what it was: an attempt to regulate the emerging social and economic institution of slavery in a way that would be most beneficial to the master.[16]

Any other rule would have created great problems for social relations. As William Wiecek has noted, "To permit these mulatto offspring to take the status of their father would not only be an anomaly—a slave woman raising her children to freedom presents obvious difficulties—but it would also lead to an unthinkable blurring of racial and social lines in a society that viewed miscegenation as a 'stain and contamination' to white racial purity."[17]

Such problems would not have been insurmountable. Under common law, children took the status of their fathers, and so bound women had raised free children in Britain. Similarly, under ancient Jewish law slave women raised the free children of their nonslave partners. But, neither bondage in Britain nor slavery in other societies outside of the New World were tied to race. However, the Virginia master class could only justify enslavement—and create bondage—by tying race to status. The "stain and contamination" of race may not have been a normative value by 1662, but clearly the legislature hoped to make it one.

This law also had an important economic component. In his *Commentaries on the Laws of England*, Blackstone explained that *partus sequitur partem* evolved as a rule for determining who owned the offspring of domestic animals because with animals the "male is frequently unknown" while "the dam, during the time of her pregnancy, is almost useless to the proprietor . . . wherefore as her owner is the loser by her pregnancy, he ought to be the gainer by her brood."[18] Of course the father of the children of black women was usually ascertainable, although social pressures might have militated against any serious attempt to determine paternity. But the notion of recompense for the loss of service during pregnancy made sense to the emerging slaveowners in Virginia.

In this law the twin engines driving Virginia toward slavery—racial difference and economic gain—merged over regulations of law, sex, and procreation. Most whites assumed (incorrectly) that mulattoes were always the offspring of white men and black women. Thus, the 1662 law helped lead to a presumption of enslavement for all blacks, to be rebutted only by showing that the mother of the person in question had been free.

In addition to striking at the uncertain status of children of mixed parentage, this law was designed to prevent miscegenation itself. Declaring that a man's child would be a slave if the mother was also a slave would not necessarily lead white men to decline to have sex with slave women—indeed, it could have been an incentive. By predetermining the status of a possible offspring, white men might have been *less* concerned about the outcome of their sexual adventures. Slaveowners were unlikely to bring bastardy charges against white fathers, because the masters, after all, would gain the value of a new slave. Furthermore, the main social (as opposed to moral) reason for bastardy laws was to make sure that illegitimate children would be fed, clothed, housed, educated, and prepared for adult life. The 1662 law obviated all these problems for the bastard children of slave women and white men: the owner of the woman would pick up the tab and be handsomely recompensed by the value of the new slave. Thus, rather than discouraging miscegenation and immoral relations between slave women and white men, this law could easily have had the opposite result.

This result might be especially true for masters who sought sexual escapades with their female slaves. Fornication normally brought legal and community sanctions. It, along with bastardy, was a minor crime, but a crime nonetheless. But fornication with a slave woman was a misdeed at which the law winked. The slave could not testify against the master (or any other white), and the master was unlikely to report his own misdeeds and moral weaknesses to the authorities. The law almost completely removed the likelihood of punishment of white masters for interracial lust directed at their own slaves, even as it appeared to raise the penalties for such activities.

The law tried to prevent such sex for the pleasure (and perhaps the profit) of the white male participant by doubling the fine for any white who was convicted of fornication with a black. The phrase "any christian" in the law clearly refers to whites. They would now pay a double fine for illegal sex with blacks. But, in fact, this "fine" would most likely fall only on white men who had relations with free black women, or white women who bore children with black men. White women who bore illegitimate mulatto children also would be prosecuted for fornication. They furthermore faced extra stigma for ignoring the emerging racial taboos of the colony.

Besides directly tying race and ancestry to enslavement, this law also led to the perverse result that masters who fathered children with their female slaves would end up enslaving their own mixed-race children. The anti-fornication provision may have been designed to prevent this. In the end it did not work very well, and instead created conditions over the next two centuries where thousands of southern white men would become the owners of their mixed-race children.

Virginia might have avoided this problem by allowing for interracial marriage. Because of the colony's gender imbalance, many black women would doubtless have ended up married to whites, and certainly more than a few white women would have married black men. A fluid and expanding frontier society was the ideal place for marriage to overcome race, as it had for John Rolfe and Pocahontas. But, that would have undermined the separation of the races—and the creation of slavery—that the legislature was trying to encourage. Thus, in the 1690s, the Virginia legislature took steps to prevent interracial marriage.

◀▷

In 1691, the House of Burgesses passed a law designed to prevent "that abominable mixture and spurious issue which hereafter may encrease in this dominion, as well by negroes mulattoes, and Indians intermarrying with English, or other white women, as by their unlawfull accompanying with another."[19] Under this law any white, male or female, marrying a nonwhite would be banished from the colony within three months. The law also provided that any free "English woman" who bore a mulatto child would pay a special fine of fifteen pounds or be sold as a servant for five years in order to raise money to pay the fine. The mulatto child would be a servant until age thirty.[20]

In both these laws, race became the key to the legal infraction. The common act of marriage became criminal, with the severe penalty of banishment, if only one of the parties was white. Giving birth to a bastard child was already a violation of the law, but this statute made the penalty much worse if the mother was white and the father was not. Moreover, this law made the child, innocent of any infraction, subject to servitude for thirty years merely because of the race of his or her parents. This servitude was imposed even though the mother might be a free white woman and the father a free black man. Significantly, this law did not affect white men who fathered children with black women. The legislature may have already assumed that most black women were slaves, and thus their children would be slaves. Mulatto slaves might be inconvenient, but would not pose any great problem for the society. Nor were they likely to become a burden on the community, since as slaves they would be fed, clothed, and subject to discipline by their masters.

The 1691 statute also prohibited any master from freeing a slave within Virginia.[21] Thus, if slaveowners did father children with their slaves, and have some compunctions about enslaving their children, they were debarred from acting on any parental instincts. They could either raise their children as slaves within Virginia or exile their children as free people. Either way, the slave children suffered for their color.

In 1705, Virginia once again tried to discourage marriages between whites and blacks. Under the colony's first comprehensive slave code, whites marrying blacks could be jailed for six months and fined ten pounds. This act reaffirmed the fifteen pounds/five years servitude penalty for white women having mulatto children. The illegitimate mulatto children of white women would be bound out by the churchwardens until age thirty-one. Unlike the earlier law, this law did not have penalties for women having children with Indians. Rather, the law only prohibited "that abominable mixture and spurious issue" of "English, and other white men and women intermarrying with negros or mulattos, as by their unlawful coition with them." Under this law, ministers performing marriages between blacks and whites could be fined 10,000 pounds of tobacco—an enormous sum.[22]

The 1705 law did not make interracial marriages null and void. This failure of the legislature to nullify such marriages was a result of canon law, and the understanding that once a marriage was solemnized, it could not be undone by mere statute. Nevertheless, given the penalties for such marriages, it is unlikely that after 1705 anyone in Virginia would have wanted to enter into them or perform them.[23]

The 1705 law also dealt harshly with the innocent mixed-race children born to free white women. The mulatto "bastard child" of any "free christian white woman" would be bound out as a servant until age thirty-one. A 1723 law further declared that any children born to females who were servants until age thirty-one would also serve the mother's master until age thirty-one. In 1765 the legislature changed this rule slightly, by reducing the period of servitude to twenty-one years for mulatto boys and eighteen for mulatto girls.[24] This reduction suggests that there were perhaps fewer and fewer white women bearing mulatto children and thus less need for regulating interracial sex.

◄▻

The success of laws punishing race mixing seems clear. Hostility to interracial marriage and children of mixed ancestry grew during the eighteenth century. So too did the female population. By the time of the Revolution, Virginia effectively regulated interracial sex. Most whites accepted the norms, created in the seventeenth century, that they should never marry a black. White men understood that they could have relations with their slaves without suffering any penalty. Because the children from such unions were born into bondage, other whites seemed unconcerned. Such acts might violate moral or religious laws, but in the eyes of the criminal code they were at worst forgivable misdemeanors for which almost no white male was ever prosecuted. Most white women, on the other hand, understood the severity of penalties for a relationship with a black man.

Thus, it is somewhat surprising that Virginia's revolutionary leaders would spend much time trying to punish what was not happening very often. But Thomas Jefferson, who in many ways spoke for his generation, was obsessed in his fear of miscegenation, especially if it involved white women. During the Revolution he used his political influence to try to exile white women who chose black mates and to punish the children of such relationships simply because they were of mixed ancestry.[25]

Shortly after he signed the Declaration of Independence, Jefferson left the Second Continental Congress to serve in the Virginia legislature. He remained there until June 1779, when he became governor. This legislative career was one of the most satisfying and creative periods in Jefferson's life. Early on he chaired a committee to completely revise Virginia's laws and was able "to set forth in due course a long-range program emphasizing humane criminal laws, complete religious freedom, and the diffusion of education, and thus to appear on the page of history as a major prophet of intellectual liberty and human enlightenment." During and after Jefferson's service in the legislature, Virginia adopted many of the committee's proposed laws, including bills for establishing religious freedom, creating public education, allowing easier access to citizenship, reforming the criminal code, and abolishing primogeniture and entail.[26]

One of Jefferson's goals was to modernize Virginia's criminal code, incorporating the humane concepts found in the new criminology of Caesar de Beccari. He reduced the number of capital crimes for white offenders to two and removed various barbaric customs from the criminal code. Jefferson also proposed a tighter slave code, increased penalties for slave criminals, and retained "most of the inhumane features of the colonial slave law."[27]

Jefferson was proud of his law liberalizing rules for white immigrants seeking citizenship. But this law, adopted just before he became governor, prohibited free blacks from becoming citizens. Under another proposed law, which did not pass, any slave manumitted in the state had to leave Virginia within a year or "be out of the protection of the laws." Another of Jefferson's proposed laws—which the legislature also rejected— would have banished any white woman bearing "a child by a negro or mulatto." If she failed to leave the state the woman would be outlawed and the child bound out for an unspecified time, after which the child would be banished from the state.[28]

Jefferson's proposed legislation for free blacks, manumitted slaves, and white women with their mixed-race children conflicts with his endorsement of the natural rights of "life, liberty, and the pursuit of happiness." A white woman could not pursue her happiness with a black mate; a manumitted slave could not exercise the liberty of living in the state of her birth with her enslaved children and husband; a free black citizen of Massachusetts, who might have been a veteran of the Continental line, could not pursue happiness in Virginia.

Fortunately for Virginia's free black population and its white female population, the legislature rejected Jefferson's harsh proposals. However, in 1792, Virginia reaffirmed its opposition to interracial marriage with an act for "preventing white men and women from intermarrying with negroes and mulattoes." This law may have reflected fears that in the post-Revolutionary environment social control might break down. Since 1782, Virginians had had the right to emancipate their adult slaves within the state. Thus the growing population of free blacks might have been seen as a threat to the "racial purity" of the white population. The 1792 law provided a $30 fine and a six-month sentence for any white man or woman who married a black. Oddly enough, not until 1849 would the Virginia legislature make such marriages "absolutely void."[29]

◀▷

Although Jefferson failed in his attempt to banish or outlaw any white woman bearing "a child by a negro or mulatto," interracial marriage remained illegal. Moreover, the social norms and legal prohibitions that Virginia created in the seventeenth century remained viable for more than two centuries in the Old Dominion and throughout the South. Virginia's early laws criminalizing interracial marriages proved to be the most durable legacy of the colonial response to race.

The anti-miscegenation laws survived the Constitution of 1787, the Civil War Amendments of 1865–70 that otherwise created a fundamentally new racial order, and even the *Brown* revolution of 1954. They remained on the books in Virginia and elsewhere in the South until 1967. At one time or another, at least thirty-eight states prohibited racially mixed marriages, not only between whites and blacks, but also, among others, between "Malayans, American Indians, Chinese, Koreans, Japanese . . . [and] Hindus." As late as World War II, thirty-one states still forbid racially mixed marriages. In 1956, the Supreme Court refused to rule on the constitutionality of miscegenation laws, in a decision constitutional law professors have difficulty explaining by any theory of law. Sixteen states still had such laws on their books, in 1967, when the Supreme Court found them unconstitutional in *Loving v. Virginia*.[30]

◀▷

Notes

1. For example, Virginia did not initially prohibit intermarriage. Instead, starting in 1705, Virginia punished the preachers who performed such marriages as well as the participants. Similarly, in 1715, Maryland fined ministers officiating over mixed marriages and in 1717 instituted servitude for the couple involved. "An Act Relating to Slaves and Servants," Act of 1715, and "A Supplementary Act to the Act Relating to Servants and Slaves," Act of May 1717, in *The Laws of the Province of Maryland Collected in One Volume*, 119, 124, 200 (Philadelphia, 1718, reprint ed., John D. Cushing, ed., 1977).

2. Frank Wesley Craven, *White, Red, and Black: The Seventeenth-Century Virginian* (New York: W. W. Norton, 1977), 26–27.

3. In 1924, at the height of the Jim Crow era, for example, Virginia defined a white person as having "no trace whatsoever of any blood other than Caucasian." But this law allowed someone to be "white" if the person had up to one-sixteenth Indian ancestry. Act of March 20, 1924, ch. 371, § 5, *1924 Virginia Acts* 534, 535. In 1950, the law of Virginia declared people to be nonwhite if they had "ascertainable any Negro blood" and no more than "one-fourth of more" of Indian blood. Pauli Murray, *States' Laws on Race and Color*, Davison Douglas, ed. (1950; reprint Athens: University of Georgia Press, 1996), 462.

4. See generally Gary Nash, *Red, White, and Black: The Peoples of Early America*, 2nd ed. (Engelwood Cliffs, N.J.: Prentice-Hall, 1982), 275–79. Nash finds a greater rate of Indian-English intermarriage in Georgia and South Carolina.

5. Edmund Morgan, *American Slavery, American Freedom: The Ordeal of Colonial Virginia* (New York: W. W. Norton, 1975), 327.

6. Morgan, *American Slavery, American Freedom*, 408, 336. Of 1,210 settlers in the colony, existing records account for 750, of these, 634 were male and only 116 were female. Gary Nash estimates that in 1720 only-one fifth of the black population in the colonies was female. Nash, *Red, White, and Black*, 281.

7. Morgan, *American Slavery, American Freedom*, 334, 155, 336. See also Warren M. Billings, "The Cases of Fernando and Elizabeth Key: A Note on the Status of Blacks in Seventeenth Century-Virginia," *William and Mary Quarterly*, 3rd Series, 30 1973; 467–74.

8. Morgan, *American Slavery, American Freedom*, 328.

9. See Jonathan A. Bush, "The British Constitution and the Creation of American Slavery," in Paul Finkelman, ed., *Slavery and the Law* (Madison, Wis.: Madison House, 1996).

10. David Brion Davis, *The Problem of Slavery in Western Culture* (Ithaca: Cornell University Press, 1966), 346; David Brion Davis, *Slavery and Human Progress* (New York: Cornell University Press, 1984), 33. *In re Sir Henry Maneringe*, in H. R. McIlwaine, ed., *Minutes of the Council and General Court of Colonial Virginia* (Richmond: Virginia State Library, 1924), 33 [Hereinafter cited as McIlwaine], reprinted in Paul Finkelman, *Law of Freedom and Bondage* (New York: Oceana Press, 1986), 10.

11. On using religion to become free, see the case of *In re John Graweere*, McIlwaine, 477 (March 31, 1641), reprinted in Finkelman, *Law of Freedom and Bondage*, 11. "An act declaring that baptisme of slaves doth not exempt them from bondage," 2 Hening 260 (September 1667), reprinted in Finkelman, *Law of Freedom and Bondage*, 16.

12. "Act Concerning Church Government," Act of March, 1642–43, 1 Hening, *Virginia Statutes at Large*, 240.

13. Edmund Morgan, *American Slavery, American Freedom*, 334.

14. Act XII, 2 Hening 170 (December 1662).

15. William Blackstone, *Commentaries on the Laws of England* 2:390 (Oxford: Clarendon Press, 1765).

16. For similar conclusions, see William Wiecek, "The Statutory Law of Slavery and Race in the Thirteen Mainland Colonies of British America," *William and Mary Quarterly* 3rd Series, 34, 1977, 282; reprinted in Paul Finkelman, ed., *Colonial Southern Slavery* (New York: Garland, 1989). Morgan, *American Slavery*, 333; and Thomas D. Morris, "Villeinage . . . as it existed in England, reflects but little light on our subject:' The Problem of the 'Sources' of Southern Slave Law," *American Journal of Legal History*, 32, 1988, 95, 112.

17. Wiecek, "Law of Slavery and Race," 263.

18. 2 Blackstone, *Commentaries*, 390.

19. "An act for suppressing outlying Slaves," 3 Hening 86–87 (April 1691). Virginia's law was not the first—thirty years earlier, Maryland prohibited miscegenation. Robert J. Sickels, *Race, Marriage, and the Law* (Albuquerque: University of New Mexico Press, 1972), 64.

20. Ibid.

21. Ibid., at 88.

22. "An Act Concerning Servants and Slaves," Chap. 49, Sec. 18, Sec. 20, 3 Hening 447, 453–54 (October 1705).

23. In 1705 at least one couple petitioned for the right to marry, despite the fact that the future husband was allegedly a mulatto. He apparently denied that he was a mulatto. H. R. McIlwaine, ed., *Executive Journals of Colonial Virginia* (Richmond: Virginia State Library, 1928) 3:28.

24. "An act directing the trial of Slaves. . . ." 4 Hening 126 at 133 (1723), the law also provided that if a female held to service until age thirty had children before her servitude ended, the children would also serve the master until age thirty. "An Act to prevent the practice of selling person as slaves who are not so, and for other purposes therein mentioned," 8 Hening 133 (1765).

25. For a fuller discussion of Jefferson's racism and fear of miscegenation, see Paul Finkelman, *Slavery and the Founders: Race and Liberty in the Age of Jefferson* (Armonk, N. Y.: M. E. Sharpe, 1996), Chaps. 5 and 6.

26. Dumas Malone, *Jefferson the Virginian* (Boston: Little Brown, 1948), 247–63, quoted at 247, 251, 263.

27. John Chester Miller, *The Wolf by the Ears: Thomas Jefferson and Slavery* (New

York: Free Press, 1977), 20; Davis, *Slavery in the Age of Revolution*, 174. The legislature eventually rejected some of the more vicious aspects of Jefferson's proposed criminal code for slaves.

28. "A Bill concerning Slaves," in Julian Boyd, ed., *The Papers of Thomas Jefferson* (Princeton: Princeton University Press, 1950), 2:470–73. "An act declaring who shall be deemed citizens of this commonwealth," 10 Hening's Statutes at Large 129 (May 1779). After Jefferson left the governorship, the legislature passed a liberalized manumission law but rejected his harsh proposal for expelling free blacks. "An act to authorize the manumission of slaves," 11 Hening 39 (May, 1782). The legislature also failed to accept the proposal to expel the white mothers of mixed-race children.

29. Act of Dec. 22, 1795, ch. 42, *1792 Laws of Virginia*, 130–35; *Virginia Code of 1849*, ch. 109, sec. 1. On the history of these laws see Peter Wallenstein, "Race, Marriage, and the Law of Freedom: Alabama and Virginia, 1860s–1960s," *Chicago-Kent Law Review*, 70, 1994, 371–438.

30. *Brown* v. *Board of Education*, 347 U.S. 483 (1954). Sickels, *Race, Law, and Marriage*, 64–65. *Naim v. Naim, appeal dismissed*, 350 U.S. 985 (1956). See Harvey M. Applebaum, "Miscegenation Statutes: A Constitutional and Social Problem," *Georgetown Law Review*, 53, 1964, 49, reprinted in Paul Finkelman, ed., *Race, Law, and American History: The Era of Integration and Civil Rights, 1930–1990* (New York: Garland, 1992), 1; *Loving v. Virginia*, 388 U.S. 1 (1967). See, generally, Wallenstein, "Race, Marriage, and the Law."

Part III

THE LOWER SOUTH

"FALSE, FEIGNED, AND SCANDALOUS WORDS"

Sexual Slander and Racial Ideology Among Whites in Colonial North Carolina

Law suits for sexual slander provide valuable glimpses into European-Americans' ideas about race in North Carolina's expanding slave society. The damaging rumors of illicit sex that European settlers circulated about each other reflected and reinforced the racial ideology by which they identified themselves as "white" and as distinct from African Americans. Significantly, these slurs underscored the notion of racial difference while expressing both class tensions and ideas about appropriate gender roles. Slanderers who used allegations of interracial sex to malign their wealthier neighbors or to denigrate white women as "whores," melded together notions of race, class, and gender, implicating each concept in the construction of the others. While historians have fruitfully examined colonial statutes to trace the legal definitions of race, slander cases demonstrate how common whites, in their interactions with each other, participated in the making of a racial hierarchy.[1]

European-American men and women from all social ranks defended their reputations against scandalous rumors by initiating defamation suits. (African Americans could not sue for slander in the colonial courts, and none of the plaintiffs in North Carolina's sexual slander suits were black.) Since white slander victims prosecuted those insults they found most damaging, the kinds of sexual slurs they took to court reveal the limits of white respectability. As the slave economy became entrenched in eighteenth-century North Carolina, allegations of interracial sex became insulting enough to prompt a court suit. Plaintiffs responded by insisting that the harmful allegation was false, and they vehemently disavowed the misconduct and professed their support for social norms. Unlawful sex persisted in practice, but courtroom disclaimers reinforced an official consensus about sexual propriety and confirmed whites' understanding that sexual intimacy with blacks had become publicly indefensible.

In these skirmishes over good reputations, the sexual double standard played a prominent role. Over the course of the seventeenth century, white men sued less and less for sexual slander, and by the turn of the eighteenth they no longer appeared in court to deny accusations of unlawful sex with a white woman. Indeed, by this time European-American men could even boast about their (real and invented) sexual exploits, defiling a white woman's name without harming their own. White men's honor had become detached from their sexual behavior, and rumors of illicit sex no longer required a refutation in court. White women, by contrast, whose good name continued to depend upon their reputation as chaste, prosecuted sexual insults with the hope that a courtroom retraction of the offending words would restore their standing as respectable women.[2]

The most degrading insults against white women contained graphic descriptions of sex with black men. By depicting sexual acts between European-American women and African-American men as especially odious— even perverse, slanderers implied that the liaison transgressed a natural boundary as well as a legal one. Vindictive slurs that linked interracial sex with other transgressions (such as sex with animals) underscored the notion that blacks and whites were naturally, and properly, distinct. Sexual slander thus bolstered the racial hierarchy at the same time that it reinforced the sexual constraints placed on white women. Rumors of interracial sex were so injurious, however, that even some white men appeared in court to refute the charge. Although only a few such cases exist, they speak beyond their numbers to the damaging potential of racial slurs for both European-American men and women. Sexual slander suits point to those insults that whites found most damaging, leaving behind clues about European-Americans' perceptions of race in the eighteenth century.

The social context for this defamation was a colony in transition from a frontier society to a more firmly established social order. Regional geography impeded the rapid growth of the colonial settlement on the Albemarle Sound just south of the Virginia border. The shifting sands of the Outer Banks thwarted efforts to establish permanent harbors, and the swamps and rivers made travel by land cumbersome. In these frontier conditions the colonial population grew relatively slowly. Many immigrants were former indentured servants who completed their terms of service in Virginia and then found they could not afford to buy land there. In 1708, the Virginia Council reported that "many of our poorer sort of inhabitants daily remove into our neighboring Colonies, especially to North Carolina." Even wealthier newcomers lagged far behind their Virginia counterparts in the acquisition of land and slaves. In 1730, when over 100,000 whites and nearly 50,000 blacks resided in Virginia, approximately 27,300 whites and 5,500 blacks lived east of the mountains in North Carolina.[3]

North Carolina soon gained a reputation as a particularly unruly colony. Government officials and Anglican ministers complained about the difficulty of imposing law and order on recalcitrant settlers who routinely refused to pay quitrents, adhere to the tenets of the Anglican Church, or show respect to local officials. The difficulty of establishing an effective government resulted in a prolonged period of social fluidity and political instability.[4]

After about 1730, however, wealthy North Carolinians began to catch up with slaveholding elites elsewhere. Prominent Albemarle planters moved to the Cape Fear region, where they and investors from South Carolina began to amass huge tracts of land and import large numbers of enslaved laborers to plant them. By 1760, there were 84,500 whites and 28,200 blacks in North Carolina. With the establishment of the colony's political structure and the entrenchment of slavery, the social hierarchy also hardened, a development which happened in all the southern colonies, albeit at different times. In the process, European Americans redefined their racial identity and sense of honor.[5]

A good reputation was a crucial asset in the credit-based economy and oral culture of early North America, and wagging tongues could severely undermine a person's standing in the community. Plaintiffs therefore sued their antagonists, demanding that they appear in court to retract their harmful utterances. Based on English common-law rules regarding defamation, maligned individuals in North Carolina could only sue against slander that caused specific harm. Words considered "actionable" in court included allegations of illegal behavior that, if true, could result in legal punishment. Or, plaintiffs could complain that the offensive words, uttered out of "spite and malice" in front of witnesses, had diminished the victim's social or economic standing. To demonstrate that scandalous rumors caused palpable injury (and not just hurt feelings), plaintiffs typically began with the formulaic statement that they had been "damnified in their good name" by "false, feigned, and scandalous words" that caused their neighbors to "more and more withdraw" from them. Male plaintiffs usually added that people no longer did business with them, while women emphasized the economic harm that ensued from their damaged marriages or marriage prospects. The fact that a plaintiff brought suit against slander did not necessarily indicate innocence: some plaintiffs initiated a suit preemptively to stave off prosecution for an unlawful deed they had actually committed. But regardless of the guilt or innocence of the plaintiff, slander suits reveal which insults whites considered damaging enough to require public refutation.[6]

White men sued most often to defend their reputations as honest and trustworthy business partners. In addition to complaining about offensive catch-all terms like "rogue" and "scoundrel" that encompassed a wide range of immoral male conduct, male plaintiffs also sued against more direct insinuations of shady business dealings. When, for example, Henry Hill announced in 1744 that Thomas Morris "was a Thief & had Stole a Beehive," Morris sued for slander in an effort to reestablish his reputation as an honest man.[7]

Ugly words exchanged during financial disputes often sparked a separate legal battle for slander. In 1695, for example, Robert Moline tangled with Captain John Hunt over the inheritance of another man's plantation. Moline said Hunt was an "old Cheating Rogue" who "got his Estate by Cheating" and that Hunt, a "darid stump handed Dog," could "kis my arse." For good measure, Moline added that Hunt's "old Cuckoldy rogue for his wife . . . played the whore with one Samuel Woodward for a stuf Gowne." Lashing out with gender-specific insults, Moline denounced John Hunt with a charge of financial corruption and smeared Elizabeth Hunt with the charge of bartering sexual favors.[8]

While allegations of financial dishonesty prompted most slander suits involving male plaintiffs, white men also protested slights against their ethnic identity. In 1755, for example, William Caron sued Thomas Gidings for saying Caron was "a dam Irish man and Damb the Scotch and Irish." In the eighteenth century, male plaintiffs refuted harmful slurs regarding financial dishonesty and ethnic identity, but they no longer brought suit against the charge of fornication with a white woman. In thirty-eight sexual slander cases brought between 1695 and 1765, only eight plaintiffs were men, and none of them sued against accusations of illicit sex with a white woman.[9]

By contrast, female plaintiffs sued primarily in defense of their sexual reputations. Chastity (virginity for unmarried women, monogamy for wives, and abstinence for widows) remained a prerequisite for female virtue and a primary measure of a white woman's standing in the community. Unmarried white women, called "spinsters," carefully defended their reputations from rumors of licentiousness, lest the taint of loose morals jeopardize their chances of making a satisfactory marriage.

Elizabeth Hacket, for example, wasted no time suing John Nichols, a bricklayer, for slander in 1744. Hacket, self-described as "a pious chast & honest Virgin never known by any Man whatsoever," was being courted for marriage. In fact, she claimed, "Several Young men of Good name Character & Credit" had "with great fervancy and protestations of Love & Sincerity Sollicited the said Elizabeth in marriage." But John Nichols intended to "deprive [her] of a happy marriage" with the false accusation that she was the "damn'd whore" of lawyer John Hull. Because this rumor threatened her nuptial prospects, Hacket sued immediately.[10]

Like Hacket, Sarah White was an unwed woman who cherished her reputation as "untouched and unsuspected of the atrocious Crime of fornication." She sued Samuel Commander in 1755 for scaring away her suitors with the appalling announcement that she was "a Damned Whore, and Run about the County a whoring, and got [her] Living by whoring and [was] the Damnest Whore in the Government." Similarly, Tamer Jones took Joseph Ferrill to court in 1754 for his public announcement that "he Knew a man that fuckt her twice one Night." Sometimes white parents sued on their daughters' behalf. In 1746, for example, John Swindal sued William Beaker for saying that he (Beaker) "did Lye with" John's unwed daughter. Four years later Mary Davisson brought Abell Bordine to court for his claim that he had "Corpelation" [copulation] with her daughter "at Sundry Times." Widows could also suffer from sexual innuendo. Widow Elizabeth Riding planned to remarry in 1763 when William Collins slandered her as unchaste. On hearing the rumors, Riding's fiancé, Hezekiah Sprewel, retracted his proposal and "doth refuse to be married" to Elizabeth.[11]

Married white women (often together with their husbands) also sued their slanderers.[12] Because a husband's legal rights included sole sexual access to his wife, the allegation that a married woman had committed adultery damaged the husband's reputation as a man in control of his household. Married women typically charged that a malicious rumor ruined not only their own reputation, but that of their spouse as well. In July 1744, for example, Elizabeth Ward sued Edward Whorton for having "declared in a loud voice" that Ward "is a whore a Publick whore and . . . he would prove it." The slander "greatly Hurt and damnified" her good name, Ward said, but "more especially," Whorton's "false feigned & Scandalous Words" angered her husband William, who "the bed & Company of the Said Elizabeth hath refused." This formulaic wording sought to establish the specific harm Elizabeth sustained from the slander, but it also protected William Ward, who officially eschewed his wife lest her sullied reputation tarnish his own. Whorton retracted his words and the Wards, "at the request" of the defendant, "Dismist the said Suit." By clearing her name, Elizabeth Ward also restored her husband's reputation.[13]

The importance of a white woman's reputation to her male kin turned sexual slander into a means of slighting the local elite. While many word-slinging encounters occurred between social equals fighting over a contested land boundary or an outstanding debt, other slanderers, white women in particular, displayed disrespect for their social superiors by accusing elite women of sexual misconduct. In 1728, for example, Mary Trotter, who ran a tavern in Edenton with her husband, scandalized the Governor's wife by announcing in public that during the voyage to America Madame Everard became a whore. Katherine Jolley was arrested in 1749 for calling justice of the peace John Harvey a "rogue" and his widowed "Doughter Molley . . . a Common Strumpit." Insults that denigrated the wives and daughters of prominent men also implied that since these patriarchs could not control the women in their families, neither were they fit to rule the public at large.[14]

Although white men could be harmed by sexual slurs against their female relatives, their own sexual behavior was not at issue in these slander suits. In fact, by the second quarter of the eighteenth century, men could brag about their sexual exploits with white women, denigrating their target without harming their own reputation (and perhaps even gaining esteem among their male peers). In July 1735, for example, spinster Ann Hosey defended her reputation from Thomas Stafford, Jr., who boasted that he had "lain with & knock't her Several times." When several witnesses testified in court that they, too, heard Stafford's claim, he confessed to the slander and added laconically "that it was false." In fact, Stafford conceded, "he had no Carnal Knowledge of hir Body Neither knoweth whether She . . . be man or woman."[15]

Stafford invented his sexual exploits and advertised them without fear of punishment; when the distressed Ann Hosey sued in her own defense,

Stafford simply retracted his statement. Not only did gender determine the parameters of acceptable sexual behavior, it also shaped one's relationship to language. Ann Hosey feared the impact of Stafford's words and responded with an immediate countercharge of slander. Stafford, on the other hand, could issue and retract his damaging statements with an ease that mocked the urgency with which Hosey was forced to respond to them.

In 1750, Robert Hill announced that Hepsebeth Minshew, a single woman under the age of twenty-one, "Came in to bed to me . . . with only her shift on." She was "a whore," he declared, for "I . . . have layn with her." The same alleged act that made Minshew a "whore" did not diminish Hill's moral stature in the least. Similarly, Demsey Trottman sullied the reputation of the unwed Mary Garrett without soiling his own when he spread the word in 1763 that he had "been seen fucking . . . Garrett two Times." By the middle of the eighteenth century, then, slander suits reflected a glaring double standard. As white men's reputations resided increasingly in their standing as businessmen, their sexual behavior became a secondary (even unremarkable) aspect of their honor. For white women, however, chastity retained its paramount importance. Allegations of illicit sex thus reflect a consolidation of the gendered split in sexual mores among whites in the eighteenth century.[16]

This sexual double standard was mediated, however, by whites' growing fixation with race. With the spread of slavery in North Carolina, lawmakers wrote increasingly detailed statutes that adjudicated race relations and prohibited interracial interactions of all kinds, including sex and (more especially) marriage. Virginia first outlawed interracial marriages in 1691, and by 1715 the North Carolina legislature had followed suit, prohibiting the marriage of a white person to "any Negro, Mulatto or indyan Man or Woman." The prohibition of mixed-race marriages prevented whites from establishing legal families with non-Europeans and declared illegitimate all mixed-race children of white women, thereby safeguarding the transference of property from one generation of white males to the next. This legislation dovetailed with the remarkable stipulation (first passed in Virginia in 1662 and then adopted by other colonies) that a child's status as slave or free followed that of the mother. This extraordinary departure from English customs of patrilineage ensured that the children of slave women by white men would be slaves; the fertility of enslaved women became a means by which slaveowners increased their human property.[17]

The new legal categories of race took hold only gradually, and, despite the prohibition, some interracial couples still got married. In 1725, for example, John Cotton officiated at the marriage of Margaret MacCarty, a white woman, to Ed Burkitt, a free black man. That same year Martha Paul, a free black woman, and Thomas Spencer, a white man, married "according to ye form prescribed by ye Church of England." Some interracial unions never received official sanction but lasted a considerable time. In 1727, for example, "Severall persons" in Edenton knew that Elizabeth Puckett, a white woman, had "left her husband and hath for Some Years cohabited with a Negro Man of Capt. Simon Jeffries." People persevered in relationships that had been outlawed relatively recently, and the imposition of a racial order took place only haltingly.[18]

The development of a racial ideology hinged on much more than legal definitions of racial boundaries, and self-imposed rules also shaped the way European-Americans thought about racial categories. European immigrants drew on informal means of differentiating themselves from Africans, underscoring their racial identity as "white" in a number of ways. The violent abuse of slaves, for example, which coincided with the courts' growing disinclination to brand or mutilate European servants, was one way in which everyday practice reinforced ideas about racial difference. Slanderous speech was another. Slanderers who antagonized their victims with taunts of interracial sex, and plaintiffs who heatedly denied such allegations, negotiated their reputations by reinscribing the boundaries of race.[19]

Accusations of interracial sex implied that whites who had sexual relations with black partners were more debased than those who had illicit sex with other whites. This was especially the case in slander that targeted white women. In 1732, for example, William Symons publicly accused Mrs. Mary Low, a white Quaker, of being "a Negro whore" (i.e., a whore with Negro men), saying "that she was a proud Bitch with a Pack [of] Dogs after her." Four days later, his wrath unabated, Symons declared that Low "was a hore & Robert Davis['] Negro could not satisfie her & [Symons] Desired her not to send for his Negro Till she had wore out the said Davis['] Negro." Symons also announced that Thomas Stafford (the slanderer who would also torment Ann Hosey) "puled a Negro fellow . . . out of Bed from the said Mary." Low denied the accusations, pleaded chastity, and said she was "Extreemly hurt & Damnified in her good name."[20]

Symons's implication that Low craved sex with, but could not be satisfied by, numbers of black men was a stunning degradation that suggested Low had voracious, bestial sexual urges. By her antagonist's account, Low's insatiable lust made her a promiscuous, irrational being. The stereotype of animalistic black male virility—a familiar theme in later eras—was not yet the focus of this slander: according to Symons, it was the white woman, Mary Low, whose excessive sexuality led her to seek intercourse with numbers of black men, showcasing her sexual depravity, Symons implied, by the very fact that she freely chose and "sent for" black sexual partners.

Mary Willabe's slanderer went a step further. William Clerk, a white laborer, declared "openly and publickly" in September 1755 that Willabe, an unmarried woman, was "a whore and the widow Godwin[']s Negro-boy has kept her Company all this Summer, and fuck't her." Not only that, Clerk continued, "My Dog . . . us'd to go this Summer to Elizabeth Vise's, and fuck Mary Willabe and Loin her." The indiscriminate sexuality that Clerk ascribed to Willabe, who allegedly had intercourse all summer with both a black man and a dog, made her seem something less than human. At the same time, Clerk's slur degraded black men by making them literally interchangeable with dogs in the accusation that Willabe had intercourse with both. Clerk's slander created a sense of perversity about interracial sex by linking it with bestiality: a white woman who had sex with a black man, the defamation implied, was likely to have sex with dogs as well. In allegations that linked projections of female sexual depravity with notions of black inferiority, ideas about sex and race built on one another and fortified the understanding that both were grounded in a natural hierarchy.[21]

White women also initiated allegations of interracial sex, although the perversity they implied generally took a different twist. Katherine Jolley, for instance, spread the rumor in 1747 that both Ann the wife and Ann the daughter of planter Thomas Partree kept company with Jefferey, a free black man. By insinuating that Jefferey had intimate relations with both the mother and daughter of the Partree family, Jolley implied that generations of the Partree women were depraved.[22]

Mary Hall added infanticide to her charge of interracial sex. In 1760, Hall told Sarah Phips that Robert Gibbs was a rogue who had testified in a suit against Hall's husband "for a great deal of money when there was none due." When Sarah replied that Gibbs "did not look to be such a man for he seemed to be very civil and his wife too," Mary replied that Judith Gibbs "was as scandalous as him for she had a negro bastard" which, on her sea voyage from Virginia, "she threw over board." Exemplifying both the gendered split in slander and the concern with interracial sex, Hall accused Robert of financial wrongdoing and slandered his wife with an accusation of interracial sex that was compounded and (given the absence of such a child) made more plausible by the claim of infanticide.[23]

Some of the venom in these allegations against white women stemmed from the fact that mixed-race children born to a white woman were free. A white woman who had sex with a black man committed multiple transgressions: not only did she engage in illicit sex, but any child born of her liaison further blurred racial boundaries and increased the population of free African Americans. Allegations of interracial sex discredited a white woman by tapping into anxieties about the maintainance of "whiteness" at a time when racial boundaries remained porous in practice, if not in law.

Despite the larger concern about interracial sex, court magistrates tended to assume that white women who engaged in sexual relations with African-American men did so of their own volition. The result was that one white woman found herself pressed to sue a male slave for slander. In May 1756, a slave named Ned boasted that he had sex with Elizabeth Flinn, an unmarried white woman. Flinn complained to a magistrate that on a Saturday night Ned "Did *Attempt* to go to bed" with her and then "out of Spite And Malice in his heart having no forethought has Degraded and Scandalously told Lyes of one Elizabeth Flinn." For this breach of the peace, Ned was arrested and brought to court to explain himself.[24]

Ned's pronouncements may or may not have reflected what happened. Flinn may have voluntarily had sex with him and then felt dismayed by his public boasts. To defend herself, she denied the encounter and called him a liar. On the other hand, if Ned had sex with Flinn by force, she may have felt unwilling to sue for rape and chose instead to represent the incident as malicious fabrication. Finally, Ned may indeed have invented his exploits with Flinn, and his talk may have been slanderous fiction as she claimed.[25]

Regardless of what actually occurred, it is significant that in 1756 Ned could make these declarations without fearing for his life. In later eras, white men in North Carolina would not have tolerated such words, even about a lower-class white woman. But in the mid-eighteenth century, it was the white woman, Flinn, who was put on the defensive by Ned's scandalous pronounce-ments. In the colonial period, slander that alleged interracial sex still func-tioned primarily as an expression of hostility between whites, and not yet as a justification for violence against blacks. The use of sexual insinuation to malign and then murder African Americans would wait another century.[26]

Plaintiffs who sued against charges of interracial sex were more likely to be female, but, in a significant exception to the sexual double standard, a few white men also sued against the charge of having sex with a black woman. In 1745, Dr. Josiah Hart prosecuted planter George Leaden for his assertion that Hart "was no Doctor" because when William Burges hired Hart to "Cure his Negro Whench's Sore Eyes," the doctor "began at the wrong end." Hart had "knockt Mr Burges' Negro Whench," Leaden continued, and was therefore "Guilty of whoredom" with her. These accusations, Hart complained, had "hurt, Blacken'd & made loose" his "Name, fame, & Credit." As a result of this deleterious "Blackening" of his reputation, Hart had "lost the opportunity & advantage of advancing his fortune by Marriage, & also much of his Bussiness and his Practice." Although Hart may indeed have taken sexual advantage of the enslaved female patient, he was effectively scandalized by the accusation of "whoredom" with a black woman and sued to clear his name.[27]

In August 1749, an indentured servant named Richard Towers spread the news that he saw Samuel Overman, the eldest son of a wealthy slaveowning Quaker, "between the Thighs of Negro Hester a Negro woman belonging to Henry Dedon." With the same phrases women used in slander suits, Overman claimed that the vicious slander caused his wife to forsake his bed. The court found Towers not guilty in July 1751, and Overman continued the case at his own expense until April 1752, when he finally dropped charges and paid the accrued court costs.[28]

In 1763, Henry Horah, who owned a number of town lots and a tavern in Salisbury Town, sued Barnaby Bowen, a laborer, for saying "[You] are a Negro Fucker. I never fucked a negroe." In an era when men generally refrained from prosecuting for sexual slander, the fact that three male plaintiffs refuted charges of interracial sex suggests that in the mid-eighteenth century, allega-tions of sexual intimacy with a black woman—when spoken by another man—could cause significant damage. In these cases, the plaintiffs were established members in their community, and while Hart and Leaden were social peers, Overman and Horah sued men of lower status than their own. Allegations of sex with a black woman became a means of nettling established men in the community, but only if the black woman belonged to another man (not the plaintiff), in which case the sexual and racial transgression was tied to the infraction of another white man's property rights.[29]

These suits do not indicate whether the plaintiff really objected to or abstained from interracial sex. They do demonstrate that white men who could brag with impunity about having "knock't" a white woman, and whose prerogatives included sex with slave women, sometimes sued against charges of sex with a black partner. In other words, by the mid-eighteenth century, white men in North Carolina did not go to court to deny extramarital sex with a woman unless she was black. Although untold numbers of white men continued to have sex with black women, the charge of interracial sex could provoke a public denial in court. Courtroom refutations of interracial sex by white men were rare, yet such cases demonstrate that sex with a black person was becoming publicly inadmissible for whites of either sex.

There is another remarkable aspect about the sexual slander cases initiated by male plaintiffs. Three men, as we have seen, opposed charges of interracial sex. One plaintiff fought allegations of sex with other men, and four others denied accusations of sex with an animal. White men sued only against those allegations of sexual behavior thought to be particularly heinous or perverted, and interracial sex was included among those transgressions. For both white men and women, slanderous allegations of sex with a black person and sex with an animal evinced in nearly equal measure a white person's alleged sexual perversion and moral debasement. Sexual insults between whites thus reflected and elaborated on racist ideas about African-Americans' inferiority, even though whites remained the overt target of the slander.

In fact, a justification of racial slavery was in the making. An Enlightenment philosophy that announced equality in a state of nature had to explain inequality in social practice, and as ancient barriers to upward mobility crumbled, ideas about gender and race conveyed the message that some hierarchies were based on inherent and immutable differences. An ideology of race that explained slavery by referencing "nature" enabled whites to find the radical legal and social innovations of the seventeenth century incontrovertibly "normal" by the nineteenth.

In North Carolina, the grounding of race in biology occurred as the economy became increasingly dependent on the staple crops grown by enslaved laborers of African descent. While legislators ensured that slavery would be permanent and hereditary, writing laws that hardened the legal categories of race, European Americans conceptualized their own "whiteness" by emphasizing their perception of innate, biological distinctions between themselves and African Americans. This did not happen smoothly or all at once, nor did this form of racialist thought become hegemonic, but the "scientific" racism that would become fully developed in the nineteenth century did gain a foothold before the American revolution.

Sexual slander played its part in ascribing natural origins to race when it evoked the presumed unnaturalness of interracial sex. As we have seen, this "unnaturalness" was strongly informed by gender. Although white men could feel the sting of allegations of interracial sex, slanderers hurled the most denigrating rumors against white women. Defamation that described a white woman's sexual liaison with a black man as a crime against nature reinscribed both gender norms and racial difference, with one apparently natural category upholding the other. As we explore further the gendered dimensions of racialist thought, it would be valuable to know when and how sexual slander shifted its focus from the figure of the sexually depraved white women as a marker of racial difference to the image of oversexed black men and women—part of a larger shift in attention from whiteness to blackness that made the former invisible and normative and the latter deviant from the (white) norm.

We also need to know more about the connection between racial distinctions and other divisions based on the body. Ideas about the anatomical differences between men and women (the sexual organs themselves) underwent a significant transformation in the late seventeenth and eighteenth centuries. While a centuries-old one-sex model supposed that women carried inside their bodies essentially the same sexual organs that men had on the outside, a two-sex model developed in the eighteenth century that described women not as inverted men, but as the complementary, inherently different, and even "opposite" sex. Presumably, the idea of men and women as anatomical opposites did not grow independently of the conceptualization of race as a biological divide, and these links require much more investigation.[30]

Slander suits demonstrate how insulting allegations of illicit sex aided in the construction of racialist thought among European Americans. Slanderers who implied that interracial sex was disgusting and degrading as well as illegal, and plaintiffs whose heated disavowals of sex with a black person left intact the supposition that interracial sex was indeed abhorrent, propped up the perception of "natural" racial difference. The slurs that European Americans aimed at one another to express personal animosity and class tensions reflected their developing ideas about race and underscored their own racial identity as white. In the context of North Carolina's growing slave economy, sexual slurs bolstered the racism that accompanied the entrenchment of slavery and provide a window into the intertwined workings of racial, class, and gender hierarchies.

◄▷

Notes

I thank Nick Biddle, William Chafe, Laura Edwards, Sabine Engel, Christina Greene, Nancy Hewitt, Marjoleine Kars, Jane Kamensky, Jennifer Morgan, David Richardson, Peter Wood, and the editors of this volume for their superb comments on the various drafts of this essay. The research for this essay was funded in part by a dissertation grant from the National Endowment for the Humanities and a Research and Creative Scholarship Grant from the University of South Florida.

1. Europeans had for centuries depicted Africans and Native Americans as savages, noble or otherwise. But such images were "not yet racist in the nineteenth-century sense of the term because they were not based on an explicit doctrine of genetic or biological inequality." George M. Fredrickson, *White Supremacy: A Comparative Study in American and South African History* (New York and Oxford: Oxford University Press, 1981), 7. It was in the eighteenth century that the idea of biologically separate races really began to take hold. See Colette Guillaumin, "The Idea of Race and its Elevation to Autonomous Scientific and Legal Status" (1980), reprinted in Colette Guillaumin, *Racism, Sexism, Power and Ideology* (London and New York: Routledge, 1995); Barbara J. Fields, "Slavery, Race, and

Ideology in the United States of America," *New Left Review*, 181, May/June 1990, 95–118; and the recent historiographical overview in Peggy Pascoe, "Miscegenation Law, Court Cases, and Ideologies of "Race" in Twentieth-Century America," *Journal of American History*, 83:1, June 1996. Although historians generally agree that a new form of "scientific" racism became full blown in the nineteenth century, the debate over what came first, racism or slavery, remains controversial. Two historiographical essays that take different positions on this issue are Alden T. Vaughan, "The Origins Debate: Slavery and Racism in Seventeenth-Century Virginia," *Virginia Magazine of History and Biography*, 97, no. 3, July 1989, 311–54 and Theodore W. Allen, *The Invention of the White Race. Vol. 1: Racial Oppression and Social Control* (London and New York: Verso Press, 1994), 1–24. I understand racial categories as social contructs with very real political and socioeconomic effects. Although the terms "black" and "white" are problematic because they reinscribe the very categories whose construction I examine in this essay, I use these terms as convenient synonyms for African American and European American.

2. For gender analyses of colonial slander suits, see Peter N. Moogk, "'Thieving Buggers' and 'Stupid Sluts': Insults and Popular Culture in New France," *William and Mary Quarterly* 3rd series, 36, no. 4, October 1979, 524–47; Robert St. George, "'Heated' Speech and Literacy in Seventeenth-Century New England," in David D. Hall and David Grayson Allen, eds., *Seventeenth-Century New England*, (Colonial Society of Massachusetts, Collections, LXIII, Boston, 1984), 275–317; Mary Beth Norton, "Gender and Defamation in Seventeenth-Century Maryland," *William and Mary Quarterly* 3rd series, 44, January 1987, 3–39; Jane Neill Kamensky, "Governing the Tongue: Speech and Society in Early New England," Ph.D. diss., Yale University, 1993; Cornelia Hughes Dayton, *Women Before the Bar: Gender, Law, and Society in Connecticut, 1639–1789* (Chapel Hill: University of North Carolina Press, 1995), Chap. 6.

3. Letter from Colonel E. Jenings, President of the Virginia Council, to the Lords of Trade, November 27, 1708, in William L. Saunders, ed., *Colonial Records of North Carolina*, 10 vols. (Raleigh: State of North Carolina, 1886–1890), v. 1, 692. Peter H. Wood, "The Changing Population of the Colonial South: An Overview by Race and Region, 1685–1790," in Peter H. Wood, Gregory A. Waselkov, and M. Thomas Hatley, eds., *Powhatan's Mantle: Indians in the Colonial Southeast* (Lincoln: University of Nebraska Press, 1989), 38.

4. A. Roger Ekirch, *"Poor Carolina": Politics and Society in Colonial North Carolina, 1729–1776* (Chapel Hill: University of North Carolina Press, 1981) Chap. 2.

5. Wood, "The Changing Population of the Colonial South," 38.

6. On the history of slander litigation in England, see J. A. Sharpe, *Defamation and Sexual Slander in Early Modern England: The Church Courts at York* (York: University of York, Borthwick Papers, No. 58, 1980); Martin Ingram, *Church Courts, Sex and Marriage in England, 1570–1640* (Cambridge: Cambridge University Press, 1987), Chap. 10.

7. *Morris v. Hill*, Declaration of Thomas Morris, October Court, 1744, Chowan Civil Action Papers, located in the North Carolina State Archives, Division of Archives and History, Raleigh, North Carolina, hereinafter cited as NCSA. On the terms "thief" and "rogue," see St. George, "'Heated' Speech and Literacy," 295–97.

8. *Hunt and wife v. Moline*, General Court, November 1694, Mattie Erma Edwards

Parker, ed., *North Carolina Higher-Court Minutes, 1670–1969*, vol. 2 of *The Colonial Records of North Carolina* [Second Series], ed. Mattie Erma Edwards Parker et al. (Raleigh: Division of Archives and History, 1963–), 210, 223–24. Moline had to pay fifty shillings and twenty shillings, respectively, for his insults against the husband and wife. For reasons of space, this essay focuses on the sexual insults themselves and not on the disposition of the cases, but, where possible, I have noted the outcome of the suits in the notes.

9. Arrest warrant for Thomas Gidings, May 15, 1755, Hyde County Civil and Criminal Action Papers. On racial prejudice against the Irish, see Allen, *The Invention of the White Race*. White women occasionally sued for being called liars or thieves, but the majority of female plaintiffs in slander suits sued for sexual defamation. On the divergence of insults brought to court by male and female plaintiffs, see Dayton, *Women Before the Bar*, Chap. 6; Norton, "Gender and Defamation in Seventeenth-Century Maryland." While lawsuits for slander made up only a tiny percentage of the overall caseload for North Carolina's colonial courts, they shed light on the dynamics of gender, race, and class in the colony.

10. *Hacket v. Nichols*, Declaration of Sarah Hacket, October Court, 1744, Chowan County Civil Action Papers, NCSA. Nichols pleaded not guilty and the case was continued until Hacket dropped the charges in July Court, 1745.

11. *Sarah White v. Samuel Commander*, June Court, 1755, Pasquotank County Civil Action Papers, NCSA. Commander pleaded not guilty and White dropped her suit in September. *Tamer Jones v. Joseph Ferrill*, October Court, 1754, Pasquotank County Civil Action Papers, NCSA. Jones won her case by default when Ferrill did not appear in court. *Swindal v. Beaker*, Arrest warrant for William Beaker, December 3, 1746, Hyde County Civil & Criminal Action Papers, NCSA. Arrest warrant for Abell Bordine, Hyde County Civil and Criminal Action Papers, July 23, 1750, NCSA. The case against Bordine was discontinued in June 1751. *E. Riding v. William Collins*, Declaration of Elizabeth Riding, Edenton District Superior Court, November 1763, NCSA. The suit was abated in May 1764 after William Collins died.

12. Single and married women sued in roughly equal numbers: of the thirty-one slandered women in this study, fifteen were married, thirteen were single, and three were widows. Married women sued male and female defendants in roughly equal numbers, while all the unwed female plaintiffs brought slander suits only against men.

13. *William Ward and Elizabeth v. Edward Whorton*, July Court, 1744, Pasquotank County Civil Action Papers, NCSA.

14. *Sir Richard Everard v. Trotter*, General Court, March 1729, in Robert J. Cain, ed., *North Carolina Higher-Court Minutes, 1724–1730*, vol. 6 of *The Colonial Records of North Carolina* [Second Series], Mattie Erma Edwards Parker et al., ed.s (Raleigh: Division of Archives and History, 1963–), 555–56. James Trotter pleaded not quilty on behalf of his wife and was acquitted by the grand jury. Arrest warrant for Jolley, August 31, 1749, Hyde County Bastardy Papers, NCSA. Katherine Jolley was fined fifteen shillings.

15. *Hosey v. Stafford*, Arrest warrant for Stafford, July 21, 1735, Perquimans County Civil Action Papers, NCSA.

16. *Hepsebeth Minshew v. Robert Hill*, Declaration of Hepsebeth Minshew, [month torn] 1750, Chowan County Civil Action Papers, NCSA. Hill was found guilty

in October 1750. *Garrett v. Trottman*, Declaration of Mary Garrett, Edenton District Superior Court, November 1763, NCSA. Garrett's case against Trottman was discontinued in that same court session.

17. This legislation meant that courts overlooked white men's liaisons with black women, while white women who had children by a black man were prosecuted for bastardy. Walter Clark, ed., *Laws of North Carolina*, vol. XXIII of Walter Clark, ed., *The State Records of North Carolina*, 16 vols. numbered XI–XXVI (Winston and Goldsboro: State of North Carolina, 1895–1906), 65. For laws about interracial sex in colonial Virginia, see A. Leon Higginbotham and Barbara K. Kopytoff, "Racial Purity and Interracial Sex in the Law of Colonial and Antebellum Virginia," *The Georgetown Law Journal*, 77, 6, August 1989, 1967–2029; Kathleen M. Brown, *Good Wives, "Nasty Wenches," and Anxious Patriarchs: Gender, Race, and Power in Colonial Virginia* (Chapel Hill: University of North Carolina Press, 1996). An overview of anti-miscegenation laws in the later periods is in Pascoe, "Miscegenation Law, Court Cases, and Ideologies of Race in Twentieth-Century America."

18. *Crown v. John Cotton*, July Court, 1725, General Court Criminal Papers, NCSA. Information made by John Blacknall, March 2, 1725, General Court Miscellaneous Papers, NCSA. Jury's presentment against Elizabeth Puckett, July Court, 1725, in Cain, ed., *Higher-Court Records*, vol. 6, 425. For other examples of sexual relations between whites and blacks in the colonies, see James Hugo Johnston, *Race Relations in Virginia and Miscegenation in the South, 1776–1869* (1937; reprint, Amherst: University of Massachusetts Press, 1970), chap. 7.

19. I discuss the role of violence in shaping white racism in "Embodiments of Power: Slavery and Sexualized Violence in Colonial North Carolina," Paper presented at the Tenth Berkshire Conference on the History of Women, University of North Carolina, Chapel Hill, June 7–9, 1996.

20. *Mary Low v. William Symons*, July Court, 1732, Pasquotank County Civil Action Papers, NCSA.

21. *Mary Willabe v. William Clerk*, October Court, 1755, Bertie County Civil Action Papers, NCSA. On the significance of gender in justifying other social hierarchies in Europe, see Joan Wallach Scott, *Gender and the Politics of History* (New York: Columbia University Press, 1988).

22. Arrest warrant for Jolley, June 15, 1747, Hyde County Civil and Criminal Papers, NCSA.

23. *Robert Gibbs and wife v. James Hall and wife*, September Court, 1760, Hyde County Civil and Criminal Papers, NCSA. Mary Hall was fined £6 proclamation money plus court costs. Six white women sued for accusations of interracial sex, and two more were accused of being themselves a "mulatto whore."

24. *Crown v. Davis's Ned*, Arrest warrant for Ned, May 22, 1756, Hyde County Civil & Criminal Action Papers, NCSA (my emphasis).

25. For the period between 1663 and 1777 I have found twelve charges of rape brought against slaves in North Carolina, only two of which occurred before 1765. Each of the black defendants was immediately convicted and sentenced to death. If Ned raped Elizabeth Flinn, she could have concealed it behind a charge of slander either to protect her reputation or save him from execution.

26. Nineteenth-century historians have argued that the myth of the black rapist was invented only during and after the Civil War. See Angela Davis, "Rape, Racism and the Myth of the Black Rapist," in *Women, Race & Class* (New York: Vintage Books, 1983), 183–89; Victoria E. Bynum, *Unruly Women: The Politics of Social &*

Sexual Control in the Old South (Chapel Hill: University of North Carolina Press, 1992); Laura F. Edwards, "Sexual Violence, Gender, Reconstruction, and the Extension of Patriarchy in Granville County, North Carolina," *The North Carolina Historical Review* 68, no. 3, July 1991, 237–60; Diane Miller Sommerville, "The Rape Myth in the Old South Reconsidered," *Journal of Southern History* 61:3, August 1995, 481–518.

27. *Hart v. Leaden*, October Court, 1745, Perquimans County Civil Action Papers, NCSA.

28. *Overman v. Towers*, April Court, 1751, Pasquotank County Civil Action Papers, NCSA. Weynette Parks Haun, *Pasquotank County North Carolina County Court Minutes (Court of Pleas & Quarter Sessions), 1747–1753, Book II* (Durham: the author, 1990), 63, 73, 78, 80, 87, 92.

29. *Horah v. Bowers*, Salisbury District Superior Court Civil Action Papers, March Term, 1763, NCSA. The case against Bowers was abated in 1764 when he died. I thank Marjoleine Kars for bringing this case to my attention.

30. On the history of one-sex and two-sex anatomical models, see Thomas Laqueur, *Making Sex: Body and Gender from the Greeks to Freud* (Cambridge: Harvard University Press, 1990). Laqueur makes the tantalizing suggestion that "scientific race . . . developed at the same time and in response to the same sorts of pressures as scientific sex." Ibid., 155.

INTERRACIAL SECTS

Religion, Race, and Gender Among Early North Carolina Moravians

Anna Maria Samuel, an African-American girl from Bethabara, North Carolina, was a bundle of anomalies. Eleven years old in 1793, she was a member of the Moravian Church, a religious fellowship that considered her one of God's elect and the spiritual equal of any white person, though the church itself owned her as a slave. Raised by English-speaking parents, she was also adroit in speaking, reading, and writing German, the native tongue of the Moravian immigrants. And in a time and region not noted for the respect given black females, Anna Maria was immersed in a church culture that exalted female spirituality and rigorously protected—even policed—white and black women's persons and sexuality.

Biographical information about African-American women and girls in the eighteenth-century South is hard to find, but the Moravian Church left a biography of Anna Maria, in German, that gives rare clues to her life inside this unusual fellowship. Her parents were Johann and Maria Samuel, the first black Moravian couple in the South. Born and baptized on Christmas Eve, 1781, Anna Maria "enjoyed as a child the care and instruction of her parents, as well as school lessons in our congregation. During her growing years one noticed a special inclination by her to sing; she diligently applied herself to learning verses and gladly attended the children's services and congregational meetings." Anna Maria flourished in this atmosphere of worship, school, and classical Moravian music, and her life's early trajectory pointed toward an identity in Christ. "She expressed so frequently her desire to be taken in the congregation . . . to live in the world only for Him alone, and to partake of the forgiveness and purification of her sins through Him, whereby she could grow and prosper in His love."[1]

The day she had long anticipated finally arrived—June 14, 1793, her entry into the Single Sisters' House, a communal dormitory in the central Moravian town of Salem where adolescent girls and single women lived. "At ten o'clock was the reception of two children, Elis. Stockburger and black Anna Maria.... After that they were seen in classes, then followed the festival homily. [During] the congregation hour, they were warmly blessed by the congregation." Anna Maria henceforth filled her days with a full routine of prayer meetings, lovefeasts, festivals, house conferences, school, and chores that made up life in the Sisters' House. With her companions in the house now a surrogate family, she was a Moravian Sister—and all the while a slave.[2]

Because of her absorption into this Germanic culture, Anna Maria Samuel's life was highly unusual. But, in another sense, it dramatizes some of the complexities creeping into southern life on a broader scale in the late eighteenth century. Anna Maria was only one of a growing multitude of African Americans to embrace Christianity during the Revolutionary period and in the early years of the new republic. Drawn by a message of universal salvation and freedom—spiritual if not temporal—thousands found acceptance in evangelical Protestant churches, most notably the Baptists and Methodists, and including the Moravians. Black Christians created diverse faiths that provided powerful religious and political sustenance in their struggle to survive slavery and racial discrimination. At the same time, evangelical communities across the South were nurseries of an emerging biracial religious culture based on spiritual egalitarianism. Black and white Christians tested the meaning of spiritual and worldly freedom in their relationships to each other and to the larger slave society. Along with a natural rights philosophy, the religion of the revivals contributed much to a new fluidity and openness of racial boundaries held ironclad for generations by slaveholding ideology.[3]

Yet we still know little about how black and white Christian worshipers viewed themselves and each other as men and women. As much as with beliefs about race and racial slavery, the Revolutionary age also saw a new flexibility in gender relations and a concerted effort by many women to claim a greater share of republican liberties. Evangelical churches proved highly attractive to women, black and white, as vehicles of spirituality, organization, and even leadership. But how did all these factors collide in a religious culture that seemed so welcoming to so many? What happened in a region where social relations among black and white southerners were prescribed not only by whether one was slave or free, male or female, but now also Christian or non-Christian?[4]

Although not widely recognized for its role in southern history, the Moravian Church has long been considered an extraordinarily important force in eighteenth-century European religious and cultural history. The church traced its roots to an early Protestant sect from Bohemia and Moravia in central Europe, the *Unitas Fratrum*, or Unity of Brethren, the followers of reformer Jan Hus, who was martyred by the Catholic Church in 1415. During subsequent centuries of religious strife, the Unity was driven underground until a small group of refugees found sanctuary in 1722 on the estate of Count Nikolaus Ludwig von Zinzendorf in nearby Saxony. Intrigued by the settlers' legacy of a simple, heartfelt faith that appealed to his own brand of Lutheran pietism, the count decided to revive the dormant sect in 1727 as the Renewed Unity of Brethren. From these humble beginnings the Unity, under Zinzendorf's dynamic leadership, would emerge as one of the most influential of all the Pietist groups and would be known by the 1730s in the English-speaking world as the Moravian Church because of its central European heritage. The Moravian Brethren's emotional rather than formalist approach to religion strongly influenced John Wesley, George Whitefield, and other important figures of the transatlantic evangelical awakening.[5]

Africans' connection with the Moravians began in the 1730s when church missionaries began preaching to slaves in the Danish West Indian islands of St. Thomas, St. Croix, and St. John. Like many Europeans, the Moravians believed slavery was ordained by God, and they regarded Africans as a socially inferior race. Unlike many Protestants, however, they believed that Christian salvation should be open to all people regardless of racial identity or worldly status, and evangelical work among the world's non-Christians was central to their self-perception as the messengers of divine redemption. By the mid-eighteenth century, missionaries attracted thousands of African converts throughout the Caribbean world.[6]

European Moravians also built settlements in North America as religious refuges and missionary bases for Native Americans. Brethren founded the communal town of Bethlehem, Pennsylvania, in 1741, and another Moravian outpost was begun on a 100,000-acre trace of land in west central North Carolina called Wachovia. The first town built there in 1753, Bethabara, was followed by a cluster of other towns and farming communities, including Salem, a so-called congregation town that became the religious, administrative, and economic center of the Moravian settlement.[7]

Because church elders feared that overreliance on slave labor would breed laziness in whites and eventually replace white workers, they generally forbade Brethren in congregation towns from owning slaves privately. Instead, the Moravian Church itself bought and owned slaves, leasing them to tradesmen or proprietors of church-operated businesses who needed workers. On less-regulated farms in the Moravian countryside, church members were given greater latitude to own slaves. Collectively and individually, Moravian slaveholding increased steadily from about twenty-five workers in 1780 to about seventy in 1800, and about 300 by 1830. African and African-American men worked on farms and in tanneries, breweries, and potteries, while women served primarily as domestics in taverns and occasionally in private homes.[8]

Some of these workers, including a number of recently arrived captives from Africa, sought admission into the Moravian Church, probably for a combination of reasons. Some, responding to the promise of universal redemption preached by the Brethren, no doubt experienced the genuine spiritual rebirth required of all converts and found the church a welcome place of worship. Others may have been intrigued by the possibility of using religious fellowship to gain protection. Many must have reasoned that because they were held as slaves in the tightly knit, exclusive Moravian communities, conversion would be more likely to win them acceptance as congregational insiders and participants in the Christian drama. The number of black Moravians was small—a dozen by 1790, several dozen by the early nineteenth century. It is difficult to know how much of an African world view these converts retained or how fully they embraced Christian concepts of sin and salvation. What is certain, however, is that their presence made the Moravian community a racially integrated Christian family. From white Brethren's perspective, black spiritual inclusion in the fellowship was in no way intended to topple worldly order. Ministers stressed that secular slavery was of relatively minor importance in any case since all the redeemed—black and white alike—were servants of a higher master, Christ.

African-American women were drawn with particular irony into the complex moral realm of Moravian congregationalism because of the status of Moravian women. The Brethren accorded women a high plane in spiritual and social life, largely because of Count Zinzendorf's insistence that men and women were spiritually equal in the eyes of God. Moravian piety was spoken of in strongly feminized terms, such as the Holy Spirit's characterization as "Mother." The church drew strong parallels between feminine virtue and the ideal of an emotional relationship with Christ, and consequently elevated the place of women as spiritual nurturers of God's elect people.

Although that principle did not necessarily mean that the sexes shared power equally in Moravian communities, Moravian society offered women critical avenues of responsibility and support. While men occupied most of the prominent administrative posts, talented women could aspire to some leadership role in Moravian theocratic structure. Women were appointed Eldresses and Acoluths (a pastor's assistant), served on important decision-making boards, and for a time were even ordained as priests. Believing that education should be open to both sexes, the Brethren sent boys and girls to separate schools. And while individual will was generally subordinated to the perceived good of the community, women were not helplessly subject to the dictates of church authorities. Decisions regarding marriage, housing, and economic status were made by the boards in consultation with women, who could ratify or deny such arrangements.[9]

Perhaps most important, a unique feature of Moravian life called the choir system guaranteed women access to important levers of power, protection, and self-expression. Moravian congregations were divided into "choirs," which were not conventional choirs as we know them—though they did sing—but rather groups composed according to affinities of age, gender, and marital status. All married women belonged to one choir, all married men to another. The elaborate breakdown also included choirs for single women, single men, girls, boys, older girls, older boys, infants, widows, and widowers—a total of eleven choirs. Each choir sat and worshiped together in church and held separate daily study and prayer sessions.[10]

Like a church within a church, the choir system provided women a vital forum for religious development. Women taught, counseled, supported, and reprimanded each other on the path to higher knowledge. Female choir lead-ers held regular interviews called *Sprechen* ("Speakings") with their charges to determine their spiritual condition and offer advice. They rigorously enforced choir rules while reining in signs of deviation from the Unity's moral codes. Though not entirely independent of male oversight—since choir leaders worked closely with ministers in supervising members—women lived and worshiped largely in a world of their own devising.

The ability to create several distinctive sisterhoods within the Moravian fellowship reached its most potent expression in the Single Sisters' House in Salem. Of all the choirs, only the Single Brothers, Single Sisters, and Widows lived in their own accommodations, the first two groups in large complexes on opposite sides of the town's central square (nuclear family units lived together but worshiped separately). Separate housing was designed to keep single con-gregants well apart; fearing the evils of temptation, church elders never allowed them even to meet or speak unsupervised. Within the enclave of the Sisters' House, several dozen single girls and women shared dormitory-style sleeping arrangements, meals, work, and prayers. Single women earned money as housekeepers, teachers, nurses, midwives, laundry workers, and many kinds of artisans.[11]

Black Sisters entered the intricate web of social relations afforded by Moravian congregational life and the choir system as thoroughly as any white woman. Regarded fully as Moravian Sisters, black women were assigned to appropriate choirs and worshiped in the heavily ritualized cycle of prayer meetings, communions, lovefeasts, and festivals that comprised the Moravian liturgy. Moravian women from Africa sat on church benches with Moravian women from Saxony and Wuerttemberg. Moravian Bishop August Spangen-berg described the extent to which enslaved church members were enmeshed in congregational life: "Because of our love to them we do not free them, for they would be in a worse condition if they got free as if we kept them. Actually they are not slaves with us, and there is no difference between them and other brothers and sisters. They dress as we do, they eat what we eat, they work when we work, they rest when we rest, and they enjoy quite naturally what other brothers and sisters enjoy." Even if allowances are made for the idyllic tone of the Bishop's claim, life probably was far less severe for black Sisters and Brothers than for the great majority of enslaved African Americans elsewhere. Because of their thorough incorporation into this society, black Moravian women adopted German ways to a degree unmatched in eighteenth- and early nineteenth-century America. They spoke and sang in the German language. They wore distinctive Moravian clothing, particularly the women's *Haube*, or cap. When they died, many black Moravian women were buried side-by-side with white Sisters.[12]

One of the first black female converts to the church in North Carolina, for example, was an African-born woman called Patty, a domestic worker in the Salem Tavern whom the Brethren bought in 1781. By the following year, the church Elders noted that Patty "has asked repeatedly about baptism." They arranged for her mistress in the tavern, Catherina Meyer, to give Patty lessons in Christianity. By July 1783, the Elders described her as still "very troubled about Holy Baptism and has urgently requested it. The necessary instruction in the redeeming truths and in Holy Baptism will be imparted to her before-hand by Brother Fritz in the English language, which she understands best." Three weeks later Patty was baptized and christened Anna. Having consented to an arranged marriage with another African-born convert named Christian, she now joined the Married Women's choir. In 1784, a Moravian diarist reported: "One hundred and twenty partook of the Holy Communion. The Negress Anna partook for the first time, after receiving the Confirmation blessing."[13] Sister Anna, like other black Moravians, was now one of the cho-sen, free in Christ's ransom, though white Brethren left no doubt what kind of liberty that was. As one enslaved convert, Jacob, was told in unmistakable terms, baptism "does not mean he becomes free and the equal of his master."[14]

Within this limited view of freedom, the Moravian choir system fostered, or was intended to foster, a common gender identity across racial lines. Women who prayed, studied, worked, and lived together would, at least in theory, see each other not as black or white but as women sharing and living in the salvation of Christ's martyrdom. It is difficult to know if practice always matched rhetoric. Surviving information tells us little, for example, about whether young Anna Maria was treated exactly as any other adolescent in the Single Sisters' House, or whether she was ever regarded as a second-class Sister. In all likelihood she partook of meals, slept in the dormitory, and wor-shiped in the prayer hall on something like an equal footing with her white companions. If so, the legal and social boundaries between slavery and free-dom may well have blurred in the self-contained daily commotion of the Sisters' world.

The church sought to instill further sense of spiritual camaraderie through the use of baptismal sponsors or godparents. Any child or adult baptized into the Unity was appointed up to five sponsors who would assume a kind of fictive kinship, reinforcing the convert's sense of being assimilated into a new family while helping to supervise the spiritual progress of the inductee. Adult converts were always assigned godparents of the same sex, usually fel-low choir members or Elders' Conference officials. The white godparents of early female African and African-American converts represented one more cross-racial affective link between the slave and her new spiritual kin. Anna's baptism, for example, was sponsored by the female Elders and Sister Meyer, her mistress in the tavern. Whether the ideal of spiritual mentorship worked in reality is another matter. One wonders how much sense of spiritual kinship African-American women felt with others who regarded their blackness as a mark of sin and a justification for their enslavement. Yet the practice of senior community leaders sponsoring or guiding initiates into a community of faith by separate gender lines was also well known among West African cultures, and different forms of that concept, such as Moravian baptismal sponsorship, were at least familiar to captive Africans in the Americas. Black Moravian con-verts might well have transferred their notions of initiation and mentorship to their new spiritual family, accepting the assistance of white godparents to ease their entry into the congregation.[15]

Congregational life afforded black Moravian women further sources of physical and social protection. At a time when slave marriages had no legal standing and masters across the South often separated families through sale, the Moravian Church sought to cultivate stable families among enslaved Brethren. This attitude showed a mix of piety and pragmatism. In the church's view, black families should have equal access to marriage, a sanctified institution reflecting a state of Christian grace. Families, as other slaveholders were discovering, also played a crucial role in social control by rooting bondspeople at home and undercutting the desire to run away. Though not legally recognized, slave marriages gained a certain sanction in the Moravian Church and other evangelical churches—an obvious incentive for African-American conversion.[16]

The church had a direct hand in negotiating marriages for white and black members alike through a complex process involving the wishes of the prospective partners, the church's interest, and the will of the Lord as determined by the lot. Congregants were permitted to marry only within the church; those who dared to marry "strangers," or non-Moravians, were swiftly expelled. A single man who wished to marry approached the Elders and proposed a match (the Elders themselves could also propose matches). If they deemed the proposal suitable, they put it to the Sister in question. If she agreed, the Elders sought final approval from the lot, and, if an affirmative answer was drawn, the couple were clear to marry. The process could break down if the Elders found the proposed match unsuitable, if the woman declined the offer, or if the lot came up negative. The intricate procedure guaranteed individuals a say in their matrimony, although women were not allowed to initiate the marriage proposal.[17]

Black church members who wished to marry, or who the Elders thought should marry, proceeded through this same elaborate series of steps. After deciding in 1780 that Brother Johann Samuel of the Bethabara congregation needed a family, for example, the Elders went to work to find him a wife. "The only baptized Negro woman here is Maria, who works in the Tavern. Thus there is no need to ask the lot about it, but rather to proceed," they decided. Samuel readily agreed to the match, and four days later the Elders reported: "Maria has willingly accepted the marriage offer. The marriage will take place Saturday in Bethabara." Johann and Maria were the first Afro-Moravian couple in North Carolina; their daughter Anna Maria was born the next year. Many other black Moravians took the same route to marriage and family life.[18]

Thus, the system of choosing or being matched to a spouse was both restrictive and empowering for enslaved Moravians. They surrendered a degree of control over family decisions to the church. Their choice of prospective partners was limited to other church members. Since single people had little or no chance to court under the watchful gaze of the Elders, marriages based on love must have been rare. On the other hand, like white Brethren they retained a voice in determining their partners. Men could take an active hand in pursuing a wife, while women theoretically could veto a match, though no black Sister is known to have done so.

Black Moravians gained assurance their marriages and families would remain intact—they were virtually guaranteed that they and their children would not be sold as long as they remained in good standing in the church. In the Moravian countryside where landowners had greater leeway to own slaves, the church pressured masters not to sell baptized slave children. One church board ruled in 1781 that when members "request to have children of their still-heathen negroes baptized, it can occur on condition that masters be bound on their conscience to raise them for the Lord, and not to sell them for Profits to outside people." The policy proved a strong lure for slave parents to have their children baptized, and this comparatively high degree of stability was no small consideration in a perilous world.[19]

Church moral codes provided an equally important defense for black women. The Moravian religious culture that so rigorously policed the conduct of its adherents and frowned on unsanctioned sexuality would have severely punished any white Brother who forced himself on a black woman, as so many slave masters did elsewhere. Victims could have reported such crimes to the Elders and appealed for justice. Black Moravian women thus lived in relative security against the sexual exploitation by whites that differentiated women's experiences from men's in slavery.[20]

Black women could also turn to ministers or church boards for intervention if they were mistreated or overworked. Anna (who was also called Nancy) appealed to the Elders for help in 1796 while working at the Bethabara tavern. "In Bethabara yesterday evening the Negress Nancy left the Steiners and came here," they reported. "Brother Hessler will talk to her and assure her that she should go back to her workplace without fear of further consequences." Such safety valves could be particularly meaningful to African-American women, who were so vulnerable to unchecked abuses under slavery. The Moravian Church sponsored and protected black Sisters even as it enslaved them. In the exclusive Moravian world where sacred and secular were so entwined, fellowship provided a code of ethics that regulated black women's relations with white women, black men and white men. Their membership in the Unity entailed an ambiguous combination of forced labor, personal safeguards, exaltation of their femininity and spirituality, and limitations on mobility and initiative.[21]

In the late eighteenth century, a fragile and flawed age of interracial fellowship seemed to guarantee black women an increased measure of respect within the Moravian Church. At the end of the century, however, their position began to erode as white Brethren rethought their ideal of including blacks in their brotherhood and sisterhood of the spirit. Throughout the post-Revolutionary South, slave restlessness often flared into overt resistance and rebellion. It now appeared to white Moravians, who were increasingly committed to slavery, that allowing blacks and whites to worship together would foster dangerous egalitarian notions among blacks. Other southern white Protestants, including many Baptists and Methodists, began reaching the same conclusions as antislavery voices previously fired by evangelical zeal waned. Besides the social implications of interracial fellowship, some white Moravians, attuning themselves to rising anti-black sentiment throughout the new republic, now disdained the black Brothers and Sisters who shared their benches. As early as 1792, a church council admonished white Brethren: "We must not be ashamed of those Negroes who belong to our community and, as has happened before, let them sit all by themselves in congregational worship and even during Holy Communion. They are our Brothers and Sisters and different treatment of them will degrade ourselves to the rank of ordinary people and will be a disgrace for the Community." Thus, when Anna Maria Samuel entered the Single Sisters' House in 1793, some congregants were questioning whether she even belonged there, though church elders insisted she did.[22]

These early refrains of resentment against blacks occurred as the Moravian Church was also turning more conservative toward women. Count Zinzendorf had shaped the Renewed Unity's views on women during its first three decades, but after his death in 1760 his successors pulled back from some of his most radical positions, instead reasserting conventional Pauline wisdom on the subordination of women to men. Women were gradually displaced from positions in the top echelon of Unity leadership and were no longer ordained as priests. This philosophical retrenchment worked its way into congregational life. Women still retained the ability to shape their own religious and social world within the choir structure, but they were gradually stripped of power in local church councils, and Moravian spirituality in general was no longer described in such glowingly feminized terms.[23]

A dramatic incident at the end of the eighteenth century suggests how the changes at work among North Carolina Moravians may have overlapped, and just how cataclysmic they were. In the Moravian farming community of Friedberg in 1797, a slave girl had been studying the Gospel with a minister in preparation for joining the church. She asked to attend a meeting of the Single Sisters and the minister agreed. Word of the plan leaked to the congregation, however, and on the appointed day, as the girl walked into the prayer hall, the Sisters stood up and stalked out in defiance. Amounting to a strike, the protest was extraordinary both as an act of organized disobedience and an expression of anti-black vehemence in a fellowship that prided itself on Christian meekness and universal inclusiveness. Elders quickly reprimanded the protesters that "not the slightest distinction between whites and blacks can be made in matters of the spirit." But any notions of gender solidarity that might have applied just a few years earlier had vanished. White Moravians now found in the negation of blacks a perfect foil to redefine their identities and declare themselves to be Germans no longer, but Americans. In the same way, as their own power in the church eroded, perhaps white Moravian women were proclaiming a newfound sense of racialized gender identity by rejecting black women, whose status as black Christians and as women was rapidly slipping.[24]

This growing sense of spiritual and social distance betweeen black and white Sisters found further expression in the baptismal sponsorships that once served to bind them. Increasingly, black women and men sponsored the baptism of other black adult converts and children. Whether this shift occurred by church design or by mutual preference among black and white congregants is not known. But by the early nineteenth century, a web of African-American godparents provided the focal points for an emerging sense of extended kinship and distinctive Afro-Moravian identity within the large Moravian church family. The emergence of such race-specific networks signaled the breakdown of cross-racial spiritual connections that had been based largely on gender. More and more, white and black women went their separate ways.

Gradually, white Brethren erected more psychological barriers between themselves and blacks. They mandated segregated burials and restricted black participation in certain rituals. No more black single men or women entered the Salem choir houses. Finally, African Americans were excluded altogether from predominantly white congregations and from the choir system in 1822, when a separate black congregation was founded. Black women now devoted their energies and organizational talents to the life of the new church, participating in worship, serving as godparents, and helping educate children. By the time of her death in 1829, the oldest communicant member, Anna, had witnessed a revolution in social relations during nearly half a century in the Moravian Church.[25]

The Moravian Church's exclusive congregational structure, choir system, complex blend of attitudes on race, gender, and power, and melding of people from central Europe, Africa, and America produced a culture unlike any other in the early South. Yet the Moravian experience also suggests ways of probing powerful social dynamics in scores of other evangelical communities that dotted the South by the late eighteenth century. In opening doors to people long shut out of power, the religion of the awakenings altered definitions of inclusion and exclusion in the social order. The ideology of spiritual freedom in the family of Christ challenged traditional assumptions that governed how the awakened, white and black, slave and free, male and female, would regard each other. Further study will reveal comparative regional and denominational differences in how these changes played out.

But if the Moravian case was exemplary of larger social currents, then for a time black women were forming ties of spiritual kinship with white women; they were sheltered under the umbrella of the Gospel from the depredations of white masters; and white people hailed their spirituality as equal to their own. That social experiment was both inspiring and threatening, and in time it collapsed under the weight of counter pressure from white men intent on reasserting themselves at the head of a paternalist order above white women and black men and women.[26] White women, it appears, also came to resent the threat of spiritual parity with black women at the expense of their own social and religious stature. With fragile alliances crumbling, the South was launched on a frightening new day of resurrected racial and gender barriers.

◄▷

Notes

The author thanks Kathy Brown and the editors for comments on several versions of this essay, as well as the Moravian Church Archives, Southern Province, for permission to use material from its collections.

1. Anna Maria Samuel's biography, or *Lebenslauf* (literally, "life course") is con-

tained in the Bethabara Church Book, February 13, 1798, trans. author. The *Lebenslauf* was a genre of writing, usually autobiographical, used in the Moravian Church. Each church member left an account describing his or her worldly life and spiritual strivings. Dozens of such life stories about black Moravians survive, though written in biographical form by ministers. All primary documentation for this essay is held in the Moravian Church Archives, Southern Province, Winston-Salem, North Carolina.

2. Single Sisters' Diary, June 4, 1793 (trans. Elizabeth Marx). Anna Maria lived with the Sisters until she was emancipated with her mother in 1795. She moved back to Bethabara and died in 1798.

3. On the outgrowth of Afro-Christianity from biracial evangelical churches, see Albert Raboteau, *Slave Religion: The "Invisible Institution" in the Antebellum South* (New York: Oxford University Press, 1978); Mechal Sobel, *Trabelin' On: The Slave Journey to an Afro-Baptist Faith*, 2nd ed. (Princeton, N.J.: Princeton University Press, 1988); John B. Boles, ed., *Masters and Slaves in the House of the Lord: Race and Religion in the American South, 1740–1870* (Lexington: University Press of Kentucky, 1988); and Sylvia R. Frey, "Shaking the Dry Bones: The Dialectic of Conversion," in Ted Ownby, ed., *Black and White: Cultural Interaction in the Antebellum South* (Jackson: University Press of Mississippi, 1993), 23–44. The flexibility of racial perceptions in the Revolutionary age is discussed in Winthrop Jordan, *White over Black: American Attitudes Toward the Negro, 1550–1812* (Chapel Hill: University of North Carolina Press, 1968); Mechal Sobel, *The World they Made Together: Black and White Values in Eighteenth-Century Virginia* (Princeton, N.J.: Princeton University Press, 1988); and Sylvia R. Frey, *Water from the Rock: Black Resistance in a Revolutionary Age* (Princeton, N.J.: Princeton University Press, 1991).

4. Gender and women's roles in the early republic are explored in Mary Beth Norton, *Liberty's Daughters: The Revolutionary Experience of American Women, 1750–1800* (Boston: Little, Brown, 1980); Linda Kerber, *Women of the Republic: Intellect and Ideology in Revolutionary America* (Chapel Hill: University of North Carolina Press, 1980); and Ronald Hoffman and Peter J. Albert, eds., *Women in the Age of the American Revolution* (Charlottesville: University Press of Virginia, 1989). A recent study of evangelical women is Susan Juster, *Disorderly Women: Sexual Politics and Evangelicalism in Revolutionary New England* (Ithaca, N.Y.: Cornell University Press, 1995).

5. On the early *Unitas Fratrum*, see Peter Brock, *The Political and Social Doctrines of the Unity of Czech Brethren* (London: Mouton & Co., 1957). The standard history in English of the Renewed Unity of Brethren is Kenneth G. Hamilton, *History of the Moravian Church: The Renewed Unitas Fratrum, 1722–1957* (Winston-Salem, N.C.: The Moravian Church, 1967). On the Moravians' place in eighteenth-century Protestant revivalism, see F. Ernst Stoeffler, *German Pietism During the Eighteenth Century* (Leiden: E. J. Brill, 1973); and W. R. Ward, *The Protestant Evangelical Awakening* (Cambridge, England: Cambridge University Press, 1992).

6. On early Moravian missionary activities, see Hamilton, *History of the Moravian Church*.

7. Standard works on Moravian settlements in colonial America include Gillian Gollin, *Moravians in Two Worlds: A Study of Changing Communities* (New York: Columbia University Press, 1967); Jacob Sessler, *Communal Pietism among Early American Moravians* (New York: Henry Holt, 1933); and Daniel B. Thorp, *The*

Moravian Community in Colonial North Carolina: Pluralism on the Southern Frontier (Knoxville: University of Tennessee Press, 1989). A recent study of the philosophy and function of Moravian congregation towns is Elisabeth Sommer, "A Different Kind of Freedom? Order and Discipline among the Moravian Brethren in Germany and Salem, North Carolina, 1771–1801," *Church History*, LXIII, 1994, 221–34.

8. Figures calculated from study of congregations registers, baptismal and burial records, diaries, and other documents. For an overview of the philosophy of Moravian slaveholding in Salem, see Philip Africa, "Slaveholding in the Salem Community, 1771–1851," *North Carolina Historical Review*, LIV, 1977, 271–307.

9. While a comprehensive study of Moravian women has yet to be undertaken, see Beverly Prior Smaby, *The Transformation of Moravian Bethlehem: From Communal Mission to Family Economy* (Philadelphia: University of Pennsylvania Press, 1988); and two conference papers from "The Quiet in the Land? Women of Anabaptist Traditions in Historical Perspective," Millersville University, June 1995: Beverly Prior Smaby, "Female Piety Among Eighteenth Century Moravians," and Elisabeth Sommer, "Weak Worktools? Female Authority in the Eighteenth Century Moravian Community."

10. On the Moravian choir system, see Gollin, *Moravians in Two Worlds*, 67–109; and Thorp, *Moravian Community in Colonial North Carolina*, 60–62.

11. No thorough study of the Salem Single Sisters' Choir has been published, but see Beverly Prior Smaby, "Forming the Single Sisters' Choir in Bethlehem," *Transactions of the Moravian Historical Society*, XXVIII, 1994, 1–14.

12. Quote from Memorandum of August Spangenberg, January 8, 1760, cited in Susan Lenius, "Slavery and the Moravian Church in North Carolina" (Honors thesis, Moravian College, 1974). Though describing congregational life in Bethlehem, the Bishop's claim also represents the church's attitude in North Carolina.

13. *Aeltesten Conferenz* (Elders' Conference minutes, trans. Frances Cumnock), December 11, 1782, July 23, 1783; Salem Diary, December 2 and 23, 1783, and August 13, 1784, in Adelaide Fries et al., eds., *Records of the Moravian Church in North Carolina*, 11 vols. (Raleigh: North Carolina Historical Commission, 1922–69), IV:1844, 1845.

14. *Aeltesten Conferenz*, July 2, 1776, in Fries, *Records*, III:1085.

15. On European varieties of godparenthood, see John Bossy, "Blood and Baptism: Kinship, Community and Christianity in Western Europe from the Fourteenth to the Seventeenth Centuries," in Derek Baker, ed., *Sanctity and Secularity: The Church and the World*, Studies in Church History, vol. X (Oxford: Blackwell, 1973), 129–43; and Stephen Gudeman, "Spiritual Relationships and Selecting a Godparent," *Man*, X, 1975, 221–37. On African and African-American concepts of spiritual kinship, see Margaret Washington Creel, *"A Peculiar People": Slave Religion and Community-Culture Among the Gullahs* (New York: New York University Press, 1988), 288–92; and Stephen Gudeman and Stuart B. Schwartz, "Cleansing Original Sin: Godparenthood and the Baptism of Slaves in Eighteenth-Century Bahia," in Raymond T. Smith, ed., *Kinship Ideology and Practice in Latin America* (Chapel Hill: University of North Carolina Press, 1984), 35–56.

16. On the wider context of black family life in the eighteenth century, see Herbert Gutman, *The Black Family in Slavery and Freedom, 1759–1925* (New York: Pantheon, 1976); Allan Kulikoff, "A 'Prolifick' People: Black Population Growth in the Chesapeake Colonies, 1700–1790," *Southern Studies*, XVI, 1977, 391–428;

and Mary Beth Norton, Herbert G. Gutman, and Ira Berlin, "The Afro-American Family in the Age of Revolution," in Ira Berlin and Ronald Hoffman, eds., *Slavery and Freedom in the Age of the American Revolution* (Charlottesville: University Press of Virginia, 1983). The Moravian Church followed North Carolina law prohibiting interracial marriage, though in the West Indies the church had sanctioned at least one such union in the 1730s between a white missionary and a free black Moravian woman.

17. Moravian concepts of family and marriage are discussed in Gollin, *Moravians in Two Worlds*, 52–62, 110–27; and Thorp, *Moravian Community in Colonial North Carolina*, 58–80.

18. *Aeltesten Conferenz*, October 4, 11, 18, and December. 6 and 13, 1780.

19. *Landarbeiter Conferenz Protokolle* (Minutes of the Country Congregation Ministers), June 5, 1781, trans. author. For a similar injunction by a North Carolina Baptist association in 1805, see Guion Griffis Johnson, *Ante-Bellum North Carolina: A Social History* (Chapel Hill: University of North Carolina Press, 1937), 537–38.

20. Cf. Sobel, *The World They Made Together*, 191–97. On African-American women's experiences during slavery, including sexual exploitation, see Jacqueline Jones, "Race, Sex, and Self-Evident Truths: The Status of Slave Women during the Era of the American Revolution," in Hoffman and Albert, eds., *Women in the Age of the American Revolution*, 293–337; and Deborah Gray White, *Ar'n't I a Woman? Female Slaves in the Plantation South* (New York: Norton, 1985).

21. *Aeltesten Conferenz*, July 20, 1796. Likewise, enslaved members of other evangelical curches sometimes gained protection from abusive masters. Raboteau, *Slave Religion*, 180–83; and Sobel, *World They Made Together*, 191–97.

22. Salem Congregational Council, December 6, 1792 (trans. Erika Huber). On African-American liberation struggles and white backlash during the period, see Frey, *Water from the Rock*; Peter H. Wood, "'Liberty Is Sweet: African American Freedom Struggles in the Years before White Independence," in Alfred Young, ed., *Beyond the American Revolution: Continuing Explorations in the History of American Radicalism* (DeKalb: Uiversity of Northern Illinois Press, 1993); Jeffrey J. Crow, *The Black Experience in Revolutionary North Carolina* (Raleigh: North Carolina Division of Archives and History, 1976); and Douglas Egerton, *Gabriel's Rebellion: The Virginia Slave Conspiracies of 1800 and 1802* (Chapel Hill: University of North Carolina Press, 1994).

23. Smaby, "Female Piety Among Eighteenth Century Moravians."

24. *Aeltesten Conferenz*, May 3, 1797. Historians have suggested that new post-Revolutionary racial barriers reflected a growing sense among whites that to be American and to be a citizen was to be white. Increasingly, that definition came to mean white and male. Jordan, *White over Black*; Ronald Takaki, *Iron Cages: Race and Culture in Nineteenth-Century America* (Berkeley: University of California Press, 1988); Nancy Cott, *The Bonds of Womanhood: "Woman's Sphere" in New England, 1780–1835* (New Haven, Conn.: Yale University Press, 1977).

25. In contrast to growing numbers of black churches, particularly in northern states, the new congregation was not independent. Though a white minister remained in control, congregants had leeway to organize services and events. Jon F. Sensbach, "Culture and Conflict in the Early Black Church: A Moravian Mission Congregation in Antebellum North Carolina," *North Carolina Historical Review*, LXXI, 1994, 401–29.

26. See Frey, *Water from the Rock*, Chap. 8; Allan Gallay, "The Origins of Slavehold-

ers' Paternalism: George Whitefield, the Bryan Family, and the Great Awakening in the South," *Journal of Southern History*, LIII, 1987, 369–94; and Rachel Klein, *Unification of a Slave State: The Rise of the Planter Class in the South Carolina Backcountry, 1760–1808* (Chapel Hill: University of North Carolina Press, 1990).

PASSION, DESIRE, AND ECSTASY

The Experiential Religion of Southern Methodist Women, 1770–1810

"My whole soul is entranced, and all that is within me shall praise the Lord—I am in debt, and in bonds, and what must be done, but that Jesus should seize my poor body."

—Sarah Jones[1]

Methodism was a religion of daily emotional experience, and for southern women like Sarah Jones, the experience involved both soul and body. Because their faith was also testimonial, Methodists strove to find language to accurately depict their sublime encounters with the divine. The rhetoric Methodists employed to describe their religious experiences exposes two interesting paradoxes. First, in an age of supposed secularization, enslaved Methodists continued to seek mystical, revelatory communion with God. Second, Methodists were often accused of a somber asceticism, of opposing fun, pleasure, and the flesh. Yet white Methodist women experienced emotional, romantic, and even physical ecstasy when communing with God.

Methodists emigrated from Britain to the South in the late 1760s and the sect steadily grew in the final decades of the eighteenth century. Methodists could count a few elite men in their ranks, but most of their southern converts were common whites and slaves. A majority were women. In the Revolutionary and early national South, there were clear distinctions in worship style and doctrine between Methodists and most other Protestants, especially Anglicans and their Episcopalian successors. The difference most important to understanding Methodists was, in biased terms they themselves used, between "heart" religion—which they believed Methodism was, and "formality"—which they believed characterized non-evangelical religion. Formality afflicted individual Methodists just as it did competing churches, and when men and women lost zeal, emotion, and bliss in their relations with God, they chided themselves for being "formal" or "cold." To avoid such spiritual death, Methodists sought frequent intense experiences of emotional intimacy with God.[2]

While proponents of the secular Enlightenment and critics of the Methodists (often one and the same) exalted reason over passion, logic over emotion, and mind over body, white Methodist women unabashedly sought out passionate, emotional, and physically expressive religion and black Methodists, male and female, sought out mystical spirituality. By embracing a faith of passion, and expressing that faith in romantic language of the senses, these converts helped mold the "experiential" religion of the early Methodists. Profoundly influenced by the distinct religiosity of blacks and white women, Methodist-style revivalism swept the South and Southwest in the antebellum years, proffering a clear alternative to the dispassionate worship of reason. Although Methodism grew increasingly conservative in the nineteenth century, the church retained its emphasis on intense emotional experience, a legacy in large measure from these founding decades.[3]

The South on the eve of Revolution was one in which white women and slaves were subordinates in a complex racial and sexual hierarchy. The values historians most often associate with the South in this era—honor and independence—are a testament to the hegemony of white patriarchs. Independence, which encompassed both self-mastery and mastery over one's household, was impossible for slaves and eluded all but the wealthiest of white widows. White women's relationship to the code of honor was always through white men. Slaves were considered to be outside the circle of honor entirely.[4]

Southern defenses of slavery in the antebellum era would include, as if it were obligatory, an analogy between the subordination of wives to their husbands and the subordination of slaves to their masters. Whether these defenses were penned by men of faith, who pointed to the Bible, or by skeptics, who pointed to "science," the implication was the same: There existed a natural hierarchy of man over woman, white over black. It is not coincidental that the critics of enthusiastic religion shared terminology with the defenders of slavery and patriarchy. White southern men ruled, it was said, because they were less emotional, governed more by reason than passion, more subject to mind than body. The mystical religion of black Methodists and the eroticized spirituality of white Methodist women challenged the devaluation of revelation, body, and emotion, and, at least implicitly, resisted the hierarchical assumptions of the southern code. Perhaps most important, these southern Methodists shaped their own imaginative universes with their distinct religiosities, universes where "honor" and "independence" mattered far less than "holiness" and "zeal." In the context of the early South, this was no small achievement.

Critics who condemned the Methodists for being both dour and enthusiastic did not understand Methodist values. The more somber side of Methodism, the side mistakenly linked with an aversion to pleasure, coexisted symbiotically with the ecstatic side. Converts did sacrifice some secular delights for religious ones. Methodists defined themselves in large part by their abstention from the worldly enjoyment of drink, dance, and gaming. Both men and women in the church would have agreed with John Littlejohn's goal "to deny myself of any pleasure . . . however pleasing to my own desires."[5] Most conversion accounts of men or women included some description of the earthly gratification left behind at conversion. As members, Methodists continued to strive for self-denial, which they variously described as "mortification" or dying to the world.[6]

Death meant rebirth, however, into a different moral universe and way of life. With this new life came different joys that more than made up, according to Methodists, for the ones abandoned. Milly Stith received God's "love and power" in her conversion, and afterward saw "new beauties and [felt] new pleasures."[7] These new pleasures were often linked through language to romantic encounters and provided a rich and vivid spiritual life that was shared communally through testimony, correspondence, and conversation.

Methodists drew language for their spiritual accounts from a number of sources. There is evidence to suggest that some white women read popular romantic fiction, at least prior to joining the church, where such works were forbidden. The Bible was, however, the most common source; even illiterate evangelicals often committed large portions of it to memory and were able to quote from it at length. Biblical descriptions of Christ as "the fairest among ten thousand" and "altogether lovely" abounded in Methodist accounts.[8]

Second in importance were John Wesley's many doctrinal tracts, letters, sermons, and journal extracts reprinted in America and voraciously consumed by American Methodists. Wesley had stressed love—fervent love—both as the basis of salvation and as God's will for his relationships with humans and theirs with one another. Equally critical to understanding southern Methodism was the fact that Wesley sanctioned "religious zeal," comparing it to having one's "passions aroused" in holiness. Mysticism and eroticized spirituality have an ancient history; Wesley was certainly not the first to stress zeal or passion. Although southern Methodists rarely alluded to early Christian texts, Wesley himself was broadly read; through his writings, his followers in the South glimpsed the older roots of the mystical, emotionally charged religiosity they would embrace.[9]

American ministers were also influential. Through sermons and exhortations, preachers related their vision of Wesley's God of love to their parishioners. Clergy tried to appeal to the heart—to emotions and passions so derided by non-evangelicals. Several of the most beloved men were known for weeping while they preached, "armed with the irresistible eloquence of tears." Members heard these powerful sermons and probably echoed some ministerial rhetoric. Clergy were the most emotionally expressive and mystical of male Methodists, many sharing with laywomen a greater tendency to spiritual visions, dreams, and encounters with spirits, Satan, or Jesus. Preacher Joseph Pinnell, for example, wrote using language that few men echoed but that many women did: "O how sweet is Love- it is the most noble [Passion] of the mind. Its sof[t] influence is spread over the believers soul- and makes every duty sweet- Its rich perfume fills Heaven."[10]

The relationship between men like Pinnell and his female parishioners was not one-sided: women influenced their clergymen as well as being influenced by them, so much so that it is just as likely that Pinnell borrowed the language of Methodist women as that they borrowed his. Ministers and women freely shared their experiences with one another. In the funeral sermon for a Baltimore woman, Christiana Lane, her minister fondly recalled that "many were the happy moments we have enjoyed with each other in waiting upon [God]." Some women so inspired their preachers that they were singled out for special praise. Jacob Young, for example, described Elizabeth Russell as "eloquent"; North Carolinian Sally Gordon had a "strong mind, and great zeal, and influence" in the church.[11]

In descriptions of pious women, preachers often emphasized the other-worldliness of women's spirituality. Francis Asbury found Sister Boydstone "heavenly" in "words, looks, and gestures." In a Kentucky service, Henry Smith witnessed a woman fall senseless to the ground from "the overwhelming power of God." After four hours, she "revived" with an "angelic countenance" and praised God using "language [that] seemed to belong to another world." Smith called her the most "enraptured soul" he had ever met. Ministers respected, admired, and at times envied women for their ecstatic religiosity.[12]

Although Methodist women clearly drew on religious sources to describe their spiritual experiences, often quoting the Bible or John Wesley, their voices emerge as more than a series of images drawn from others. Some women used biblical language to describe a divine encounter without biblical precedent. Others took a biblical metaphor, such as the idea of Jesus preparing a banquet, and embellished it with details of their own choosing. Women's accounts of communion with what they saw as a living God were, above all, intimate. They shared God's message of love or his beauty with others, but during the moment of communion, divine attention was focused on the individual woman.[13]

Because of the Methodists' close-knit communities, some of their rhetoric and experience transcended race, class, and gender. White men in the church certainly had visions and dreams and sometimes claimed to have seen Jesus or to have touched a heavenly spirit. Although far less often than white women, white men also occasionally fell unconscious or paralyzed during services, and claimed otherworldly experiences when coming to. The differences between the language of white men and women are nonetheless stark. White women tended to use more of the five senses in their communions with God, while men rarely described scents or touches.

White men's visions of God, moreover, were often tableau from the Bible, with the crucifixion being the most common. Benjamin Lakin, a profoundly mystical Methodist preacher, had a waking vision in which he saw Christ "sweating blood" for Lakin's sins. Lakin also saw numerous signs of God in the actions of birds, although birds seem to have been a more common motif in the visions and dreams of women than men. Other white men, like white women, heard the voice of God or, as one man did, felt the "blood of Jesus as great drops washing my soul." But men as visionary as Lakin were not the norm, and few were as vivid and sensual as women. Even rarer was the man who used erotic language to describe his encounters with God.[14]

The direct testimony of black Methodists is less abundant than that of white women, but extant evidence suggests some parallels and differences. Like white women and unlike white men, black men and women seemed more comfortable with physical expressions of religion. Critics, for example, noted that white women and African Americans shared a thirst for expressive religion, often lumping them together derisively. One man claimed that "no one but negroes and weak-minded women" were susceptible to Methodist enthusiasm. The few surviving black-authored accounts from southerners who converted before 1810 describe encounters where Jesus appeared, talked, and touched the converts. The authors do not, however, employ eroticized language to describe communion with God.[15] Most evidence comes from white ministers, men who may well have been reluctant to report any eroticized language used by African Americans. It is also possible that slaves and former slaves eschewed such rhetoric on purpose, to counter insidious racist stereotypes of blacks as oversexed.

Although she may not represent the normative experience for black Methodist women, the religious memoir of a woman identified only as "Old Elizabeth" does suggest that slave and white women experienced God in distinct ways. Wealthy and middling white women were able to set aside a number of hours each day for communion with God. But, as a young slave, Elizabeth often had to steal time with God while working for her master. White women could retire to the woods for daily prayers; Elizabeth poured out her "sorrow" in "the corners of the field, and under the fences." Consider too the difference between her conversion and that of many white women. White women even of lower-class families, while "seeking" religion, were often incapacitated physically and emotionally. Several remarkable white women were said to have remained paralyzed for days—a Virginia woman for nine. William Ormond met a young woman who had visions of heaven and hell during a thirteen-day fast. Elizabeth, in contrast, was in "seeking" for six months, when she "could do nothing but weep" and "lost my appetite." During this time, she recalled, "still I was required to do all my duty." For a slave, there could be no lengthy paralysis or extended fast if they interfered with a master's profits.[16]

Contrast as well the experience of white women who were unable to work while in ecstasy with Elizabeth's account: "many times while my hands were at work, my spirit was carried away to spiritual things." The sense of transport she described when a slave is much closer to the language used by Richard Allen, who when he was working to purchase his freedom found that "while my hands were employed to earn my bread, my heart was devoted to my dear Redeemer." If Allen and Elizabeth were typical, it would seem that moments of private physical rapture were not as crucial to enslaved Methodists as the daily spiritual interaction with God through which they could psychically distance themselves from enslavement.[17]

Elizabeth reported that her first direct encounter with a divine presence was witnessed "with my spiritual eye," an expression similar to that a preacher used to describe an African-American woman who was blind, but who "sawe by an eye of faith." White women often had their first contact with Jesus himself. Elizabeth, like the black Baptists of Mechal Sobel's study, was led to Christ by a "director, clothed in white raiment," who "took me by the hand and said, 'come with me.'" She shared with white women the touch and sight of the divine, but Elizabeth's vision of hell was more elaborate than most white women reported. She saw a "fiery gulf" and an "awful pit" and peered "to the belly of hell." Crying out to God for mercy, with each cry Elizabeth was lifted further from the pit until she saw "the Saviour with His hand stretched out to receive me." Her director showed her a vision of a heaven of "light and love" with "millions of glorified spirits in white robes." Her account is surprisingly similar to that of white minister Freeborn Garrettson, to whom "heaven and hell were disclosed to view" and who was personally approached by two spirits, one good and one evil, before Jesus appeared to him.[18]

Elizabeth's encounter ended not with an ecstatic bodily experience, but with a command of social purpose. She was "shown the world lying in wickedness, and was told I must go there, and call the people to repentance." Still, some of Elizabeth's language resembled that used by white women. She related that "all my *desire* was to see the Saviour," that she was "filled with sweetness and joy" and was a "vessel filled with holy oil." Many times she was "anointed" or filled with light, but in only one occasion did she refer to the physical nature of her relationship with God: "I was so full I hardly knew whether I was in the body, or out of the body." Even here, her emphasis is on the mystical aspects of rapture and not the physical.[19]

Elizabeth's experience might not be representative of black women in the early church, nor may her memoir reflect her full experience. Her oral account was transcribed (and edited) for publication, the unidentified transcriber noting that "her simple language has been adhered to as strictly as was consistent with perspicuity and propriety." Moreover, Elizabeth reported that "many" white clergy she talked with claimed that "they did not believe in revelation" as she did. She thus may have consciously shaped her account to conform more to the conventions of the white ministry. Consider the case of a unnamed black woman of Maryland who asked for William Colbert's help in interpreting her vision. In Colbert's words, she asked "what she must say when she goes to pray, telling me that she sometimes sees something like milk streaming down her breast; at other times something like a cake of ice or snow, and sometimes something like a young child siting[sic] on her shoulder. She wanted to know what these things meant." Colbert told the woman it was "not in my power to tell her" but that his duty was to encourage conversion and holiness. Sarah Jones, who described Christ as a nursing mother several times, might well have interpreted (and transcribed) this woman's vision in a more erotic idiom.[20]

Yet it may also be the case that slaves, who in services were physically expressive, had private experiences of God distinct from free converts. Jarena Lee, a New Jersey woman who preached in the North after 1811, described physical encounters with Jesus and used romantic language in her journal. So too did other free black northern women.[21] African-American Methodist women in the South experienced religion in ways shaped by gender, but the fragmentary records currently available suggest that race and civil status were equally important factors in shaping their religiosity, and these factors may account for the dearth of erotic imagery in their testimony.

White women's direct testimony is more available than that of blacks, but is still not ubiquitous. Fortunately for modern researchers, many of the letters of one of the most influential southern Methodist women, Sarah Jones, were preserved and published following her death.[22] These letters offer needed insight into the inner life and spirituality of Methodist women, and along with other evidence, demonstrate that for many white southern women, religious passion was to be courted and not feared.

Women variously described their quest for intimacy with God in romantic language. Margaret Anderson wrote of her "ardent desires to behold" God and how her "heart panted" for Jesus to "take possession" of her. Sarah Jones experienced what she called the "fainting of my soul" and "longings of my spirit" when she sought more of God: "I sink, I burn, I die, I glow to be fully possessed of all thy killing charms, thy soul transporting smiles." When successful, she felt "floods of extatic joy and peace." While men in the church occasionally wrote of their "desire" or "longing" for Christ, women were more effusive and more exact in the details of their encounters with Jesus. Men rarely, for example, claimed to have been smiled at literally by the Lord or to have seen Christ blushing.[23]

Male and female observers also noted women's religiosity using rhetoric of rapture and ecstasy. "Mrs. Killen," a Maryland Methodist, was said to have surpassed all others Ezekiel Cooper had observed "in the magnitude and constancy of her ecstacy and joy." Cooper found her so "enraptured in love to God" on her death bed that he believed her "anxious to meet the Bridegroom." Killen expressed her resignation in the face of death and longing to be with Jesus in terms of union: "O Jesus take me to thyself! . . . O come! come! come! let me see thy face! Come receive me and let me receive and join with thee in glory!"[24]

The different meanings that common language might have had for men and women is clearly discernible in terms like "Bridegroom." Methodists had a multitude of biblical synonyms for God, Christ, and the Holy Spirit, but used "Bridegroom" more with women than men. It is significant that among men in the church, the image of being the bride of Christ was primarily one used by ministers. Preacher Daniel Shine, Jr., for example, told his disappointed parents that he had nothing "against affinity" but that "singularity is my station." "I am espoused to and wed[d]ed to one Bridegroom," he explained, "who is call'd Jesus." The vast majority of ministers, like Shine, were single. The church discouraged preachers from marrying because married men, it was believed, could not balance a life in the itineracy and their obligations to a wife and children, and because the financially struggling church did not want to oblige its members to support a minister's family.[25]

Most women, unlike preachers, could expect to have more than a metaphorical bridegroom at some point in their life. The comparison of Christ's relationship to the church with earthly marriage may well have had a more profound and literal meaning for women. John Littlejohn assured one woman that God would "clothe" her "with the wedding garment." Women themselves spoke of Christ as a spouse, and as the following accounts indicate, sometimes described Jesus as if he were a suitor wooing them. Christ was, for example, Prudence Hudson's "first love." While God the father could be stern and patriarchal, and therefore much like the southern masculine ideal, Christ was like a sweet and caring husband, who returned women's love and, perhaps, their carnal desire as well.[26]

White women experienced the divine and his love with all of their senses. They shared with other Methodists the two most common sensory perceptions of God: sight and sound. "Old Elizabeth," the freedwoman discussed above who converted while a slave in Maryland, heard "a voice" that told her to "rise up and pray," an image common to male and female conversion accounts. There is a qualitative difference between some aspects of men's and women's visions, however. An inspired Sarah Jones spoke of Christ's "lovely face" and "charming voice," and often saw him smiling at her, while men tended to see, if they saw him smile at all, God smiling "on" them. While white men conventionally heard Christ or a heavenly spirit describe Hell or Heaven, urge them to convert, or comfort them with assurances they were saved, women had a wider range of conversations, and in their accounts, the voice of Jesus or angels was gentle and tender.[27]

Margaret Anderson claimed that while lying in bed a spirit "whispered in my ears softly, arise and pray." Describing Jesus as a being who had words for her alone, Sarah Jones wrote that he "answered to my heart; and O, I may just say I heard the noise of his voice, and he uttered things which I cannot unfold." The intensely private speech of God to southern women, whether directly to the heart or whispered in their ears, was only one of the ways women personalized their encounters with the Lord.[28]

Women, more than men, used language of taste. While men in the church spoke of the "Lord's table" both literally when describing the sacrament and figuratively when describing Heaven, women could sometimes picture and taste the bounty. Prudence Hudson, a Delaware Methodist, exhorted those around her to "taste the sweets of religion." When writing to fellow Methodist Anne Smith, Sarah Jones mixed spiritual and literal metaphors. She likened seeking Christ to gathering "delicious fruit"—rare melons that she shared with him at a nightly banquet.[29]

Jones consumed and was consumed by Jesus: "I love him till I am swallowed up. I am eating my honey with my honey-comb, and drinking my wine with my milk, wrestling, diving and rising in hope extatic." Here she was the aggressor, reaching Jesus "by holy violence, breaking into the magazine of divine jewelry." As she became part of him through taste in a quasi-eucharistic devotion, he "swallowed" her as well, with the result of their union being ecstasy. In another "sacred banquet" with Jesus, Jones described having "drunken with my beloved, until I am sick of love, and roll in tumbling oceans of bliss immortal." Jones was consumed on this occasion by God's "flames" that "boils my life and drinks my very vitals."[30]

Women also remembered the scent of Jesus or Heaven. One woman, after a moving service in her home, claimed the house was "perfumed with the

Glory of God." Sarah Jones was entranced by the smell of Christ's garments, which "exhaled a fragrancy like a field which the Lord had blessed." Women's use of the language of sight, sound, taste, and smell undoubtedly made their accounts more vivid when related to others. Their rhetoric shows as well how intense their experiences of God were.[31]

The most remarkable of all sensory perceptions of God that women experienced included the touch of Jesus or an aspect of him. Some of the images women used were common to both male and female believers, although ministers were much more likely than laypeople to use sensory language in depicting God. One metaphor men and women shared was describing Christ as a fountain or likening communion with God to swimming in an infinite ocean. Preacher John Kobler wanted to be like a drop of water in an ocean, "swalowed up" in God's will.[32]

Methodists often spoke of being washed clean with Christ's blood (or "the blood of the Lamb"), but women less frequently saw visions with blood. When they did describe Christ's blood, it was connected with the sacrifice of the cross or the atoning power of the crucifixion. Sarah Jones told Susannah Williams that she hoped "to meet your blood-besprinkled soul above, to rest forever in the arms of Jesus," but in her many letters, blood was a rarely used image. Instead, Christ was like a fountain or ocean. "In him is a pure fountain where I wash, and bath[e] my weary soul with the ointment of his name," Jones described. On other occasions, she wrote of "swimming in the very ocean of his amazing, singular, astonishing love" or of swimming "in the full rivers that issued from the throne of God" where "such seas of bursting glory came rolling from Heaven, I screamed out—weakness overpowered my limbs."[33]

Some women experienced the sacred touch in dreams or religious visions. Margaret Anderson dreamed as a child that Christ had come into her bedroom "and took me up in his arms and blessed me." African-American women in the church had similar experiences. "Old Elizabeth" saw Christ filled with "an indescribably glorious light." He then offered his hand to her.[34]

While many Methodists described the recently deceased as being "in Abraham's bosom" or in Jesus' arms, white women occasionally believed they embraced God in this world. Sarah Jones vividly related one such encounter with Christ: "Jesus's hands, his soft and lilly[sic] hands! I as sensibly, through faith, handled the sacred touch . . . . O, I leaned on his bosom till streams of tears answered in witness." Her ecstasy was immense. She felt "transported, intranced, captured, delighted," as, she wrote, "my heart flutters, my soul blazes, my flesh trembleth, and my hands are so weak I can just set up." Being with Christ wrought profound emotions in Jones, who wrote that "Sometimes I feel like my breath would cease in his embraces." Like a lover struck by Cupid's bow, Jones felt Christ's eyes leave "an arrow in my heart." In another devotional moment, Jones was given such a beautiful vision of Heaven that she almost leapt out of her window, but remarked that "I found my arms clinched around [Christ], and restraining power to hold me back."[35]

Women occasionally experienced many different sensory perceptions during the same devotional. Warning her fellow Methodists to "trim their lamps" because the "Bridegroom cometh," Sarah Jones depicted a lover-God who poured her wine: "I was buried in the ocean of shoreless, boundless love immense. All my veins kindled and flamed, set on fire by Jesu's radient smiles; he looked like kindness itself, when he poured such a flagon of sweet wine for me . . . the perfume is yet with me; the odours fly through my passions."[36]

If sometimes women used all of their descriptive powers to explain their communion with God, at other times they found language inadequate to the task. Women's claims of the failure of words were so frequent that they bear closer analysis. Sally Eastland wrote a minister about "Jesus and his Love," but found that "oh my feeble pen—it, fails, it, fails, my unskillful hand falls short here." Fanny Lewis wished she had the powers of "an Addison or a Pope" to convey her feelings at a camp meeting, but "alas! all description fails," she concluded. Susan Wyval, on her deathbed in 1810, was "in extacy, pouring out her soul in torrents of praise to God, in language which seemed almost more than human!" Wyval's joy was indescribable: "O that I could tell you what I feel; and what views I have of glory!—My tongue cannot express it!" Margaret Anderson's conversion came "when a stream of love and joy flowed into my soul," but such "inexpressible joy, as I must forever remain unable to express or describe."[37]

Even the exceedingly vivid language Sarah Jones employed was inadequate for her at times. "What do words signify, or figures mean, or nature's voice with all terrestrial things possess, to show my pleasures this morning?" she asked in one letter: "They faint, grow dumb, and expressive silence points the task beyond their skill: they borrow all that's grand or eloquent below the sun, but all is but a shadow, pale and glimmering." Jones's words are, despite her claims of their inadequacy, revealing. Her God bears some resemblance to the unknowable Lord of John Calvin, but only in that both Gods transcend human powers of representation. Where Calvin sought the awful stillness of the divine, Jones found the silence of language's failure to represent "expressive" and pleasurable. Southern Methodist women were comfortable conceding the limitations of words, further testimony to their belief that faith was to be experienced and not rationalized.[38]

Although little is known about the relationships of some Methodist women to their husbands, Jones's spouse, Tignal, was described by a preacher as a man "of violent passions and a most ungovernable temper." He had ordered Sarah to avoid the Methodists, and had threatened to shoot her if she disobeyed. She did not obey him, however, and he aimed his gun at her on one occasion. Sarah was resolute, and "accosted him mildly" by saying "'My dear, if you take my life, you must obtain leave from my heavenly Spouse." Tignal's "virulent temper" was eventually "softened and subdued," but the wealthy slaveowner still retained control over his affairs and children. Sarah wanted Tignal to free their slaves, but he refused. She also, because of Methodist values, objected to the worldly dress of her children, but Tignal insisted that their children dress as others of their class did.[39]

Sarah wrote few words about their relationship and in her prolific correspondence with other Methodists, she mentioned her husband rarely, and never in the intimate manner she used to describe her affection for Brothers and Sisters in the faith. She had several passionate but evidently platonic and spiritual friendships with Methodist men and women. Her love and ardor for Jesus and those who, like her, longed for "all Christ's mind" more than "did a suckling desire the breast" stands in marked contrast to the absence of ardor revealed for Tignal. In response to a letter from William Spencer, Jones wrote in terms she never used for her husband: "My burning heart thrills with quicked life at reading the copy of love in golden capitols flaming from your breast."[40]

Her covenant partners—those people she had agreed to pray with at a set time every day, even though physically separated—evoked strong emotions. "Come along—," she wrote Jeremiah Minter, "I am ready to meet you in earth or in Heaven. . . . Fire, fire blazes, and I am happy, happy, thrice happy; I feel at emulous war with you." Once, when Minter had just left her home for another preaching appointment, she went to the guest room, "fell on my knees upon the carpet, believing there you had lifted your hands and heart to my adorable JESUS. . . . God came down and I *held him* and *would not let him go*." She even had visions of a feminized Christ nursing her and Minter simultaneously, telling Minter "Sometimes by faith I see us around a rich table, and how careful you are to help me; and at other times both spirits on Jesu's breast as twins, swallowing the streams of Love."[41]

Jones's ties to Minter—who published her *Devout Letters*, merit special attention, for they illustrate how some women's friendships with other Methodists involved a shared religious passion that may have rivaled or exceeded in intensity the marital bond. Few women had a friend as odd as Jones had in Minter, for he caused one of the greatest scandals in southern Methodism. Minter, as an act of self-denial, had himself surgically castrated and consequently was expelled from the itinerancy. His relationship with Sarah Jones seems not to have troubled Tignal. Although Sarah and Minter were close before and after Minter became a self-described "eunuch," any fear or jealousy on Tignal's part was quite likely alleviated by Minter's surgery. Nonetheless, some rumors persisted, even after Minter's castration, that he and Jones had a "carnal" relationship.[42]

Celibate though their friendship, which Sarah Jones termed "our union, in Jesus," probably was, it was emotionally charged and spiritually intimate, as were her friendships with other devout members. Jones's circle of local Methodist friends shared their spiritual correspondence with each other, reading the letters together and inspiring one another. "Sister Taylor" showed a letter she had received from Minter to Sarah and Sally Eastland. His words "set" the three women "on fire." Jones's male covenant partners she addressed as "my beloved brother" or "my very dear Brother," or "precious Brother." Susannah Williams, who described one of her own visions to Jones, was "My very well beloved." Tignal, in contrast, she referred to dispassionately as "Mr. Jones." The most affectionate term she used for him in her numerous letters was "my dear companion."[43]

Tignal's power to thwart what Sarah believed were moral imperatives helps account for her detachment. In a letter reporting how his decision about their children's dress grieved her, she called him "my head" and wrote that he "positively commands my children to dress as others do." Sarah agonized more deeply over Tignal's refusal to liberate his slaves. In 1788, striving to reconcile her religious duty and her legal powerlessness as a wife, she took some refuge in the idea of an omnipotent God who knew her "inmost mind" was opposed to slavery and of a wrathful God who would "avenge" slaves by loosing his sword on Virginia's proud slaveholders. Although she did not meditate on patriarchal privilege, she clearly regretted her inequality and the moral dilemmas it raised for her: "I am bound, and must go on beneath it," she wrote. Over a year later, still struggling for inner peace, haunted by her perception that "the oppressed [the family's slaves] stare me through," she resolved to "try to be clear of their blood." Finding comfort in Isaiah's promise that those who "despiseth the gain of oppressions" and "walketh righteously" would not be consumed by God's "devouring fire" at judgment, she renewed her commitment to holy living. It is little wonder that Sarah's rhetoric cooled when it came to Tignal, the man whose intransigence and power placed her in such moral quandaries.[44]

Sarah Jones was warmly attached to her fellow Methodists, but she reserved her most fervent prose for encounters with Christ. Comparing the language she used to describe her unequal relationship with Tignal and her unequal relationship with her "heavenly Spouse," it is evident that for her Jesus was a preferable master. If she was "bound" to Tignal by law and custom, and obliged to "go on beneath it," her bondage to Christ was altogether different: "I am imprisoned, Love with golden chains hath bound my head, my heart and hands, and I can truly say 'tis a pleasing pain.— I feel my widening soul a sacrifice to love." Surrounded by slaves who were literally bound in chains, committed to the idea that Christians could not be saved if they were "clouded in Ethiopes blood," Jones sought to clearly distinguish her bondage to God from her subordination as a wife and from the cruel bondage of slavery. Both Christ and Tignal had power over Sarah, but Christ ruled with ardent love, not with the callous fiat of a southern patriarch.[45]

In other ways, it is possible to contrast her view of Tignal and Christ. Tignal's "virulent temper" had in the past been directed against Sarah, but Jesus's wrath was meant for unbelievers. To Jones, Christ was "kind and tender," "my dear JESUS," "my adorable, matchless, shining JESUS," or "my sparkling Jesus." He could fill her with holy zeal to combat Satan or unbelief, but one on one, Jones and her God shared sweet moments. If she lacked emotional fulfillment in her marriage, which the available evidence suggests, she found it in Christ.[46]

Her eroticized language also suggests that she was physically as well as spiritually fulfilled by communion with Jesus. Once when praying, she "felt faint" while love "blazes through my soul, as sharpened daggers." The scene of her rapture grew more vivid, as "Trees of Life dropped their delicious mellons; the fertile soil became a Paradise, a garden of sweets . . . more delightful than rosebuds in June." When Jesus "draws nigh," she continued, the "effulgent beams of his brightness have overcome me. . . . I burn, I melt, I blaze, I sicken, all faint with love divine . . . the fire of Jesu's love hath taken possession of all my soul, and every vein beats with young life and sweet salvation." She wrote almost two years later of "a continual violent motion, exerting every faculty of body and mind," as she communed with God.[47]

Jesus, in Jones's visions, was neither stern nor demanding; she revealed that "my choicest hours are with him alone." She elsewhere penned that "the smiles of my Jesus opened in a blush. . . . His full glory, and beaming countenance, contended with all my sense and passions, until overwhelmed, I yielded a solid sacrifice to love. . . . And I rolled in the spicey presence of the fountain of gardens, drowned in the essence of beauty and comeliness." Although Minter substituted asterisks for one word in Jones's following description, it is clear that her reaction was spiritual and physical: "my adorable Jesus unveiled his rosy face; and his sparkling eyes almost made me faint: I fell on the ground and again pitched glory unto Heaven, it darted like lightning, and the thunderbolt struck somewhere about ***** I thought."[48]

In the patriarchal, honor-driven white masculine culture of the South, many white Methodist women faced opposition and even violent retribution from male relations because of their beliefs. Some women were beaten by husbands and fathers who tried to keep them from the Methodist church. Many women were threatened with violence for their religion. The white patriarchal ethos demanded that husbands and fathers assert their will and enforce it. By opposing Methodist women with violence or threats of violence, southern men only heightened the contrast between themselves and the sweet and caring Jesus of women's experience. Although southern women's faith was not solely compensatory, the fact remains that some, like Jones, might have sought in religion the eros, love, and solicitude that eluded them in marriage.[49]

Enslaved Methodists, in contrast, were violently opposed by their owners and white ruffians. For them, religion may have filled the void created by monotonous and back-breaking labor, slave owner cruelty, and callous disregard for their humanity. The God that "Old Elizabeth" and Richard Allen experienced when enslaved was "kind and gracious," but was not a lover. He was merciful and powerfully infused them with a sense of self-worth and purpose, but he was also a judge: Allen, like Elizabeth, feared for a time that "hell would be my portion." For slaves, who could expect little justice on earth, a judging God who would avenge the wrongs done to them might well have been more attractive than the romantic partner depicted by white women.[50]

Most white southern women in the church did not commit their experiences to writing. Those who did shared much of Sarah Jones's rhetoric. Sally Eastland wrote that "when I hear from [Jesus], some times my poor [Eastland drew a heart here] desolves in love." During Jesus's "love visits," as she termed them, "He's left me as it [were] help less on the ground, ah sweet momentes, how fain would I faint away in his arms." Eastland's mixture of her own fainting and Christ's embrace was part of a distinct idiom. So too was the language of Mary Avery Browder, who, when praying, "felt [God's] power in so wonderful a manner that it occasioned my trembling body to fall down befor[e] Him."[51]

The public ecstasy of white women and black men and women became a hallmark of Methodist services and camp meetings. Paintings and sketches of revivals often depicted a group of white women in swoons or lying prostrate before makeshift altars. Literary evidence of black responses also abounds, from both sympathetic Methodists and hostile critics. Henry Boehm arrived as a lovefeast for blacks was in progress: "The dear people was shouting and praising that God [had] maid them and redeemed them and converted them. . . . it apeared as if glory was opened upon earth, see one and another hoisted out through a window that was overcome with the power of God. They carried them out and laid them under a tree, after they lay there a while, they would get up and praice God."[52]

In camp meetings and churches across the South, Methodists, especially white women and blacks, experienced God with both soul and body. This physical and emotional style of religious rapture became identified with southern Methodism. For white women, physical ecstasy was also part of their private religious experience. For enslaved Methodists, mystical religiosity, the evidence suggests, was primary. The "experiential" religion of these southerners posed a clear alternative to the growing emphasis on what opponents called "rational" religion and what Methodists termed "formality."

In the later decades of the nineteenth century, evangelical-style romanticism would pervade the secular southern world as well as the religious. Jan Lewis shows how even non-evangelical elites of Jefferson's era began to use the language of emotion and to seek intense emotional fulfillment in marriage and family life.[53] Novelists of the antebellum years would attempt to combine secular romance and religion in their works, portraying heroines with strong religious values who sought romantic love from worthy men. Few non-evangelicals, however, captured the intense emotional and physical experience of early Methodists' religiosity.

Mary Ann Peaco, who converted shortly after the Revolutionary War and died in 1817, might effectively represent so many of her contemporaries. She exemplified the zealous faith Wesley and his American missionaries hoped to kindle in all southern hearts. In her eulogy, a minister recalled her "salutary instructions" to himself and others, and Peaco's frequent prayers, both alone and in public. Her religion, he claimed, was "evangelical" and he contrasted it favorably with opposing intellectual currents: "She had not the unfeeling philosophy of the stoic, nor the dry and insipid religion of the formalist, that only renders its subjects frigid and inanimate in devotion; but that which warms the heart with fire from the heavenly altar."[54]

The romantic and at times erotic language white Methodist women used to describe their heartfelt encounters with Christ and the mystical transporting experiences of enslaved Methodists reveals that for this small but growing number of southerners, the secular Enlightenment and its devaluation of the passions, body, and feelings had little appeal. Instead, white women embraced—literally and figuratively—a God who deeply affected those aspects of the human experience that were associated by male critics with women's "weaker" nature. In exalting these so-called feminine characteristics as evidence of special grace and intimacy with the divine, these women inverted the rankings of male intellectuals. Black Methodists do not seem to have used erotic imagery in their accounts, but their visions of heavenly beings who personally appeared to them, who spoke to them, and who displayed heaven and hell in vivid detail indicate their rejection of "unfeeling philoso-phy" and secularized Christianity. In fashioning their own systems of value and meaning, white women and slaves refused to define themselves by a code they did not create.

These inner worlds deepen our understanding of the early South, adding layers of complexity to seemingly ordinary scenes. When "Old Elizabeth" was at labor, was her master aware that she was sweetly communing with her God, hearing words meant only for her to hear? When Sarah Jones was on her knees, praying in the grove, did those who saw her comprehend the heights of her rapture? The religious lives of women such as these reveal a far different mentality than historians usually associate with the early South. Perhaps we have listened too well to the critics, to elites who dismissed enthusiastic reli-gion as the province of "weak-minded women," to men who never cared to look below the surface. For beneath the somber exterior of Methodist asceti-cism and self-denial, beneath the exuberance of camp meetings, enslaved Methodists experienced a soul-transporting, joyous intimacy with God that gave meaning and purpose to their lives and white women experienced a rich and vibrant world of passion, desire, and ecstasy.

◄▷

Notes

Research for this essay was funded in part by a National Endowment for the Humanities Doctoral Dissertation Fellowship.

1. Sarah Jones to Edward Dromgoole, copy, n.d., Edward Dromgoole Papers, Southern Historical Collection, University of North Carolina at Chapel Hill.
2. The literature on early southern evangelicalism and Anglicanism is vast. See, for example, Richard R. Beeman, *The Evolution of the Southern Backcountry: A Case Study of Lunenburg County, Virginia, 1746–1832* (Philadelphia: University of Pennsylvania Press, 1984); John B. Boles, *The Great Revival, 1787–1805: The Origins of the Southern Evangelical Mind* (Lexington: University Press of Ken-tucky, 1972); Rhys Isaac, *The Transformation of Virginia, 1740–1790* (New York: W. W. Norton, 1988); Donald G. Mathews, *Religion in the Old South* (Chicago: University of Chicago Press, 1977); A. Gregory Schneider, *The Way of the Cross Leads Home: The Domestication of Early American Methodism* (Bloomington: Indi-ana University Press, 1993); Albert J. Raboteau, *Slave Religion: The "Invisible Institution" in the Antebellum South* (New York: Oxford University Press, 1978).
3. Some scholars argue that evangelicals were from the outset conservative. See Rachel Klein, *Unification of a Slave State: The Rise of the Planter Class in the South Carolina Backcountry, 1760–1808* (Chapel Hill: The University of North Car-olina Press, 1990), for the most compelling recent statement of this interpreta-tion.
4. For southern honor, independence, and patriarchy, see Bertram Wyatt-Brown, *Southern Honor: Ethics and Behavior in the Old South* (New York: Oxford Univer-sity Press, 1982); Victoria E. Bynum, *Unruly Women: The Politics of Social and Sex-ual Control in the Old South* (Chapel Hill: University of North Carolina Press, 1992); Joan E. Cashin, *A Family Venture: Men and Women on the Southern Frontier*

(New York: Oxford University Press, 1991); Lacy K. Ford, Jr., *Origins of Southern Radicalism: The South Carolina Upcountry, 1800–1860* (New York: Oxford University Press, 1991); Stephanie McCurry, *Masters of Small Worlds: Yeoman Households, Gender Relations, and the Political Culture of the Antebellum South Carolina Low Country* (New York: Oxford University Press, 1995); T. H. Breen, *Tobacco Culture: The Mentality of the Great Tidewater Planters on the Eve of Revolution* (Princeton: Princeton University Press, 1985); Kenneth Greenburg, *Masters and Statesmen: The Political Culture of American Slavery* (Baltimore: Johns Hopkins University Press, 1987).

5. July 26, 1777, The Journal of John Littlejohn, typescript, Baltimore-Washington United Methodist Historical Society, Baltimore, Maryland. For more information on the Methodist ethos, see Cynthia Lynn Lyerly, "When Worlds Collide: Methodism and the Southern Mind, 1770–1810," Ph. D. diss., Rice University, 1995, Chap. 2.

6. John Lednum, *A History of the Rise of Methodism in America* (Philadelphia: n.p., 1859), 341; Nancy Simms to Ezekiel Cooper, May 17, 1793, Ezekiel Cooper Letters, Ezekiel Cooper Collection, Manuscripts Library, Garrett-Evangelical Theological Seminary, Evanston, Illinois; *Methodist Magazine*, August 1820, 302–303.

7. Milly Stith to [Francis Asbury?], December 17, 1802, *Extracts of Letters, Containing Some Account of the Work of God Since the Year 1800* (New York: Totten for Cooper and Wilson, 1805), 69.

8. Margaret Anderson read novels that "neither tended to piety or excited to virtue" before converting to Methodism in 1809. *Methodist Magazine*, August 1820, 303. For a man who described Christ as "altogether lovely," see "The Experience of Richard Graves," in *Extracts of Letters*, 23.

9. Many of John Wesley's tracts, books, and sermons were reprinted by American Methodists. One of his most popular was "The Character of a Methodist," cited here from *Methodist Magazine*, January 1797, 7–9. For Wesley on "zeal," see *Arminian Magazine*, November 1789, 526–27, an idea Sarah Jones echoes after reading one of Wesley's sermons in *Devout Letters: Or, Letters Spiritual and Friendly. Written by Mrs. Sarah Jones, ed. Jeremiah Minter* (Alexandria: Jeremiah Minter, 1804), 48. For Wesley as a "seductive" preacher who "made his followers fall in love with him"(xii), see Henry Abelove, *The Evangelist of Desire: John Wesley and the Methodists* (Stanford: Stanford University Press, 1990).

Wesley and his followers on both sides of the Atlantic had no patent on the imagery discussed below. Any reader of the Song of Solomon could appropriate the erotic language found therein and shape an experience of God to conform to that language. Mystics were more likely to be found in Methodist churches than Episcopalian, not because mystical rhetoric was unavailable, but because Episcopalian clergy discouraged visions. Baptists, some Presbyterians, even Quakers of the era had religious experiences that sometimes included visions. The analysis that follows should thus not be read as making unique claims for southern Methodists. Nonetheless, accounts by travelers and other observers conventionally cite the Methodists as being the most enthusiastic, the most physically expressive, the most mystical of southern Protestants. The Wesleyan doctrines of free will (not shared by the vast majority of other groups in this era) and holiness (condemned by the vast majority of other Protestants in this era as a conceit) predisposed Methodists to an intimacy (one might say familiarity) with God beyond most other believers.

10. Thomas Ware, "Sketches of the Life and Travels of Rev. Thomas Ware," in William R. Phinney et al., eds., *Thomas Ware, a Spectator at the Christmas Conference* (Rutland: Academy Books, 1984), 174; Joseph Pinnell to Brother and Sister Shine, March 16, 1805, Daniel Shine Papers, Special Collections, Duke University, Durham, North Carolina.

11. Rev. Prior, *A Funeral Sermon, Preached by the Rev. Mr. Prior, Minister of the Methodist Church at Baltimore, on the Death of Miss Christiana Lane, Who Departed This Life, Friday, October 5, 1792* (Baltimore: Samuel and John Adams, 1792), 11; Jacob Young, *Autobiography of a Pioneer: Or, the Nativity, Experience, Travels, and Ministerial Labors of Rev. Jacob Young* (Cincinnati: Swormstedt & Poe, 1857), 128; for Sally Gordon, see Historical Sketches, Wilkes County, Methodist Church Papers, Special Collections, Duke University.

12. Elmer T. Clark et al., eds., *The Journal and Letters of Francis Asbury*, (London: Epworth Press, 1958), 1:518; Henry Smith, *Recollections and Reflections of an Old Itinerant* (New York: 1848), 82.

13. Scholarly works on religious eroticism and imagery that influenced the readings in this essay include Caroline Walker Bynum, *Fragmentation and Redemption: Essays on Gender and the Human Body in Medieval Religion* (New Work: Zone Books, 1991), Chaps. 4 and 6 and *Jesus as Mother: Studies in the Spirituality of the High Middle Ages* (Berkeley: University of California Press, 1982), Chap. 4; Elizabeth Alvida Petroff, *Body and Soul: Essays on Medieval Women and Mysticism* (New York: Oxford University Press, 1994).

14. Lakin, "The Journal of Benjamin Lakin," in William Warren Sweet, ed., *Religion on the American Frontier, 1783–1840. Volume IV: The Methodists.* (Chicago: The University of Chicago Press, 1946), quotation on 215, birds also on 217–29, 232; Robert Drew Simpson, ed., *American Methodist Pioneer: The Life and Journals of the Rev. Freeborn Garrettson, 1752–1827* (Rutland: Academy Books, 1984), 198. For women and bird visions, see Clark, et al., eds., *The Journal and Letters of Francis Asbury*, 1:441 and J. B. Wakeley, *The Patriarch of One Hundred Years; Being Reminiscences, Historical and Biographical, of Rev. Henry Boehm* (New York: Nelson & Phillips, 1875), 74.

15. James Jenkins, *Experiences, Labours, and Sufferings of Rev. James Jenkins, of the South Carolina Conference* (n.p.: 1842), 184. For black-authored accounts by pre-1810 converts, see David Smith, *Biography of Rev. David Smith, of the A. M. E. Church* (Xenia, Ohio: Xenia Gazette, 1881); "Old Elizabeth," *Memoir of Old Elizabeth, A Coloured Woman* (1863: repr. in *Six Women's Slave Narratives* (New York: Oxford University Press, 1988).

16. *Memoir of Old Elizabeth*, 4; Minton Thrift, *Memoir of the Rev. Jesse Lee with Extracts from His Journals* (1823: repr. New York: Arno Press & The New York Times, 1969), 296–97; September 11, 1800; William Ormond Papers, Special Collections, Duke University, Durham, North Carolina.

17. *Memoir of Old Elizabeth*, 7; Daniel A. Payne, *History of the African Methodist Episcopal Church* (Nashville: Publishing House of the A. M. E. Sunday-School Union, 1891), 74.

18. *Memoir of Old Elizabeth*, 5–6; July 13, 1802, Henry Boehm Journals, Manuscripts Division, Drew University, Madison, New Jersey; Mechal Sobel, *Trabelin' On: The Slave Journey to an Afro-Baptist Faith* (Princeton: Princeton University Press, 1988), 113–14; Simpson, ed., *American Methodist Pioneer*, 44. Unlike the accounts Sobel cites, Elizabeth does not describe her director as a "little man."

19. *Memoir of Old Elizabeth*, 7, 14, emphasis added.

20. *Memoir of Old Elizabeth*, 3, 17–18; August 24, 1794, William Colbert Journals, Garrett-Evangelical Theological Seminary, Evanston, Illinois.

21. For Lee and other black Northern women, see *Spiritual Narratives* (New York: Oxford University Press, 1988).

22. Jones's *Devout Letters* were edited by Jeremiah Minter, but the rhetoric and rhythm of the published letters are so similar to the unpublished letters found from Jones to Edward Dromgoole in the Edward Dromgoole Papers, SHC, that a careful reader must conclude the words are essentially her own.

23. *Methodist Magazine*, August 1820, 301; *Methodist Magazine* October 1820, 377; Sarah Jones to Pemberton Smith, n.d., *Devout Letters*, 85. For a man who, after being inspired by a conversation with Sarah Jones, felt "desire . . . for more of Mind of my dear well beloved," see James Meacham, "A Journal and Travel of James Meacham," [Trinity College] *Historical Papers*, 1912, 87. Here again, however, the language may well be influenced by Sarah Jones, whom he greatly respected.

24. Ezekiel Cooper to John Dickins, October 1, 1789; Ezekiel Cooper Collection.

25. June 9, 1794, Daniel Shine to Daniel Shine, Sr., Daniel Shine Papers. See also May 17, 1777, The Journal of John Littlejohn, 43.

26. The Journal of John Littlejohn, 33; *Methodist Magazine*, November 1826, 409, emphasis added. Hudson converted in 1779. For women calling Christ their "spouse," see the account of Sarah and Tignal Jones.

27. "Old Elizabeth," *Memoir of Old Elizabeth*, 5; Jones to Enoch George, October 11, 1792, *Devout Letters*, 125.

28. *Methodist Magazine*, October 1820, 375; Jones to William Heath, November 16, 1791, *Devout Letters*, 99. Contrast such language with that of John Littlejohn, who heard a "small still voice" in The Journal of John Littlejohn, 10.

29. *Methodist Magazine*, November 1826, 408; Jones to Smith, n.d., *Devout Letters*, 89–90.

30. First scene is from Jones to Smith, n.d., *Devout Letters*, 89–90; second from Jones to Mr. Loyed, n.d., *Devout Letters*, 63–64.

31. Simpson, ed., *American Methodist Pioneer*, 181; Jones to William Spencer, December 5, 1791, *Devout Letters*, 102.

32. February 11, 1790, The Rev. John Kobler's Journal, Baltimore-Washington United Methodist Historical Society.

33. The quotations of Jones are, in order, from her letters to Susannah Williams, n.d., 87; to Mr Loyed, n.d., 112–13; to Jeremiah Minter, January 13, 1793, and to Jeremiah Minter, January 25, 1790, 9–10, all from *Devout Letters*. The different meanings of "blood" for men and women may help account for this disparity in images. For women who associated blood with menstruation, the image of washing oneself clean with blood or bathing in blood may have had little appeal.

34. *Methodist Magazine* August 1820, 301; "Old Elizabeth," *Memoir of Old Elizabeth*, 6.

35. Jones to Jeremiah Minter, n.d., 21–22; to William Spencer, November 18, 1790, 61; to Minter, n.d., 42, all in *Devout Letters*.

36. Jones to William Spencer, n.d., *Devout Letters*, 134.

37. Eastland to Edward Dromgoole, February 21, 1790, Edward Dromgoole Papers; *Extracts of Letters*, 88; *Methodist Magazine* (May 1818): 181; *Methodist Magazine*, October 1820, 376.

38. Jones to Jeremiah Minter, July 21, 1790, *Devout Letters*, 29.

39. Quotations from Thomas Ware, "Sketches of the Life and Travels of Rev.

Thomas Ware," 168–69. For her disputes with Tignal over slavery and dress, see Jones to Jeremiah Minter, December 1, 1788, *Devout Letters*, 2; Jones to Minter, January 25, 1790, *Devout Letters*, 7; Jones to Susannah Williams, n.d., *Devout Letters*, 88.

40. Both letters are from Jones to William Spencer, January [?], 1790, and November 18, 1790, *Devout Letters*, 57 and 62.

41. Jones to Minter, n.d., *Devout Letters*, 38, 44–45, 34.

42. Minter, *A Brief Account of the Religious Experience, Travels, Preaching, Persecutions from Evil Men, and God's Special Help in the Faith and Life, Etc., of Jerem. Minter, Minister of the Gospel of Christ, Written by Himself, in His 51st Year of Age.* (Washington, D.C.: n.p., 1817), 13–14, and Jones to Minter, December 22, 1792, *Devout Letters*, 138.

43. The reference to "My beloved brother" is from Jones to Edward Dromgoole, n.d., copy, Edward Dromgoole Letterbook, Edward Dromgoole Papers. The remaining quotes are, in order, from Jones to Minter, May 14, 1790, 16; to Minter, n.d., 36; to William Spencer, January [?], 1790, 57; to Minter, May 14, 1790, 15; to Susannah Williams, n.d., 135; to Minter, May 14, 1790, 18; to Minter, January 25, 1790, 9, all in *Devout Letters*.

44. Jones to Susannah Williams, n.d., 88; to Minter, December 1, 1788, 2; to Minter, January 25, 1790, 7, all in *Devout Letters*.

45. Jones to Edward Dromgoole, copy, n.d., Edward Dromgoole Letterbook, Edward Dromgoole Papers; Jones to Jeremiah Minter, December 1, 1788, *Devout Letters*, 2.

46. Ware, "Sketches of the Life and Travels of Rev. Thomas Ware," 169 and Jones to Jeremiah Minter, May 15, 1791, 51; Jones to Minter, January 2, 1790, 4; Jones to Minter, n.d., 39, 41, all in *Devout Letters*.

47. Jones to William Spencer, January [?], 1790, 57–58; Jones to William Heath, November 16, 1791, 98, both in *Devout Letters*.

48. Jones to Edward Dromgoole, copy, n.d., Edward Dromgoole Letterbook, Edward Dromgoole Papers and Jones to William Spencer, December 5, 1791, 102; Jones to Minter, May 14, 1790, 20, both in *Devout Letters*. The omission of the noun in this letter is interesting. Jones was alone in a grove when "the thunderbolt struck," so the reference is most likely to a part of her body, although there is no way to be positive.

49. Jan Lewis, *The Pursuit of Happiness: Family and Values in Jefferson's Virginia* (Cambridge: Cambridge University Press, 1983); for opposition to Methodist slaves and white women, see Lyerly, "When Worlds Collide: Methodism and the Southern Mind, 1770–1810," Chap. 7.

50. Payne, *History of the African Methodist Episcopal Church*, 71, 75.

51. Eastland to Edward Dromgoole, February 21, 1790, and Browder to Dromgoole, November 1777, copy, Edward Dromgoole Letterbook, both in Edward Dromgoole Papers.

52. July 19, 1800, Henry Boehm Journals. Because of the length of this quotation, for clarity I have removed Boehm's many unneeded punctuation marks, added an "e" to past tense verbs and a "y" to his "the."

53. Lewis, *The Pursuit of Happiness*.

54. *Methodist Magazine*, July 1818, 273, 276.

THE SEXUAL POLITICS
OF RACE AND GENDER

Mary Musgrove and
the Georgia Trustees

Early Saturday evening on August 12, 1749 the white residents of Savannah learned that several dozen Lower Creek warriors and their chiefs, accompanied by Mary Musgrove, her third husband Reverend Thomas Bosomworth, and his brother Abraham, were nearing town. "Alarmed by the beat of the drum" and fearing an Indian attack, the residents called out the militia, who prepared to fire on the visitors as they approached the Upper Square. The colony's leaders wisely chose this moment to intervene, inviting the chiefs and Reverend Bosomworth to engage in wine and talk rather than combat. Mary Musgrove, once the most respected arbiter of Anglo-Creek relations in the colony, was excluded from this session.[1]

As James Oglethorpe's principle interpreter between 1733 and 1743, negotiator for many thorny problems between the Creeks and the white colonists, and the most popular Indian trader south of Augusta, Mary Musgrove, the adult daughter of a Tuckabachee Creek woman and a white Carolina trader, was insulted at her exclusion.[2] So great was her anger at the white leaders' blatant snub and her concern that her authority over both the Lower Creeks and the English settlers had been sabotaged, that after several hours of waiting, she entered the meeting room unbidden and proceeded to berate the leaders and their "white town" for the successive abuses she and the Creek people had endured at their hands. The white men responded to her outburst by treating the nearly fifty-year-old woman like a child, admonishing her "to go home, go to Bed and not expose herself."[3] To the astonishment of all in attendance,

Musgrove not only refused to leave but rebuked those present for not recognizing her status as leader of the Creek Nation. The Creeks in the room, she stated, were "her People." She added that all who resided on Creek lands, including the English settlers, were subject to her sovereignty.[4]

Mary Musgrove found herself in these circumstances because she was the progeny of an interracial sexual relationship between a Creek woman and an English man.[5] Such interracial unions aided the exchange of cultures that hastened both English colonization and Native American acculturation in southeastern North America in the eighteenth century. No wonder then that some English authorities sanctioned interracial marriage between Native American women and Englishmen. Through these unions, colonizers sought more than the fostering of peaceful relations with Native Americans—they sought their conquest.[6] History and myth have linked famous Native American women from Pocahontas to Sacagawea to virtually every so-called successful encounter, from the European point of view, between Europeans and Native Americans in the New World. But the scores of anonymous Native American women who engaged in sexual liaisons with European men, and the children these liaisons produced, acted as mediators between these two cultures and played an equally significant and enduring role in colonial history.[7]

This was especially evident in the Southeast where the history of native peoples' colonial encounters differed in kind from those in the northeastern and mid-Atlantic regions of North America.[8] For southeastern native groups, including the Creeks, Choctaws, Apalachees, and Catawbas, contact with Europeans began with the Spanish who arrived in North America in the sixteenth century. The conquistadors were the first European colonizers to introduce the diseases that decimated the southeastern native populations. They also introduced the native societies to the material culture that eventually involved them, if only peripherally, in the transatlantic trade system.

Unlike native peoples to the north, the southeastern indigenous groups had adapted their reduced populations, political organizations and cultural practices in response to the Spanish presence over several generations of time and prior to settlement by the English in Carolina. Thus English merchants and their traders, eager to procure furs and deerskins from these Indians, discovered in the late seventeenth century that the native peoples of the southeast were already familiar with Europeans, their ways, and their goods. This familiarity, along with native customs that sanctioned premarital intercourse and exogamous marriage, made sexual relationships and marriages between Native American women and white traders acceptable practice in most southeastern native societies in the late seventeenth and early eighteenth centuries.[9]

Although acceptable practice, neither sex or marriage between Native American women and European men ensured that Native American women's subsequent lives, or the lives of their children, would be ordinary by Native American standards. Instead, these women and their bicultural children were forced to assume the mantle of "cultural broker." Caught between two worlds, they found themselves occupying the contested terrain between distinctly different cultures. Both of these worlds, moreover, anticipated not only that cultural brokers understood the differences that separated them, but could "broker" some measure of understanding between them.[10]

Despite their significance to the history of British settlement in the colonial southeast, the voices of these women and their progeny are virtually absent from the historical record with a few exceptions—almost always "half-breed" sons such as Alexander McGillivray of the Creeks and John Ross of the Cherokees who came to assume important leadership positions in their societies in the last half of the eighteenth and early nineteenth centuries. Mary Musgrove, however, the daughter of an interracial union herself, achieved significant standing among both the white settlers and the Lower Creeks in the first half of the eighteenth century. Though she is probably the most frequently cited woman in the history of colonial Georgia, Mary Musgrove remains an enigmatic figure. She has alternately been celebrated for her critical role as Oglethorpe's interpreter, vilified by those who view as extortion her demand for prime coastal lands given her by the Lower Creeks, and pitied by those who see her as the unwitting dupe of her conniving husbands and their grandiose schemes.[11]

While very few extant records document Musgrove's own words, the texts that describe her prove as revealing as those she penned herself. These documents indicate that Musgrove's status as a "mixed-blood" woman proved useful, at least at times, as she moved back and forth across two different cultures for some five decades. The privileges Musgrove garnered as well as the drawbacks she endured by virtue of her perceived racial and gendered status, however, were not unique to her alone. We simply know more about Musgrove because her life experiences and their impact on the colonial enterprise assured their inclusion in the official record. Musgrove was exceptional in that she wielded substantial power as a cultural broker for the settlers and the Lower Creeks alike during the first two decades of white settlement in Georgia. Yet her circumstances, because they are relatively well documented, can also help us begin to understand how scores of other women in colonial Georgia, also the daughters of intercultural unions, negotiated the same changing boundaries of race, gender, sex, and culture.

Historians have only recently come to appreciate the important role cultural brokers played in the process of colonization. But the work produced, particularly Richard White's pathbreaking *Middle Ground*, has been both sophisticated and compelling.[12] As James Merrell has convincingly argued, charting the cultural transformations in language, trade, and diplomatic customs that took place between indigenous societies and European colonizers is as important for understanding the destruction of Native American societies as the history of war, disease, and settlement.[13] The examination of competing notions of gender represents yet another critical battleground on which Native Americans waged and eventually lost an important cultural war with Europeans.

Mary Musgrove carefully cultivated her identity in response to the racial and gendered boundaries she encountered in the colonial culture of Georgia. As a "subjugated body," her choices were shaped by each successive phase of

English settlement. Like all bicultural women, her body literally and figuratively linked these two distinct societies. Musgrove's life, then, can be used to exemplify the process of colonization and the importance of shifting racial and gendered boundaries in that process. Through Musgrove's experiences we see how and on what terms the English colonizers dominated and excluded from the increasingly hierarchical world they were constructing those individuals and social groups who proved most threatening to the establishment of their authority.[14]

Little about Mary Musgrove's youth can be fully documented since original accounts about her and by her differ greatly. She was probably born between 1700 and 1708 to a Lower Creek woman and a South Carolina trader who lived together in the Creek town of Tuckabachee, near the Chatahoochee River. Though many historians dispute her version of her lineage, she claimed late in life that her mother was the sister of two important Creek leaders, Brim and his brother and successor Chigelli, thereby entitling her to call herself "Princess Coosaponakeesa." Musgrove also related that, at the age of seven, she "was brought Down by her Father from the Indian Nation, to Pomponne in South Carolina; There baptized, Educated and bred up in the principles of Christianity." She returned to her Creek town shortly after the Yamasees and their allies attacked the Carolina frontier in the Yamasee War of 1715, living with her relatives for as many as ten years before marrying Johnny Musgrove.[15]

Johnny Musgrove was also the child of an interracial liaison. His mother was either a Tuckesaw or Apalachicola Creek woman, whose identity is unrecorded; his father, John Musgrove, was a wealthy South Carolina planter. Mary and Johnny probably married in 1725 and lived in South Carolina for seven years before moving to the Yamacraw settlement in 1732, near the future site of Savannah. The Yamacraws, perhaps a hundred in number, were a mixed group of Creeks and Yamasees who had settled on this coastal site only a few years before Oglethorpe's arrival. The Musgroves had been invited to establish a trading post at this settlement at the request of the Governor of Carolina and Tomomichichi, the Yamacraw leader.[16]

By the 1720s, Creek leaders had concluded that the best strategy for contending with the influx of European colonizers was to maintain respectful but removed relations with all three: the Spanish, French, and English. But from the vantage point of the English, relations with the Creeks needed to be far more cordial if the colony of Carolina and the proposed colony of Georgia were to succeed.[17] The Musgroves came to the aid of the English by negotiating peaceful relations between the settlers and the Creeks and Yamacraws. Shortly after the official founding of Georgia in 1732, Mary Musgrove quickly became Oglethorpe's favorite interpreter, helping him secure two treaties and two land cessions before his final departure from Georgia in 1743.[18]

If the Musgroves were brokers in this exchange of cultures, their trading post was the intersection where such exchanges took place. The Creeks and Yamacraws who bartered deerskins for blankets, guns, and rum turned the Musgrove store into a kind of cultural crossroad where Creek and Yamacraw families, traders, merchants, and English authorities exchanged not only goods but information. As a result, the Musgrove settlement came to serve diplomatic and military purposes as well as commercial ones.[19] The Musgroves' ability to facilitate this cultural exchange brought them prosperity as well as influence. Their holdings came to include not only their trading house, but a 500-acre land grant from the King, a plantation six miles up the Savannah River, several cowpens, indentured servants, and at least three Indian slaves. In addition, the couple collected some 1,200 pounds worth of deerskins each year from local hunters, assuring them good credit with the merchants of Charleston.[20]

Because Mary Musgrove was especially influential with the Creeks, due as much to her savvy as her alleged royal relations, Oglethorpe took great advantage of her willingness to aid him. When war with the Spanish loomed on the horizon, Musgrove successfully urged the Creeks to stand by the English, much to Oglethorpe's relief. Worried about the colony's weak borders, Oglethorpe subsequently convinced the Musgroves to establish a trading establishment sixty miles up the Altamaha River, where Mary Musgrove could watch the Spanish and monitor Creek loyalties. Oglethorpe consistently relied on Mary Musgrove as translator, fact gatherer and mediator during almost all his negotiations with the Creek leaders during his decade in Georgia. Nor did Mary Musgrove's influence falter with the death of her husband in 1735.

Shortly after John Musgrove's demise, Mary wed Jacob Matthews, her former indentured servant and the current commander of twenty rangers stationed at her Altamaha trading house, Mount Venture.[21] She continued to assist Oglethorpe, who secured a substantial land cession from the Creeks in 1737–1738 with her aid. Although some Savannah residents felt she had married beneath her—while Matthews was an Englishman, he was also her former servant—no one could contest her continued influence with Oglethorpe and the Creeks and the benefits this relationship reaped for the colonists.

In the fall of 1738, the leaders of four Lower Creek towns invited Oglethorpe to meet them, with Mary Musgrove acting as interpreter. At this meeting the chiefs informed Oglethorpe that they were bestowing on Mary Musgrove some 300 prime coastal acres south of Savannah (on the old Yamacraw tract). A surprised Oglethorpe found himself forced to acknowledge this exchange, though he had no legal right under English law to approve it. Yet by witnessing this event, Oglethorpe had in fact sanctioned it, at least in the eyes of the Creek leaders and Mary Musgrove. All three parties clearly understood that for Oglethorpe to challenge Musgrove's right to this land would threaten far more than his relationship with his trusted interpreter; it would threaten the hitherto cordial relationship between the Creeks and the English, since the Creeks had bestowed gifts of land to the English under similar circumstances. Oglethorpe's unfortunate but calculated presence at this event would not only cost him much of his credibility with the other trustees but would generate a host of problems for the colonists in years to come.[22]

Respect for Oglethorpe's leadership skills waned from this date forward. Two years later, England's war with Spain and the tensions between the Cherokees and the Creeks that ensued meant that relations between the

Creeks and the English were at their weakest in nearly a decade. Oglethorpe's increasing ineffectualness compelled the Georgia Trustees to assess his nego- tiations in a more critical light. One of their first decisions was to condemn his spending habits, which had included many gifts for the Native Americans, and to take over the financial reins of the colony for themselves. This action had serious repercussions for Creek relations; Mary Musgrove and her new hus- band Jacob Matthews now had far fewer presents to dispense at their trading post, which exacerbated bad will between the Creeks and the English. Mean- while Mary Musgrove, because she had been providing food and supplies to needy colonists and Creeks alike and had frequently been forced to leave her store unattended to assist Oglethorpe, lost money and business.

Despite her legitimate disgruntlement with the English leaders, Musgrove continued to act as an intermediary for Oglethorpe. Yet the new colonial gov- ernment refused to pay not only for the costs encumbered by hosting Creeks, Yamacraws, and traders at her trading post but for her services as interpreter as well. The leaders also refused to recognize her stake in the coastal property awarded her by the Creeks.[23] Still, the colony's leaders did not want to alien- ate her completely, for she remained an influential ally and diplomat. The trustees, therefore, chose to stall her request for legal recognition of her lands by initiating a Trustee's Grant that required lengthy legal procedures on the other side of the Atlantic.[24]

In June 1742, Jacob Matthews died, which compelled Musgrove to leave their home, the Mount Venture post on the Altamaha. Most of the Creeks who had settled with her in the area departed as well. In their absence, the Spanish and their new allies the Yamacraws destroyed the place, straining Musgrove's declining resources even more. Then in the spring of 1743, Oglethorpe was ordered to depart the colony just as relations between the Creeks and the English soured anew in the wake of England's successful repul- sion of the Spanish. Before leaving Georgia, Oglethorpe gave Musgrove 100 pounds and a diamond ring from his own hand as payment for her services and the losses she suffered at Mount Venture. He also promised her an annual salary of 100 pounds.[25]

Despite these gifts, Oglethorpe left Mary Musgrove in a precarious situa- tion. The leadership that had replaced him encouraged further deterioration of Creek–English relations. The new governor would honor neither the gift- giving traditions that had smoothed these relations in the past nor the conces- sions Oglethorpe had reached with the Creeks in 1738–1739. Meanwhile, Musgrove's appeals to the colony for legal recognition of her Yamacraw tract lands were denied.[26]

Especially vulnerable at this time of her life given her reduced resources, Oglethorpe's departure, and her widowed status, Mary Musgrove chose to marry a third time to Thomas Bosomworth, an Anglican minister in the town of Savannah. The two had met during a boat voyage in June 1743 and were wed shortly thereafter. Bosomworth retained his title as minister but moved with Mary to her plantation where the two of them renewed her battle for legal right to the Yamacraw tract. Over the next four years, the trustees summarily rejected Musgrove's successive requests despite the passionate memorials she and her husband penned.

By the winter of 1746–1747 both Mary Musgrove and the Creeks were at loggerheads with the colonial government. As chief Chigelli explained in December 1746 to colonial leaders in a talk translated by Mary Musgrove, the Creek people now distrusted "the white people" who had a history of making "false claims" to Mary Musgrove and the Creek nation.[27] Recognizing that such disastrous relations with the Creeks spelled danger, the colonists feared imminent attack. Despite the personal and political tensions between Musgrove and the colonists, colonial leaders still asked her to intercede with the Lower Creeks on their behalf, tacitly concurring with Colonel Alexander Heron who stated of Musgrove at this time:

> I have had personal knowledge of her merit since my first arrival in this country, and I am highly sensible of the singular service she has done the country (a great part of the expence of her own private fortune) in continueing the Creek Indians in friendship and alliance with the English.[28]

Fortunately for the colonists, Mary Musgrove agreed to intervene once more, for she hoped to reconcile Creek–English differences and secure her right to her land as reward for her actions. The tensions among all three parties only worsened, nonetheless, over the next two years. War in Europe had ended in 1748. The peace treaty that ensued vanquished fear of Spanish invasion in Georgia. At the same time, some two thousand settlers, largely self-sufficient landholders, now resided in the colony which was experiencing slow but steady economic growth. These changing diplomatic and economic realities turned the historic relationship between the Creeks and the colonists on its head. Previously courted by the English, the Creeks suddenly found themselves scrambling for their suitor's favor. The tensions between the Creeks, Mary Musgrove and the colony that accompanied this transformation culminated in the fateful visit of Mary Musgrove, her husband Thomas Bosomworth, and several dozen Creek men to Savannah on a steamy summer evening in 1749.

Once the arbiter for all significant Anglo-Creek discussions, Mary Musgrove was pointedly excluded by white leaders from the session that followed the delegation's arrival. Distraught at the larger significance of this action, she broke into the meeting without invitation to deliver her extraordinary speech before the Creek chiefs and the colonial leaders. An unsympathetic white male eyewitness described Mary Musgrove's entrance and words as follows:

> [She] rushed into the Room, in the most violent and outrageous manner, that a Woman spirited up with Liquor, Drunk with passion, and disappointed in her Views could be guilty of. . . . She then, if possible, grew more outrageous, and in the most insulting manner declared, She was Empress of the Upper and Lower Creeks, Yea, went so far in her imaginary Sovereignty,

as to call herself King, and that she should command every Man in these Nations to follow her, and We should soon know it our cost. It is needless to repeat, the threatening and irritating language used by this woman, indicating both her and [her] husband's wicked designs.[29]

The white male officials present responded to Mary Bosomworth's impassioned speech by putting her under temporary custody. They were convinced that she was out of her mind or at the very least in a drunken rage. While we can never truly know her actual state, it seems likely that her accusers were attempting to justify their punitive actions against her by identifying her behavior as flagrantly inappropriate in accordance with their expectations about racial and gendered behavior. By labeling her either crazy or "just another drunken Indian," the colonial authorities could dismiss the deeper meanings behind her actions. Although too little evidence exists to assess Mary Musgrove's condition, it seems highly likely that she was both sane and sober and that her speech was a heroic act to preserve her authority in a society that was shifting the terms of colonization and settlement to suit itself.

Thomas Bosomworth himself was clearly aware that his wife's relationship to the colonists had been dramatically altered by her speech and her subsequent imprisonment. He responded to this turn of events by asserting his authority as a white man and a husband within this marriage. The day after his wife's impromptu oration, he publicly apologized to the colony's leaders for her behavior, stating that henceforth he would speak on behalf of the couple and that any and all utterances made by his wife should be ignored.[30] Mary Musgrove herself later claimed that from that day forward she was "no longer countenanced by the White People," despite her significant record of diplomacy and trade that had contributed so enormously to the colony's successful venture.[31]

Mary Musgrove's verbal assault on the officials was a desperate measure by a desperate woman. She had come to understand that the colony no longer appreciated either her skillful negotiations with the Creeks or her right to lay claim to lands she had earned. She also had come to recognize that the role she had carved out for herself as Christian helpmeet to the colonists was no longer tenable.

By renouncing the colonial leaders and their "white Town," by reclaiming her Creek identity, Mary Musgrove not only lost the respect of the white male European leaders but was subsequently silenced by them. It did not help her cause that she had chosen such an inappropriate way for a woman in this society, particularly a Christian woman born of a Creek mother, to convey her anger. In the eyes of the colony's stewards, she had transformed herself overnight, reduced to the status of outcast and heathen. Even her spouse understood the implications of her debacle when he publicly declared himself her spokesman. While Mary Musgrove and her third husband would continue to seek legal right to the Creek lands awarded her for another decade, eventually securing a compromise deal that allowed her to claim St. Catherine's Island as her own, along with the money made from the public sale of Ossabaw and Sapelo Islands, she never regained her former status as cultural broker to the colony.[32]

This denouement should not be too surprising. Mary Musgrove's speech in essence had denigrated every Anglo-American premise on which the white leaders had erected their colony and on which she had allegedly acted, with the understandable effect of turning the entire white colony against her. Although Mary Musgrove had supposedly been negotiating on behalf of the colonial leaders' best interests for years, her speech indicated that her allegiance now clearly lay with the Creeks. She had turned her back in a most deliberate and spectacular fashion on the white officials who believed she had embraced them as her own. Despite the serious consequences of her actions, one suspects that after years of negotiating the sexual, racial, and gendered boundaries of the Anglo-American male world as a woman of "mixed blood," she breathed a long sigh of relief at being able to shed the conflicting identities she had carefully negotiated for so long.

As a young girl, she had learned that her acceptance in white society necessitated her acquisition of a Christian education. Likewise as a young woman, she had recongized that by establishing herself as a good Christian wife, she had slightly improved on the subordinate status accorded her as a woman and a "half breed." The fact that the Methodist Minister John Wesley spent some time with the Musgroves at their plantation shortly after his arrival in Georgia in 1735, and appears to have been tutoring Creek and mixed blood children there, suggests the degree to which Mary Musgrove supported this doctrine.[33] Moreover, Wesley's visit to her home must have curried favor with the local white authorities who believed in the language of the promotional materials distributed in England on behalf of the colony: "The Encrease of our People, on this Fruitful Continent, will probably, in Due Time, have a good effect on the Natives, if we do not shamefully neglect their Conversion." What better ally for converting local Indians than Mary Musgrove, a convert herself.[34]

From an Anglo-American vantage point, the conversion of Native Americans to Christianity signaled a willingness to accept white values and the social hierarchies associated with them. Thus when Mary Musgrove in her ill-fated speech declared herself the Queen of all the lands on which the whites had settled, Colonel Stephens turned in astonishment to Governor Reynolds and asked him whether she had been baptized, received the sacrament, or stood as a godmother for children. Musgrove replied before Reynolds could respond to Stephens, stating that she had accomplished all three. Stephens then asked her, using an interpreter although Musgrove was obviously fluent in English, whether she was an Indian or a white person. She replied that she was an Indian. Stephens was aghast. He believed that as a Christian woman she had long since renounced her Indian identity.[35]

Mary Musgrove's earlier credibility in the colony then had originated in large part from her conversion to Christianity, which whites believed had erased the signficance of her mixed lineage and Creek upbringing. These same beliefs about Native American conversion to Christianity also convinced colonists that Musgrove had mastered those Anglo behaviors and attitudes considered appropriate to her gender. In many respects, Mary Musgrove was unlike any Christian woman the colonists had ever known. She had lived in remote settlements surrounded by rough men, sold them rum and guns, and traveled with Indians and traders to the distant Creek Nation, a world she knew intimately, to secure their cooperation with the colonists. Yet once they had proof that she was a Christian woman, they were convinced that she shared their world view.

By contrast Oglethorpe and his men had not considered Mary Musgrove a particularly worthy woman on making her acquaintance in 1732. Knowing little of her background, they used English notions about fashion and status as well as race and gender to mark her among the lower sort in social rank, observing that "she appeared to be in mean and low circumstances, being only cloathed with a red stroud petticoat and Osnabrig Shift." Yet Mary Musgrove soon earned their respect despite their initial assessment, proving her worth to Oglethorpe and the colony as a whole. These Englishmen discovered that the social codes embedded in notions of gender and race as well as dress and behavior, which structured their views of both Old World and New, were far from accurate in the early days of English settlement in Georgia.[36]

Over time Mary Musgrove's authority as a cultural mediator was legitimated in English eyes more by her status as a good Christian helpmeet than by her rough attire or Creek background. Thus, while an earlier generation of historians pinned Musgrove's willingness to remarry so quickly following on the deaths of her husbands on her lusty nature, an assumption with unsavory undertones about status and sexual desire, another interpretation is well worth considering. Musgrove may have known that prolonged widowhood would have made her vulnerable to scandal as a single woman on a remote frontier working with men of all races. Marriage, especially to an Englishman, offered her reputation some measure of protection, especially since the institution was sanctified by the Church. Taken in that light, Musgrove may have held her third and final marriage to the minister Thomas Bosomworth as the most significant. In a society in which she remained in most ways an outsider, marriage to someone as venerable as a minister raised her social standing and protected her reputation. Widowed white women were legally permitted to retain their property in colonial Georgia, and Mary Musgrove was one of the largest women landholders in a colony where land afforded its owners status and independence as well as subsistence.[37] Yet Musgrove may have chosen not to remain single, despite her relative wealth and influence, because of her marginal status as a mixed-blood woman.

Although Musgrove spent most of her adult life as a married woman, she bore children only with her first husband and none of them lived to adulthood. Yet she knew the signficance that the English settlers tied to their prescribed gender roles. Childless by the 1740s, she publically upheld maternal feelings and used the term "Maternal Affection" to describe her relationship with "the Infant Colony" of Georgia. Musgrove's claim to be the Mother of the Colony, despite its grandiosity, remained grounded in Christian notions about a woman's special calling. Musgrove used this metaphor in her memorial to the trustees in 1747 since its meaning was understood by the white leaders. Through it she inferred that she was not a greedy powermonger, bent on shaping the colony to her will, but a Christian woman fulfilling her female duty as best she could.[38]

Mary Musgrove employed similar language to cast herself as a willing public servant wronged by the colony's leaders.[39] In her quest for legitimate control of the Yamacraw tract, she described herself as "having sacrificed my own private Interest to the Publick Welfare." And she reminded her audience that in "her past services of Maternal Affection" she had been forced to deal with "loads of infamy and reproach" and was "branded and stigmatized" for her noble efforts.[40] It is significant that she attempted to justify her role on behalf of the colony with Anglicized notions about the relationship between femininity and Christianity.

Regardless of Mary Musgrove's efforts to present herself as a good Christian woman, she could not always escape the derogatory judgments of whites. Throughout her life she was served notice that she was not fully accepted as a member of the white community, despite her crucial contributions to the colony's security and prosperity, her wealth, and her status as Christian helpmeet.

When her first husband John Musgrove traveled to England as interpreter for Oglethorpe and the Creek chiefs going to meet the King in the summer and fall of 1734, Mary and John's partner, a white man named Joseph Watson, was left to mind the store with Mary. Unfortunately, Watson was an unsavory fellow who drank excessively. On one occasion, when Mary Musgrove and her Creek customers fell into an argument with him, the inebriated Watson responded by yelling at Musgrove and trying to shoot her. Mary Musgrove eventually brought charges against him and the magistrates ruled in her favor.[41]

But Watson in the meantime had been wagging his tongue, calling Musgrove a witch and claiming she had the power to "bewitch" other people. Watson resorted to this accusation in a society where Musgrove's "race," her trade and her property, along with her ability to negotiate with the Creeks, singled her out as a highly unusual woman. It is likely that Watson was not the only colonist to claim Musgrove had "supernatural" powers in a society where her status as a woman and a "half-breed" of some authority necessitated an explanation for those white men who were not faring as well as she.[42]

Musgrove's difficulties with Watson, symbolic of her difficult relationship with white society, did not end with his accusations. After his argument with Musgrove, Watson and a Yamacraw named Skee proceeded to drink heavily. Skee died under somewhat mysterious circumstances shortly after their binge. Watson himself boasted that he had drunk Skee to death. Still angry with Musgrove, he then locked her out of the storehouse, preventing her from doing business. Watson's collective actions prompted Skee's lieutenant, Estichi, to break open the storehouse on Musgrove's behalf and then hunt down Watson to seek revenge for Skee's death. During his pursuit of Watson, Estichi accidently killed Musgrove's slave Justice. The authorities, convinced both men must be located since each allegedly committed a murder, eventually found them. Fearing an incident with the local Creeks, who blamed Skee's death on Watson, the magistrates returned Estichi to the Yamacraw tract without a trial.

Meanwhile Watson's anticipated fate became the talk of Savannah. Some believed he was a "lunatick" and therefore not accountable for his bizarre behavior. Others sought his banishment from the colony since he had jeopardized the colonists' good relations with the Creeks. But, most significantly, others wanted him released from jail because, they argued, "it is cruel to imprison [Watson] on account of an Indian."[43] That any Savannah residents were sympathetic to Watson seems amazing, until we factor in their virulent racism, a racism Musgrove constantly confronted.

This particular series of events and their reception in the white community suggest that Mary Musgrove must have recognized that many white colonists viewed her as an outlandish member on the fringes of their community. Her power and authority challenged Anglo notions about who deserved privilege and status. In their minds, a "half-breed woman" could be a good Christian helpmeet, a squaw trader, and little more.[44] Musgrove was slandered and called a witch precisely because her status challenged the colonists' ideas about gendered behavior and race difference.

The complexities and contradictions that surrounded Mary Musgrove throughout her life were manifold. The daughter of a white father and a Creek mother, raised among whites, and the recipient of a Christian education, she aided both the Creeks and the English settlers as an interpreter and a trader, accruing substantial property, servants, and slaves throughout the 1730s and early 1740s. As the colonial leaders perceived that Musgrove's usefulness to the maturing colony was on the wane, however, and as Musgrove sought formal recognition of the lands the Creeks had bestowed on her, the English authorities who dealt with Musgrove reassessed her value to the colony. As they did so, they also reconceptualized her racial and gendered identity to suit their changing needs. Musgrove's influence with the Lower Creeks, along with her knowledge of English and Creek cultures, had made her an invaluable ally to the Georgia Trustees during the earliest stages of settlement. Her careful negotiations had in fact assured the relative success of the colonial venture. But by 1749 she was forced to contend with a new series of ordeals and confrontations at the hands of the latest colonial government. These challenges to her authority reflected the leadership's lowered opinion of her value to the Georgia colony. Colonial leaders had shifted the terms, demanding that she adhere to their conceptions of race and gender difference in order to diminish her authority and power. Henceforth she would be expected to observe a whole new set of boundaries to fit into their world.

Certainly Mary Musgrove was a product of, as well as a contributor to, the evolution of the triracial cultural encounter in Georgia and therefore defies easy analysis. After all, the limited nature of the sources makes it difficult to determine with absolute certainty where her allegiances really lay and how they changed over time. Nor can it be determined precisely how the shifting boundaries of race, class, gender, and sex in early Georgia influenced the kinds of choices she made, though again the sources seem suggestive. Was Mary Musgrove struggling to survive the personal circumstances of the cultural encounter? Or was she struggling for more power and influence given her special authority and status? The latter seems far more likely.

At the very least, Mary Musgrove clearly understood the cultural differences that separated the Creeks and the English. Moreover, she used that knowledge to wage a fierce contest, to triumph, however briefly, in this new society. Her life story demonstrates that colonial mix in Georgia was far more complicated than any simple depiction of violent conquest. Mary Musgrove's words, actions, and authority defy any essentialist interpretations that hinge on the good Indian woman's loss of status and respect in the evil Christian world of the white colonialists. Far more complex interactions were at play here.

In the end, Mary Musgrove was powerful only as long as she used her knowledge and influence to aid the colony and its leaders. When she used her knowledge and influence to pursue her own gains, the trustees ceased to view her as useful. Over time, Musgrove and her ambitions threatened the authority of the white leaders and when that happened she became a problem. Her value as a cultural broker declined precisely when the colonial government pushed to establish its dominance over the Creeks, to set more firmly into place patriarchal institutions, its English legacy. Colonial leaders applied the racial and gendered hierarchies implicit in these institutions to judge, demean, and belittle Mary Musgrove in the wake of her infamous speech. They cast aspersions on her character at the same time that a series of successfully negotiated treaties with the Creeks stripped her of authority. Her response was unexpected. Undaunted by the costs, Musgrove renounced her status as good Christian helpmeet to reclaim her Creek identity, casting aside white notions of social hierarchy in the process.

In one stroke Mary Musgrove had been forced to confront the reality she had worked so hard to escape. Despite her many accommodations to white society, despite the many ways she had aided the colony, the white leaders retained the upper hand, changing the rules when most convenient and to their advantage.

◀

Notes

The author owes a great debt to Catherine Clinton whose thoughtful suggestions have vastly improved this essay. She also wishes to thank Colleen Gillespie for her helpful comments.

1. Allen D. Candler, ed. *The Colonial Records of Georgia*, v. 6, (Atlanta, Ga.: The Franklin Printing and Publishing Company, 1908), 260–68 (hereafter cited as *CRG*); *CRG*, v. 7, 269–80.

2. Historians have debated the identities of Mary's parents for more than 150 years. The latest and probably most accurate discussion of Mary Musgrove's lineage can be found in Rodney Baine, "Notes and Documents: Myths of Mary Musgrove," *Georgia Historical Quarterly*, LXXVI:2, Summer 1992, 428–35. Determining how to identify Mary Musgrove is almost as problematic as identifying her parents. Because she married three different men, her English last name

changed three times, from Musgrove to Matthews to Bosomworth. In her later years, she signed herself Princess Coosaponakeesa on petitions she sent to Georgia leaders and to the King of England.

3. *CRG*, v. 6, 283.

4. *CRG*, v. 6, 260–68; v. 7, 269–80.

5. I have chosen to use the term "interracial" because it fits early eighteenth-century Anglo-American ideas about difference. I recognize, however, that the term "intercultural" more accurately reflects these differences as discussed in Dina Birman, "Acculturation and Human Diversity in a Multicultural Society," in Trickett, Watts, and Birman, eds., *Human Diversity: Perspectives on People in Context* (San Francisco, Jossey-Bass Publishers, 1994), 261–84.

6. Clara Sue Kidwell, "Indian Women as Cultural Mediators," *Ethnohistory*, 39:2, Spring 1992, 101; Eirlys Mair Barker, "'Much blood and treasure': South Carolina's Indian Traders, 1670–1755," Ph.D. Thesis, College of William and Mary, 1993, 162–65.

7. Kathryn Holland Braund, "Guardians of Tradition and Handmaidens to Change: Women's Roles in Creek Economic and Social Life During the Eighteenth Century," *American Indian Quarterly*, 14, 1991, 248–50; Kidwell, "Indian Women as Cultural Mediators," 98–103; Barker, "'Much blood and treasure,'" 150.

8. Joel W. Martin, "Southeastern Indians and the English Trade in Skins and Slaves," in *The Forgotten Centuries: Indians and Europeans in the American South, 1521–1704*, Charles Hudson and Carmen Chaves Tesser eds., (Athens: The University of Georgia Press, 1994), 305–307.

9. Martin, "Southeastern Indians and the English Trade," 305–306.

10. Margaret Connell Szasz, "Introduction," in *Between Indian and White Worlds: The Cultural Broker*, ed. by Szasz (Norman: The University of Oklahoma Press: 1995), 4, 6, 18–19.

11. E. Merton Coulter, "Mary Musgrove, 'Queen of the Creeks': A Chapter of Early Georgia Troubles," *The Georgia Historical Quarterly*, XI:1, March 1927, 1–30; John Pitts Corry, "Some New Light on the Bosomworth Claims," *The Georgia Historical Quarterly*, XXV:3, September 1941, 196–234; Edward S. Sell, et al., *The Story of Georgia* (Atlanta: Science Research Associates, 1942), 104, 120–21; Phinizy Spalding, *Oglethorpe in America* (Athens: The University of Georgia Press, 1984) reprint ed., orig. pub. 1977, 92–93; Doris B. Fisher, "Mary Musgrove: Creek Englishwoman," Ph.D. diss., Emory University, 1990; Rodney M. Baine, "Myths of Mary Musgrove," 428–35.

12. Richard White, *The Middle Ground: Indians, Empires, and Republics in the Great Lakes Region, 1650–1815* (New York: Cambridge University Press, 1991).

13. James H. Merrell, "'The Customes of Our Countrey': Indians and Colonists in Early America," in *Strangers Within the Realm: Cultural Margins of the First British Empire*, Bernard Bailyn and Philip D. Morgan eds. (Chapel Hill: The University of North Carolina Press, 1991), 117–56.

14. Anna Laura Stoler, *Race and the Education of Desire* (Durham: Duke University Press, 1995), vii, 1–12; Michel Foucault, *The History of Sexuality, Vol. 1: An Introduction* (New York: Random House, 1978), 25–26.

15. Baine has pieced these dates together with other available evidence to produce a highly plausible time frame, which I have relied on for this essay. See Baine, "Myths of Mary Musgrove," 428–35.

16. John T. Juricek, ed., *Georgia Treaties, 1733–1763* in Alden T. Vaughan, ed., *Early*

American Indian Documents:Treaties and Laws, 1609–1789, Vol. XI (Frederick, Md.: University Publications of America, 1989), 3–4; Baines, "Myths of Mary Musgrove," 433; Mary Bosomworth, Memorial to Col. Alexander Heron, August 10, 1847, in Charles C. Jones, Jr., *The History of Georgia*, Vol. 1 (Boston, 1883), 387.

17. Juricek, *Georgia Treaties*, xxii–xxiii.
18. Juricek, *Georgia Treaties*, xxii–xxiii.
19. Juricek, *Georgia Treaties*, 6, 24–26.
20. Juricek, *Georgia Treaties*, 6, 28–29.
21. Juricek, *Georgia Treaties*, 12, 70–73.
22. Juricek, *Georgia Treaties*, 79, 86.
23. Juricek, *Georgia Treaties*, 83.
24. Juricek, *Georgia Treaties*, 84.
25. Juricek, *Georgia Treaties*, 84–85.
26. Juricek, *Georgia Treaties*, 110.
27. *CRG*, v. 36, 298–303.
28. *CRG*, v. 36, 310–11.
29. *CRG*, v. 7, 277.
30. *CRG*, v. 6, 276.
31. *CRG*, v. 25, 412–23.
32. Juricek, *Georgia Treaties*, 228–33.
33. *CRG*, v. 21, 77.
34. "England Will Grow Rich by Sending Her Poor Abroad. Of Refugees, Conversion of Indians, Small Offenders, Roman Colonies," in *The Most Delightful Country of the Universe: Promotional Literature of the Colony of Georgia, 1717–1734*, intro. by Trevor R. Reese (Savannah: Beehive Press, 1972), 139.
35. *CRG*, v. 27, 173–74.
36. *CRG*, v. 6, 269–280.
37. Lee Ann Caldwell, "Women Landholders of Colonial Georgia," in *Forty Years of Diversity: Essays on Colonial Georgia*, Harvey H. Jackson and Phinizy Spalding eds. (Athens: The University of Georgia Press, 1984), 183–97.
38. Memorial of Mary Bosomworth to Col. Alexander Heron, *CRG*, v. 36, 256–73.
39. *CRG*, v. 36, 285–86.
40. Memorial of Mary Bosomworth to Col. Alexander Heron, *CRG*, v. 36, 256–73.
41. *CRG*, v. 29, 196; Juricek, *Georgia Treaties*, 40–41.
42. *CRG*, v. 29, 196; Juricek, *Georgia Treaties*, 40–41.
43. Juricek, *Georgia Treaties*, 28.
44. Rayna Green, "The Pocohontas Perplex: The Image of Indian Women in American Culture," *The Massachusetts Review*, 16, Autumn 1975, 698–714.

◆ Part IV

THE
GULF
SOUTH

"IN CONSIDERATION OF HER ENORMOUS CRIME"

Rape and Infanticide in Spanish St. Augustine

On the night of October 6, 1787, St. Augustine slaveowner, Juan Salom, awoke to find that his slave, Juana, and her two children, were missing from their usual sleeping place on the floor next to his bed. He assumed they had fled. Before returning to sleep he went out to the patio well to get a drink and discovered the two small bodies of Juan Baptista Salom, age five, and Isabel Anna Salom, age two, floating in the dark water. He ran to inform the Sergeant Major and at 9:00 the next morning the governor's tribunal opened an investigation into the deaths of Juana's children.[1]

The criminal case against Juana illuminates central questions of race, sexuality, and gender in eighteenth-century Spanish Florida. The court's detailed attempts to assess the truth of Juana's story and its willingness to accept the testimony of female slaves against a white male owner stand in sharp contrast to legal procedures in the Anglo South. The verbatim statements the slave women give in this case are also an extremely rare and valuable window into the sensitive issues of race, sexuality, and gender. Juana's final punishment and the resolution of the case are classic examples of Spanish efforts to achieve compromise and restore community order through a combination of *derecho* (customary law) and *ley* (written law).[2] Because the case involved non-Spanish slave owners subject to Spanish law, the testimonies of the various parties also illuminate cultural differences in the treatment of slave women.

Spaniards constructed particular political and social identities for women that drew on a variety of sources including Roman and Visigothic law, Aristotelian theories, theological principles of the Roman Catholic Church, and centuries of customary law and practice in a racially and ethnically diverse metropolis.[3] In the thirteenth century, King Alfonso X (the Wise) codified Spain's varied legal traditions in the *Siete Partidas*. This code identified women, along with children, invalids, and delinquents, as in need of supervision but also deserving of familial and societal protection. Spain was a patriarchal society and a woman was subject to the will of her father, brothers, or uncles until either they died, or she reached twenty-five years of age or married, at which point she was subject to her husband's will. Should a woman marry against the advice of the responsible male of the family, she was liable to be disinherited.[4] Such juridical categorization obviously limited, at least temporarily, a woman's legal autonomy and economic power.

Nevertheless, women also enjoyed specific protections based in the same medieval Spanish law and customs that limited them. For example, women could inherit, hold, and disperse property left them by either parent, including real property, and it could not be seized for the debt of their husbands. Moreover, by law, women and men inherited equally from their parents, except in very notable exceptions. A husband could not alienate the dowry or *arras* (the groom's marriage gift) of his wife, and with her husband's written license, or power of attorney, a woman could, and did, enter into a wide variety of legal transactions. Women could also testify in secular courts and seek redress for grievances.[5]

The *Siete Partidas* also guaranteed Spanish slaves a legal personality and voice. Slaves in Anglo Saxon law, on the other hand, were considered chattel. Drawing primarily on Roman law, which recognized slavery as an accident of fate and against the laws of nature, the *Siete Partidas* detailed the rights as well as the obligations of slaves. In theory, these rights included personal security and legal mechanisms by which to escape a cruel master; conjugal rights and the right not to be separated from children; and the right to hold and transfer property and initiate legal suits.[6] In the Americas, that allowed slaves to purchase themselves or family members through an institution called *coartación*.[7] Slave women might also secure their freedom or that of their children through uncompensated manumission, which sometimes, but not always, involved a sexual relationship with their owners.

Spanish traditions of Christian charity and paternalism required magnanimity and generosity toward dependents and inferiors, including slaves. Not only divine reward but status were achieved by public acts of beneficence such as almsgiving, feeding and clothing the poor, or visiting the ill or imprisoned. Those who could afford to might endow charity hospitals and orphanages or establish funds to dower young girls. Appeals to a Christian governor would trigger certain requirements—to shelter fugitives, extend the benefit of the 'True Faith' to those seeking it, and defend the miserable, especially women and children. These public acts of goodness were carefully recited in any requests for appointments, grants, or titles and could have tangible rewards in Spanish society, just as they might expiate sin in the hereafter.[8]

If necessary, the Church also interceded "paternally" on behalf of members of the miserable classes, including slave women of African descent, supporting the sanctity of the family and the rights of slaves to freely choose their spouses. Informal institutions such as the extended kinship group *parentela*, which included blood relations, fictive kin such as godparents, and even household servants and slaves, and *clientela*, which bound powerful patrons and their personal dependents into a network of mutual obligations, were also useful to slave women. They were so deeply rooted that, according to one scholar, they might have been the "primary structure of Hispanic society," and slaves learned that mistreatment of servants and household slaves or their obvious hunger or poverty would dishonor the patriarch/owner.[9] While social conventions were no guarantee that Spanish slaveowners would not abuse their property, the combination of a real fear of eternal damnation and peer pressure was powerful enough to shape many master/slave relations, as slaves well understood.

Although women of African descent have long been thought to be doubly "victimized" by their race and gender in the Anglo South, and, if enslaved, legally oppressed as well, across the linguistic, political, and cultural divide that separated Florida from its northern neighbors they enjoyed access to courts that, in turn, gave them an historically recorded voice. Recent studies of the rich notarial records of Spanish "borderland" colonies such as Florida, Louisiana, and Texas verify that even on somewhat remote frontiers, law was adhered to, and that African and African American women in Spanish communities, both free and enslaved, seemed to enjoy legal protections and social opportunities significantly better than those of their counterparts in Anglo settlements. Moreover, in a small town such as St. Augustine, where both legal and religious institutions were readily available and where neighbors monitored each others' social behavior, slave women were assertive about pursuing both.[10]

The widespread acceptance of miscegenation no doubt affected master/slave relations in Spanish Florida. By the eighteenth century, European-African unions were very common. Many of Florida's wealthiest ranchers, planters, government officials, and merchants created large mulatto families with formerly enslaved women (sometimes in addition to white families). They recognized and freed their mulatto children, educated them, and provided for them and their mothers in their wills. Even in cases involving concubinage, the law and community consensus protected their widows and heirs. In Spanish Florida, free African women and their children managed plantations, operated small businesses, litigated in the courts, and bought and sold property, including slaves.[11]

And slave women in Florida, as elsewhere throughout the Spanish circum-Caribbean, also exercised rights that might not have been possible across the northern border. Slave women filed legal grievances against their owners, petitioned for manumission, hired out their own time, managed their own property and economy, and solicited changes in owners when they could find a more likely candidate to purchase them.[12]

This is not to suggest an absence of racial prejudice in Spanish settlements or to minimize the often horrific circumstances of Hispanic slavery. As the tragedy of the slave woman, Juana, graphically illustrates, slavery could be cruel and perverse anywhere. However, had Juana lived north of the Florida border, she would not have had the legal opportunity to defend herself in court and accuse her owner of rape and abuse, or to have her testimony supported by her fellow slaves.

Despite Juana's slave status, and the horror of her "unnatural" crime of infanticide, meticulous Spanish bureaucrats conducted her investigation as they would any other.[13] They followed all legal requirements and took great care to gather available physical evidence as well as lengthy testimony from the involved parties. They followed up on testimony to resolve differences or points of uncertainty and they tried to be sure that Juana understood the charges against her, as well as the religious and legal implications of her acts. Because they uncovered important mitigating circumstances in her crime, the St. Augustine court even referred the case to a higher court, seeking its guidance on her punishment.

This careful prosecution was extended to someone who could well have been considered an "outsider," and who lacked important personal connections within the community. Juana had been born in New York and raised among Protestant Anglos. Because she was illiterate and spoke only English, Juana's testimony was recorded by a bilingual interpreter who asked a set of questions about the crime, but also allowed Juana to add any statements she wished to make. The same format was followed with each of the other witnesses. The multiple and, sometimes conflicting, testimonies and perspectives on the case not only illumine the intimate, and often hidden nature of master/slave relations, but also how much the community knew about and monitored these.

Juana's owners, the Saloms, were also in a sense, outsiders. They were Minorcans, not Spaniards, and had been residents of St. Augustine less than a decade.[14] Although Salom's occupation was not stated, Minorcans in St. Augustine were commonly associated with the petty trades and petty agriculture and the Saloms were probably of the lower-middling class. At the time of the trial the Saloms still rented their house and farm lands.[15] But the court afforded Salom the same opportunity it gave Juana to present testimony, offer explanations about the crime, and defend himself against the serious accusations made by his slave.

Three days after Juan Salom discovered Juana's dead children in his well, she was captured and jailed in St. Augustine's stone fortress, the Castillo de San Marcos, where her interrogation took place.[16] A bilingual interpreter asked Juana if she knew why she was in prison, and she answered for drowning her children.[17] Asked how she accomplished the deed, Juana alleged that without knowing what she was doing she jumped into the well with them and that she had no idea how she found herself back out. Asked why, if she did not know what she was doing, she fled, Juana answered that she was afraid and beside herself (*fuera de sí*). Almost immediately upon discovery of the crime, Governor Vicente Manuel de Zéspedes had ordered an investigation of the murder site. The man who had retrieved the children's bodies from the well had been unable to get out without assistance, and so Juana's contention that she jumped into the well with a child under each arm, was kept afloat by her clothes, and got out unassisted, and in some unknown manner, raised questions. Although interrogators voiced their opinion that the story was unlikely, Juana stuck to it. When the interpreter asked Juana's motive for drowning her own children, her story began to unfold.

Juana related that on the night of the crime her owner had told her to say farewell to her children, because he had sold her to a new owner who would take her to Havana the following day. When Juana added that her owner had mistreated her for some time, the translator asked her to elaborate.

Juana reported that Salom continually solicited her to have sexual intercourse, and that when she refused him, Salom beat her. Solicitation was a serious charge under Spanish law, and if proven, the *Siete Partidas* required the court to remove Juana from the owner's household. Juana said that often when Salom propositioned her, his wife, with whom he also had sexual relations, was asleep in the bed next to which Juana slept. Asked if there were any witnesses to Salom's solicitations, Juana replied that he usually accosted her when she was working in the fields alone, but that occasionally he also harassed her in the house. One time her protests attracted another slave whom Juana stated overheard Salom threaten to beat her if she did not comply and also heard Juana's resistance. Sadly, Juana added that on many occasions Salom had his way, "by force of blows."

Only a few nights before the crime her owner had chained Juana next to his bed. As soon as his wife fell asleep, Salom awoke Juana with a kick and promised that if she would have sex with him, he would remove her chains. The interrogators asked Juana why she did not tell Salom's wife of these multiple offenses, and Juana responded that she had tried to but that the wife called her a liar and helped punish her. At this point the translator interjected that it was unlikely a wife would not do something about her husband's misdeeds if she knew the circumstances. In fact, Salom's wife, Margarita Neto, obviously suspected her husband, for Juana stated that she frequently asked Salom why he wanted to be alone with Juana. But Margarita was the mother of two small children in a precarious economic position and may not have felt it wise to confront this situation directly. Margarita, like Juana, was under Juan's control—physical and economic.[18] Margarita accepted her husband's denials, as so many wives of slaveowners did, but she also took out her frustrations on Juana. Once again, the interrogators gave Juana the opportunity to add to her statement and in an attempt to define her own character in terms the court would appreciate, Juana stated that even her owners would testify to her good service. (A good servant was an obedient servant.)

The translator next asked Juana if she had ever tried to find a different owner. In St. Augustine, as in many other Hispanic areas, a slave could seek a new owner willing to pay the old owner's asking price and, if the former owner agreed, change venues. Juana had actually found two different people willing to buy her, but when she told Salom about her prospects he did not believe her. Nor would Salom allow her to bring the prospective buyers to his house, but apparently understanding her determination to get away, Salom sold Juana to a resident of Havana.

Juana was listed in the records as an "infidel" because although she had been baptized into the New Light sect in New York, she said she never had been taught any prayers. Given this lack of religious instruction, the translator attempted to determine if she understood that killing her children and attempting suicide were wrong and deserving of punishment. Juana replied she knew it well, but that she was blinded by the problems she had described. The translator inquired why she had not gone to the priest for help, as she had a right to do. Juana said she would have but Salom told her he had already spoken to the priest and that the clergyman had signed papers allowing her sale. This was untrue, but Juana had no way of knowing that, and, seeing no way out, she admitted she had attempted to end all their lives.

The day after Juana began telling her story, her owner, Juan Salom, appeared before the governor to voluntarily give up custody of Juana, "in consideration of her enormous crime," and leave her "in the hands of Justice." A female slave of Juana's age and condition would have been valued at several hundred pesos, or the equivalent of several hundred dollars, so this was an expensive gesture for Salom. As it soon became clear, there were reasons for his largesse.

Juana had testified that another slave overheard Salom proposition her and Governor Zéspedes called that slave, María, to testify. Like Juana, María had been raised in the Anglo north, and was not a Catholic. She was a forty-six-year-old mulatta and illiterate, but certainly not without "voice." María lived in the adjoining house and so knew of Juana's plight, saying she would have had to "stuff her ears not to hear what she did." María testified that Juana had been sold to a new owner in Havana and that she heard Salom tell the distraught Juana, "Every ounce of flesh and each bone in your body belongs to that woman" (*todas sus carnes y cada hueso de ella era de dicha señora*). He taunted Juana to look one last time at the children which were not hers, but his.

The governor asked María about Juana's response and she said she heard Juana agree that her owner had a right to sell her, but that Juana had also reminded him he was obliged to sell her children with her. It is clear from this that although Juana was not a Catholic, she understood elements of the Church requirements that were critical to her welfare. The court also asked María if Salom had starved or punished Juana frequently, mistreatment that the *Siete Partidas* forbade of slaveowners.[19] María answered that Juana got abundant food but that once when Salom discovered Juana had spent the night elsewhere he gave her "about a dozen lashes" and locked her up.

María had not spoken with Juana since the night of the murders and so the court had no reason to believe she may have conspired to support Juana's version of the crime. Given the open windows, close proximity of houses, and relatively unrestricted movement of slaves throughout the city, the court simply assumed María would have knowledge of Juana's treatment by her owner. María testified that Juana complained that Salom would not allow her to see the black man with whom she had a relationship (possibly the father of the children) and that Salom's motive was to have Juana to himself. On that note María testified that one afternoon the previous summer she was in the street and saw Salom's wife leave the house. María said she approached an open window and had stuck her head in to talk with Juana when she heard Salom call

Juana and ask her to get in bed with him. She heard Juana refuse and tell her owner he had "his own woman." At that moment María had to leave her listening post because Salom's wife, Margarita, made a sudden reappearance. It is possible that she was investigating her suspicions about her husband. Once Salom's wife was inside the house, María returned to the window and heard her query Juana about what she was doing at the top of the stairs. Juana responded that Salom had called her up there and when his wife asked her why, Juana replied, "If I tell you, you'll whip me." That time the wife encouraged her to confess, saying she had overheard all anyway. Here María interjected that it was untrue Salom's wife had overheard, but that she only wanted to get the story. Trapped, Juana told the wife the truth, and this time Salom's wife marched to the bedroom and proceeded to slap Salom repeatedly.

María's lively and verbatim testimony caused the court to question how she understood the Catalan exchanges among the three, and María stated that she knew that language after living with two different Minorcan families for the past eight or nine years. She was also asked if the Saloms spoke English, which she confirmed they did. The court did not question the veracity of her statement; however, it wanted the legal record to be clear that María had, indeed, been able to understand and faithfully report the conversations she overheard. Slaves living in St. Augustine had often mastered at least three languages and sometimes more, and many were commonly bilingual.[20]

It was true that Spanish justice, like Spanish society of the time, suffered from a certain snobbism and commonly gave greater credit to testimony by elite witnesses.[21] Had María been telling such tales about members of the Governor's circle, she may have had a more difficult time being believed. But Salom was not of that strata, was not even Spanish, and had once been an indentured servant himself, so he was due no assumed superiority in the case. To further discredit him, and as if to emphasize Salom's guilt, María testified that when his wife was attacking him he never said a word, nor did he try to stop the physical abuse.

The following day the thirty-six-year-old illiterate Juan Salom appeared in court to give his version. Salom acknowledged that Juana had killed her children because she was about to be separated from them, but he said she had heard the news from her new owner, not from him. Salom said he had told Juana that in Havana she would be taking care of the new owner's child, but she ought to be happy because Havana was a prosperous city, and she would be able to earn money with which to buy her liberty and return to Florida to see her children.

From the various testimonies, Juana is known to have worked in the fields, in domestic service, and as a wetnurse, but she had no highly valued skills, and Salom's statement implied that Juana had little chance in St. Augustine of earning the funds required to buy herself and her children. Since the average price for a healthy woman of Juana's age was approximately 250 to 300 pesos and the cost of her children's freedom would have added another 100 to 200 pesos, and since the average day's pay for a man was a half peso, and women commonly earned less, Salom may have been right. Buying freedom was an arduous process, no doubt, however, other of Juana's contemporaries managed it, as she well knew.[22] The unnamed father of Juana's children might have also been able to help her work toward that goal. The fact that Salom introduced that idea into testimony may signify that Juana had been discussing the possibility.

The court signaled some sympathy for Juana when it asked Salom if the "true and sole" motive for Juana's actions was "the pain she felt to find herself sold to a country across the water, leaving behind her children." Given the opportunity to paint a darker picture of Juana, Salom had to agree that it seemed her grief was to blame. The court also asked Salom to say how and why he punished Juana and he answered that in the two years he had owned Juana he had once given her a few slaps (*bofetones*) and only on two other occasions had he struck her—once for refusing to get dressed on time to go to a wetnursing appointment and once for leaving the house.

Salom's version of why Juana left his house differed dramatically from the story Juana told María and María told the court. Salom said that his wife was going to punish Juana one time and Juana refused to allow it, biting his wife on the arm, and running away. Juana ran to the governor's house (once again illustrating that she understood from whom to seek protection), but Salom's wife followed her there and proceeded to punish her on the spot, until the governor intervened and chided Margarita Neto for disrespecting his house. It is significant that Governor Zéspedes, who was hearing the case, had witnessed some of Juana's mistreatment and had interceded for her on at least one occasion. Moreover, Margarita's public and unseemly display at the governor's house would have been regarded with public disapproval. No upper class woman would have conducted such a scene, and with this catfight, Margarita had, in effect, lowered herself to Juana's status.

The court then proceeded to the more serious charges made by Juana and asked if Salom had solicited his slave or ever had carnal knowledge of her. Salom said he never had and, in an eerily contemporary vein, said the charges were incredible because "my wife is pretty" (*la mujer que tiene es bonita*). The court asked him to better refresh his memory on this matter (*repase mejor la memoria*) since several previous testimonies had alleged otherwise, but Salom repeated his denials. He was asked specifically about the afternoon solicitation described by Juana and María, and once again denied it.

Meanwhile, St. Augustine's master carpenter and one other appointed official had concluded their examination of the crime scene. They reported that it would have been impossible for Juana to have committed the crime as she said she did, and that she would not have been able to get out of the well unassisted because it was too deep and narrow. This would seem to indicate that either Juana threw the children in and did not jump in herself, or that someone whom Juana was protecting by her silence had helped her get out.

Although Governor Zéspedes had full authority to decide this case, the severity of the crime, and of the allegations Juana made against her owner, led him to refer the case to the next level of justice—the royal audiencia in Havana. He forwarded the case testimony to Havana and by the following January that court had rendered a decision. The audiencia's dictate was that "there were not conclusive or clear enough proofs of the malice" required to hang Juana, which would have been the normal sentence for a capital crime. It added that the crime may have been involuntary or impetuous on the mother's part since she was driven almost mad by the pain of leaving her children forever in the custody of a feared owner. Rather than execution, therefore, the audience recommended a severe punishment to be left to the discretion of the governor. The higher court suggested lashes in the pillory and that "the delinquent" be made to wear an iron collar for six years to satisfy her punishment and at the same time "cleanse" the community of the evil of infanticide. No mention was made of Juana's charges of sexual harassment, because Salom had already given up custody of Juana. Had he not, the court would have been required to remove him from her home. Lastly, the court ordered Juana's sale at public auction to defray the court costs in Florida and Havana. This decision illustrates the standard legal effort to find compromise in contention and render justice in a manner that would reduce conflict and restore order to the community.

On receipt of the dictate from Havana, Florida's governor sentenced Juana to 200 lashes at the public pillory and to wear an iron collar as recommended. Such a harsh whipping would seem impossible to survive, but on February 14, 1788, her sentence was administered by the free black, July, and Juana was afterwards returned to the Castillo to await her sale. Bidders offered such low prices for Juana that the governor suspended two auctions. He also turned down the Royal Hospital's request to buy Juana as a laundress. Finally, on February 26, after almost five months in prison, Juana was sold at a third public auction to Pablo Villa for a low 135 pesos and her historical trail disappears.[23]

Juana escaped execution due to the extenuating circumstances of the crime, which she and her friend, the slave, María, were able to present to the court in their unconstrained testimonies. Nevertheless, she was severely whipped and humiliated in a staged morality play and forced to remind the populace of her punishment for infanticide by wearing the mark of her crime every day for six years. More horribly still, she lived with the knowledge that she had killed her children in the mistaken belief that the priest had authorized her separation from them. Juana remained a slave, but she was free of Salom's harassment, and it seems doubtful that a new owner would attempt similar mistreatment given the serious attention the governor's tribunal had paid to Juana and María's testimonies.

Salom and his wife escaped any punishment other than the public scandal that surrounded them. Not only were the details of their intimate relations made public, but the story of Salom's physical abuse by his wife (an inversion of the "natural order" of Spanish gender conventions) would surely have been the stock of popular jokes in that day. Perhaps there was little surprise that the Saloms had not behaved as "proper" Christian slaveholders were supposed to. Their low status probably made it easier for the court to believe Juana and María's stories about Salom's sexual abuse and his wife's silent complicity. More serious than their disgrace to the Saloms was the economic loss of Juana and her services, and the potential profits they may have made on the later sale or services of her children. Their downfall, like Juana's, was a lesson to be read by the community.

This is only a single case study, yet it clearly indicates that several important institutional, political, and social factors operated to guarantee even
enslaved women some rights and protections in Spanish Florida. One was the
observance of a legal code that upheld the rights of women generally and supported their access to the courts. In this legalistic society, all could make their
voices heard. Another was the particular geopolitical circumstances of Spanish
Florida. Bordered by a competing culture that practiced chattel slavery—first
English, then American—it sought advantage in its different treatment of
slaves. From the sixteenth through the eighteenth centuries, Spanish Florida
sought to weaken northern competitors by attracting and then freeing their
slaves, to the consternation of generations of Carolina and Georgia slaveholders.[24] More important, the conservative and family-based religious and
social systems and the gender conventions operating in Spanish Florida
required charity and moderation toward miserable classes, women, and slaves.
In a small town such as eighteenth-century St. Augustine, it was relatively easy
for inhabitants to monitor one another, and scandals and notorious abuses
would usually be corrected in the interest of community order. Finally, after
centuries of experience, Spaniards were accustomed to Africans and African
Americans in their communities and extended them legal rights, if not always
freedom. This access to legal recourse and "voice" generated a rich documentary record for African and African-American women in the Hispanic South
that allows historians to explore issues of race, sexuality, and gender more fully
than they might through Anglo-American records of the same period.

◆

Notes

1. All the material on the case is found in "Autos seguidos . . . contra Juana, esclava
   de Juan Salom, por haver ahogados dos niños suyos en un pozo de su casa," East
   Florida Papers, "Miscellaneous Legal Instruments and Proceedings,
   1784–1819," on microfilm Reel 110, no. 33, P. K. Yonge Library of Florida
   History, Gainesville (hereafter cited as PKY).

2. Lyle N. McAlister, *Spain and Portugal in the New World, 1492–1700* (Minneapolis: University of Minnesota Press, 1984), 24–26.

3. On the legal and social position of women in Spain, see Heath Dillard, *Daughters of the Reconquest: Women in Castilian Town Society, 1100–1300* (Cambridge:
   Cambridge University Press, 1984), 12–35. On the Spanish colonies, see Asunción Lavrin, "Introduction" and "In Search of the Colonial Woman in Mexico:
   The Seventeenth and Eighteenth Centuries," in Asunción Lavrin, ed., *Latin
   American Women: Historical Perspectives* (Westport, Ct.: Greenwood Press:, 1978),
   3–22, 23–59.

4. Dillard, *Daughters of the Reconquest*, 36–67, 96–126. Unmarried women over the
   age of twenty-five and widows actually enjoyed even more freedom than their
   married counterparts in colonial Latin America. David E. Vassberg, "The Status of Widows in Sixteenth-Century Rural Castile," in John Henderson and
   Richard Wall, eds., *Poor Women and Children in the European Past* (London, 1994),
   180–95; Asunción Lavrin, "The Colonial Woman in Mexico," in Asunción

Lavrin, ed., *Latin American Women: Historical Perspectives*, 30, 41. Others who
have written insightfully on women and marriage in colonial Latin America are
Patricia Seed, *To Love, Honor, and Obey in Colonial Mexico: Conflicts over Marriage
Choice, 1574–1821* (Stanford: Stanford University Press, 1988), Susan Migden
Socolow, "Love and Marriage in Colonial Latin America," paper delivered at the
Conference on Latin American History, December 1991, and Ramón A. Gutiér-
rez, "From Honor to Love: Transformations of the Meaning of Sexuality in
Colonial New Mexico," in Raymond T. Smith, ed., *Kinship Ideology and Practice
in Latin America* (Chapel Hill: University of North Carolina Press, 1984),
237–63.

5. Dillard, *Daughters of the Reconquest*, 26–30; Asunción Lavrin and Edith Couturier, "Dowries and Wills: A View of Women's Socioeconomic Role in Colonial Guadalajara and Puebla, 1640–1790," *Hispanic American Historical Review*,
59:2, 1979; 280–304; Edith Couturier, "Women and the Family in Eighteenth-
Century Mexico: Law and Practice," *Journal of Family History*, 10:3, Fall, 1985;
294–304. For the contrasting position of contemporary women in nearby South
Carolina, see Marylynn Salmon, "Women and Property in South Carolina: The
Evidence from Marriage Settlements, 1730–1830," *William and Mary Quarterly*,
39, October 1982; 655–85. Salmon argues that marriage settlements became
more common in South Carolina during the eighteenth and early nineteenth
centuries as a way of protecting women from the legal disadvantage and loss of
personalty they suffered under common law. She also points out, however, that
marriage settlements were not common and that women may have deferred to
male antipathy to them.

6. William D. Phillips, *Slavery from Roman Times to the Early Transatlantic Trade*
(Minneapolis: University of Minnesota Press, 1985), 154–70; Ruth Pike, *Aristo-
crats and Traders: Sevillian Society in the Sixteenth Century* (Ithaca: Cornell University Press, 1972), 170–92; Herbert S. Klein, *African Slavery in Latin America
and the Caribbean* (New York: Oxford University Press, 1986).

7. Hubert H. S. Aimes, "*Coartación*: A Spanish Institution for the Advancement of
Slaves into Freedom," *Yale Review*, February 1909; 412–31.

8. Maureen Flynn, "Charitable Ritual in Late Medieval and Early Modern Spain,"
Sixteenth-Century Journal, 16, Fall 1985; 1–30 and *Sacred Charity*, 44–74; Amy
Bushnell, "The Expenses of *Hidalguía* in Seventeenth-Century St. Augustine,"
El Escribano, 15, 1978; 23–36.

9. This does not mean, of course, that owners never neglected slaves. There are
numerous examples throughout colonial Spanish America where they did. However, the prohibition against the neglect at least gave slaves accepted legal
grounds on which to grieve against their owners. McAlister, *Spain and Portugal
in the New World*, 133–52. For an excellent look at how these systems actually
operated, see Stephanie Blank, "Patrons, Clients and Kin in Seventeenth-Century Caracas: A Methodological Essay in Colonial Spanish American Social History," *Hispanic American Historical Review*, 54, May 1974; 260–82. An older, but
still useful study is by George M. Foster, "Cofradía and Compadrazgo in Spain
and Spanish America, "*Southwestern Journal of Anthropology*, 9, 1953; 1–28.

10. In 1788, St. Augustine's total population was only 1,878, and was composed of
651 whites, 588 slaves, and 63 free blacks. Blacks, free and enslaved, formed 37
percent of the population. Report of Vicente Manuel de Zéspedes, October 2,
1788, Cuba 1395, Archivo General de Indias, Seville, Spain. For comparable
findings on Louisiana, see Kimberly S. Hanger," 'The Fortunes of Women':

Spanish New Orleans' Free and Slave Women of African Descent," in Patricia Morton, ed., *Discovering the Women in Slavery* (Athens: University of Georgia Press, 1995). On similar legal initiative (and success) demonstrated by Indian women in Spanish Texas, see Ana María Castillo Crimm, "Indian Slavery, Indian Freedom: The Case of María Gertrudis de la Peña on the Spanish Frontier, 1760–85," paper delivered at the Conference on Latin American History, Washington, D.C., 1992.

11. Jane Landers, "Black Society in Spanish St. Augustine, 1784–1821," Ph.D. diss., University of Florida, 1988, 106–45. Daniel L. Schafer, *Anna Kingsley* (St. Augustine: St. Augustine Historical Society, 1995).

12. Jane Landers, "Traditions of African American Freedom and Community in Spanish Colonial Florida," in David R. Colburn and Jane L. Landers, eds., *The African American Heritage of Florida* (Gainesville: University Press of Florida, 1995), 29–31.

13. Dillard, *Daughters of the Reconquest*, 208–10. Because children were highly valued in the Reconquest era, when colonizing an ever-advancing frontier was critical, infanticide was harshly punished and men and women were usually executed for this crime. Women convicted of such a grave crime were usually burned alive. In other parts of early modern Europe, women were more often drowned for this crime and more women were executed for this crime than for any other, except witchcraft. See Merry E. Weisner, *Women and Gender in Early Modern Europe* (Cambridge: Cambridge University Press, 1993), 51–52.

14. Juan Selom (sic) was among the Minorcans indentured and transported by Andrew Turnbull to New Smyrna, Florida in 1768. This group suffered such horrible conditions on Turnbull's indigo plantations that in 1777 they rebelled and escaped to St. Augustine where Governor Patrick Tonyn freed them. Selom signed the Minorcan declaration of loyalty to Governor Vicente Manuel de Zéspedes on July 13, 1784. Joseph Byrne Lockey, ed., *East Florida, 1783–1785: A File of Documents Assembled and Many of Them Translated* (Berkeley: University of California Press, 1949), 233.

15. Salom cultivated 3 1/2 acres of rented land according to the Spanish census of 1783–1784, and the house in which the crimes took place (on lot #290) was described in the 1788 inventory of the royal engineer, Mariano de la Rocque, as "timber frame house, in bad condition." Salom also rented that house. Mariano de la Rocque, "Plano Particular de la Ciudad de San Agustin," State Archives, Tallahassee, Florida. For a fine study of Minorcan culture and Minorcan integration into Spanish St. Augustine, see Patricia C. Griffin, "Mullet on the Beach: the Minorcans of Florida, 1768–1788," *El Escribano*, 27, 1990.

16. Juana had run west to the ferry where she found a black man willing to transport her across the San Sebastian River in his canoe, but before her escape was accomplished, a white man took her prisoner and took her to the Castillo. By that time, Father Thomas Hassett had presided over the Christian burial of Juana's children in the town's Catholic cemetery. There is no record of Juana's reaction to this news. The burial records definitively list the children's race as negro (Ethiops vulgo negro), ruling out the possibility that Juan Salom was their father. Burials of Juan Baptista Salom and Isabel Anna Salom, October 7, 1787, Black Burials, Catholic Parish Registers, on microfilm reel 284 L, page 4, nos. 11 and 12, PKY.

17. In many African cosmologies, bodies of water are seen as the boundary between this world and the next, and African slaves commonly believed that after death

they would be carried across the Atlantic to be reborn in their homeland. There are many colonial accounts of suicides by drowning, but water also held sacred meanings associated with purification. See Robert Farris Thompson, *Flash of the Spirit: African and Afro-American Art and Philosophy* (New York: Vintage Books, 1984), 134–38 and *Face of the Gods, Art and Altars of Africa and the African Americas* (New York: Museum for African Art, 1993).

18. I am indebted to Patricia Griffin for information on Salom and his family. On Father Thomas Hassett's census conducted in 1786, one year before this trial, the Salom family was household number 36 and included Juan Salom, age thirty-five, a native of Alayor (Minorca), his wife, Margarita Neto, age thirty, from San Felipe (Minorca), their children, Juan, seven, and Clara, four, and two male and two female slaves, unnamed and not baptized. The Mariano de la Roque index of town properties shows that in 1787 the family lived in a wooden house on the street of the jail.

19. Slaves who asked the court for changes of owners or to initiate self-purchase often charged that their owners had not properly clothed or fed them (as required by the *Siete Partidas*). This seems to have been an effective argument and it was used repeatedly. Denying a slave access to church was also an effective complaint. Landers, "African American Traditions," 29.

20. Just as slaves learned new languages, they also adapted to a variety of new legal and social systems. For a fascinating study on the Minorcans in St. Augustine, see Patricia C. Griffin, "Mullet on the Beach: The Minorcans of Florida, 1768–1788," *El Escribano*, 27, 1990.

21. For a discussion of Spanish interrogatories and the relative weight assigned to witnesses of different statuses, see Alexandra Parma Cook and Noble David Cook, *Good Faith and Truthful Ignorance: A Case of Transatlantic Bigamy* (Durham: Duke University Press, 1991), 87–89, 91–103, 112–14.

22. Landers, "Black Society," 146–73.

23. "Autos seguidos contra la esclava Juana."

24. Jane Landers, "Gracia Real de Santa Teresa de Mose: A Free Black Town in Spanish Colonial Florida," *American Historical Review*, 95, February 1990, 9–30.

COPING IN A COMPLEX WORLD

Free Black Women in Colonial New Orleans

Colonial New Orleans' free blacks or *libres*[1] inhabited an intricate, complex, and ambiguous world. Free black women, in particular, found themselves living within a plantation slave society in which racial discrimination and a hierarchy ordered by race, class, and gender interacted to subordinate them as women and as nonwhites. Laws and customs purposefully delineated differences among Spain's subjects, constructing and maintaining inequalities based on race, religion, occupation, gender, wealth, and lineage; from the Spanish perspective it went against nature for all people to be equal.[2] In reality, however, demographic, economic, and political conditions in New Orleans created a frontier, small-scale society in which relationships between persons of different race, status, and gender were fluid, mutable, and highly personalistic. Many libres strove to move up within the hierarchy and a few worked to dismantle it entirely, especially during the late eighteenth century's era of revolution. They desired that the distinctions between themselves and whites be dissolved altogether, claiming to be "free like you" and asserting "a universal equality among men," with only "their method of thinking, not color," differentiating them.[3]

Libre women in New Orleans were no exception, and they would extend the desire for equality beyond the confines of gender. Free black women used advantages unique to them and generally not available to white or slave women to confront limitations imposed on them as defined by their race and gender and images of their sexuality. They exercised more control than slave women did over the choice of a husband or a more casual consort. In many ways they also had more options than white women, who were controlled by the *patria potestad* (authority excercised by the male head of the household) and for whom society dictated that they marry honorably, produce and raise children, and in general retreat from a public life. One must keep in mind, however, that married white women, especially those of the elite class, enjoyed a material standard of living, degree of legal protection, and social status higher than that of any nonwhite woman.

Free black women were not expected to marry, a societal prescription that could give them greater independence but, as mentioned, could also circumscribe the resources available to them in a patriarchal society like New Orleans. They could maintain formal and informal relations with white, libre, or slave men, and if they chose to remain single or widowed, they could exercise greater independence in the economic sphere than slave women or married women. Many more free black than white women headed households.[4] Libre women who arranged interracial unions with white men often did not live with these men, and thus they and their daughters did not have to endure a day-to-day existence within the confines of a strong patriarchal household and were not subjected to the patria potestad, under which the patriarch of the family exercised authority over their wives, single daughters, and other single women in the household.

These alternatives, however, often came at a high cost. Although they might have had greater control over business enterprises, property, and their daily lives, free black women also suffered discrimination and diminished resources because they lacked the protection of powerful patriarchal allies who could represent their interests within a society that valued the opinions, wage-earning potential, and honor of males, especially white males. For most libre women work was a necessity, not an option; many a free black woman appealed to the mercy of the court as a *"pobre muger"* whose family depended on her *jornales* (daily wages) to survive. They faced circumscribed choices of occupation—primarily as domestics, boardinghouse keepers, retailers, and publicans—that paid less than men's work,[5] and the property that white consorts donated to them and their *casta* (mixed-race) children could be taken back or contested by legitimate heirs.

Libre women had to tread carefully and artfully within a patriarchal society that valued males more than females but that did not afford them the paternal protection due the weaker sex because they ostensibly did not possess honor and virtue—attributes accorded only to whites. Caught in between the interests of officials and residents, of white, free black, and slave men, free black women fought daily oppression and sought to assert their identity, in part by striving to attain what was important to them: freedom for themselves, friends, and relatives; stable, long-lasting unions that produced children and cemented kin networks; prosperity for themselves and future generations; and respect as hardworking, religious members of the community. Free black women utilized to the best of their advantage a unique hybrid of choices *and* constraints that white and slave women rarely experienced. Despite their best efforts, in most cases these women faced an uphill battle.

Demographic and other material conditions found along the Gulf Coast and elsewhere across New Spain's northern border somewhat tempered New Orleans' social hierarchy and contributed to the limitations and opportunities available to libre women. Issues of honor and status associated with consensual interracial unions and out-of-wedlock children were tempered by demographic realities found in many peripheral regions of the Spanish empire. Relationships among the various racial groups that inhabited this borderland were common, and the stability offered by marriage and family formation along patrilineal lines was often shaken by the specter of early death. Given New Orleans' unhealthy semitropical climate and low-lying, mosquito-infested terrain, it is not surprising that inhabitants died frequently and at tender ages. Children in particular were subject to the ravages of smallpox, yellow fever, influenza, and malaria, women to the tortures of childbirth, and men to the uncertainties of warfare. The median age at death for white males was 30.6 years and white females 18.1 years; the figures for free blacks were even more dismal, although reversed by sex, with a median age at death for free black males of 8.1 years and for free black females 30.3 years.[6] Interracial unions and the offspring they produced resulted at least partly from these demographic circumstances, as well as from a shortage of white women and an abundance of libre and slave women. White male New Orleanians outnumbered white women (with a sex ratio of 175 males per 100 females in 1777, 162 in 1791, and 115 in 1805) and free black females outnumbered free black males about two to one. In urban centers like New Orleans, there were even more females than males among slaves, although the disparity was not so great (a sex ratio of 82 in 1777, 95 in 1791, and 76 in 1805).[7]

Because white women were scarce and died young, white men often sought partners among the more numerous and longer-lived free black and slave women of New Orleans. Such unions—most of them unsanctioned by church and crown—confounded official efforts to keep bloodlines "pure," marriages legitimate, and women subordinate to men. "Family values" and kinship patterns were complex and constantly changing. There was a lack of stability and consensus in Louisiana, where the hierarchy was marked by "a degree of social fluidity," as in other peripheral regions of the Americas.[8]

Spanish law further cut across boundaries of the social hierarchy by establishing and protecting the property rights of all women, regardless of their race, status, or class. Women exercised control over their own possessions, which for the wealthy could be considerable. When a woman married, her parents or other relatives furnished her with a dowry; the groom could also make a present of one-tenth of his estate, known as the *arras*. All property acquired during their marriage was considered communal and divided equally between husband and wife. If the husband predeceased his wife, she received her original dowry, arras, half the communal property (*bienes gananciales*), and any goods inherited by her during their marriage, all before the royal treasury or any other creditors could make a claim on the estate. This wealth remained hers even if she remarried. The intent of Spanish law was not to favor the woman as an individual, but to protect the property of her family. Spanish law also promoted the integrity and importance of the family as a corporate body by upholding partible inheritance, whereby each child, whether male or female, received a part of his or her parents' estates and could not be disinherited. This legislation applied to all women and children—white and nonwhite, slave and free, wealthy and poor.[9]

Increasingly over the eighteenth century, however, legislation regarding marriage sought to redraw and reinforce the boundaries between persons of different races and statuses. In addition to the general populace's hostility and opposition toward mixed marriages, crown officials made it more difficult for whites to marry nonwhites, especially when their parents opposed such unions. The *Real Pragmática* (Royal Pragmatic), issued by the crown in 1776 and applied to its American colonies in 1778, codified this move toward restricting marriage choice and preventing "unequal" alliances. Concerned with any impact that the "passions of youth" might have on the economic stability of elite families, Spain required all persons under age twenty-five (the age of majority) to obtain parental permission to marry. The Pragmatic exempted castas and blacks because it assumed that they were illegitimate or did not know who or where their parents were. Such perceptions had the effect of giving nonwhites more flexibility while at the same time reinforcing negative stereotypes about them. Of greater consequence, the Royal Pragmatic additionally conferred on parents the right to prevent the marriage of their offspring to someone of "substantial social inequality." Inequality was officially defined in racial terms but also could be interpreted in terms of wealth, occupation, and status disparities. Marriage was intended to take place between social equals, and thus most interracial unions were consensual and not recognized by the church.[10]

Nevertheless, after receiving special permission and the consent of their families, a white and free black couple could marry in the Catholic church in many colonial societies, including New Orleans. Indeed, most church authorities continued to promote the doctrine of free will in the choice of marriage partners, but they did so in opposition to the rising power of the state and thus increasingly to little avail. One scholar of Saint-Domingue notes that "even during the last few decades of the colony, marriage between . . . impecunious white Frenchmen and comfortably placed women of color were common enough to inspire bitter comment."[11] In New Spain, as well, marriages between whites and blacks, while generally tolerated in the sixteenth and seventeenth centuries, became an issue of contention in the eighteenth century, when "Spanish elites responded defensively to the efforts of increasingly well-to-do mulattoes to intermarry with their ranks."[12] Interracial marriage, however, was primarily of concern to status-conscious white elites; few poor Spanish and prosperous mixed-race families objected to unions between their members and darker-skinned castas.

Although official unions between whites and free blacks were not common in New Orleans, they occurred frequently enough for fray Firso de Peleagonzalo to assume that don Juan Antonio Lugar and the free *parda* María Juana Prudhome (alias de Justis) were wed, when actually they had lived in a state of public concubinage for four years. A native of Havana, Prudhome was herself the natural daughter of Mr. Prudhome and Angélica Forest, a *morena* libre.

After Prudhome bore Lugar a daughter in 1793, she presented herself to the priest in order to receive benediction. In his own words Peleagonzalo expressed his surprise: he "had not even suspected that [Prudhome] was not the legitimate wife of Lugar, as there were in New Orleans other whites married to *mulatas*."[13] One such marriage between a free black and a white involved Bautista Rafael, a free moreno and the legitimate son of two other free morenos, and María Andrea Gitana, the white widow of Vilime Alemán. Church officials recorded their wedding date of May 1, 1779, in the nonwhite registers.[14] Such marriages and even less formal unions between black males and white females were especially rare and deemed unnatural and odious according to the double sexual standard set by Spanish society. While an illicit relationship with someone of another race did not permanently dishonor a white male, it doomed a white woman to ignominy and loss of virtue.[15]

In Spanish New Orleans, free blacks interacted frequently with slaves as well as whites—at work and at play, in the streets, markets, homes, and religious institutions of the city—and occasionally married them, even though such bonds were also considered to be forged between "unequals." Disproportionate sex ratios in the free black population prompted some free women of color to seek mates among slaves as well as among whites. Of the 136 marriages recorded in the black registers between 1777 and 1803, ten (7.4 percent) were between a free person of color and a slave, and in six of the ten cases the bride was the free partner.[16] Only two of the twenty partners were light-skinned, both of them free pardo men. In addition, both libre men and women who wed while in slavery continued their relationships with still-enslaved partners.

A few free people of color acted as prescribed by the church and crown and married persons of the same race and status. Of the ninety-three marriages recorded in the black registers between 1777 and 1803 in which both bride and groom were libres, seventy-one (over three-quarters) involved partners of the same phenotype; for the remaining cases, in thirteen the male was lighter and in nine the female was lighter.[17] One of those nine united Catarina Labastille (also known as Lafrance), a *cuarterona*, and Bartolomé Bautista, a *grifo*, in 1788. Catarina had consented to marry Bartolomé, but her father, a white plantation owner named Pedro Pablo Labastille (Lafrance), objected to the marriage on grounds of *la desigualdad de los contrayentes respecto ser la dicha mi hija quarterona, y el subrodicho Bartolomé grifo* (inequality of the marriage partners because my daughter is a cuarterona and the above-mentioned Bartolomé is a grifo), all within his rights according to the Royal Pragmatic. Arrested and imprisoned, Bartolomé pleaded for justice before a civil court, claiming that he was not forcing Catarina to marry him against her will and requesting expediency with regard to the marriage ceremony because he needed to harvest his crops. When convinced by "sensible persons" that there was no "diversity of class" between the parties, don Pedro Pablo finally relented and dropped his objections. The court referred the case to the commissioner of the Inquisition so that he could arrange for the wedding celebration, which took place the next day. In the marriage record, the priest recorded Catarina as the legitimate daughter of Pablo Lafrance and María

Charles, the offspring of an official union between a white man and a free woman of color.[18]

Although there is no record of how long Catarina and Bartolomé remained together,[19] many unions between free blacks endured several years, indicating the value they placed on such family relationships. In her will, the free morena Angélica stated that she had been married to Roberto Horry, moreno libre, for thirty-five years and that they had had two children.[20] When the free parda Naneta Manuela Carrière (alias Cádiz) died in 1800 at the age of forty-one, she had been married to Pedro Bahy (Bailly), a free pardo businessman and militia officer, for twenty-two years. Their marriage produced five children, two of whom died at ages three and nine; their oldest son Pedro was also a member of the free pardo militia, as were Pedro, Sr.'s two illegitimate sons, Narciso and Alejandro, who also took the name of Bahy. Alejandro had been born prior to Pedro's marriage to Naneta, Narciso slightly afterward. Apparently Pedro—like many white and black men of his era—subscribed to the double standard of sexual honor. In this case, Bahy's illegitimate sons were also his slaves. They sued him and won both recognition as his sons and their freedom, despite Bahy's appeal to a higher court in Havana.[21]

Whereas Naneta and her siblings were the offspring of an unwed mixed-race union, they and their children chose to marry persons of the same phenotype and to legitimate their marriages in the Catholic Church, as did many second- and third-generation libres.[22] Naneta's younger sister María Genoveva Morín Montreuil married twice within a short time as a result of the death of her first husband, Juan Francisco Mercier, a free pardo. When María Genoveva wed Juan Francisco in 1793, she brought a dowry of 450 pesos given her by her mother Fanchon Montreuil, alias Carrière, a free morena *panadera* (baker).[23] Fanchon had provided her other daughter Naneta with 390 pesos when she married Bahy in 1778. By the time María Genoveva's son Carlos Saint-ville was born in September 1795, she had already remarried, this time to a pardo militia officer, Gabriel Gerónimo.[24] Naneta's and María Genoveva's brother Carlos Montreuil married Constanza Juan Luis, a free parda and the legitimate daughter of a free pardo and a free morena, when he was forty-eight years old and "gravely ill" on what he thought was his deathbed in 1792. The entry of their marriage in the sacramental registers stated that Carlos and Constanza had begotten several children, who were now legitimate. One of these children, Agata, sought the sanction of a church wedding from the very beginning of her relationship with a free pardo native of Haiti in 1805.[25]

As noted previously, most New Orleanians in the colonial period did not marry before church officials and lived together in what today would be considered common-law marriages. Many of these relationships were interracial—involving white males and nonwhite females in particular—and "tended to be consensual rather than legal," as they were in Cuba and other peripheral regions of Spain's eighteenth-century empire.[26] Even though interracial informal unions were nominally illegal, New Orleans officials generally looked the other way and occasionally engaged in them themselves (including at least one lieutenant governor and scores of army officers). In one case a white man was actually prosecuted for living with a woman of color without benefit of marriage, but only because he stated so at a trial concerning another matter.[27] Rather ironically, these interracial unions were tolerated in part because of the value white society placed on the patriarchal family. The man's desire to shield his casta offspring and potential heirs also helped secure some protection for his female consort, an advantage not overlooked by libre women.

Don Pedro Darby and the morena libre Naneta had a representative interracial relationship. In his will dated 1803 Darby, a native of New Orleans and single, acknowledged his seven natural children by Naneta, ranging in age from thirty-three to ten years. The children's ages attest to a lengthy relationship between don Pedro and Naneta. Darby donated half his animals and a slave to Naneta, and left the rest of his estate (two plantations, furniture, and half the animals) to the children. He appointed their eldest son guardian of the minor children.[28] Another white man who freely recognized his long-term union with a free woman of color was don Pedro Cázelar. In his will dated June 1797 Cázelar—single, thirty-two years old, and a native of New Orleans—affirmed that he and the free cuarterona Carlota Wiltz had produced four daughters, all between the ages of five and ten. He left the mother and daughters a morena slave and her four children, furniture, household goods, 1,000 pesos, and a farm. A sixth heir was added when Carlota bore don Pedro a son in 1800.[29]

Despite what might be perceived as the generally "positive" experiences of Cázelar's and Darby's consensual partnerships, there were distinct disadvantages to such informal unions, whether between whites and blacks, free persons and slaves, or "equals." Libre women struggled to overcome these obstacles, and although they might have secured some privileges for themselves and their children, in the larger arena of public opinion they failed. Free black women who engaged in sexual relationships with white men, and even those who did not, were often condemned as "lewd," "lascivious," and "licentious," in New Orleans and throughout the Americas.[30] One late eighteenth-century observer of New Orleans lifestyles, Claude C. Robin, denounced the many white men who were tempted to "form liaisons with these lascivious, coarse, and lavish [libre] women" and subsequently were "ruined."[31] He, however, primarily blamed the women for such sinful practices, as did physician Paul Alliot, who believed that free black women inspired "such lust through their bearing, their gestures, and their dress, that many quite well-to-do persons are ruined in pleasing them."[32] Of course, the objects of this derision did not perceive themselves as such and resisted efforts to denigrate them as women and nonwhites.

Nevertheless, most libre women found that they exercised little leverage in convincing white partners to legitimate their relationships, due in part to these negative stereotypes. The dominant society assumed that nonwhite, especially casta, women were illegitimate offspring who lacked pure bloodlines (*limpieza de sangre*) and wealth and thus had no honor, whether defined in terms of virtue or status.[33] This concern for their own and their families' honor dissuaded most white males from seeking official church weddings with their free black consorts, and religious authorities rarely forced them to legitimate these unions or uphold marriage promises. In 1779 the free parda tavernkeeper María Teresa Cheval petitioned the ecclesiastical tribunal in New Orleans to enforce the promise of marriage that Phelipe Lafarga (la Farge), a white French tailor, had made her in Havana. Before the marriage banns were proclaimed, Lafarga and Cheval had left Havana for New Orleans, where they lived for two years without completing the banns. One witness testified that Cheval's owner in Havana had manumitted her specifically so that she could marry Lafarga.[34] Although the record is incomplete, Cheval apparently was unsuccessful in attempting to restore her lost honor, which the court did not recognize anyway because she was not of pure European ancestry; she remained unmarried, while Lafarga married a white woman. Cheval and Lafarga, however, continued to engage in business transactions, buying and selling slaves and real estate and making loans to each other. Cheval also maintained a close business and personal relationship with another white man, the Spaniard Bernardo Izurra, a tavernkeeper like herself.[35]

Another drawback to common-law marriage was that the state as well as the church did not recognize the union, and thus parents could not guarantee the transmittal of property and status to children and surviving partners. The laws of partible inheritance, by which no legitimate child could be disinherited, did not apply to natural or illegitimate offspring. These children, however, could inherit up to one-third the value of their parent's estate, and the consort up to one-fifth the estate's value, either through an *inter vivos* donation or by testament.[36] One's claim to and hold on this property was tenuous and required the cooperation of legitimate heirs (some of whom contested the wishes of their relatives), executors, and the judicial system. Occasionally, even the donors changed their minds, reneging on their obligations as a means of expressing their displeasure toward or controling the behavior of the object of their magnanimity. When don Luis de Beaurepos discovered that his former consort, the free parda Magdalena Canelle, was living "in a state of concubinage" with another white man, he seized the female slave he had given Canelle seven years earlier. According to witnesses, it was common knowledge that Beaurepos had made the slave a "pure gift" to Canelle in order to serve her and the two daughters she had had by Beaurepos during their eight-year relationship. Even though Beaurepos claimed to be ignorant of such things and dismissed her witnesses as "some mulatas, libertines like herself," Canelle maintained that he had also bestowed on her a plantation across the river "to recompense her for the concubinage that he had with her and for the advantages of their two children." The court initially returned the slave to Canelle, but a new judge ruled in favor of Beaurepos and jailed Canelle until she turned the slave over to her former lover. One year later Canelle appealed the case to a superior court in Havana, where the Louisiana record ends.[37] By this time court costs surely surpassed the value of the slave. Canelle probably continued arguing the case as a matter of principle, an option few nonwhite and even white women could afford or had the tenacity to pursue.

Of course, even an official marriage did not assure the wife and children a large or even comfortable inheritance, especially if one's mate squandered all their property, earned jointly or brought by the wife into the union. Several free blacks lived in poverty, barely better off than slaves. Even those women who had accumulated estates through hard work and/or inheritance could see them slip away under the legal jurisdiction of husbands who through lack of judgment, neglect, or deliberate fraud misused their wives' property.

These women bore what the free parda María Gentilly termed the "yoke of matrimony." She tried—but failed—to preserve her property from what she perceived as malicious deception on the part of an inept husband, unjust favoritism toward slaves, and discrimination against women—married women in particular. When Gentilly's husband Esteban Lalande borrowed money from a slave named Luis Dor and could not repay the loan, he was thrown in jail and Gentilly's house was seized with the intent of auctioning it and settling the debt. Gentilly protested that the house was part of the property she had inherited from her white father prior to her marriage and as such entirely belonged to her. In addition, Lalande had forged her mark on the promissory note to Dor, a fraudulent act to which he eventually admitted.

Lalande died in prison, and the slave then proceeded against his estate. Once again Gentilly contested what she perceived as Dor's unjust pretensions on her dowry, reiterating that "the woman's dowry is always sacred, and protected by royal laws and natural laws" no matter what it was used for, even the manumission of a slave, especially one whose value was grossly overestimated by his greedy white master. Nevertheless, Dor convinced the tribunal that Lalande and Gentilly had both contributed to the purchase of the previously seized house in New Orleans and that it should be considered community property. The judge ordered the house sold at public auction, with half the proceeds going to Gentilly and half to satisfy Lalande's debts.[38] Thus Gentilly reluctantly relinquished much of the estate she had brought into her marriage twenty years before. Even though Spanish civil law offered her some protection, it could not prevent the manipulation of women, especially nonwhite women, in a society that valued patriarchy, European blood, and freedom.

Gentilly's experience and that of other married women might have convinced the majority of libre women to remain single or enter into consensual unions that were more easily dissolved when the relationship proved disadvantageous. María Luisa Venus Doriocour was one woman who chose cohabitation with a white man over marriage to a free black. For two months Doriocour had refused to marry her free moreno lover of seven years—Antonio de Noyan, alias Conway—when he declared his intention to marry another free woman of color. Doriocour promptly objected to the wedding on the grounds that Conway had already given her a promise of marriage; she apparently did not want him, but did not want another woman to have him either. Witnesses testified that Doriocour had indicated to them that she did not want to marry Conway because she had initiated a relationship with a white Spanish warrant officer who provided her with gifts and everything she needed in exchange for living with him illicitly.[39] Doriocour apparently perceived greater advantages in cohabitating with an influential, well-to-do white than in marrying a free black. At the same time, her reluctance to let her former free black lover marry another woman reveals her feelings of uncertainty toward the permanancy and future prospects of the interracial cohabitation she eventually elected.

Concubinage to white and libre males definitely was exploitative, especially of slave women who rarely had any say in the matter, but for some free black women—like Doriocour—it was also a choice. They accepted consensual union as a viable alternative when white men would not marry them because bonds across racial lines stained their honor. Although considered an "inferior form of mating," concubinage could provide opportunities, especially for successive generations; it secured material advantages and a lighter phenotype for children born into an acquisitive society that valued racial lightening. Although libre women probably would have preferred the stability and honor associated with an official marriage, they made the best of the situation, attempting to maintain long-term relationships with their consensual partners, secure comfortable lifestyles, bear children, and subsequently arrange for their advantageous marriages.[40]

A few libre women went so far as to "pass" into white society. Indeed, one way for a white male to maintain his honor and still marry a woman of African descent was to redefine her race as white, or lacking that as Native American. In most of Spanish America, *indios* and especially *mestizos* ranked above morenos and pardos within the social hierarchy, although still beneath whites.[41] The lighter and closer in resemblance to a white person an individual was, the higher up the status scale he or she could climb. Usually this process transpired over several generations as nonwhites sought to "marry lighter," but it could occur in one's own lifetime. Such was the case of doña Clara López de la Peña, a free cuarterona or mestiza, and don Luis Declouet, a white officer in the Spanish regiment. Although they wed on October 1, 1797, it was not until November 20, 1801, that a priest entered their marriage into the white register and made a notation that the children born to them (a total of six) were now legitimated, by decree of the vicar general. Two years earlier, López de la Peña had instituted proceedings before an ecclesiastical tribunal to prove her descent from whites and Native Americans rather than from whites and Africans and to have her oldest daughter Luisa's baptismal record transferred from the nonwhite to the white books. Baptisms of the most recently born children were already recorded in the white registers, exemplifying the temporal nature of the whitening process. López de la Peña, however, most likely *was* of African descent, but even for persons of native descent, it was rare to pass as white and gain the title of "doña" as López de la Peña did.[42] Thus, given enough wealth and power, a family could modify its racial heritage to correspond with its social standing, although in López de la Peña's case it also meant rejecting one's identity as a nonwhite in order to pass as a white and thereby gain honor.

In many ways, though, López de la Peña is to be envied because at least she exercised some control over her destiny, as did many other libre women in colonial New Orleans. They seemed to have more freedom to choose their fate than did slave and even white women, who, if they acted as prescribed by society, rarely could own and operate businesses, enter into legal contracts without the consent of their fathers or husbands, serve as heads of household, and marry or cohabit with someone of "unequal" status. All New Orleans women—white, slave, and libre—operated within a patriarchal, hierarchical system that viewed them as inferior merely because of their gender. But this society also cared less about the conduct of libre women because they had no honor; with less to lose, free black women had more flexibility to maneuver within the system. Although subordinated not only by their gender but also their race and class, libre women worked within a limited sphere to improve their own condition and that of future generations. Through their words and actions, it is apparent that most free black women endeavored to create lasting, stable unions with men of all races, to attain higher status for themselves and their children—which often meant accepting European religion, language, and values and attempting to "marry lighter"—and to win the honor and virtue accorded white women in their society.

◆

Notes

Research for this essay was made possible through generous assistance from the Program for Cultural Cooperation Between Spain's Ministry of Culture and United States Universities, an Alfred G. Beveridge Grant for Research in the History of the Western Hemisphere, the American Philosophical Society, the Oklahoma Foundation for the Humanities, the University of Tulsa Faculty Development Summer Fellowship Program, and the University of Tulsa Faculty Research Grant Program.

1. Throughout I use the inclusive somatic terms "free black," "free person of color," and "libre" to encompass anyone of African descent—that is, any free nonwhite person whether he or she is pure African, part white, or part Native American. The exclusive terms *pardo* (light-skinned) and *moreno* (dark-skinned)—preferred by contemporary free blacks over *mulato* and *negro*—are utilized to distinguish elements within the nonwhite population. Occasional references delineate further between *grifo* (offspring of a pardo(a) and a morena(o), and in some cases of a pardo(a) and an *india(o)*), *cuarterón* (offspring of a white and a pardo(a)), and *mestizo* (usually the offspring of a white and an indio(a) but in New Orleans sometimes meaning the offspring of a pardo(a) or moreno(a) and an india(o)).

2. Lyle N. McAlister, "Social Structure and Social Change in New Spain," *Hispanic American Historical Review*, 43:2, April 1963; 349–70 and *Spain and Portugal in the New World, 1492–1700* (Minneapolis: University of Minnesota Press, 1984), 24–40, 398–401.

3. The documents from which these quotes are drawn are "Criminales Seguidos por don Pedro Fabrot contra María Cofinie, parda libre, sobre palabras infuriosas," Louisiana State Museum Historical Center, Spanish Judicial Records (hereafter cited SJR), June 8, 1795, and "Testimonio de la Sumaria contra el Mulato libre Pedro Bailly, Theniente de las Milicias de Pardos de esta Ciudad, por haver prorrumpido especies contra el Govierno Español, y haver manifestado adicto a las máximas de los Franceses rebeldes," Archivo General de Indias, Estado, legajo 14, no. 60, February 11, 1794.

4. Kimberly S. Hanger, "Household and Community Structure Among the Free Population of Spanish New Orleans, 1778," *Louisiana History*, 30:1, Winter 1989; 63–79.

5. Hanger, "'Almost All Have Callings': Free Blacks at Work in Spanish New

Orleans," *Colonial Latin American Historical Review*, 3:2, Spring 1994; 141–64.

6. Data for computing the median age at death for whites were drawn from funeral records dating 1785 through 1803 (except for a few entries between 1772 and 1776, all funeral records for whites until October 1784 perished in the Great Fire of 1788) and numbered 1,526 for males and 741 for females, with an additional 179 and 69, respectively, having no given ages and thus not used in computations. For free nonwhites, the funeral records date from 1774 through 1803 and numbered 441 for males (plus 61 with no given age) and 574 for females (plus 116 with no given age). Beginning in 1777, all sacramental records were kept in separate books for whites and nonwhites and are now housed at the Archdiocese of New Orleans Archives.

7. Census of 1777, Archivo General de Indias, Papeles Procedentes de Cuba (hereafter cited AGI PC), legajo 2351, May 12, 1777; Census of New Orleans, November 6, 1791, Louisiana Division, New Orleans Public Library; Matthew Flannery, comp., *New Orleans in 1805: A Directory and a Census* (New Orleans: Pelican Gallery, 1936).

8. Verena Martínez-Alier, *Marriage, Class and Colour in Nineteenth-Century Cuba: A Study of Racial Attitudes and Sexual Values in a Slave Society*, 2nd. ed. (Ann Arbor: University of Michigan Press, 1989), 124.

9. For an expanded discussion of Spanish legislation pertaining to women and family and its contrast with English common law, see Edith Couturier, "Women and the Family in Eighteenth Century Mexico: Law and Practice," *Journal of Family History*, 10, Fall 1985; 294–304; James M. Murphy, *The Spanish Legal Heritage in Arizona* (Tuscon: University of Arizona Press, 1966), 31, 32, 38; and Rosalind Z. Rock, "'Pido y Suplico': Women and the Law in Spanish New Mexico, 1697–1763," *New Mexico Historical Review*, 65, April 1990; 145–59.

10. Ramón A. Gutiérrez, *When Jesus Came, the Corn Mothers Went Away: Marriage, Sexuality, and Power in New Mexico, 1500–1846* (Stanford: Stanford University Press, 1991), 315–18; Martínez-Alier, *Marriage, Class and Colour*, xiv–xv; Patricia Seed, *To Love, Honor, and Obey in Colonial Mexico: Conflicts over Marriage Choice, 1574–1821* (Stanford: Stanford University Press, 1988), 205–56.

11. Gwendolyn Midlo Hall, "Saint Domingue," in David W. Cohen and Jack P. Greene, eds., *Neither Slave nor Free: The Freedmen of African Descent in the Slave Societies of the New World* (Baltimore: The Johns Hopkins University Press, 1972), 187.

12. Seed, *To Love, Honor, and Obey*, 152.

13. Court Proceedings of Esteban de Quiñones, no. 1, fols. 30–44, April 12, 1779. Prudhome subsequently bore Lugar another daughter, and then in 1801 wed a free pardo, the natural son of a free morena and white man and the father of four children by his first wife, another free parda. When Lugar died that same year, he named his two natural daughters as his heirs, but also left half the value of his house to Prudhome's oldest daughter by another white man she had known previous to Lugar in Havana (Nonwhite Baptisms, book 5a, October 1, 1792–April 29, 1798, [all sacramental records cited are for St. Louis Parish]; Nonwhite Marriages, book 1, entry no. 66b, March 10, 1801; Will of don Juan Antonio Lugar, Acts of Pedro Pedesclaux, no. 39, fol. 444, July 20, 1801).

14. Nonwhite Marriages, book 1, entry no. 13, May 1, 1779.

15. Seed, *To Love, Honor, and Obey*, 148–52.

16. Nonwhite Marriages, book 1.

17. Nonwhite Marriages, book 1.

18. "Bartlomé Bta. Grifo libre contra Juan [sic] Lafrance sobre impedir este el matrimonio de su hija con el dicho Bartlomé," SJR, September 6, 1788; Nonwhite Marriages, book 1, entry no. 41, September 12, 1788.

19. Caterina and Bartlomé's marriage lasted at least fourteen years. In 1802, they had two daughters, Barbara and Eulalia, baptized in the St. Louis Cathedral (Nonwhite Baptisms, book 7a, entry nos. 501 and 502, March 7, 1802).

20. Acts of Leonardo Mazange, no. 4, fol. 891, November 5, 1781.

21. Marriage Contract between Pedro Bahy and Naneta Cadis, Acts of Andrés Almonester y Roxas, fol. 251, April 25, 1778; Nonwhite Baptisms, books 3a, 4a, and 5a; Acts of Narciso Broutin, no. 2, fol. 13, 29 January 1800; Free Moreno and Pardo Militia Rosters, AGI PC, legajo 160a, fols. 342–45, May 1, 1801; Acts of Carlos Ximénez, no. 15, fol. 499, June 26, 1798.

22. Some recent works on Louisiana's Creoles of Color confirm this. See Carl A. Brasseaux, Keith P. Fontenot, and Claude F. Oubre, *Creoles of Color in the Bayou Country* (Jackson: University Press of Mississippi, 1994), 8–11; Lois Virginia Meacham Gould, "In Full Enjoyment of Their Liberty: The Free Women of Color in the Gulf Ports of New Orleans, Mobile, and Pensacola, 1769–1860," Ph.D. diss., Emory University, 1991), 215–17; and Gary B. Mills, *The Forgotten People: Cane River's Creoles of Color* (Baton Rouge: Louisiana State University Press, 1977).

23. Acts of Pedro Pedesclaux, no. 18, fol. 580, July 12, 1793.

24. Even though Carlos Saint-ville was baptized as the legitimate son of Montreuil and Gerónimo, the author has not found registration of his parents' marriage.

25. Marriage of Carlos Montreuil and Constanza San Luis, Nonwhite Marriages, book 1, entry no. 57, September 12, 1792; Marriage of Juan Francisco Dutreuil and Agata Montreuil, Nonwhite Marriages, book 1, entry no. 95, January 4, 1805; Nonwhite Baptisms, books 4a, 5a, 6a, 7a. It turned out that Carlos survived his illness and lived until 1825. He and Constanza produced four more legitimate children prior to 1803, when this study ends.

26. Martínez-Alier, *Marriage, Class and Colour*, 63.

27. Carlos Budé went to jail when evidence at a trial revealed that he was involved in an illicit affair with a parda slave. Ironically, Budé had instituted the initial proceedings against a free morena for striking and slandering him. He lost the case and was arrested ("Criminales Seguidos por Carlos Budé, contra la Negra Libre Nombrada Rosa, sobre palabras Infuriosas," SJR, February 16, 1786).

28. Acts of Narciso Broutin, no. 5, fol. 291, June 18, 1803.

29. Acts of Francisco Broutin, no. 46, fol. 118, June 17, 1797; Nonwhite Baptisms, book 6a.

30. For a discussion of the images whites held of black women, see Barbara Bush, *Slave Women in Caribbean Society, 1650–1838* (Bloomington: Indiana University Press, 1990), 11–22.

31. Claude C. Robin, *Voyage to Louisiana, 1803–1805*, trans. Stuart O. Landry, Jr. (New Orleans: Pelican Publishing, 1966), 250.

32. Paul Alliot, "Historical and Political Reflections," in *Louisiana Under the Rule of Spain, France, and the United States, 1785–1807*, trans. and ed. James Alexander Robertson, 2 vols. (Cleveland: Arthur H. Clark, 1911); I:146–47.

33. For a discussion of changing definitions of honor, see Gutiérrez, *When Jesus Came* and Seed, *To Love, Honor, and Obey*.

34. Court Proceedings of Esteban de Quiñones, no. 1, fols. 30–44, April 12, 1779.

35. In her will, Cheval declared that all the *aguardiente* (cheap rum), three barrels of

coffee, and other merchandise in her house belonged to Izurra. She named him as her heir, along with her three sisters (Acts of Pedro Pedesclaux, no. 20, fol. 6, January 5, 1794).

36. Judith K. Schafer, "'Open and Notorious Concubinage': The Emancipation of Slave Mistresses by Will and the Supreme Court in Antebellum Louisiana," *Louisiana History*, 28:2, Spring 1987; 165–82.

37. "Magdalena Canella, Mulata libre contra don Luis Beaurepos para la liberación de su esclava Adelaida," SJR, January 20, 1777.

38. Materials for the Dor/Lalande/Gentilly trial are drawn from "Luis Dor, negro esclavo contra Estevan Lalande, pardo libre," Court Proceedings of Francisco Broutin, fols. 1–99, January 31, 1793 and "Luis Dor, negro esclavo de Dn. Joseph Dusuau contra la Sucesión de Estevan Lalande, mulato libre," Court Proceedings of Francisco Broutin, no. 31–A, fols. 1–43, January 10, 1794. Special thanks to Jane Landers for her invaluable help in translating these documents.

39. Court Proceedings of Esteban de Quiñones, no. 5, fols. 357–61, September 22, 1789 and fols. 362–88, September 29, 1789; Nonwhite Marriages, book 1, entry no. 47, October 31, 1789.

40. Martínez-Alier in her work *Marriage, Class and Colour* has found similar attitudes prevailing in colonial Cuba.

41. In her study of marriage choice in New Spain, Seed finds that "Black ancestry was clearly far more a problem than Indian ancestry" in obtaining parental permission to marry (*To Love, Honor, and Obey*, 153).

42. Each generation lightened and eventually passed as white. Clara López de la Peña's parents were Luison Marigny de Mandeville, also known as Brunet, and don José López de la Peña, a native of Galicia in Spain and officer in the Spanish military. Luison Brunet is alternately listed as a mulata libre, cuarterona libre, or mestiza libre in documents, and her mother María Juana as a negra or india slave. After bearing four daughters and one son by don José, Brunet married Francisco Durand, a free pardo widower with four children. Their marriage lasted nine years, when both partners died in 1794, and produced no children (Nonwhite Marriages, book 1, entry no. 27, September 27, 1785; Acts of Carlos Ximénez, no. 6, fol. 27, January 27, 1794).

"A CHAOS OF INIQUITY AND DISCORD"

Slave and Free Women of Color in the Spanish Ports of New Orleans, Mobile, and Pensacola

Shortly after arriving in Pensacola in 1821 to serve as the Territorial Governor of Florida, Andrew Jackson was drawn into an imbroglio that proved to have international consequences. The incident began when Maria Josepha de las Mercedes Vidal, a free woman of color, requested Jackson's aid in recovering documents of her late father's estate. Mercedes Vidal's father, Don Nicholas Vidal, who was a Spanish official, first in Louisiana and then in Florida, had accumulated property in both colonies. After Vidal's death, however, his daughters, Mercedes and Carolina, believed that the executor of their father's estate, John Innerarity, had fraudulently settled the estate. They also suspected that the Spanish officials in Louisiana and Florida had protected him. Mercedes Vidal had attempted and failed to obtain the documents for over fifteen years when she approached Jackson. Jackson, in response, requested that the then Spanish Governor, José Callava, turn the documents over to him, but Callava refused, which infuriated Jackson so much that he had Callava jailed and seized the documents.

What is not completely clear is why Callava refused to relinquish the documents. Under the agreement of the Adams-Onis Treaty, any papers involving property rights were to be turned over to the United States at cession. Furthermore, if the estate had been settled fraudulently, as Mercedes and her attorney declared, it was done many years before, by the executor, under the tenure of an earlier governor. One must ask why, then, if the estate had already been settled, would Callava have put his freedom at risk?

It cannot be said with absolute certainty, but it appears that the conflict occurred as a result of the fundamental difference between the way in which the Spanish governor viewed the women and their rights and the way in which the women viewed themselves and their rights. To fully understand not only these differences but also their implications, it is necessary to understand something of the law and custom of the region.

Spain, France, and Britain vied throughout the eighteenth century for the region that bordered the northern Gulf. Pensacola was founded first, by the Spanish, in 1698. The French placed a settlement a year later at Biloxi. They founded Mobile in 1702. New Orleans was settled in 1718. All three ports remained under the governance of their founders until the Treaty of Paris of 1763. Louisiana, west of the Mississippi, was ceded to the Spanish with the treaty; however, the Spanish did not gain control of the colony until 1768. Mobile and Pensacola and the regions around them were ceded to the British with the Treaty of Paris. Mobile remained under British rule from 1763 until 1780, when it was captured by the Spanish. Pensacola was captured a few months later, during 1781. The entire region remained under Spanish control until each port and the region around it was successively ceded to the United States. Louisiana was ceded first, in 1803. Mobile went next, in 1811. Neither Pensacola nor the rest of Florida was officially turned over to the Americans until 1821.[1]

During the century that France, Spain, and England competed for control over the territory that bordered the Gulf, their colonists struggled to survive. Colonial officials encouraged their earliest settlers to establish farming communities. The settlers, however, had other ideas. In specific, colonists in Louisiana and Florida demanded that their officials import African slaves so they might establish a plantation society. There were already some slaves in the colony. A few had accompanied the early governing officials as personal servants. The first few pages of the sacramental records of the Cathedral of the Immaculate Conception in Mobile shed light on these first Africans who came to the region. The first African slave baptized at Mobile was Jean Baptiste, the seven-year-old *negre* slave of Jean Baptiste Le Moyne, Sieur de Bienville. Jean Baptiste was baptized June 11, 1707. It is unlikely that Jean Baptiste was born in Louisiana, since the colony was not that old. Yet, it is probable that two of Bienville's other slaves who were baptized in Mobile in 1707 were born in the colony. These slaves were the three-year-old Joseph and the newborn Antoine Jacemin. The records only state that the mother or mothers of these children belonged to Bienville. The only father recorded was that of Antoine Jacemin. His father was François Jacemin, a slave of Captain Chateauguay's.[2]

It was only after 1719 that thousands of Africans were imported into the region for the purpose of plantation agriculture. Between 1719 and 1731, twenty-two ships carrying nearly 6,000 slaves arrived in Louisiana's various ports. These ships brought slaves into the Gulf region from Juda (Whydah), Cabinda (Angola), and Senegal. After 1731, only one other ship carrying slaves imported directly from African landed in French Louisiana. That was the *St. Ursin*, which debarked 190 slaves in 1743 from Senegal. Yet, despite the best efforts of the slaves and their masters, a suitable crop was not found. Instead, local settlers, slave and free, tried unsuccessfully to consistently produce indigo, sugarcane, tobacco, and rice. With their hopes for a profitable plantation economy dashed and with few other resources, white settlers and their African slaves struggled to survive by forming face-to-face networks based on subsistence farming and trade with the local Native Americans and one another. Subsistant farming and trade in clay, lumber, and deer hides, not plantation agriculure, defined the local economy.[3]

The failure of plantation agriculture not only redefined the economy but also had a definitive effect on the social relations of the population. Unable to establish economic and political dominance, neither planters nor merchants were able to fully subjugate their slaves. Slaves struggled with their owners for control, and in many cases managed to establish some power over their daily lives. It was more usual than not for slaves to cultivate their own plots of land and to use Sundays for worship, rest, and marketing. Nor was it unusual for slaves in the ports to live away from their owners. Slaves in colonial New Orleans, Mobile, and Pensacola often provided housing, food, and clothing for themselves and their families. Antoine LePage DuPratz wrote in 1734 that slaves in Louisiana preferred to take care of their own needs.[4]

And it was not unusual for slaves to gain their freedom during the economically and politically unstable colonial period. Some Africans and their descendants simply escaped into the swamps that surrounded the ports. Others were freed in return for faithful service and performing outstanding military feats. Still others were freed as a consequence of their ties to the free white community. The first evidence of a freed slave can be found in the sacramental records of the Cathedral of the Immaculate Conception. According to a baptismal record dated July 26, 1715, Janneton, the former slave of "Mr. Charlie," brought her son, Michel, to the church to be baptized. Janneton declared in the record that her son's father was a French soldier named La Terrier. Since Janneton was freed before she gave birth and the condition of a child followed that of its mother in Louisiana and Florida, her son was born free. Slave women, like Janneton, often found their freedom in their relations with free men. The records do not say, but it is more than likely that La Terrier purchased Janneton's freedom from "Mr Charlie" before the birth of their first child. Such interracial liaisons as that between Janneton and La Terrier routinely evolved in the socially fluid frontier ports, and it was not unusual for the men to purchase the freedom of the slave women with whom they cohabited. If they could not or did not free the women before they had children, they often freed them along with their children when they could. In fact, it was from just such relations as that of La Terrier and Janneton that the large and relatively influential free colored population in the Gulf region emerged.[5]

Many of the secular and religious officials viewed the interracial liaisons that were so common in the region as threatening to the social order. Father Henry La Vente, a Catholic clergyman in Mobile who wrote a memoir of his experiences in Louisiana after he returned to France in 1713, noted that the cause of the colony's spirit of irreligion was the generalized concubinage. The white settlers, he pointed out, refused to marry white women; instead, preferring to "maintain scandalous concubinages with young Indian women, driven by their proclivity for the extremes of licentiousness." The bachelors, the pastor wrote, had "bought the women under the pretext of keeping them as servants, but actually to seduce them, as they in fact have done." It was not unusual, he concluded, for the mixed couples to expose or strangle their offspring in order to avoid detection by the authorities.[6]

Father Raphaël complained in a letter to Abbé Raguet in 1726 that "the number of those who maintain young Indian women or negresses to satisfy their intemperance . . . remain enough to scandalize their church and to require an effective remedy." Admonitions from officials, however, appear to have been completely ignored by the region's inhabitants. The practice of white settlers taking slave women and free women of color as cohabitants continued unabated throughout the early decades of the colony. In 1766, just three years before the Spanish officially took control of the colony, Father Clements de Saldaño stated that it was so common for white men to keep slave women and free women of color as mistresses that no one commented on it.[7]

In order to establish a more orderly slave society, French officials in Louisiana implemented the *Code noir* in 1724. The *Code noir*, or slave law, was modeled after the 1685 *Code noir* that France had originally devised for its Caribbean Islands. By its intent, the *Code* embodied the planter philosophy of Catholicism, white supremacy, and patriarchal rule. It regulated the fundamental rights of slaves by guaranteeing them a minimum of food and clothing and providing for their baptisms and marriages. Besides regulating their fundamental rights, the *Code* also stated that slaves could not be freed without the consent of the Superior Council. After restricting slaves' access to freedom, officials placed restrictions on their ability to receive property. Freed slaves and their descendants, according to the *Code*, were prohibited from receiving donations *inter vivos* or *mortis cause* from whites. (Donations made between living persons were *inter vivos* and those made by a person after death were *mortis cause*.) The restrictions the French placed on freedom and the distribution of property were aimed at undermining relations between white men and slave women and free women of color. The *Code*, it is clear, was meant to protect the race-based hierarchical nature of the social system.[8]

Despite the best efforts of the French, the *Code* did not prevent white settlers from cohabiting with African women and their descendants. Nor did it prevent men from freeing their cohabitants and their racially mixed offspring and providing them with property. Indeed, by the time the Spanish arrived in New Orleans in 1768, there was an already rapidly growing population of racially mixed free people of color. That is not to suggest, however, that the Spanish welcomed interracial liaisons any more than the French did. Spanish attitudes can be found scattered throughout their official correspondence. In an edict issued in 1776, Charles III of Spain emphasized that the newly appointed Governor of Louisiana, Bernardo Galvez, establish public order and proper standards of morality. After setting forth instructions for the governance of the colony's slaves, the King pointed out that public immorality had produced a large class of "mulattos," that a large number of "mulatto" women who were "given over to vice" lived in public concubinage with whites. If they did not marry and enter into proper employment, the King informed Galvez, he should see to their deportation.

The Spanish, in response to the King's demands, implemented specific restrictions against interracial liaisons in the Black Code of 1777. The code forbid white men from living in concubinage with free women of color or with slaves. It ordered that fines be levied against illegitimate children born of any such liaison. The fine for a child born of a free women of color and a white man was sixty piasters, which was a considerable sum. If the woman was a slave, the fine was unspecified and the child was confiscated.

It is not difficult to understand why Spanish officials, or, for that matter, officials in any of the New World slaveholding societies, believed that such liaisons threatened the social order. Since slavery in the New World was based on race, it was imperative for the white dominant class to protect its identity, or status, from contamination by those of African descent. The Spanish believed that purity of blood—*limpieza de sangre*—was necessary for the protection of the hierarchical nature of the social system, which, in turn, reinforced the distribution of property. *Limpieza de sangre* was originally a religious convention devised by the Spanish to distinguish and exclude Jews and Moors, whom they defined as "impure," from the Christians, whom the considered "pure." At the time that the custom of *limpieza de sangre* was dying out in Spain it was adapted to the colonial situation. There it was used to distinguish those of "pure" or white Caucasian European descent from those of "impure" or African descent. In his essay on New Spain, the commentator Baron Alexander Von Humböldt noted at the beginning of the nineteenth century that, "In Spain it is a kind of title of nobility not to descend from Jews and Moors." It is different in America, he notes, for there it is the skin, more or less white, that "dictates the class that an individual occupies in society." Whites, Von Humbölt writes, even when riding barefoot on horseback, consider themselves members of the nobility. The distinction between black and white, slave and free, which is evident in Von Humbölt's writings, was the most important one in any society in which slavery was based in race.[9]

Indeed, the increasingly lighter skinned, racially mixed offspring of white men and women of color, both slave and free, offered the clearest manifestation of the false assumptions on which slavery was based. John H. B. Latrobe described the way in which the so-called black and white populations blurred together when he recounted a conversation that he had while taking a stroll through the streets of New Orleans.

> Hah—what's that. A fine figure, a beautiful foot, an ankle like an angel's—an air quite distinque, and then so strange, and characteristic—so Spanish, with that long black veil over the head—`Allons, we will pass her. Why she's a mulatto—Fie—not at all—don't let her hear you—that's a quadroon. A quadroon!
>
> Well, I'll know better next time. Are those quadroons on high there, in the balcony that projects from that Spanish looking house with ornamented cornice and window frames and flat roof? One of them has a veil, and all that I see are darker than she we have passed. Heavens no, they are creoles—

natives, whites—Spaniards and French mixed—born in the country—very good society. No indeed they are not quadroons. You must make a distinction. Faith so I perceive—And here are more balconies, and more females— and . . . two old ladies, quadroons—No, those are mulattos, well be it so— the two old mulattos are also smoking cigars.[10]

The blurring of the population that Latrobe described so graphically was later so alarming to Esteban Miró, who was appointed governor of Spanish Louisiana in 1786, that he addressed the problem in his *bando de buen gobierno,* or proclamation of good government. Newly appointed governors of the Spanish colonies, like Miró, usually addressed those issues that they found the most daunting in their inaugural addresses or *bandos.* It only takes a glance at Miró's *bando* to demonstrate that his foremost concern was the behavior and appearance of the region's free women of color. Recognizing that free women of color threatened the social stability of the region, Miró ordered them to abandon their licentious ways from which they subsisted and to go back to work with the understanding that he would be suspicious of their indecent conduct. The extravagant luxury of their dress, which was already excessive, he warned, would compel him to investigate the mores of those who persisted in such display. To ensure that their status was clearly identifiable, he ordered them to reestablish the distinction that had been manifest in their headdress. Finally, he prohibited them from wearing feathers or jewels in their hair. Instead, they were to cover their hair with headkerchiefs as was formerly the custom.[11]

Miró, like officials in Spanish America as well as Europe and other European colonies, believed that social station or status was visibly expressed through dress. In general, most of the Spanish colonial sumptuary restrictions were adapted to the colonial situation from traditional Spanish law. Spanish colonial legislation usually prohibited women of color from wearing silks, gold, silver, pearl jewelry, or mantillas. Some legislation went even further by forbidding them to wear slippers ornamented with silver bells, own canopied beds, or sit on rugs or cushions while attending church. Miró's sumptuary legislation directly reflected other attempts by colonial governors throughout Latin America and the Caribbean to prevent free women of color from obscuring the visible expression of status. Miró's *bando* that remanded the women of color in the Gulf colonies to wear the headkerchief was a completely symbolic ploy.[12]

The symbolism that Miró hoped to establish was that of women tied to slavery. After all, the slave women in the region were most closely and officially associated with work, and they were the women who traditionally wore kerchiefs to cover their heads. Thus, the intent of Miró's sumptuary law was to return the free women of color, visibly and symbolically, to the subordinate and inferior status associated with slavery. His order ignored the legal status of these women, but it also ignored their economic condition and their ties to the white community. To Miró, it was necessary for women of color who had become too light skinned or who dressed too elegantly, or who, in reality, competed too freely with white women for status and thus threatened the social order, to symbolize their ties to slavery through the simple head-kerchief.[13]

There is no evidence that officials in the Gulf ports ever enforced the "tignon law," as it became known. Yet whether officials enforced the law or not, it appears that the free women of color obeyed it by adopting the habit of wearing the headkerchief. However, in acquiescing to Miro's order, free women of color thwarted it by adapting the kerchief into the stylish and flattering tignon that became a badge or mark of distinction of their race, their status, and their gender. Liliane Crété notes that the women exchanged their elegant coiffures for a tignon or a "brilliant silk kerchief, artfully knotted and perhaps enhanced with a jewel." The image seems to have attained such social prominence that, in some ways, it bound very different women together in an act of defiance.[14]

Despite their rhetoric and the laws that prohibited interracial liaisons, in reality, Spanish officials could do little to discourage white men from cohabiting with slave and free women of color. In fact, certain Spanish laws and traditions motivated slave women and free women of color to participate in liaisons with white men. For instance, Spanish law allowed masters to free their slaves by a simple act recorded by a notary. It also implemented the more lenient custom of *coartación*, or self-purchase. *Coartación*, as practiced throughout Spanish America, was an arrangement in which slaves were permitted to free themselves by agreeing with their masters on a purchase price or by arbitrating a sum through the courts. Such a policy not only allowed slaves the possibility of freedom—not only suggested to them that it was their natural right by its implications of liberty and humanity; but, in effect, loosened their master's control over them. Once freed, free people of color were allowed by Spanish law to receive *inter vivos* and *mortis causae* donations from whites. Spanish law, as implemented in New Orleans in 1769, in Mobile in 1780, and in Pensacola in 1781, encouraged a practice that had already become common. Cohabitation that had been mostly beneficial to white men during the earliest years of settlement now more directly and openly benefited their African cohabitants and their racially mixed offspring.[15]

The records do not offer evidence of the type of arrangement that Eufrosina Hisnard, the mother of Mercedes and Carolina Vidal, and their father, Don Nicolas Vidal, had. Some general information about the couple, however, does exist. For instance, it is clear that Don Nicolas Vidal arrived in New Orleans in 1791 as the *Auditor de Guerra* of the colony and that he began to cohabit with Eufrosina Hisnard shortly after he arrived. There is also evidence that Vidal's liaison with Hisnard was not his first with a free woman of color. He had left a daughter, Maria Josefa, a "quarterona libre," and her mother, Rosa Noriega, who was described as a "mulata libre," in Cartegena. Eufronina Hisnard, on the other hand, was a native of New Orleans. As the daughter of Maria Grondel, who was described as a "negra libre," and the white Don Francisco Hisnard, she was described as a "mulata libre." She was approximately fifteen years old when she became Vidal's *concubinato*. A year after Hisnard began living with Vidal, on October 22, 1792, she bore him a daughter, Carolina Maria Salomé Vidal. Two years later, on January 10, 1795, she bore him another daughter, Maria Josepha de las Mercedes. Eufrosina Hisnard bore Vidal at least one other child, Nicolas Eustaqui de las Mercedes Vidal, who was born on September 20, 1795, but died seven days later. Nicolas Vidal, Euphrosina Hisnard, and their children remained comfortably in New Orleans until it was ceded to the French in 1803. With cession, they moved to Pensacola where Vidal continued his duties as *Auditor de Guerra*. Vidal died in Pensacola in 1806, after naming Hisnard and their daughters as his heirs.[16]

Euphrosina Hisnard's extralegal liaison with Nicolas Vidal was not uncommon since the demographic imbalance in the population encouraged white men and slave women and free women of color to cohabit. A sampling of census data in the colonial ports reveals the trend. For instance, the Spanish census of New Orleans for 1788 includes 5,321 inhabitants. Of those, 2,370 were described as white, 820 as free people of color, and 2,131 as slaves. The adult portion of the white population for the city had a sex ratio of 68+, which suggests that there were only 68 women for 100 men in that segment of the population. The sex ratio for the white population, however, is insignificant when compared to that of the free-colored population, which was 677+. That number meant that there were 677 free women of color for every 100 free men of color in the port in that year.[17]

A census taken in Mobile in 1805 reported that of the 1,537 inhabitants in the city in that year, 448 were white, 255 free people of color, and 612 slaves. The sex ratio for the white population, which included 383 males and 292 females, was 76+—only 76 white women for every 100 white men. The 255 free people of color living in the port in 1805 had a sex ratio that was nearly even in that year. It was 105+.[18]

The 1819 Census of Pensacola reported 992 inhabitants in the port. Of those, 432 were described as white, 217 as free people of color, and 343 as slaves. The white population included 234 males and 198 females, which indicates a sex ratio of 85+. The sex ratio for the free people of color was 197+— 197 adult women for every 100 adult men. White men, absent white partners, would have turned to slave women and free women of color. Free women of color, absent free men of color, would have turned to other free men, even if they were white. Few free women of color chose to tie themselves to slave men, although there are a few examples of women who did.[19]

The demographic imbalance in the region does not, however, tell the entire story. Other evidence suggests that white men preferred cohabiting with slave women and free women of color rather than marrying white women. C. C. Robin wrote soon after Louisiana was ceded to the Union that "travelers, Creoles, residents, and everyone else in New Orleans forms alliances with these colored women and many have children of them. This license extends also to the rural regions, where the Creoles prefer to live with these women rather than to give to a white woman the title of spouse." Perrin du Lac agreed with C. C. Robin's impression of the preference of white men for women of color. "As in all colonies their taste for women extends more particularly to those of color, whom they prefer to the white women." The impression that some free women of color preferred to cohabit with white men rather than cohabit with or marry free men of color that was expressed by

Robin and Du Lac is verifed by all the region's censuses. There are many examples of white women who were of marriageable age, yet lived with their parents, and other cases in which single white women were described as heads of households.[20]

It was also reported that some free women of color and slave women preferred liaisons with white men. John F. Watson wrote in his journal in the summer of 1805 that there were beautiful yellow women in New Orleans who had no more ambition than to become the concubine of a white gentleman. They were content, he noted, "to live at an expense of about four hundred dollars a year. Many are so maintained." He noted again, about a month later, that the women who entered in liaisons with white men were faithful. "They never desert their *maris* (de facto husband) in any case of adversity. They do not marry, because custom holds that to be odious; but that not being their fault, they are, in all respects, good as wives in general, frugal in their habits and innocent in their lives and deportment." Liaisons with white men offered slave women and free women of color opportunities they would not have found elsewhere. Again census data supports Watson's allegations that some women preferred cohabiting with white men by including multiple examples of free men of color living alone or with other free men of color. The records also demonstrate that it was also common for free men of color to cohabit with or marry slave women.[21]

It can be said without reservation that any relationship in which power was as unequal as that between white men and women of color in the early Gulf ports was exploitive. But it must also be pointed out that many of these liaisons would have been mutually beneficial to the couple and their children. As Marcus Christian, a Creole descendant of the early African and European population in New Orleans, observed over a century later, while "the female slaves were peculiarly exposed . . . to the seductions of an unprincipled master," most of the liaisons were mutually sought. White men, perhaps like Nicolas Vidal, could formulate liaisons with women outside the formal institution of marriage, and without social stigma. And women of color could acquire freedom, or property, or status and influence from their liaison with white men. There is more than a little evidence to support the argument that women of color, both slave and free, sought liaisons with white men knowing that they could exert at least a modicum of control over them. A woman who rejected one white man to form a liaison with another was Magdalena, the slave of Nicolas in New Orleans. Magdalena complained to the court that La Pedro Cabanne, a white man, approached her on the steps of her master's house "and begged her to concede him the favors as she had been accustomed to do before." La Cabanne, according to Magdalena, told her that he had "not eaten, nor slept, nor drunk for three days." Magdalena, however, testified that she told him that her relationship with him "had passed and that she did not want anything more to do with him." Later, however, according to the court records, La Cabanne entered the window of Magdalena's cabin and threw himself on his knees. At that point, Magdalena testified that she "threatened to waken her master if he did not go away," but Cabanne continued to harass her for a while longer, even "throwing stones on the roof of her cabin." Later that evening, according to the testimony, as Magdalena lay in bed with Claudio Chabote, another white man, Pedro La Cabanne broke into her cabin and wounded them with a sword or knife. Thus, while Magdalena might not have been in absolute control of her life, she had the ability to exercise some choice in her mate.[22]

Another woman, Maria Juana, who was the slave of Juan Suriray, petitioned the court in New Orleans in 1776 for her freedom on the grounds that she had been the concubine of her master for many years, but that when she refused to consort with him after he married a prominent white woman, he had abused her—even to deprive her of her shoes and stockings and forcing her to wear rags. Preferring to spend her time in jail rather than with Juan, Maria Juana was no longer willing to be his concubine or his slave.[23]

Yet while some slave women obviously had great difficulty in their relationships with white men, others found considerable advantage. The manumission records for New Orleans, Mobile, and Pensacola support the evidence for sex ratios derived from the analysis of the census records. Approximately three times as many women and children were freed than men, and a large number of these women found their freedom and the freedom of their children in relationships with white men. One of countless examples is that of the white Juan Robin of New Orleans who manumitted his forty-eight-year-old slave Maria and their three children: Juan Luis, eighteen; Maria Juana, twenty-seven; and Isabel, twenty. Juan Robin also freed Isabel's two daughters: Juana and Francisca.[24]

While it is impossible to calculate with certainty the frequency of interracial liaisons, a sample of the sacramental records, and in particular the baptismal records, of the St. Louis Cathedral in New Orleans suggest just how common such liaisons were. Of the 314 infants and children of slave women and free women of color baptized in the St. Louis Church in 1793, 2 were described as mestizo. Of the 312, excluding the mestizos, 217 were slaves and 95 were free, or 70 percent were slaves and 30 percent were free. The 217 slaves included 83, or 38 percent, who were described as racially mixed. Of the 83 infants born to slave mothers, even though five of the children had been freed and had their freed papers with them at the baptismal font, 3 were acknowledged by their white fathers and 67, it can be inferred by their phenotype, had white fathers. The other 13 had racially mixed parents. Of the 95 infants born to free mothers in that year, 81, or 85 percent, were described as racially mixed. Of those, 10 were acknowledged by their white fathers and another 49, it could be inferred by their phenotype, had white fathers. That total of 59 suggests that 73 percent of the infants of free women of color had white fathers. To summarize the data, the baptismal records of 1793 demonstrate that 38 percent of the slave infants baptized were racially mixed while 85 percent of the children of free women of color were racially mixed. Racial mixing was consequently one of the more common features of the culture.[25]

And racial mixing frequently, but not always, led to freedom. This is particularly evident from the data from the 1793 baptismal records of the St. Louis Church. That data demonstrates that 38 percent of slaves in that year were racially mixed. Confirmation records for the 64 slaves confirmed in the

Plaza and at Fort Barrancas in the District of Pensacola in May 1798 demonstrate that 27, or 42 percent of the slaves then confirmed were described as being racially mixed. Some racially mixed slaves baptized or confirmed in the ports were later freed, but many spent their lives in bondage. Some of the port's slaves were even described as extremely light-skinned or even white. Eliza Potter, a free woman of color who lived a few months in New Orleans, witnessed a slave auction in which several women were sold. According to Potter, a great many of the women were as "white as white could be." It is not difficult to assume that all these women were racially mixed. Other documents affirm the presence of slaves who appeared to be white.[26]

Some women and their children, however, did effect their freedom and that of their children from their liaisons with white men. The census schedules demonstrate the dramatic growth of the free people of color in these ports. For example, the 1788 census of New Orleans shows that the free-colored population made up approximately 25 percent of the entire free population. By 1805, however, free people of color totaled approximately 34 percent of the free population. The population of Mobile had a similar structure. By 1805, the number of free people of color there had reached 250, or 27 percent of the entire free population. The Pensacola Census of 1802 reports that free people of color made up approximately 21 percent of the free population. By 1820, however, the free people of color in the city constituted approximately 36 percent of the free population.[27]

Some slaves attained their freedom without the aid of whites. But the relationship between freedom and skin color, or racial classification, is unmistakable. For instance, of the 74 free people of color in Pensacola in 1802, 56, or 76 percent, were described by the census taker as "mulattos." Of the 145 slaves in the port in that year, 40, or 28 percent, were racially mixed. The 1787 census of Mobile offers a similar picture. There were a total of 64 free people of color in the port in that year. Of those, 49, or 77 percent, were described as racially mixed. The slave population totaled 726 and, of those, only 86, or 12 percent, were described as racially mixed. There were 743 free people of color in New Orleans in 1791. Of those, 575, or 77 percent, were racially mixed. In the same year, there were 1,889 slaves. Of those, 285, or 15 percent, were described as racially mixed. Thus, it is clear from the available data that interracial liaisons were not only common but it was also common for white men to free their cohabitants and their children.[28]

Freedom, however, was not all that slave women and free women of color gained from their extralegal liaisons. Many women and their children also received property. Hundreds of deeds, wills, and inventories of estates contain evidence of property transferred from white men to slave and free women of color and their children. One woman who inherited a sizable estate from her de facto marriage with a white man was Louison Chastang. The tenor of her relationship with her cohabitant, Jean Chastang of Mobile, can be found in Jean's last will and testament, written in 1805. In that document Juan wrote that he bequeathed to his "beloved worthy friend and companion, Louison, a free negro woman, who has resided with me for twenty years past and has been my sole attendant in health and particularly so in sickness" all of his real estate and dwellings—"lying on the opposite side of the River Mobile." The property that John owned across the river from Mobile was not all that he bequeathed to Louisan. He also left her a lot in Mobile, four slaves, cattle, silverware, furniture, his corn crop, and his other provisions. Jean Chastang also specified in his will that the property that he left to his "beloved companion" was to be divided equally among his mulatto children after Louison's death. Louison's relationship with Jean lasted for over thirty years and produced at least ten children, who were acknowledged by their father.[29]

Louison Chastang was only one of many propertied, influential free women of color in the Gulf ports who found at least a part of their identities through their white cohabitants and/or white fathers and their other ties to the white community. Mercedes Vidal was another. Her ties to her father, her influence in her community, her knowledge and insistence on her rights, were as surely a part of her identity as the African origins and ties to slavery that she inherited from her mother. It would, therefore, be shortsighted to simply dismiss interracial liaisons as unimportant, as many have done, by pointing solely to their exploitive nature. For to focus only on the exploitive nature of the relations between white men and slave women and free women of color would be to ignore the reality of the world in which they lived. And to ignore that world would be to ignore the way in which the women participated in redefining it, despite the fears they inspired in secular and governing officals.

◀▷

Notes

1. The will of Nicolas Vidal is dated 1798 and located in the Notarial Archives, New Orleans. The baptismal records of Carolina and Mercedes Vidal are located in the sacramental records of the St. Louis Cathedral. Clarence E. Carter, "Transactions in the Floridas under Governor Jackson," *American State Papers*, Miscellaneous 2 (Washington, D.C.: U.S. Government Printing Office, 1934–1962), 799–875.
2. First Book of Baptisms, entry dated June 11, 1707, Archives of the Cathedral of the Immaculate Conception, Mobile, Alabama.
3. The information on the importation of the early slaves can be found in Gwendolyn Midlo Hall, *Africans in Colonial Louisiana: The Development of Afro-Creole Culture in the Eighteenth Century* (Baton Rouge: Louisiana State University Press, 1992); James Thomas McGowan, "Creation of a Slave Society," Ph.D. diss., University of Rochester, 1976; "William S. Coker and Thomas D. Watson, *Indian Traders of the Southeastern Spanish Borderlands: Panton, Leslie & Company and John Forbes & Company, 1783–1847* (Gainesville: The University Presses of Florida, 1986); Daniel Usner, *Indians, Settlers, and Slaves in a Frontier Exchange Economy: The Lower Mississippi Valley Before 1783* (Chapel Hill: The University of North Carolina Press, 1992).
4. Antoine LePage Dupratz, *Histoire de la Louisiane*, 3 volumes (Paris, 1758), vol 1, 333–35.

5. First Book of Baptisms, entry dated July 26, 1715, Cathedral of the Immaculate Conception.

6. Father Henry La Vente, *Memoire de la Louisiane*, written in 1713 and 1714, *Archives des Colonies*, Series C 13a, vol. 3.

7. Fr. Raphael to Abbé Raguet, May 19, 1726, *Archives des Colonies*, Series C, 13a, *Louisiane: Correspondence generale*; Father Clements de Saldaño's to Joseph Antonio de Armona, New Orleans, March 30, 1766, *Biblioteca Nacional* (Madrid), Ms. Vol. 18.

8. *Le Code noir ou Edit du Roi*, Versailles, 1724; *Le Code noir, ou loi municipal, . . . entreprit par Delidération du Cabildo en vertu des Ordres du Roi . . . consignés dans sa Lettre faite à Aranjuez le 14 de Mai 1777* (1778). Copy in Parsons Collection, Humanities Research Center Library, University of Texas at Austin. Paul LaChance, "The Formation of a Three-Caste Society," *Social Science History*, 18, 2, Summer 1994.

9. Verena Martinez-Alier, *Marriage, Class, and Colour in Nineteenth Century Cuba: A Study of the Racial Attitudes and Sexual Values in a Slave Society* (London: Cambridge University Press, 1974), 20–41. There are examples of documents in which heritage is explored in the Notarial Archives in New Orleans. For instance, a document details the blood lines of Magdalena Margarita de la Ronde and Joseph Xavier de Pontalba in New Orleans in 1789. The couple wished to marry and, since each was from an elite family, their lineages were explored and recorded. Margarita Vils (Wiltz) also documented her "purity of Blood" in New Orleans in 1773. For these and other cases, see the Court of Governor Unzaga, Escribano J. B. Garic, No. 14. Virginia Dominguez argues in *White by Definition* that identity was determined by blood and that blood ties, both lineally and collaterally, carried not only social and economic rights but also obligations. Racial identity and class membership were determined by blood. Property was not just a corollary of racial classification, but also a criterion. The Spanish Crown enacted the *Pragmatica Sançion* in 1776 to prevent unequal marriages, and it was extended to the colonies in 1778. Parental consent, according to the *Pragmatica*, was a formal requirement for those under twenty-five years of age who wished to marry and parental objections repeatedly focused on the inequality of the race, hence the social status, of the couple. The protection of family integrity was essential; disinheritance was the penalty for disobedience. Although in colonial Louisiana and Florida, the threat was hardly effective since those who had migrated there left little behind. But, as Martinez-Alier explains for Cuba, the "metropolis laws on intermarriage, far from constituting an imposition, did no more than provide a legal framework for preexisting racial attitudes." Also see Frederick P. Bowser, "Colonial Spanish America," in David Cohen and Jack P. Greene, eds., *Neither Slave nor Free: The Freedmen of African Descent in the Slave Societies of the New World* (Baltimore: The Johns Hopkins University Press, 1972); Alexander Von Humböldt, *Ensayo Politico sobre El Reino de la Nueva España* II (Mexico, Porrbua, 1973), 262.

10. John H. B. Latrobe, *Southern Travels*, Samuel Wilson, Jr., ed. (New Orleans: The Historic New Orleans Collection, 1986).

11. Esteban Miró's *bando de buen gobierno* was first proclaimed in the Cabildo, June 2, 1786. See Actas, III, Minutes for that date, Articles 3, 6, 9, 10 on microfilm at the New Orleans Municipal Library. For one translation of the document, see Gayarré, *History of Louisiana: The Spanish Dominion*, Vol. III, (New Orleans: James A. Gresham, 1879).

12. Caroline Maude Burson, *The Stewardship of Don Esteban Miró, 1782–1792* (New Orleans, American Printing Company 1940). Frederick P. Bowser, *The African Slave in Colonial Peru, 1524–1650* (Stanford: Stanford University Press, 1974), 311–12.

13. Bowser, *The African Slave in Colonial Peru, 1524–1650*, 311–12; François Boucher, *20,000 Years of Fashion: The History of Costume and Personal Adornment* (New York: Barry N. Abrams, Inc.) 179–202; Michael and Ariane Batterberry, *Fashion: The Mirror of History* (New York: Greenwich House, 1977), 1–12; Berquin-Duvallion, *Vue de las colonie espanole du Misissipi, ou des provinces de Louisiane et Floride occidental*, 201–47; Records of the Cabildo, June 2, 1786; *Recopilacion de Leyes de los Reynos de las Indias* (Madrid: *por Ivlian de Paredes, Ano de 1681*), *Libro VIII and Titulo V*. Also, for a sampling of Spanish American sumptuary restrictions aimed at free women of color, see Richard Konetzke, *Colleçion de documentos para la historia de la formacion social de hispanoamerica* (Madrid: Consejo Superior de Investigaciones Cientificas, 1962), Vol 2: 11–12, *El Prado, 22 de Noviembre de 1593*, 319–22; *Madrid, 29 de septiembre de 1628*. John Fanning Watson, *Notitia of Incidents at New Orleans in 1804 and 1805, American Pioneer*, II, No. 5 (May 1843), 233–36.

14. Liliane Crété, *Daily Life in Louisiana, 1815–1830*, trans. by Patrick Gregory (Baton Rouge: Louisiana State University Press, 1981), 81.

15. Hans Baade, "The Law of Slavery in Spanish Louisiana," in Edward F. Haas, ed. *Louisiana's Legal Heritage*, (Pensacola: Perdido Bay, 1983), 43–67.

16. *Testamentaria de Don Francisco Hisnard que Falleció en el Puesto de Opelousas*, Judicial Records, RG 2, 27 August 1798; Birth of Carolina Maria Salomé Vidal recorded in the Records of Baptisms of Slaves and Free People of Color, St. Louis Church, New Orleans, October 22, 1792. The baptism of Maria de Los Mercedes Vidal is recorded in the same record, January 10, 1795. The birth of Nicolas Eustaqui is also in the baptism records of this church. For other information, see the will of Nicolas Vidal, April 25, 1798, New Orleans Notarial Archives, Pedro Pedesclaux. Also see the American State Papers, vol 21.

17. Spanish Census of New Orleans, 1788, AGI PC 1425.

18. *Resumen General del Padron Hecho en la Provincia de la Luisiana. Distrito de la Movila y Panzacola, 1788, legajo* 1425.

19. Spanish Census of Pensacola, June 1, 1819, AGI *legajo* 1876–B.

20. C. C. Robin, *Voyages to Louisiana*, translated and edited by Stuart O. Landry, Jr. (New Orleans: Pelican Publishing Co.), 250; Perrin DuLac, *Travels Through the Two Louisianas . . .* (London: Richard Phillips, 1807).

21. John F. Watson, "Notitia of Incidents at New Orleans in 1804–1805," in *American Pioneer*, II, 5, May 1843, 233–36.

22. The criminal prosecution of Pedro La Cabanne and the mulatress, Magdelena, who belonged to Nicolas Perthuis, are located in the records of the escribano Juan B. Garic, published in the *Louisiana Historical Quarterly*," Index to Spanish Judicial Records of Louisiana," Vol. 13, 339. Christian's remarks can be found in "Genealogy: The Creoles of Louisiana, White Men and Negro Women," the Marcus Christian Collection, Special Collections, The University of New Orleans.

23. Court proceedings of Maria Juana, the slave of Juan Suriray, Spanish Court Records, February 28, 1774.

24. For the best discussion of manumission in Spanish New Orleans, see Kimberly S. Hanger, "Personas de Varias Clases y Colores: Free Persons of Color in the

Spanish New Orleans, 1769–1803, Ph.D. diss., University of Florida, 1991.

25. The practice of self-purchase in New Orleans is evident in the Notarial Archives of the Spanish period located in the Civil Court Building in New Orleans. Also for the debate surrounding the liberality of the Spanish practice of *coartaçion*, see Gwendolyn Midlo Hall, *Social Control in Slave Plantation Societies: A Comparison of St, Domingue and Cuba* (Baltimore: The Johns Hopkins University Press, 1971), 81–135; Rebecca J. Scott, *Slave Emancipation in Cuba: The Transition to Free Labor, 1860–1899* (Princeton, N.J.: Princeton University Press, 1985), 13–14; Franklin W. Knight, *Slave Society in Cuba During the Nineteenth Century* (Madison: The University of Wisconsin Press, 1970), 130–31; Elsa Goveia, "The West Indian Slave Laws in the Eighteenth Century," in Laura Foner and Eugene D. Genovese, eds., *Slavery in the New World*, (Englewood Cliffs, N.J.: Prentice-Hall, 1969), 113–38; McGowan, "Creation of a Slave Society," 175–217; Baade, "The Law of Slavery in Spanish Louisiana," 67–70; Fierher, "The African Presence in Colonial Louisiana," 24. For the nearly complete records of manumission for the Spanish colonial period in New Orleans, see the *cartas de libertad* included in the Notarial Acts, 1769–1803, housed in the Civil Court Building in New Orleans. Also, a few court cases that consider the subject of self-purchase are located in the Court Records for the Spanish period that are housed in the Louisiana State Museum in New Orleans.

26. Eliza Potter, *A Hairdresser's Experiences in High Life* (Cincinnati: By the Author, 1859), 173–74. Confirmations Conferred in the Plaza of Pensacola, the seventh day of May, by the Most Reverend Señor Don Luis Peñalver y Cardenas, First Worthy Bishop of this Diocese, in the present year of 1798 and the Confirmations Conferred at the Fort of Barrancas of the District of Pensacola, the twenty-first of May 1798. The Confirmation lists are published in William S. Coker and G. Douglas Inglis, *The Spanish Censuses of Pensacola, 1784–1820: A Genealogical Guide to Spanish Pensacola* (Pensacola: The Perdido Bay Press, 1980).

27. The Spanish Census of New Orleans, 1797: New Orleans in 1805: A Directory and Census (New Orleans, 1936). *Census de Mobile, Septembre 12, 1805, Legajo 142*, Territorial Papers, Jackson Mississippi; *Padron de Panzacola, 1802 AGI PC Legajo, 59*; Coker and Inglis, *The Spanish Censuses of Pensacola, 1784–1820*.

28. The Census of Pensacola, May 15, 1802, *AGI PC legajo 59; General de la Jurisdiction de la Mobila del Primero de Enero del Año 1787, AGI PC Legajo 206*. Mississippi Territorial Archives, Jackson, Mississippi. Census of New Orleans, November 6, 1791, Louisiana Collection, New Orleans Public Library.

29. Will Book 2, 112, Mobile County Records, Mobile County Courthouse, Mobile, Alabama. All of Jean Chastang's children, except for Françoise, were the children of Louison. Françoise was the daughter of the free woman of color, Catherine.

AFRICAN WOMEN IN FRENCH AND SPANISH LOUISIANA

Origins, Roles, Family, Work, Treatment

The popular culture of Louisiana has had a profound impact on the United States since 1803 when the vast Louisiana Territory was incorporated into the nation. After the Civil War and Reconstruction era, Louisiana and Black Belt culture from along the Mississippi Valley spread throughout the country in waves, northward to Chicago, eastward to the northeast corridor, and westward to California.

Louisiana was, and is, a truly, multicultural society that developed very differently from the thirteen original Anglo colonies. In the early English colonies, Europeans came mainly in families. The white population increased rapidly, Indians declined, and Africans were introduced gradually and in small numbers. Many of these blacks came from the British West Indies rather than directly from Africa and they spoke English when they arrived.

In colonial Louisiana, however, an entirely new Creole culture was created from the knowledge, skills, folk art, and world views of Africans, Native Americans, and Europeans. Its population came from diverse nations speaking a variety of languages and practicing many religions. The most widespread, common language spoken was Creole: a new language created there during the first few decades of colonization by slaves brought directly from Africa and by the first generation of their children. Unlike the English mainland colonies, no stable, pervasive European culture could be imposed.

This essay is informed by the understanding that it is women—especially mothers and surrogate mothers—who primarily mold the new generations.

They most often speak, sing, and tell stories to impressionable infants and small children, passing on their verbal and body language, manners of expression and communication, feelings, perceptions, and values. In no other colonial culture of the United States did African women play such a central role.

African women and their descendants were especially influential in colonial Louisiana because of the nature of the colony and the patterns of introduction of its population. Throughout the colonial period, it was a frontier society that had primarily strategic rather than economic value to the colonizing powers. It was located outside normal routes of trade and communication. Frequent warfare erupted among rival European powers and their Amerindian allies. There was widespread smuggling and piracy and political and military control remained weak.

Louisiana was founded as a small, military outpost in 1699. Its civilian population became significant with the founding of New Orleans in 1718 and the arrival of the first slave trade ships coming directly from Africa in 1719. The colony was then administered by the Company of the Indies while it, at the same time, administered Senegal in West Africa. The Louisiana colony was vast and its population mainly native American. Its European population was small and diverse. Immigrants and forced immigrants, African and European, were overwhelmingly male. Two-thirds of the slaves introduced from Africa were male. Among adult slaves (more than fourteen years old) there were 158 men to each 100 women during French rule (1699–1769) and 144 men to each 100 women during Spanish rule (1770–1803). Some Frenchmen and Canadians, mainly single men, some German families and later, some Acadian (Cajun) families came voluntarily.

Europeans of both genders were especially vulnerable to Louisiana's semi-tropical climate and environment. The death rate among newly arrived Europeans from hunger and thirst as well as from disease was overwhelming. In 1729, the Natchez Indians, with substantial help from African slaves, wiped out 10 percent of the surviving French population. Many of the remaining French colonists, survivors of disease, starvation, and massacre, abandoned Louisiana after 1729, leaving a substantial majority of Africans in French settlements throughout the colony. A clear African majority in settlements during the earliest stages of colonization, extensive race mixing, and the insecure, strategic nature of the colony contributed to its unique dynamics and complexion.

Many French settlements had been established in Indian villages. Enslaved Indians were overwhelmingly women. Among adults there were fifty-one women and twenty-three men listed as Indians ("Sauvage") in documents from the French period. Indian women of these villages as well as female Indian slaves were quickly absorbed into the Franco-African communities through concubinage and intermarriage.[1]

The Senegal region of West Africa supplied two-thirds of Louisiana's African slaves during the French slave trade to Louisiana (1719–1743). Senegambia was the site of the great medieval Ghana, Mali, and Songhi trade empires. This region supported extensive interactions of diverse and sophisticated peoples, creating a significantly unified culture throughout the region.[2] The Wolof are the main ethnic group in Senegal today and are rapidly absorbing other ethnic groups. While French remains the official language, the use of the Wolof language is expanding while other languages are dying out.

A substantial number of Bambara were brought down from the upper Senegal and Niger River region to the coast of Senegal, sold into the Atlantic slave trade, and transported to Louisiana. But they were almost entirely young men captured in warfare. The Bambara maintained a language community in early Louisiana. They were powerful due to their numbers, flexible social structures, technical skills, and military experience. But there were very few women among them.[3]

Although only one-third of the Africans brought to Louisiana were women, almost all of them came from the coast and were probably mainly Wolof, called Senegal in Louisiana. Wolof women played the most crucial role in forming and passing on Louisiana Creole culture. Their influence resulted, not simply from their numbers, but because they arrived in Louisiana first, and largely reared the first generation of Louisiana Creoles of all statuses and racial designations. Wolof women played a crucial role as wives, concubines, and mothers as well as workers in Louisiana. The Wolof Bouki-Lapin folktales survived in the Louisiana Creole language and were later adapted and translated into English as the Brer Rabbit stories. *Bouki* means hyena in Wolof. *Nar*, the Wolof name for Moor, means "burn," a preferred technique of warfare among the Moors. The nation designation *Nar* is found on Louisiana documents dating from the Spanish period (1770–1803).[4] While the Bambara clung tenaciously to their traditional religion, a substantial proportion of the Wolof had been at least nominally Islamized since the eleventh century when the Ghana Empire was overthrown by the Almoravides and the Mali Empire established. Many slaves in Louisiana had Wolof and Islamic names. Among women, Fatima (daughter of Mohammed) and Pinda (a uniquely Wolof name) were common. We see these names on lists of slaves loaded on slave trade ships in Senegambia as well as on estate inventories and other Louisiana documents.

Some of the open patterns of gender and race relations implanted in Louisiana were carried over from French experience in Senegal where French officials and workers were extremely dependent on women of the Wolof nation. The Wolof, living along and near the Atlantic Coast, had sustained contact with French officials and workers since the mid-seventeenth century. French officials and chroniclers testified to the beauty, intelligence, and remarkable adaptability of Wolof women. French men in Senegal admired Wolof women for their lustrous, very dark skins, and their elegant dress. Wealthy and influential Wolof women were involved in trade networks in Senegal. French officials and workers stationed there eagerly sought sustained relationships with these women in order to accumulate wealth through pooling their trade contacts with their companions, and to assure their care during the frequent illnesses that devastated Europeans in West Africa. A wealthy and influential Euro-African community developed in Senegal among children born to these couples and their descendants. Many French men working in

Senegal adopted Wolof marriage and inheritance practices. French fathers customarily purchased a slave for each of their children. There is at least one example of this custom being carried out in Louisiana.[5]

French colonists in the Caribbean as well as in Louisiana sought out Wolof women for slaves, especially as domestics, because of their remarkable beauty, intelligence, adaptability, and linguistic talents. Many of these women became wives, concubines, mothers, and surrogate mothers of the first generation born in Louisiana. Another Wolof marriage practice carried over to Louisiana was when a freeborn man married a slave woman, she and her children were accorded freeborn status.[6] There were few formal interracial marriages in Louisiana, but concubinage was frequent, and the custom of freeing the mothers and the children born of these relationships was quite common. With few exceptions, women as well as men considered white in Louisiana accepted the principle that slave concubines and mixed-blood children of white men should be manumitted, even at the expense of legitimate heirs. Substantial amounts of property were passed on to their concubines and children by white male fathers.

While the French slave trade took place entirely between 1719 and 1731 except for one voyage in 1743, by the late 1750s, an illegal British slave trade became important and a much greater variety of African ethnic groups were introduced. After Spain established control of the colony (1770–1803), the African slave trade increased dramatically. Both the Bight of Benin and Senegambia remained important sources for slaves, although their proportion in the slave population was reduced. Slaves from Central Africa of various ethnic groups—almost all of whom were designated as Congo in Louisiana— became prominent. Ibo slaves (from the Bight of Biafra) began to appear in the documents by the 1760s. A few slaves were brought from Mozambique, listed mainly as Makua.

It is possible to pinpoint the African nations introduced into Louisiana over time, the proportion of women among them, their marriage patterns, and their fertility rates, as well as many other characteristics of the slave population in colonial and early American Louisiana thanks to a database created by this writer and her collaborators. This database contains 93,265 descriptions of individual slaves (records) with 121 possible comparable pieces of information (fields) about each slave. These slaves were listed in a variety of documents found throughout Louisiana. We did not sample. Every existing document was studied and its data entered into the database. These documents consist of inventories of the property of masters after their deaths, manumissions, testimony of slaves (mainly runaways), marriage contracts, mortgages, leases, wills and other types of documents. Much of the information in this essay was calculated from this Louisiana Slave Database.[7]

Now, we ask, which Africans? A plurality of slaves came from Senegambia during the Spanish period, followed by the Bight of Benin. Slaves from Upper Guinea continued to appear. The Bight of Biafra (mainly Ibo) and Central Africa grew in importance during the Spanish period. Those from Central Africa were almost all listed as Congo, although they were actually a variety of peoples speaking mutually unintelligible languages.

The continued, large-scale importation of slaves from Senegambia involved the tradition and preference of slaveowners. As we have seen, two-thirds of the slaves brought to Louisiana during the French period came from Senegambia. During the Spanish period, Senegambia had become a minor area for exporting slaves in the international slave trade. But Louisiana slave traders sent ships directly there, and many other Senegambians were tran-shipped from Caribbean ports. Very few slaves from the Gold Coast were brought to Louisiana, reflecting the importance of Jamaica as a point of trans-shipment to Louisiana of newly arrived Africans. Jamaican planters preferred Gold Coast slaves and evidently were happy enough to sell their Senegambian slaves to slave traders supplying Louisiana and keep slaves arriving from the Gold Coast for themselves. Senegambians were well represented in the slave population of rural Spanish Louisiana, and even better represented among *commandeurs* (slave foremen), half of whom were Africans and more than half of them from Senegambia.

Domestic slaves were especially important in socializing the new genera-tions. Some historians have argued that masters chose domestic slaves based on how closely their skin color and culture resembled their own: In other words, light-skinned Africans, mixed blood slaves, the most socialized slaves, preferably Creoles, were chosen as domestics. If this were true, cultural influence of domestic slaves would tend to be removed by one or more gener-ations from Africa. But this was not true for colonial Louisiana. Women born in Africa continued to play a crucial role in socializing the children designated as white as well as black and racially mixed. Racial designations of Creole domestic slaves by and large reflected those of Creole slaves as a whole during the colonial period. During both the colonial and the early American periods (to 1820), there were a number of African nations represented among domes-tic slaves in higher proportion to their numbers in the slave population than were Creole domestics. During the colonial period, they were Aja, Kissy, and Mina (Ewe). During the early American period, they were Mozambique, Arada, Fon, and Ibo. These data reflect preferences among masters and/or mistresses, as well as talents and ambitions among women of various African nations.

The first generation of Africans brought to Louisiana largely succeeding in forcing their masters to recognize the integrity of their marriages and their families. African women slaves were almost always listed with mates on estate inventories from the French period. The role of the Catholic Church was minimal in protecting the slave family. There were few slave marriages listed in the sacramental records of the Catholic Church, and slave children bap-tized in the church were almost always listed as born of unknown fathers. The civil rather than the ecclesiastic records best reveal patterns of family forma-tion among slaves. At first blush, one might conclude that the provisions of the *Code Noir,* which prohibited the separate sale of husband, wife, and children under the age of fourteen, explains the integrity of the slave family under French rule. But much less attention was paid to the slave family in the French West Indies: St. Domingue, Martinique, and Guadeloupe during the same time period. A more likely explanation is that the first generation of slaves in

Louisiana were all Africans and they were in a relatively powerful position within the society. Another possible factor was perhaps a pronatalist policy among slaveowners because their slaves could no longer be replaced through the French slave trade that practically ended after 1731.

The slave population of early Louisiana did not reproduce itself. In order for a population to be self-sustaining, it has to produce two surviving children for each woman of childbearing age. Since there were substantially more men than women in Louisiana, there had to be more than 2 children per woman. Early Louisiana never even approached these norms. During the 1740s, the proportion of children to women peaked (1.582 children under 15 years of age for each woman of childbearing age). This was the only decade when the price for women was higher than for men. This exceptional decade reflected the positive impact of ending the African slave trade.

The overall figures for early Louisiana, however, are indeed gloomy. During the French period as a whole, there were only 1.164 live children per woman of childbearing age, dipping to 1.117 during the Spanish period, and rising slightly to 1.294 during the early American period. The small numbers of children appears to reflect high death rates more than low fertility rates. The reproductive powers of women were generally devalued. The price differential between female and male slaves of prime age increased substantially over time. Women sold for 93% of the price paid for men during the French period, dropping to 83% during the Spanish period and plunging to 80% during the early American period. It is clear that female slaves were devalued, not only as workers, but also as mothers and potential mothers.

The slave family came under sharp attack with the advent of Spanish control (1770–1803)—an assault that intensified during the early American period (1803–1820). Neither Spanish law nor practice protected the slave family, and the baptismal records kept by the Catholic Church displayed even fewer incidents of slave marriage or the indication of who the father of the slave child was. Within a few years after Spain took control of Louisiana, children over age six or seven began to be routinely inventoried and sold separately from their mothers. This destructive process is shown clearly in our Louisiana Slave Database. During the French period, 51% of all slaves were listed in families. The figures dropped to 28% during the Spanish period and 26% during the early American period. The percentage of children under age 14 inventoried with their mothers dropped from 65.8% during the French period to 42.9% during the Spanish and 42.8% during the early American. The percent of slaves listed with mates dropped from 20.5% during the French period to 3.1% during the Spanish and 1.8% during the early American.

During the Spanish period of effective rule (1770–1803) when marriage and the family, especially the designation of husband and father, were under sharp attack, it was the Africans rather than the Creoles who had the greatest success in forcing recognition of the husband and father. Surely, husbands and fathers existed without being recognized as such in the documents. But when an estate was inventoried to be sold, this formal recognition led to placing a single price on the family group. Sometimes family members were sold separately anyway, but this was, in practice, rare.

During the Spanish period, a variety of African nations were introduced into Louisiana. An understanding of the mating patterns of these newly arriving Africans helps us begin to understand the very complex acculturation process that was taking place. Women from two nations with deep roots in Louisiana, the Wolof and the Mina, showed the highest incidence of marriage to men of their own nation and of nations from their own region of Africa. The husbands of twelve Wolof women were all from Senegambia except for three Creoles who were most likely descendants of Senegambian slaves and one whose nation could not be identified. Their African mates were five fellow Wolof, one Mandingo, and two Bambara. Only two Bambara women were listed as married, one to a fellow Bambara, the other to an African whose nation was listed as "Guinea." Among the five Mandingo women listed as married, one had a fellow Mandingo mate, two were married to men listed as Congo, and two to men of unidentified nation.

It is particularly interesting to consider the contrasting marriage and parenting patterns among Wolof, Mina, Ibo, and Congo women, each of them coming from a different region of Africa. Among Africans of identified nations, Wolof women coming from Senegambia were only 7.9 percent of women, but 18.2 percent of women married to men of identified nations and mothers of 13.1 percent of the children. The child/woman ratio among Wolof women was 0.313 (313 childen under age five per 1,000 women of childbearing age), approaching that of Creole women which was 0.327. There was a relatively high proportion of females among Wolof slaves: 40.6 percent (219 females, 321 males).

The Mina of the Bight of Benin were 6.6 percent of women of identified African nations, and 9.1 percent of those listed with mates of identified nations. The husbands of six Mina women were five fellow Mina and one Chamba, all coming from the Bight of Benin, and five from unidentified nations. They were mothers of 8.4 percent of the children with a child/woman ratio of 0.238. The proportion of females among them was quite low: 30.7 percent (184 females, 415 males).

Ibo women from the Bight of Biafra were 8.8 percent of identified African women, 19.7 percent of married women and mothers of 16.5 percent of the children. The child/woman ratio among Ibo women was 0.289. The proportion of females among Ibo slaves was quite high: 45.4 percent (234 females, 281 males). The mates of Ibo women were varied in origin. The fourteen Ibo women listed with mates were married to four fellow Ibo, two Chamba, two Congo, one Bambara, one Mandingo, one Yoruba, one Bermudan, one Creole, and one of unidentified nation.

Congo women were least likely to marry and/or bear children. Although they were 33.2 percent of African women of identified nations, they were only 9.1 percent of women listed with mates. They were mothers of only 19% of the children. The child/woman ratio among Congo women was only 0.148, the lowest end of the scale. The proportion of females among Congo slaves was low: 31.3 percent (923 females, 2,026 males). Congo women were married to three fellow Congo, three Mina, and four men of unidentified nations.

Creole women definitely stuck to their own kind, but their marriage rate was very low. Among the forty-one Creole women with mates of identified nations, thirty-seven were married to fellow Creoles, one to a Yoruba, and two to Africans of unidentified nations. The nations of the mates of fourteen more Creole women were unidentified.

These variations in patterns of family formation and parenting among African slaves raise a number of questions, some of which will bring us back to Africa for the answers. The most fertile women, the Wolof and the Ibo, lived near the coast. Were they less damaged physically and emotionally than their sisters who were captured and transported from the interior? African women were probably torn away from some of their children born in Africa and those born in Louisiana reflected only a portion of their reproductive lives. But the contrast in fertility among women from the same regions of Africa reinforces the likelihood of the use of birth control among certain African nations.

The resiliency of family life among African-born slaves despite extreme handicaps in Spanish Louisiana is striking. They substantially outperformed Creole slaves in forcing masters to recognize the family status of husbands and/or fathers. While the percentage of slaves listed as married was very low, especially compared to the French period, a significant number of Africans did indeed force their masters to recognize husbands and fathers. Does a relatively high rate of marriage and fathering of children among African men of various nations reflect higher levels of status and power? The evidence is contradictory. Slaves listed as Mina (Ewe) were a numerous, well-organized ethnic group in Louisiana whose presence was noted as early as the French period. They were the largest single nation from the Bight of Benin, so their prominent role as husbands and fathers is not surprising. On the other hand, there were very few Bambara or Mandingo listed as husbands or fathers. And Mandingo women had very few children in proportion to their numbers. Their child/woman ratio was only 0.169. The child/woman ratio among Bambara women was even lower: a mere 0.143. These questions remain to be explored in the context of Atlantic and African Diaspora history.

It is past time to forcefully reject the vicious, racist, sexist stereotypes published in travelers accounts of the early nineteenth century that have often been accepted as historical truths. These stereotypes are insulting to black and mixed-blood women as well as to the men with whom they were allied.[8] The only value of these accounts is to reveal the attitudes of these writers who were no doubt reporting prevailing prejudices arising from growing racism with the advent of American rule. African women and their descendants, whether they were concubines of white men or not, worked hard to purchase their freedom as well as the freedom of members of their families. Many manumitted slave concubines earned their status through efficient management of the household and sometimes the plantation in addition to the more engendered roles of sexual partner, mother, and nurse to the many sick and dying in the colony. These women were not sex toys. As one proud free woman testified in New Orleans in 1795: "I did not earn my freedom on my back." (*No he ganado mi libertad sobre las espaldas.*)[9]

The nature of sexual relationships between white men and nonwhite women varied greatly. It does not help to stereotype them. In this brief essay, we can discuss only the most benevolent and the most sadistic. A more nuanced discussion will be presented in this writer's forthcoming book.

There were a few African and Indian women legally married to French colonists, especially during the early years of colonization, but almost all the African women involved with white men were informal wives or concubines. These women were often the only mate of white men and the mothers of their only children. There is extensive documentation involving white fathers of nonwhite children who recognized them, freed them, and passed property on to them either during their lifetime or under their will.[10] Paul Lachance's study of wills probated in New Orleans between 1804 and 1812 demonstrates that 33.3 percent of white men born before 1740, 25.8 percent born between 1740 and 1759, and 19 percent born between 1760 and 1779 indicated in their wills that they were involved in consensual unions with women of color and passed on property to their concubines and their natural children.[11] Some of these relationships ended up in court after the death of the masters, but they are surprisingly few. They were usually complaints brought by white women whose husbands had freed, or intended to free and pass on property to, their slave concubines and mixed-blood children, and they often focused on the widow's property rights. Marie Claude Bernard (white), widow of Comte Pechon, an infantry officer, pointed out that she was beneficiary of all her husbands acquisitions and conquests according to their marriage contract signed in 1758. She complained that it was quite enough that she had consented to the manumission of Marie Negresse and her newborn son François Mulâtre in 1760, two years after her marriage. She then enumerated large sums of money, slaves, and valuable land that her deceased husband had donated during his lifetime to his natural son, François Mulâtre Libre, then ten years old. These donations were disguised in the form of sales from son to father. Her argument was based, not on race, but on the limited rights of natural children to inherit their father's property.[12]

The widow of Simon Lacour of Pointe Coupée challenged her deceased husband's will manumitting his two mulatto children by his slave concubine, but her challenge was not successful. One disputed inheritance in New Orleans involved the children of Maria Teresa, a free griffe[13] woman whose three children were the heirs of their deceased white father. Their father had appointed a trusted friend as executor of his estate to avoid a disputed inheritance, but the executor died before he could pass the property on to them. The court appointed two physicians to examine these children to determine if they could be the biological children of the deceased, because one of them was white, the other was black, and the third was described as grif, with the explanation that this term meant a mixture of black and Indian. The doctors concluded that, since they were the biological children of the same mother, they could be the biological children of the same father as well. But since they were illegitimate, the inheritance was denied to them. After several years of litigation, the children finally were given their inheritance.[14]

A contrasting attitude was displayed by the three legitimate white children of François Lemelle of Opelousas who renounced all their rights to hold Marie Jeanne Quarteronne Libre or any of her descendants as their slaves

based on verbal wishes expressed by the deceased to his wife. They acknowledged Marie Jeanne's right to one-fifth of the deceased's estate as provided by
his will.[15]

Many if not most white men having nonwhite concubines were single.
Some of these women were treated in every possible respect as wives. Pierre
Belly, a judge and by far the wealthiest planter of Iberville Parish, owned
ninety-seven slaves when he died in 1814. His concubine Rose was a Nago
(Yoruba) woman whom he had bought from an African slave trade ship. He
freed her and their five daughters during his lifetime. Several years before his
death, he passed much of his property on to Rose who managed it and provided for their children. Rose accepted a cash settlement from Belly's forced
heirs in France in return for renouncing her claims to the remainder of his
estate.[16] François Grappe, a white slaveowner of Natchitoches, bought his
concubine and several of his children from his mother after the death of his
father and then bought his oldest daughter and her children from another
planter. He then freed all of them, expressing in this manumission document
his pride in the fecundity of his concubine, a black woman named Marie
Louise, age forty-five. They had twelve children, the oldest of whom was a
daughter age thirty and their youngest was a son who was one year old. He
also freed their eight grandchildren. All twenty of these slave descendants of
their white master were freed in the same document.[17]

The gender imbalance in New Orleans favored female slaves. They were
likely to be employed as domestics at the inns, boardinghouses, bars, and
saloons that dotted this seaport town. Although the isolation of rural slaves
has been greatly exaggerated, there is no doubt that urban slaves, especially in
port cities, had more contact among themselves, with whites, and with travelers. Slave women working in New Orleans had greater physical mobility than
those in rural areas. Because of their prominent role in marketing, including
street vending, they had greater possibilities of earning money as well. There
was, in fact, a trading company operated by San Luis La Nuit and Gota, male
and female free blacks living in New Orleans, which supplied a large variety of
valuable goods to residents of St. Martin, Opelousas, and the Attakapas Post
during the 1770s and 1780s.[18] Interaction and mobility would open more
opportunities for interracial unions, and concubinage sometimes became a
realistic way out of slavery for urban women slaves, although interracial concubinage was quite common in rural areas of colonial Louisiana as well. Many
of the descendants of these unions passed into the population classified as
white.[19]

While nonwhite concubines and mixed-blood offspring of white men were
most likely treated with more consideration in colonial Louisiana than elsewhere in colonial United States, at the same time brutality toward slave
women was probably unmatched. A few of these cases appear in the documents after complaints were made, usually by persons with pecuniary interests
in the abused slaves. The earliest case involved Jacques Charpentier dit Le
Roy who was brought to court in 1727 by the owner of the slaves he rented
because Charpentier was destroying them by depriving them of food and
drink, overwork, flogging, raping the women in the open fields, and beating

them to force them to abort when they became pregnant. There is the terrible case of Jacques Ozenne of Opelousas. Cher de Clouet, comandante of the Attakapas Post, complained to the Governor of Louisiana that Ozenne made a game of being barbarous with his slaves despite reiterated warnings. Babet Mulâtresse, one of his slaves, was kept entirely nude. Her master had placed a piece of metal in her mouth to prevent her from eating and had torn up her body from head to foot by lashings. When a local man named Boutte saw this, he reported it to the comandante whose wife insisted that Babet be treated by a doctor. The comandante brought Babet to his house, put her under a doctor's care, and insisted that Ozenne sell Babet to another slaveowner. Ozenne replied that he had a right to punish his slave in any way he saw fit as long as he did not break any bones. The comandante sent M. Boutte to the governor with the piece of metal that had been removed from Babet's mouth, reporting that she was near death. She evidently died of her wounds.[20] Ozenne continued to own slaves, including Babet's brother Jacques and Babet's daughter. In 1793, Babet's aunt, Cecilia India Libre, sued to free her nephew Jacques as well as the daughter of her deceased niece Babet from Jacques Ozenne on the grounds that they were descended from an Indian woman and, under Spanish law, could not be held in slavery. Cecilia Indian Libre's efforts failed, but she and her family were deeply involved in the Point Coupée Conspiracy of 1795 that sought to abolish slavery in Louisiana.[21] Other documents from rural Louisiana also reveal several other cases of torture of slave women by their masters.

Most slave women worked hard and performed backbreaking, unskilled tasks far out of proportion to slave men. During the French period, there were 1,483 females of working age. Only 55 (3.7 percent) were listed as having one or more skills. The colony was not rich enough, especially during the French period, to employ large numbers of female slaves primarily as domestics. Many of them were also field hands. During the French period, a high proportion of domestic workers were males (fifty-one female, forty-two male, or eighty-two men for each 100 women). All personal servants and all bakers and confectioners were males. There were sixteen male cooks and only seven female. Laundresses, wetnurses, and seamstresses were all female. Among general domestics, who included butlers and housekeepers, eighteen were male and thirty-four female. Women slaves were longshoremen, woodcutters and haulers, field workers, and laborers. Four of them wielded pickaxes.

During the French period, male slaves from Senegambia brought technological knowledge and many vital skills sorely lacking in Louisiana. Many, if not most, performed highly skilled, and less physically demanding labor than women. There were 2,439 males of working age listed during the French period. Among them, 294 (12.1 percent) were listed with one or more skills. These included 37 *commandeurs* (drivers or foremen), 10 gardeners, 19 cowboys, 11 hunters, 16 wagon drivers, 10 coach drivers, and many skilled tradesmen including 13 blacksmiths, 2 tailors, 2 locksmiths, 2 cartwrights, 19 carpenters, 11 cabinetmakers, 8 masons, 18 indigo makers, 2 charcoal makers, 19 lumber squarers, 12 longsawyers, 11 hunters, 15 butchers, 1 rummaker, 4 goldsmiths, 1 silversmith, 4 ship caulkers, 2 sailors, 4 rowers, 10 coopers, 3 surgeons or healers, 1 good violinist, 1 innkeeper, and 2 executioners. Only twenty-nine males were listed as field workers or pick-axemen. Traditional gender roles appear to have been eagerly enforced in household tasks as well as in occupations. For example, Esions, an unbaptized Nago (Yoruba) slave whose testimony had to be interpreted, explained that he ran away because his master had given him a wife to gather wood and cook his meals and then took his wife away from him.[22]

During the Spanish period the skills listed for females increased substantially in numbers, if not in variety. There were 8,764 women of working age listed. One or more skills were listed for 551 (6.3 percent) of them. There were ninety-seven laborers, field hands, and pickaxewomen among them. The rest were mainly domestics, cooks, laundresses, seamstresses, or a combination of one or more of these skills. There were seven street vendors, a hairdresser, three health care workers including a midwife, and a watchwoman. Women were highly valued as vendors.

Among the 13,315 males of working age encountered during the Spanish period, 1,409 (10.6 percent) were listed with one or more skills, including all the skills listed for the French period, with the addition of metalworkers, tanners, leatherworkers, saddle-makers, horse trainers, *tallistas* (woodcarvers, sculptors, or engravers), upholsterers, makers of fine china, potters and glazers, ropemakers, charcoal makers, sugar refiners, navigators, sail makers, tobacco stemmers, and cigar makers. The proportion of females among domestic workers rose sharply. There were 446 female domestics and 128 male: twenty-nine males for each 100 females.

There are few specific descriptions of illnesses among female slaves during the French period. Three were listed as blind, two as one-eyed, two as old and weak, one as insane, and two as epileptic. The most common physical defects among the 286 listed for slave women during the Spanish period included 27 as insane, 14 epileptics, 26 with vision problems including blind or one-eyed, 21 with heart disease, 19 with gynecological disorders and breast problems, 18 with leprosy, 11 with hernias or ruptures, 8 with lung diseases including asthma, 8 alcoholics, and 6 with venereal disease. The rest were crippled or missing members or suffered from various other internal illnesses. The high proportion of epilepsy and mental disease among illnesses described for slaves, male and female, might not reflect a true, high incidence of these disorders but the legal obligation to declare them at inventory or sale of slaves since these were not visible disorders.

There is a high proportion of females listed as chronic runaways or helpers of runaways: five women and seven men during the French period and fifty-three women and 105 men during the Spanish period. Throughout the Americas, runaway slaves were overwhelmingly male. It is possible that these slave women were reacting to the beatings and tortures discussed here. In documents describing slaves with wounds, cuts, and scars, some from being lashed, there were six males and only one female during the French period and six males and twelve females during the Spanish period: evidence for increased torture and physical abuse of females during the Spanish period. Males were most likely to be listed as thieves and/or drunkards, although some women were also so categorized. Juliet, an English slave listed on a New Orleans estate in 1792, was a lumber squarer described as a runaway and a thief. Four women were listed as *libertinas* or sexually promiscuous. Such behavior in men was evidently not considered a character defect.

The experience of African women in colonial Louisiana reflected a broad continuum ranging from the most brutal forms of economic and sexual exploitation to impressive upward social mobility and economic power. Colonial Louisiana was a rough, violent, frontier world where slave women were overworked, driven beyond the limits of their physical endurance, tortured, and victimized. But it was also a challenging world, desperately short of human resources, especially women. While the vast majority of women of all statuses and racial designations doubtlessly suffered deeply in this exceptionally brutal environment, women had some bargaining power because of their scarcity and some of these remarkably resourceful women were able to maintain their resiliency and make the most of their situation. African women and women of African descent were crucial in the creation of this new and unique Louisiana Creole language and culture. Their hands rocked many cradles: those of their own children, and of many white children as well.

We no longer look exclusively to the thirteen original colonies along the Atlantic Coast, especially to New England, to find the roots of American culture. Our forebears were women as well as men. They were Africans and Native Americans as well as Europeans. When the United States took over Louisiana in late 1803, it did not enter a cultural vacuum. Incoming Americans encountered a lively, heavily Africanized Louisiana Creole culture that continues to influence the culture of the United States and of the world through its strong, universalist folk culture that has produced our truly unique classical music—jazz.

◀▷

Notes

1. Joseph Zitomerski, "Urbanization in French Colonial Louisiana, 1706–1766," *Annales de Demographie Historique*, 1974, 263–77. For a discussion of Indian women in colonial Virginia, see Peter Wallenstein's essay in this volume.
2. Boubacar Barry, "Senegambia from the Sixteenth to the Eighteenth Century: Evolution of the Wolof, Serer, and 'Tukuloor.'" *UNESCO General History of Africa*, vol. V: B. A. Ogot, ed., *Africa from the Sixteenth to Eighteenth Century*, (Paris: UNESCO, 1992).
3. Gwendolyn Midlo Hall, *Africans in Colonial Louisiana: The Development of Afro-Creole Culture in the Eighteenth Century*, (Baton Rouge: Louisiana State University Press, 1992), 28–55, 96–118.
4. The nation-designation *Nar* was identified by the audience during my lecture opening the West African Research Center in Dakar in November 1993.
5. Hall, *Africans in Colonial Louisiana*, 257.
6. George E. Brooks, Jr., "The Signares of Saint-Louis and Gorée: Women Entrepreneurs in Eighteenth-Century Senegal," in Nancy J. Hofkin and Edna G. Bay, *Women in Africa. Studies in Social and Economic Change*, (Stanford: Stanford University Press, 1976), 19–44.

7. The database was created with generous support from the National Endowment for the Humanities, the Louisiana Endowment for the Humanities, Rutgers University, Northeastern University, the University of New Orleans, the Historic New Orleans Collection, the Program for Cultural Cooperation Between Spain's Ministry of Culture and United States Universities, the Ministry of Culture of France, and the John Simon Guggenheim Foundation. More detailed and varied results and analysis of this and other topics will be published in this writer's book, *Slavery and Race Relations in French, Spanish, and Early American Louisiana: A Comparative Study*, (Chapel Hill: University of North Carolina Press, forthcoming). All quantitative information in this chapter was calculated from Gwendolyn Midlo Hall and Patrick Manning, *Louisiana Slave Database 1723–1820.*

8. See the essays by Virginia Gould and Kimberly Hanger in this volume.

9. June 8, 1795, *Pedro Fabrot* v. *Maria Coffigny*, Spanish Judicial Records, Louisiana Historical Center, Louisiana State Museum, Document No. 1795.06.08.02. For a fuller discussion of this case as well as patterns of self-purchase among slaves in Spanish New Orleans, see Kimberly S. Hanger's excellent book, *Bounded Lives, Bounded Places: Free Black Society in Colonial New Orleans*, (Durham, N.C.: Duke University Press, forthcoming).

10. See, for example, Lois Virginia Meacham Gould, "In Full Enjoyment of their Liberty: The Free Women of Color of the Gulf Ports of New Orleans, Mobile, and Pensacola, 1769–1860," Ph.D. diss., Emory University, 1991, 71–131.

11. Paul F. Chance, "The Formation of a Three-Caste Society: Evidence from Wills in Antebellum New Orleans," *Social Science History*, 18:2, Summer 1994. See also Judith Kelleher Schafer, *Slavery, the Civil Law, and the Supreme Court of Louisiana*, (Baton Rouge: Louisiana State University Press, 1994).

12. July 6, 1769, document 2. Réquisition de Marie Claude Bernard, Vve. Comte Pechon, Records of the Superior Council of Louisiana, Louisiana Historical Center, Louisiana State Museum, New Orleans.

13. Griffe usually meant a mixture of African and Indian, but it sometimes meant three-fourths black and one-fourth white, the definition used in St. Domingue (Haiti).

14. January 24, 1789, Spanish Judicial Records, Louisiana Historical Center, Louisiana State Museum, New Orleans.

15. December 15, 1789, document 261, Agreement between the heirs of François Lemelle in favor of Marie Jeanne, free quadroon, Opelousas Courthouse, St. Landry Parish, Louisiana, microfilm.

16. Ulysses S. Ricard, Jr., "Pierre Belly and Rose," *Chicory Magazine*, Vol. 1, No. 1, Fall 1988; February 16, 1809, Presentation by Pierre Belly to Rose a free negress for love and affection, transfers for her support and livelihood goods valued at $66.896, including the following slaves: 27 men ($17,550), 25 boys ($7890), 24 women ($10,950), and 6 girls ($1575); March 23 and April 16, 1819, Agreement Between Rose Belly and her children with Pierre Belly's family in France, Original Acts, Iberville Parish Courthouse, Conveyance G. Under French law, the deceased was forced to leave a certain portion of his estate to his legitimate family including parents, siblings, nieces, and nephews.

17. November 13, 1796, Original Acts Natchitoches Parish, Natchitoches Courthouse.

18. July 24, 1781, Bill presented by Goton Negra Libra of New Orleans to Various

Inhabitants of the Posts of Attakapas and Opelousas, Original Acts, Volume 2, copies, St. Martin Parish Courthouse, St. Martinville, Louisiana.

19. Hall, *Africans in Colonial Louisiana*, Chap. 8, 237–74. For racial passing throughout Louisiana, see Virginia R. Dominguez, *White By Definition: Social Classification in Creole Louisiana* (New Brunswick: Rutgers University Press, 1986).

20. November 12 and 14, 1782, Comandante Cher de Clouet to Governor, Papeles Procedente de Cuba, Archivo General de Indias, Seville, Spain.

21. For more information about Cecilia India Libre and support networks, among women see Hall, *Africans in Colonial Louisiana*, 337–41.

22 February 16, 1765, Interrogation of Nègre Esion, Louisiana Historical Center, Louisiana State Museum, Records of the Superior Council of Louisiana, Document No. 1765.02.16.01.

◄ Epilogue

Finding one's bearings along the devil's lane of early southern history is no easy task. Many have tried, choosing to forge a deceptively straight and narrow path through complicated terrain rather than pay attention to the unique and intricate landscapes of time, place, identity, and difference along the way. The travelers in this volume, however, have chosen a different route from that of their predecessors. They have taken as their starting point the assumption that the social constructs of race, sex, and class that are so fundamental to our understanding of the nineteenth- and twentieth-century South underwent evolution and transformation over the course of the colonial and revolutionary eras. This vantage point has enabled them to map the complex interrelationships between sex, race, and gender within the larger framework of a slave society in the making.

Their work has raised as many questions as it has answered, reminding us that while the contours of the devil's lane have begun to emerge, more exploration is needed. To this end we must consider the larger meanings intendant on the wealth of "thick and deep descriptions of social change" proffered here. How different does the history of the early South look when examined through the lens of sex and race instead of the conventional focus on government and war?

European settlement in the American South marked the meeting of old and new and the often desperate dance that ensued between the two. Native Americans, Africans, African Americans, British Americans, French Americans, and Spanish Americans, men and women, the enslaved, the indentured and the free, found themselves carving out a social identity in unfamiliar settings wrought with uncertainty, incoherence, and danger.

At the same time, the very absence of a shared social order and imposed communal values in the earliest stages of settlement permitted Europeans a measure of social freedom and personal choice unknown in the Old World. This fluidity defies customary expectations about the rootedness of sexual and racial difference throughout the southern past. The society that emerged in the American South by the early nineteenth century, one in which freedom for some rested on the enslavement of many, had evolved slowly over time. The notions of race difference, sexual misconduct, and gendered behavior that came to define who was free and who was not, who had power and who did not, were neither organic or monolithic in the early South. Instead fledgling communities, like those of Thomas(ine) Hall's and the slave woman Juana's, painstakingly crafted these definitions out of their own particular circumstances—the cultural, demographic, and political realities unique to each colony and settlement.

Over the course of the colonial era, nonetheless, certain patterns emerged that served to unite this diverse region. Virtually all communities and colonial governments, under the Spanish and French as well as the English, wanted to establish a stable social order that could withstand the external threats posed by hostile Native American and greedy European rivals. As the essays by Peter Wallenstein, Diane Miller Sommerville, Paul Finkelman, Jane Landers, and Kirsten Fischer suggest, the European colonists also sought a stable social order able to withstand the internal threats posed by the settlement of so few in a new world peopled by such diversity. This social order was as desirable for Floridians as for Virginians and Carolinians. The experiences of these inhabitants, along with the absence of many traditional social institutions, the imbalanced sex ratios and the radically altered social structures, the plentiful land and resources, and the indentured servants and African slaves who became the laboring classes, circumscribed traditional patterns of Native American, European, and African settlement and community and together transformed them into something new.

European Americans, who came to wield the most power in this cultural encounter, in time created systems to label inhabitants according to dominant theories of race difference, permissible sexual behavior, and perceived social status. These conceptions bolstered the influence and authority of a select few—generally the wealthy white male leaders within each colony—while silencing the voices of others, especially those of women, Native Americans, and African Americans.

This development, and its important implications for sex and race in the early South, seems linked in the most fundamental of ways to the market. Across the early South, the encroachment of the transatlantic commercial economy and the kinds of social differentiation it fostered came to determine who defined socially acceptable behavior and who constructed social hierarchies, who enforced them and who was victimized by them. The more a colony participated in the exchange of agricultural commodities, the more property and prosperity such exchanges fostered, the greater the social stratification and rigidity that ensued.

Engagement in the commercial economy differed from colony to colony. By the seventeenth century, the Spanish empire concerned itself far more with political unity and religious conformity than transatlantic trade. In contrast, England's imposition of its mercantilist policies on its Atlantic colonies after the first half of the seventeenth century transformed British settlement. Does this contrasting approach to New World empire explain the relative freedom and social mobility that Kimberly Hanger and Ginger Gould discovered among slaves and free blacks, especially women, within these groups in the Spanish Gulf? Would greater participation in this developing commercial economy have altered in fundamental ways the world in which these black women lived?

Moreover, would race difference and sexual codes of conduct have assumed such importance in the new United States by the early nineteenth century without the intrusion of market forces and the accompanying spread of plantation agriculture with its nearly insatiable desire for cheap labor? Or would the need for some semblance of social order have encouraged the imposition of the language and law of difference regardless of the nature of exchange? Were colonists so desperate for a harmonious society given their frontier circumstances that defining who and what one was or was not became just as much of a prerequisite for community-building as market developments and their demands? Again, the contrasting example of the Spanish Gulf does seem to suggest that the timing and intrusion of the commercial market and the degree to which England propelled its Atlantic colonies into it did in fact shape the racial nature of Anglo-American slavery in the British colonies as well as the sharply defined sexual division of labor among free whites. But more careful analysis is required to follow up on such suggestive conceptions.

Black labor was coerced in the American South. What role then did violence play in enforcing racial difference? And how was violence used to define women's place within these emerging communities? Violence traditionally has been associated with settlement in the early South: from the warfare during the earliest cultural clashes in the New World to the warfare between colonists and Mother Country during the American Revolution. Violence was in fact interwoven into the very fabric of everyday life throughout the seventeenth and eighteenth centuries. A powerful weapon to enforce race and gender divides and maintain hierarchies, violence provided a last resort for individuals who failed to meet socially prescribed roles and duties. How central was this violence—rape, castration, murder, and physical brutality in general—in shaping social behavior in the early South? Did everyday acts of violence represent a crucial arena where colonial players came to test their social status and identity? To what degree did violence against slaves and against white women take on similar form and meaning in the Gulf South as well as the Anglo-American South? And to what extent were these kinds of expressions of violence as critical for understanding the dynamics of early southern society as formal warfare between nations?

While institutions and authorities used the threat of violence to press marginal members of colonial society, especially slaves and women, into positions of social subordination, what do we make of those who fought back? Violence in the colonial South was not a one-way street. The oppressed could and did turn the tables. Violence might be self-inflicted as well as directed at oppressors. Violent acts might reflect the indignities suffered by the most powerless within colonial culture. Thus, in Spanish St. Augustine, Juana the slave woman perhaps resorted to violence against her own children to retaliate against the master who raped her.

Women and slaves in the South found by the late eighteenth century that only the church could provide them with a relatively safe public space where they might find their voices. Within religious expression, society's marginal members articulated their passion for God, albeit in "acceptable" ways. Both women and blacks could find some measure of community and experience some measure of freedom. As the essays by Jon Sensbach and Lynn Lyerly suggest, southern churches may have been the most important institutions for forging female culture at this time. And as Betty Wood argues, biracial evangelical churches in the South permitted enslaved African Americans to claim at least one right, the right to worship alongside whites, in the wake of the American Revolution. These findings about religious institutions in the fledgling southern states beg comparative questions: Did the Catholic Church serve its female and enslaved worshippers in the eighteenth-century Gulf South in similar ways? Were these avenues for personal expression abstract enhancements or could they lead to concrete measurable improvements in individuals' lives?

Joan Gundersen has suggested that women in eighteenth-century Virginia found news ways of creating a female culture in the void men left behind as they rushed to embrace citizenship and commerce, areas increasingly relegated to white propertyholding men. Was this development unique to Virginia? Did it take different shape in the Carolinas and Georgia or in the Gulf South? In rural and in urban areas? Across racial or ethnic boundaries?

Gwendolyn Hall's provocative essay, with its emphasis on the nativities of the African population in colonial Louisiana, reminds us that answering such comparative questions is absolutely essential to fully comprehending the early South. Hall suggests that to appreciate the diversity of the slave experience in the Gulf South, one must recognize the integral relationship between ethnic origins and cultural practices, its influence on family formation, occupational patterns, and even health and mortality. Her careful demographic research invites comparison with Atlantic seaboard colonies where we know only that the ethnic origins of the African populations were quite different from those within Louisiana but lack the detailed analysis that Hall has provided for this Gulf colony.

Scholars have traced the transformation of ideas about gendered power from rigidly patriarchal expressions in the seventeenth century to new notions reflecting ideas about public and private spheres in the post-Revolutionary republic. And one wonders to what extent this fundamental shift in social thought actually predicated the sets of events that led to the Revolution—a developmental stage that caused one commentator, de Tocqueville, to single out American women as the new nation's most distinctive cultural feature. Perhaps equally significant was the rigid stratification of racial differences during the expanded settlement of the American South. While this diminished fluidity flowed from the post-Revolutionary social reordering, the essays in this volume repeatedly illustrate that maintaining permanent, binding racial and gender lines was a lengthy process. Then, did the American Revolution merely offer southerners an enhanced opportunity to codify pre-Revolutionary developments in their new state legal systems, or did these changes come from transformations wrought by war and subsequent peace? We invite you to travel further down the devil's lane and examine these and other questions for yourself.

◆ Suggested Readings

Early southern history has a long and distinguished literature. Colonial southerners themselves took great pride in recounting their own beginnings, from Robert Beverly's *The History and Present State of Virginia* (1722) to Thomas Jefferson's extensive chronicles. These native sons showcased exclusively the accomplishments of white men. It took several generations before scholarship broadened to include questions of race and sex, to encompass the people of color in the region and the white women who together outnumbered the white male minority within the early South.

Colonial southern women have been shamefully neglected in the explosion of work in the field of women's history during the past quarter century. The "New Englandization" of early women's experience in American history remains a sore subject. The Southern Association for Women Historians honors the remarkable Julia Cherry Spruill by giving a prize to the best book in southern women's history to commemorate her pioneering contribution. Spruill's life is highlighted in Anne Scott's bittersweet tribute to the first generation of southern women historians, *Unheard Voices* (1994). Indeed, no monograph has been published that replaces Spruill's monumental *Women's Life and Work in the Southern Colonies* (1938) and it has been twenty years since Lois G. Carr and Lorena S. Walsh published their influential "The Planter's Wife: The Experience of White Women in Seventeenth Century Maryland" in the *William and Mary Quarterly* (1977). Both these models of scholarship endure, but we look forward to expanded accounts that include African Americans and other women of color as agents within the culture.

It is not unusual to have important articles and monographs remain central for several decades. Colonial historians of the South still look to Wesley Frank Craven's *The Southern Colonies in the Seventeenth Century* (1949) in Louisiana State University's "History of the South" series, while the volume on the eighteenth century remains unwritten. A recent edition of Verner Crane's *The Southern Frontier, 1670–1732*, published in 1929, demonstrates its vitality, especially Crane's treatment of the Yamassee War (1715–16). At the same time a large crop of anthologies and monographs have broadened and diversified our understanding of this crucial era of white settlement, from T. H. Breen's *Shaping Southern Society: The Colonial Experience* (1976) to Charles Hudson's comprehensive *Southeastern Indians* (1976) and Richard Beale Davis's massive *Intellectual Life in the Colonial South, 1585–1763* (1978).

Our vision of the seventeenth- and eighteenth-century South has been seasoned and improved by the excellent studies produced by Richard Beeman (Virginia), Russell Menard (Chesapeake), Gloria Main (Maryland), Rachel Klein (South Carolina), Phinizy Spalding (Georgia), Joyce Chaplin (South Carolina), Aubrey Land (Maryland), T. H. Breen (Virginia), Alan Gallay (Georgia), Darrett and Anita Rutman (Virginia), and Peter Coclanis (South Carolina).

Our ability to reconstruct the lives of the forgotten first southerners, the native peoples who shaped settlement and conflict throughout the colonial period, has been measurably improved with the work of James Axtell, most notably his *The Invasion Within: The Contest of Cultures in Colonial North America* (1985), and James Merrell's *The Indians' New World: Cawtawbas and Their Neighbors from European Contact through the Era of Removal* (1989), Kathryn Braund's *Deerskins and Duffels: The Creek Indian Trade with Anglo-America* (1993), Peter Wood, Gregory Waselkov, and M. Hatley's *Powhatan's Mantle: Indians in the Colonial Southeast* (1989), and James O'Donnell's bibliographical contribution, *Southeastern Frontiers: Europeans, Africans and American Indians* (1982).

Many prizes have been garnered by chroniclers of race relations and slavery's indelible impact in the early South. Notable contributions to this field include Winthrop Jordan's *White over Black* (1968), Gerald Mullin's *Flight and Rebellion* (1972), Peter Wood's *Black Majority* (1974), Edmund Morgan's *American Slavery, American Freedom* (1975), Daniel Littlefield's *Rice and Slaves* (1981), Rhys Isaac's *The Transformation of Virginia* (1982), Betty Wood's *Slavery in Colonial Georgia* (1984), Allan Kulikoff's *Tobacco and Slaves* (1986), Mechal Sobel's *The World They Made Together* (1987), and Sylvia Frey's *Water from the Rock* (1991).

Exciting inroads are made by assessing material culture and archeological excavations, creating an entirely new body of historical work that sharpens our senses and sensibilities about evidence. Scholarship on the colonial South has been enriched by such impressive studies as John Michael Vlatch's *The Afro-American Tradition in Decorative Arts* (1978), Ivor Noel Hume's *Martin's Hundred* (1988), and Leland Ferguson's *Uncommon Ground* (1992).

The forgotten multiculturalism of early exploration in colonial North America, the real blend of cultures in the Gulf South has only recently taken center stage. Like a tenacious vine, the evidence of Spanish and French influences in the New World persists, despite the lack of recognition these cultures and their scholarship have endured. We are grateful for the pioneering work by David J. Weber's *The Spanish Frontier in North America* (1992), Paul Hoffman's *A New Andalucia and a Way to the Orient* (1990), and Gwendolyn Midlo Hall's *Africans in Colonial Louisiana* (1992).

The central transforming experience of the eighteenth century has been examined and revisited by American historians beginning with Mercy Otis Warren, whose three-volume *History of the Rise, Progress and Termination of the American Revolution* (1805) launched studies of the war and its impact. Warren was a New Englander who, like too many scholars who followed, ignored the crucial role the southern colonies played in military strategy. Work on the American Revolution remains all too segregated. If you want to know about southern contributions, you must look for titles specifically on the South, such as John Alden's *The South in the American Revolution* (1957) and Jeffrey Crow and Larry Tise's *The Southern Experience in the American Revolution* (1978). Exceptional scholars who have done extensive research on the South, such as Robert Weir and Jack P. Greene, manage to be enlightening and integrative in their approaches.

There have been important volumes examining questions of sex and questions of race touching on the early South. We are most indebted to three volumes: Ira Berlin and Ronald Hoffman's *Slavery and Freedom in the Age of the American Revolution* (1983), Ronald Hoffman and Peter Albert's *Women in the Age of the American Revolution* (1989), and Ira Berlin and Philip Morgan's *Cultivation and Culture* (1993). The Chancellor's Symposium at the University of Mississippi produced the volume *Race and Family in the Colonial South* in 1987. Paul Finkelman's multivolume series provided an excellent anthology of published articles, entitled *Slavery, Race and the American Legal System, 1700–1872* (1988).

Readers seeking insight specifically into questions of gender, race, and sex in the early South may find the following selections useful both as background and as guideposts for future work in the field.

◄►

Alden John. *The South in the American Revolution, 1763–1789*. Baton Rouge: Louisiana State University Press, 1987.

Arnade, Charles W. "The Avero Story: An Early Saint Augustine Family with Many Daughters and Many Houses," *Florida Historical Quarterly*, 40, #1, July 1961.

Axtell, James. *The Invasion Within: The Contest of Cultures in Colonial North America*. New York: Oxford University Press, 1985.

Beeman, Richard R. *The Evolution of the Southern Backcountry: A Case Study of Lunenburg County, Virginia, 1746–1832*. Philadelphia: University of Pennsylvania Press 1984.

Berkin, Carol and Clara M. Lovett, eds. *Women, War and the Revolution*. New York: Holmes and Meier, 1980.

Berlin, Ira and Ronald Hoffman, eds. *Slavery and Freedom in the Age of the American Revolution*. Charlottesville: University Press of Virginia, 1983.

Berlin, Ira and Philip D. Morgan., eds. *Cultivation and Culture: Labor and the Shaping of Slave Life in the Americas*. Charlottesville: University Press of Virginia, 1993.

Beverly, Robert. *The History and Present State of Virginia*. Edited with an introduction by Louis B. Wright. Chapel Hill: University of North Carolina Press for the Institute of Early History and Culture, 1947.

Billings, Warren S. "The Case of Fernando and Elizabeth Key: A Note on the Status of Blacks in Seventeenth Century, Virginia," *William and Mary Quarterly*, 3rd, 30, July 1973.

Boatwright, Eleanor. "The Political and Civil Status of Women in Georgia, 1702–1860," *Georgia Historical Quarterly*, 25, 1941.

Boles, John B. *The Great Revival, 1787–1805: The Origins of the Southern Evangelical Mind*. Lexington: University Press of Kentucky, 1972.

Boyle, Susan C. "Did She Generally Decide? Women in Ste. Genevieve, 1750–1805," *William and Mary Quarterly*, 3rd, 44, October 1987.

Brasseaux, Carl A., Keith P. Fontenot, and Claude F. Oubre, eds. *Creoles of Color in the Bayou Country*. Jackson: University Press of Mississippi, 1994.

Braund, Kathryn M. Holland. *Deerskins and Duffels: The Creek Indian Trade with Anglo-America, 1685–1815*. Lincoln: University of Nebraska Press, 1993.

Breen, Timothy, ed. *Shaping Southern Society: The Colonial Experience*. New York: Oxford University Press, 1976.

————. *Tobacco Culture: The Mentality of the Great Tidewater Planters on the Eve of Revolution*. Princeton: Princeton University Press, 1985.

Breen, Timothy and Stephen Innes. *"Mine Owne Ground": Race and Freedom on Virginia's Eastern Shore, 1640–1676*. New York: Oxford University Press, 1980.

Brown, Kathleen M. *Good Wives, "Nasty Wenches," and Anxious Patriarchs: Gender, Race, and Power in Colonial Virginia*. Chapel Hill: University of North Carolina Press, 1996.

Bush, Barbara. *Slave Women in Caribbean Society, 1650–1838*. Bloomington: University of Indiana Press, 1990.

Bushman, Richard. *The Refinement of America: Persons, Houses, Cities*. New York: Random House, 1993.

Calvert, Karin. *Children in the House: The Material Culture of Early Childhood, 1600–1900*. Boston: Northeastern University Press, 1992.

Carr, Lois G., Philip D. Morgan, and Jean B. Russo, eds. *Colonial Chesapeake Society*. Chapel Hill: University of North Carolina, 1988.

Carr, Lois G. and Lorena S. Walsh. "The Planter's Wife: The Experience of White Women In Seventeenth Century Maryland," *William and Mary Quarterly*, 3rd, 34, October 1977.

————. "Economic Diversification and Labor Organization in the Chesapeake, 1650–1820," in Stephen Innes, ed., *Work and Labor in Early America*. Chapel Hill: University of North Carolina Press, 1988.

Clinton, Catherine. *The Plantation Mistress: Woman's World in the Old South*. New York: Pantheon Press, 1982.

Cody, Cheryll A. "Naming, Kinship, and Estate Dispersal: Notes on Slave Family Life on a South Carolina Plantation, 1786–1833," *William and Mary Quarterly*, 3rd, 39, January 1982.

Cohen, David W. and Jack P. Greene, eds. *Neither Slave nor Free: The Freedmen of African Descent in the Slave Societies of the New World*. Baltimore: Johns Hopkins University Press, 1972.

Colburn, David R. and Jane L. Landers, eds. *The African American Heritage of Florida*. Gainesville: University Press of Florida, 1995.

Cook, Alexandra Parma and Noble David Cook. *Good Faith and Truthful Ignorance: A Case of Transatlantic Bigamy*. Durham: Duke University Press, 1991.

Courturier, Edith. "Women and the Family in Eighteenth Century Mexico: Law and Practice," *Journal of Family History*, 10, #3, Fall 1985.

Crane, Verner. *The Southern Frontier, 1670–1732*. Anne Arbor: University of Michigan Press, 1978.

Craven, Frank. *The Southern Colonies in the Seventeenth Century, 1607–1689*. Baton Rouge: Louisiana State University Press, 1949.

Crow, Jeffrey. *The Black Experience in Revolutionary North Carolina*. Raleigh: Division of Archives and History, 1983.

————, and Larry Tise, eds. *The Southern Experience in the American Revolution*. Chapel Hill: University of North Carolina Press, 1978.

Crowley, John E. "Family Relations and Inheritance in Early South Carolina," *Histoire Social/Social History*, 17, 1984.

Davis, Richard Beale. *Intellectual Life in the Colonial South, 1585–1763*. Knoxville: University of Tennessee Press, 1978.

Deegan, Kathleen A., ed. *Spanish St. Augustine: The Archeology of a Colonial Creole Community*. New York: Academic Press, 1982.

Dunn, Richard S. "A Tale of Two Plantations: Slave Life at Mesapotamia in Jamaica and Mount Airy in Virginia, 1799–1828," *William and Mary Quarterly*, 3rd, 34, January 1977.

Ferguson, Leland G. *Uncommon Ground: Archaelogy and Early African America, 1650–1800*. Washington, D.C.: Smithsonian Institute Press, 1992.

Finkelman, Paul, ed. *Slavery, Race and the American Legal System, 1700–1872*. 16 vols. New York: Garland, 1988.

Frey, Sylvia. *Like Water From the Rock: Black Resistance in a Revolutionary Age*. Princeton: Princeton University Press, 1991.

Galenson, David W. "'Middling People' or 'Common Sort?' The Social Origins of Some Early Americans Reexamined," *William and Mary Quarterly*, 3rd, 39, January 1982.

Gillespie, Michele. "Planters in the Making: Artisanal Opportunity in Georgia, 1790–1830" in *American Artisans: Crafting Social Identity, 1750–1850*. Ed. by Howard B. Rock, Paul A. Gilje, and Robert Asher. Baltimore: Johns Hopkins University Press, 1995.

Gladwin, Lee. "Tobacco and Sex: Some Factors Affecting Non-Marital Sexual Behavior in Colonial Virginia," *Journal of Social History*, 12, 1978.

Green, Rayna. "The Pocahontas Perplex: The Image of Indian Women in American Culture, " *The Massachusetts Review*, 16, Autumn 1975.

———. "Native American Women," *Signs*, 6, Winter 1980.

Greven, Philip. *The Protestant Temperament: Patterns of Child-Rearing, Religious Experience, and the Self in Early America*. New York: Alfred A. Knopf, 1977.

Griffin, Patricia C. "Mary Evans: A Woman of Substance," *El Escribano*, 1977.

Guderman, Stephen. "Herbert Gutman's *The Black Family in Slavery and Freedom, 1750–1929*: An Anthropologist's View," *Social Science History*, 3, 1979.

Gunderson, Joan. "The Double Bonds of Race and Sex: Black and White Women in a Colonial Virginia Parish," *Journal of Southern History*, 52, August 1986.

———. "The Noninstitutional Church: The Religious Role of Women in Eighteenth Century Virginia," *Historical Magazine of the Protestant Episcopal Church*, 51, #4, December 1982.

———, and Gwen V. Gampel. "Married Women's Legal Status in Eighteenth Century New York and Virginia, *William and Mary Quarterly*, 3rd, 39, January 1982.

Gutman, Herbert. *The Black Family in Slavery and Freedom, 1750–1929*. New York: Pantheon, 1976.

Hall, Gwendolyn Midlo. *Africans in Colonial Louisiana: The Development of Afro-Creole Culture in the Eighteenth Century*. Baton Rouge: Louisiana State University Press, 1992.

———, and Patrick Manning, *Slaves in Louisiana, 1735–1820*. (forthcoming)

Heyrman, Christine. *Southern Cross*. New York: Knopf, 1997.

Higginbotham, A. Leon and Barbara K. Kopytoff, "Racial Purity and Interracial Sex in the Law of Colonial and Antebellum Virginia," *Georgetown Law Journal*, 77, 1989.

Hoffman, Paul. *A New Andalucia and a Way to the Orient: The American Southeast During the Sixteenth Century*. Baton Rouge: Louisiana State University Press, 1990.

Hoffman, Ronald and Peter J. Albert, *Women in the Age of the American Revolution*. Charlottesville: University of Virginia Press for the Capitol Hill Society, 1989.

Holmes, Jack D. L. "Do It! Don't Do It!: Spanish Laws on Sex and Marriage," in Edward F. Haas, ed., *Louisiana Legal Heritage*. Pensacola: Perdido Bay Press, for the Louisiana State Museum, 1983.

Hudson, Charles M. *Southeastern Indians*. Knoxville: University of Tennessee Press, 1976.

Hughes, Sarah. "Slaves for Hire: The Allocation of Black Labor in Elizabeth City County, Virginia, 1782–1810," *William and Mary Quarterly*, 3rd, 35, April 1978.

Hume, Ivor Noel. *Martin's One Hundred*. New York: Knopf, 1982.

Isaac, Rhys. *The Transformation of Virginia, 1740–1790*. New York: W. W. Norton, 1988.

Jones, Jacqueline. *Labor of Love, Labor of Sorrow*. New York: Basic Books, 1985.

Jordan, Winthrop. *White over Black: American Attitudes Toward the Negro, 1550–1812*. Chapel Hill: University of North Carolina Press, 1968.

Kerber, Linda. *Women of the Republic: Intellect and Ideology in Revolutionary America*. Chapel Hill: University of North Carolina, 1980.

Klein, Rachel. *Unification of a Slave State: The Rise of the Planter Class in the South Carolina Backcountry, 1760–1808*. Chapel Hill: University of North Carolina Press, 1990.

Kulikoff, Allan. *Tobacco and Slaves: The Development of Southern Cultures in the Chesapeake, 1680–1800*. Chapel Hill: University of North Carolina, 1986.

Land, A. D., Lois G. Carr and E.C. Papenfuse, eds. *Law, Society and Politics in Early Maryland*. Baltimore: Johns Hopkins University Press, 1977.

Landers, Jane. "Gracia Real de Santa Teresa de Mose: A Free Black Town in Spanish Colonial Florida," *American Historical Review*, February 1992.

Lavrin, Asuncion, ed. *Sexuality and Marriage in Colonial Latin America*. Lincoln: University of Nebraska Press, 1989.

Lebsock, Suzanne. *Free Women of Petersburg: Status and Culture in a Southern Town, 1784–1820*. New York: W. W. Norton, 1984.

Lee, Jean B. "The Problem of Slave Community in the Eighteenth Century Chesapeake," *William and Mary Quarterly*, 3rd, 42, July 1986.

Lewis, Jan. *The Pursuit of Happiness: Family and Values in Jefferson's Virginia*. New York: Cambridge University Press, 1983.

———. "Domestic Tranquillity and the Management of Emotion Among the Gentry of PreRevolutionary Virginia," *William and Mary Quarterly*, 3rd, 39, January, 1982.

———. and Kenneth Lockridge. "'Sally Has Been Sick:' Pregnancy and Family Limitation Among Virginia Gentry Women, 1780–1830," *Journal of Social History*, 22, #1, Fall 1988.

Littlefield, Daniel. *Rice and Slaves: Ethnicity and the Slave Trade in Colonial South Carolina*. Baton Rouge: Louisiana State University Press, 1981.

Lockridge, Kenneth. *On the Sources of Patriarchal Rage: The Commonplace Books of William Byrd and Thomas Jefferson and the Gendering of Power in the Eighteenth Century*. New York: New York University Press, 1992.

Main, Gloria. *Tobacco Colony: Life in Early Maryland, 1650–1720*. Princeton: Princeton University Press, 1982.

McEwan, Bonnie G. "The Archeology of Women in the Spanish New World," *Historical Archeology*, 25, #4, 1991.

Menard, Russell. "Immigration to the Chesapeake Colonies in the Seventeenth Century: A Review Essay," *Maryland Historical Magazine*, 67, 1973.

———. "The Maryland Slave Population: 1658 to 1730: A Demographic Profile of Blacks in Four Counties," *William and Mary Quarterly*, 3rd, 32, January 1975.

———. "From Servants to Slaves: the Transformation of the Chesapeake Labor System" *Southern Studies*, 16 Winter 1977.

Merrell, James. *The Indians' New World: Catawbas and Their Neighbors from European Contact Through the Era of Removal*. Chapel Hill: University of North Carolina Press, 1989.

Mills, Gary. "Coincoin: An Eighteenth Century 'Liberated Woman,'" *Journal of Southern History*, 42, May 1976.

Moogk, Peter N. "'Thieving Buggers' and 'Stupid Sluts': Insults and Popular Culture in New France," *William and Mary Quarterly*, 3rd, 36, October 1979.

Morgan, Edmund. *Virginians at Home: Family Life in the Eighteenth Century.* Williamsburg, Va.: Colonial Williamsburg, 1952.

———. *American Slavery, American Freedom: The Ordeal of Colonial Virginia.* New York: W. W. Norton, 1975.

Morgan, Philip. "Work and Culture: The Task System and the World of Lowcountry Blacks, 1700–1880," *William and Mary Quarterly*, 3rd, 39, October 1982.

Morton, Patricia, ed. *Discovering the Women in Slavery.* Athens: University of Georgia Press, 1995.

Mullin, Gerald W. *Flight and Rebellion: Slave Resistance in Eighteenth Century Virginia.* New York: Oxford University Press, 1972.

Myers, Kathleen A. "A Glimpse of Family Life in Colonial Mexico," *Latin American Research Review*, 28, #2, 1993.

Nash, Gary B. "The Image of the Indian in the Southern Colonial Mind," *William and Mary Quarterly*, 3rd, 39, April 1972.

Nicholls, Michael. "Passing Through this Troublesome World: Free Blacks in the Early Southside," *Virginia Magazine of History and Biography*, 92, 1984.

Norton, Mary Beth. *Founding Mothers and Fathers: Gendered Power and the Forming of American Society.* New York: Knopf, 1996.

———. *Liberty's Daughters: The Revolutionary Experience of American Women, 1750–1800.* Boston: Little Brown, 1980.

———. "Eighteenth Century American Women in Peace and War: The Case of the Loyalists," *William and Mary Quarterly*, 3rd, 33, July 1976.

———. "'What an Alarming Crisis Is This:' Southern Women and the American Revolution," in Jeffrey Crow and Larry Tise, eds., *The Southern Experience and the American Revolution.* Chapel Hill: University of North Carolina Press, 1978.

———. "Gender and Defamation in Seventeenth-Century Maryland," *William and Mary Quarterly*, 3rd, 44, January 1987.

O'Donnell, James. *Southeastern Frontiers: Europeans, Africans and American Indians.* Bloomington: Indiana University Press, 1982.

Ransome, David R. "Wives for Virginia, 1621." *William and Mary Quarterly*, 3rd, 48, January 1991.

Rutman, Darrett and Anita Rutman. *A Place in Time: Middlesex County, Virginia, 1650–1750.* New York: W. W. Norton, 1984.

Salmon, Marylynn. *Women and the Law of Property in Early America.* Chapel Hill: University of North Carolina Press, 1986.

———. "Women and Property in South Carolina: The Evidence from Marriage Settlements, 1730–1830," *William and Mary Quarterly*, 3rd, 39, October 1982.

Schafer, Daniel L. *Anna Kingsley.* St. Augustine: St. Augustine Historical Society, 1994.

Schwartz, Philip. *Twice Condemned: Slaves and the Criminal Laws of Virginia, 1705–1865.* Baton Rouge: Louisiana State University Press, 1988.

Scott, Anne Firor. *Unheard Voices: The First Historians of Southern Women.* Charlotteville: University Press of Virginia, 1993.

Seed, Patricia. *Ceremonies of Possession in Europe's Conquest of the New World, 1492–1640.* Cambridge: Cambridge University Press, 1995.

———. *To Love, Honor and Obey in Colonial Mexico: Conflicts over Marriage Choice, 1574–1821.* Stanford: Stanford University Press, 1988.

Shammas, Carole, Marylynn Salmon and Michel Dahlin. *Inheritance in America: Colonial Times to the Present*. New Brunswick, N.J.: Rutgers University Press, 1987.

————. "Black Women's Work and the Evolution of Plantation Society in Virginia," *Labor History*, 26, 1985.

Smith, Daniel B. *Inside the Great House: Planter Family Life in Eighteenth Century Chesapeake Society*. Ithaca: Cornell University Press, 1980.

————. "Mortality and Family in the Colonial Chesapeake," *Journal of Interdisciplinary History* 8, 1977–78.

Sobel, Mechal. *The World They Made Together: Black and White Values in Eighteenth-Century Virginia*. Princeton: Princeton University Press, 1987.

Speth, Linda. "More than Her 'Thirds': Wives and Widows in Colonial Virginia," *Women and History*, 4, 1982.

Spindel, Donna. *Crime and Society in North Carolina, 1663–1776*. Baton Rouge: Louisiana State University Press, 1989.

Spruill, Julia Cherry. *Women's Life and Work in the Southern Colonies*. Chapel Hill: University of North Carolina Press, 1938.

Stevenson, Brenda. *Life in Black and White: Family and Community in the Slave South*. New York: Oxford University Press, 1996.

Tate, Thad W. and David Ammerman, eds. *The Chesapeake in the Seventeenth Century: Essays on Anglo-American Society*. Chapel Hill: University of North Carolina Press, 1980.

————, Winthrop Jordan and Sheila Skemp, eds. *Race and Family in the Colonial South*. Jackson: University of Mississippi Press, 1987.

Usner, Daniel H. *Indians, Settlers & Slaves in a Frontier Exchange Economy: The Lower Mississippi Valley Before 1783*. Chapel Hill: University of North Carolina, 1992

Vlach, John Michael. *The Afro-American Tradition in Decorative Arts*. Athens: University of Georgia Press, 1978.

Walsh, Lorena. "The Experiences and Status of Women in the Chesapeake," in Walter J. Fraser, Jr., Frank Saunders, and Jon L. Wakelyn, eds., *The Web of Southern Social Relations: Women, Family and Education*. Athens: University of Georgia Press, 1984.

Watson, Alan. "Women in Colonial North Carolina: Overlooked and Underestimated," *North Carolina Historical Review*, 58, 1981.

Weber, David J. *The Spanish Frontier in North America*. New Haven: Yale University Press, 1992.

White, Deborah. *"Aren't I a Woman?" Female Slaves in the Antebellum South*. New York: W. W. Norton, 1985.

Wood, Betty. *Slavery in Colonial Georgia, 1730–1775*. Athens: University of Georgia Press, 1989.

Wood, Peter. *Black Majority: Negroes in Colonial South Carolina from 1670 through the Stono Rebellion*. New York: Alfred A. Knopf, 1974.

————, Gregory Waselkov and M. Hatley, eds. *Powhatan's Mantle: Indians in the Colonial Southeast*. Lincoln: University of Nebraska Press, 1989.

Zuckerman, Michael. "William Byrd's Family," *Perspectives in American History*, 12, 1979.